Extending Research Horizons in Applied Linguistics

Extending Research Horizons in Applied Linguistics

Between Interdisciplinarity and Methodological Diversity

Edited by

Hadrian Aleksander Lankiewicz

SHEFFIELD UK   BRISTOL CT

Published by Equinox Publishing Ltd.

UK: Office 415, The Workstation, 15 Paternoster Row, Sheffield, South Yorkshire S1 2BX

USA: ISD, 70 Enterprise Drive, Bristol, CT 06010

www.equinoxpub.com

First published 2023

British Library Cataloguing-in-Publication Data
A catalogue record for this book is available from the British Library.

ISBN-13   978 1 80050 363 2   (hardback)
          978 1 80050 364 9   (paperback)
          978 1 80050 365 6   (ePDF)
          978 1 80050 405 9   (ePub)

Library of Congress Cataloging-in-Publication Data

Names: Lankiewicz, Hadrian, 1966- editor.
Title: Extending research horizons in applied linguistics : between
  interdisciplinarity and methodological diversity / edited by Hadrian
  Aleksander Lankiewicz.
Description: Sheffield, South Yorkshire ; Bristol, CT : Equinox Publishing
  Ltd., 2023. | Includes bibliographical references and index. | Summary:
  "The book is targeted at professional scholars as well as language
  students who plan their own research in the fuzzy field of applied
  linguistics, while working on their degree papers, or doing an any
  academic work related to language study. The uniqueness of the volume
  consists in its methodological character which is made operational and
  thus the book may function as a methodological manual"-- Provided by
  publisher.
Identifiers: LCCN 2023008958 (print) | LCCN 2023008959 (ebook) | ISBN
  9781800503632 (hardback) | ISBN 9781800503649 (paperback) | ISBN
  9781800503656 (ePDF) | ISBN 9781800504059 (ePub)
Subjects: LCSH: Applied linguistics--Research--Methodology. | LCGFT:
  Essays.
Classification: LCC P129 .E96 2023 (print) | LCC P129 (ebook) | DDC
  418.007--dc23/eng/20230717
LC record available at https://lccn.loc.gov/2023008958
LC ebook record available at https://lccn.loc.gov/2023008959

Typeset by Sparks Publishing Services Ltd – www.sparkspublishing.com

Contents

Preface   vii
Hadrian Lankiewicz

1   Building translation sub-competences of foreign language students in telecollaboration   1
Małgorzata Godlewska

2   How does language become a skill? Analysing languaging in a problem-solving activity using a multimodal methodological framework   35
Grzegorz Grzegorczyk

3   Integrating duoethnography with ethnolinguistics in an endeavour to reconstruct the profiles of education in the discourse of third-year students of applied linguistics: A case study   80
Magdalena Grabowska

4   The four perspectives model for psychological/psychiatric case formulations in analysing the discourse of clinical-diagnostic case reporting   105
Magdalena Zabielska

5   The application of projective techniques to render linguistic repertoires of plurilingual language learners at the tertiary level   130
Emilia Wąsikiewicz-Firlej

6   Deconstructing ethnic insults by means of dual character concepts: Finding evidence of newly emerging contemptuous meanings with recourse to philosophical concepts and corpus linguistics   172
Anna Szczepaniak-Kozak

7   Focus group interview in the ecological perspective on language study: An insight into critical language awareness of L2 users with regard to translingual practices of plurilinguals   208
Hadrian Aleksander Lankiewicz

Index   251

Preface

Hadrian Lankiewicz

The term "applied linguistics", even if it has a relatively short history, has undergone a remarkable development over the years which reflects its viability and justifies the need for the divergence from traditional "pure" linguistics. Nonetheless, there is still much "uncertainty surrounding applied linguistics as an academic enquiry" (Harris, 2001: 99). The bone of contention is both the purview of academic interest, in other words, what is to be studied (language as an object of research, but in what sense) as well as methodological ground (how to go about doing viable and legitimate research pertaining to language related issues, which researchers who identify themselves as linguists consider their exclusive territory). The proper definition of applied linguistics within these two areas is crucial for recognizing it as an independent discipline, especially if it tries to be different from a well-established branch of knowledge such as linguistics.

Historically, applied linguistics emerged in the field of L2 teaching, in which language issues needed to be perceived from a new perspective, reaching beyond traditional linguistics. The "applied aspect" pertained initially to second language teaching, to make it more "academically driven", as initiated by the University of Michigan, at which in 1941 the English Language Institute was created to confront this issue (Richards & Rodgers, 1986: 45). This initiative soon met with the formation of similar units at other universities and was accompanied by professional journals and associations for which applied linguistics became synonymous with language teaching, extended to include language literacy and language arts (Liddicoat, 2010: 14.7) Hence, the strong legacy of language learning and teaching in applied linguistics is accentuated in its various definitions (cf. Harris, 2001). In this context, it is worth considering Widdowson's (1980, 2000a) differentiation between "applied linguistics" and "linguistics applied". While the former calls for legitimate research based on a practice-before-theory paradigm, accommodating more ethnographic perspectives to language related real-world problems, the latter foreshadows the primacy of linguistic theories to be simply applied to reformulate these problems.

Language learning and teaching, at its onset, was strongly influenced by linguistic theories adopted and applied on a pedagogical level in a top-down way. With time, however, as applied linguistics left the fledgling stage, the practice-before-theory paradigm took over, and the sociocultural reality of the processes of learning and teaching, as well as individual personality features, came to the forefront of attention. In some countries, academic circles dubbed this part of applied linguistics glottodidactics (e.g. Poland and Germany) triggering research going far beyond linguistics and dictating new frameworks for language units to be taught. Some scholars, allowing for the ecology of language learning and teaching, and the place of language in education in general, have proposed a transdisciplinary academic endeavour termed educational linguistics (van Lier, 2004: 2, Spolsky, 2000: 157) to account for language-related aspects which fall outside the area of interest and methodology available to theoretical linguistics.

Another area of study which diversified the scope of applied linguistics at its early stage of development was automatic translation, as may be inferred from the papers presented at the Congress of the *Association Internationale de Linguistique Appliquée* held at Nancy University in France in 1964. They "were solicited in two distinct strands – language teaching and automatic translation" (Tucker, 2022). The translation component in the early definition of applied linguistics is also mentioned in Corder's view of the discipline (1973, after Liddicoat, 2010: 14.7). These two lines of applied linguistics research were, in turn, reinforced by the newly emerging discipline of psycholinguistics, and second language acquisition (SLA), in which research in the field of language processing and language acquisition motivated the theories and practices of language teaching. In fact, informed language teaching and translation triggered the bulk of studies carried out on the fringes of various academic domains, and ultimately applied linguistics became a multifaceted discipline promoting context sensitive research allowing for *variability* rather than *stability* in SLA.

Despite the dominance of language pedagogy in publications classified as pertaining to applied linguistics, today, the investigative orientations of applied linguistics encompass research areas far beyond teaching and translation, but the scope of academic enquiry of this discipline still remains vague, shrouded in its being "multidisciplinary" and "practical", as argued by Harris (2001: 110–111). Finding a single, all-encompassing and exhaustive, definition is impossible. Available delineations of this discipline are biased by the academic affiliations of their authors, which boils down to the problems highlighted by Widdowson (1980, 2000a) of how much linguistics is in applied linguistics and how far its research scope has methodologically expanded over the years. Thereby, any definition is unsafe and politicised in the face of the diversity of contemporary academics who classify themselves as applied linguists.

In fact, the scope of enquiry of applied linguistics is *ostensive* without demarcating any limits of the field (Davies, 2007: 1), and it is mainly derived from the formulations of the aims and objectives of numerous professional journals, applied linguistics associations or names of academic institutions (cf. Harris, 2001).

Liddicoat (2010: 14.4), referring to other scholars, presents the following macro-level of applied linguistics interests: "theoretical and empirical investigation of real world problems in which language is a central issue", "problems in the world in which language is implicated", "a practice-driven discipline that addresses language based problems in real world contexts". In this regard, the range of activities of AILA (Association Internationale de Linguistique Appliquée/International Association of Applied Linguistics) may be interesting, encompassing problems related to language teaching, language planning, discourse analysis, interpreting and translating, language and media, language and ecology, language and business, language and gender language contact and language change, lexicography and lexicology, second language acquisition, psycholinguistics, rhetoric and stylistics, and many more (cf. Liddicoat, 2010: 14.5).

This inherently diverse focus on language problems and the thematic vagueness of applied linguistics still generates doubts and misgivings towards it as academic enquiry (Harris, 2001: 100). Yet, as others point out (Widdowson, 2000: 3), the lack of boundaries and its ever-expanding scope of interest have certainly contributed to its development. These two features became constitutive elements of this academic field, since the preference for the study of local and practical issues in a particular context accounts for its dynamic nature.

Even if, in common terms, applied linguistics incorporates the notion of linguistics, the analysis of its research may indicate that linguistics informs it less than other disciplines (Liddicoat, 2010: 14.8). Those who follow this line of thinking clearly propound applied linguistics as an independent discipline, not a subfield of linguistics in the form contested by Widdowson (1980, 2000a).

In this vein, Lars S. Evensen (2013) tries to find a consensus for this fragmented discipline by suggesting an integrated research paradigm and an elaboration of a third-space, a platform of collaboration for applied linguists representing different research areas. He builds this space upon the Bakhtinian concept of dialogism. Drawing on poststructural thinking, he contends, in epistemological terms, the emancipatory character of applied linguistics in its knowledge interest, and presents it as questioning the institutionalized (technical) approaches to doing science. Additionally, the epistemological category of the object of research allows him to claim that applied linguistics research is problem-driven, as opposed to the theory driven approaches typical of linguistics. As he admits, the latter informed applied linguistics issues in the burgeoning stages, like, for example, the application of contrastive analysis theories and behaviourist psychology to language teaching.

Opting for a problem-driven approach, Evensen accentuates the mediatory role of applied linguistics (hinted at earlier by Widdowson, 2000b), consisting in solving "real-world problems related to language-mediated communication, where the language system functions as a resource and not as the exclusive target of research"

(Infante, 2021; 125). His integrated research paradigm based on a *tertium compa-rationis* (third space) is solidly supported with theoretical consideration regarding an integrated model of communication at micro- and macro level predicated upon the dialogic theory of Bakhtin. One of the turning points in applied linguistics, free-ing it from linguistics, is found in language teaching informed by Vygotskian psy-chology, which sees language development as intermental mediation, rather than the computer metaphor of mind posed by the Chomskyan tradition. This argument echoes Harris's (2001: 107–109) recognition of the search for an applied linguistics model for language pedagogy associated with the British tradition of communica-tive language teaching (CLT), anchored in bottom up research.

Ultimately, the third space in doing applied linguistics research is visualised by Evensen (2013) in the potential of participatory action research, "representative of the collaborative, interactive, and ethical problem-driven orientation of applied lin-guistics scholarship" (Infante, 2021: 126). Keeping in mind the emancipatory char-acter of applied linguistics, this research orientation is the most promising for social transformation.

An interesting concept in the context of applied linguistics as an independent discipline is put forth by Li (2018). He proposes conceptualising translanguaging as a practical theory of language. His attempt is evocative of Kramsch's (2015) call for formulating a practical theory of language, representative of applied linguistics, a theory which would "capture the dialectic between social structure and human agency and how social beings, with their diverse motives and their diverse inten-tions, make and transform the world" (Li, 2018: 10). His is informed, among oth-ers, by the "so-called dialectical materialist approach to knowledge acquisition that knowledge is wrought through practice" (ibid.), a stance which diverges form Even-sen's point of view (cf. Infante, 2021: 126). Without going into details, however, it needs to be admitted that Li's underlying ideas fit well into a general predication for bottom-up production of theories in an interpretative way, rather than offering top-down predictions and solutions. In his mind, "Translanguaging as a practical theory of language offers better interpretations […] of language practice […] and the kinds of theoretical questions it can raise in relation to some of the most cen-tral issues in linguistic science" (Li, 2018: 11). His theory challenges the myth of a pure form of language, and allows for the ongoing semiotic agency of language us-ers who make the most of their linguistic repertoires in the Post-Multilingualism era. It calls for the reassessment of both the notion of language and communication. The latter, in the 21st century, is basically multimodal, going far beyond linguistic means. Drawing on ecolinguistic theories, he discloses instances of how the idea of translanguaging works as an all-encompassing theory for human language-related activities, including thinking, and "takes us beyond the linguistics of systems and speakers to a linguistics of participation" (Li, 2018: 15). In the conclusion to his considerations, Li underscores the fact that translanguaging is not merely a disruptive label for certain practices typical of the 21st century, it rather "offers a practical theory of language that sees the latter as a multilingual, multisemiotic, multisensory, and multimodal resource that human beings use for thinking and for communicating thought" (ibid., 26).

It is commonly agreed that applied linguistics escapes rigid understanding of disciplinarity and scholars frequently point to the fundament tenet of interdisciplinarity, which is of a particular importance for this publication. Modern applied linguistics relies on interdisciplinary research more than ever, since, as Carole L. Palmer (2001) points out, "[t]he real-world research problems that scientists address rarely arise within orderly disciplinary categories, and neither do their solutions" (p. vii; after Repko, 2008: 3). Its interdisciplinary character manifests itself in the wide scope of research done on the border of linguistics and well-recognized academic fields such as, e.g. education, psychology, communication, sociology, philosophy, or anthropology and methodology, drawing on various disciplines. It would not be far-fetched to claim that, from its outset, research in applied linguistics has always transgressed the compartmentalization of doing science.

Yet, it is important to stress here that interdisciplinarity should not be understood as a mere application of research methodology from one academic discipline to another, but rather its application should help redefine initial research problems and pursue them in a new way, to offer new insights and ultimately impart a new type of knowledge, which alternatively would be unattainable. Thereby, those for whom interdisciplinarity is more than "any form of dialog or interaction between two or more disciplines" (Moran, 2010: 14, after Repko, 2008: 4) accentuate integration "by which ideas, data and information, methods, tools, concepts, and/or theories from two or more disciplines are synthesized, connected, or blended" (Repko, 2008: 4). As a result, some researchers question the interdisciplinary placement of applied linguistics, since "interdisciplinarity is not possible because no interaction of disciplines will leave those disciplines in their pristine form, one discipline will modify another to accommodate to its own perspectives" (Widdowson, 2005: after Liddicoat, 2010: 14.8). This radical view assumes that applied linguistics adopts methods and theories from other disciplines in an eclectic way. Conversely, however, this opinion may be used as an argument for its disciplinarity, because the incorporation of methodologies is more adaptive than adoptive. Thereby, the interdisciplinarity in question results in the field dubbed as applied linguistics being defined not only by its focus, but also by its incorporative methodology used for solving language-related real-life problems which other disciplines would not consider. Li's (2018: 10) words, that "the disciplines from which we have borrowed concepts and methods pay relatively little attention to what we as applied linguists have done in return", may be important in this regard.

In this volume, the authors will try to accentuate this integrationist aspect of applying research methods and techniques from other disciplines to the domain of language studies to meet the challenge of theoretical or practical complexity. They will stress the emerging value of going beyond clear-cut methodological purity, while striving after their research objectives (inherently irresolvable within border disciplines). It is worth mentioning here that a remarkable body of research in applied linguistics is the result of the integrationist approach, especially that pertaining to multilingualism, second language acquisition, language pedagogy, translation studies, or forensic linguistics. Research goals for the applied fields necessitate theoretical and methodological transgressions, and help to obtain more comprehensive insights – an added value. New knowledge space gained this way blurs disciplinary borders and promotes, in some contexts, interdisciplines, which acquire the status of subdisciplines.

In the field of applied linguistics, and not only, the end of the 20th century has been defined as a "discursive turn", "cultural turn" or "critical turn". The beginning of the 21st century is marked by a "trans turn" standing for the dethroning of monolingual ideologies in language studies. The new linguistic reality – psycholinguistic plurilingualism, sociolinguistic multilingualism and multiculturalism, facilitated by globalization processes – forces academics to look for new pathways for delving into linguistic issues which slip away from a structural mindset. A tangible example of transgressing a structural framework in doing linguistic research is the field of plurilingualism, which required academics to reformulate the theoretical background for the conceptualization of plurilingualism as a single underlying multi-competence, rather than a monolingual poly-competence (separate competence for any single language). As a result, research objectives shifted from contextual code-switching to more inherent translingual practices, illuminating instinctual language processing among plurilinguals (Li, 2011). Accordingly, problems highlighted by critical approaches come into play, questioning linguistic formativeness, political standardization, linguistic planning, linguistic empowerment, or marginalization of non-native speakers, or issues of linguistic identity. All of the issues need the application of methodologies from bordering disciplines and many a time go beyond conversation analysis, critical discourse analysis or language processing protocols and employ phenomenological observation, more typical of ethnographic studies, articulated in the form of narratives analysed in a variety of ways to account for contextual language use.

The aim of this publication is to highlight the possibilities of applying selected methodologies or a theoretical apparatus derived from other fields of research into the area of language study (or a language-related problem which requires an interdisciplinary approach) in the era of the poststructural and multidisciplinary approach to doing research. Poststructuralism necessitates the use of new methods and data collection techniques to account for language fluidity, or non-fixity (Harris,

1981), and the need for deep contextualization to provide the ecological validity (van Lier, 2004: 168) of any linguistic study, on the one hand, and open-minded, cross-disciplinary methodological stances, on the other. Basically, this approach favours qualitative, interpretative research, but does not exclude quantitative methods and techniques. Thereby, this volume promotes less frequent methodologies, articulating their topical suitability (face validity), overall reliability, and advantages as well as their shortcomings. The authors stress the latent potential of the presented methodology to confront elusive and transitory linguistic phenomena which may be difficult to research via more traditional approaches.

Interdisciplinarity has become a signpost to a new age of scientific advancement in Europe (LERU universities, cf. Wernli & Darbellay, 2016). In applied linguistics, it is necessitated by the pervasiveness of language in many areas of human activities, which are academically divided into various disciplines. We foresee the future of applied sciences such as applied linguistics not only in the application of methodologies derived from overlapping disciplines, but in sharing interdisciplinary boundary experiences (cf. Clark, Laing, Leant, Lofthouse, Thomas, Tiplady & Woolner, 2017) since dialogue between people from different disciplines offers a transformational potential for finding practical solutions to language-related problems and strengthens the face validity of academic research in the area. This, however, requires the application of a process-oriented research approach (Kumar, 2011) and new interdisciplinary programs training critical skills and competences for effectuating this type of research (Tobi & Kampen, 2018). Nonetheless, this volume is very modest in its character and offers only a step forward towards interdisciplinarity in its full compass. Contributions presented in this volume only delineate tentative horizons derived from the application of new research methodologies, and in this way they lie somewhere between interdisciplinarity and methodological diversity, a constitutive element of applied linguistics research, articulated earlier in this preface.

The book consists of seven chapters, each of which is dedicated to a selected methodology incorporated form the outside of the linguistic domain, yet applied to linguistic issues which are interdisciplinary in their character. They either occupy a "contested space between disciplines", need interdisciplinary insights and require methodological or theoretical integration. Ultimately, this integration offers "a more comprehensive understanding" of the researched problem (cf. Repko, 2008: 8).

Thereby, Małgorzata Godlewska, in Chapter 1, investigates the collaborative strategy rooted primarily in social sciences, specifically in pedagogy and psychology, and transferred in her research into subfields of applied linguistics – translation studies and translation teaching. The methodology, founded on the socio-constructivist approach and the social psychology of knowledge, validates collaboration as a method to examine the stimulation and development of translation sub-competences in the process of shared expert knowledge building.

Grzegorz Grzegorczyk (Chapter 2) suggests we turn to methods typically used in Anthropology, Sociology and Communication and Media Studies when analysing face-to-face linguistic interactions. His argument is that, since language is not a code but an activity in which vocalisations, prosody, gesture, facial expression, body movement, and artefacts of the immediate environment play a significant role, the ways we use to study talking should go far beyond the research methods traditionally used in linguistics. He postulates multimodal analysis as a holistic methodological approach addressing the embodied and distributed nature of language.

Magdalena Grabowska (Chapter 3) draws our attention to duoethnography, a qualitative method developed in social, health and educational research. The author finds its application useful for the study of profiles and profiling, concepts developed in the field of ethnolinguistics. The main thrust of this academic endeavour is to understand how people of difference who are in the course of collaborative interaction conceptualize education.

Magdalena Zabielska (Chapter 4) adopts the four perspectives approach to case formulations as utilised in psychology/psychiatry, in order to examine the specialised discourse of clinical-diagnostic case reporting from an applied perspective. Although the two micro-genres represent two conceptually different disciplines, this primarily content-related generic macro-scheme can aid the selection of particular linguistic resources in the clinical-diagnostic context to render the uniqueness of each patient's case, which may be of interest from the perspective of Language for Specific Purposes courses. Apart from examining two data types, the study draws on the combination of qualitative research with the quantitatively oriented computer-aided analysis.

Emilia Wąsikiewicz-Firlej (Chapter 5) integrates projective techniques, introduced in clinical psychology and currently successfully applied in marketing and consumer research, with metaphor analysis to study young adults' multilingual repertoires. The novelty of the method used is that it focuses on the figurative representation of multilingual repertoires and the analysis of visual and verbal metaphors generated in the construction of the language portrait and accompanying narrative. The employed multimodal approach enabled the participants to represent their attitudes and experiences in a figurative, creative way and to view their linguistic repertoires from a holistic perspective by developing narratives that connect the dots between their biographies, language and identity. From a methodological perspective, the interdisciplinary approach and the combination of different data collection and analysis methods has provided rich and insightful data, and enabled the researcher to triangulate the findings and reject criticism directed at projective techniques.

Anna Szczepaniak-Kozak (Chapter 6) applies the notion of the dual character of words, derived from experimental philosophy and cognitive psychology, to discuss how racist and xenophobic hate speech could be more easily identified as part of public awareness, and dealt with legally in court. The dual character concept supports her research based on corpus linguistics tools and critical discourse analysis. The dual character of the words is evidenced with partial support of data mining and concordance analysis, in order to demonstrate how specific linguistic choices adopted by the authors of hate messages reveal their contemptible prejudice.

Hadrian Lankiewicz (Chapter 7), in the linguistic search for critical language awareness among plurilinguals, applies a focus group interview methodology, which basically derives from social sciences. He justifies its use in the context of the ecological approach to language study and the concept of ecological validity, and stresses the benefits derived from its application for the research area, compared to a traditional one-to-one interview or a survey study or observation.

We hope our proposal proves to be insightful, practical and will inspire other scholars to do similar interdisciplinary research in the field of applied linguistics.

REFERENCES

Clark, J. Laing, K. Leat, D. Lofthouse, R. Thomas, U. Tiplady, L., and Woolner, P. (2017). Transformation in Interdisciplinary Research Methodology: The Importance of Shared Experiences in Landscapes of Practice. *International Journal of Research & Method in Education,* 40(3): 243–256.

Corder, S. P. (1973). *Introducing Applied Linguistics*. Harmondsworth: Penguin.

Davies, A. (2007). *An Introduction to Applied Linguistics: From Practice to Theory* (2nd ed.). Edinburgh: Edinburgh University Press.

Evensen, L. S. (2013). *Applied Linguistics: Towards a New Integration?* Sheffield and Bristol, CT: Equinox Publishing Ltd.

Harris, R. (1981). *The Language Myth*. London, Duckworth.

Harris, T. (2001). Linguistics in Applied Linguistics: A Historical Overview. *Journal of English Studies*, 3(2): 99–114.

Infante, P. (2021). Review: Applied Linguistics: Towards a New Integration? Lars Sigfred Evensen (2013). *Language and Sociocultural Theory*, 7(2): 123–127.

Kramsch, C. (2015). Applied linguistics: A theory of the practice. *Applied Linguistics*, 36: 454–465.

Kumar, R. (1999/2011). *Research Methodology: A Step-by-Step Guide for Beginners*. Third edition. Los Angeles, London, New Delhi, Singapore, Washington DC: Sage.

Li, W. (2011). Moment Analysis and Translanguaging Space: Discursive Construction of Identities by Multilingual Chinese Youth in Britain. *Journal of Pragmatics*, 43(5): 1222–1235.

Li, W. (2018). Translanguaging as a Practical Theory of Language. *Applied Linguistics*, 39/1: 9–30.

Liddicoat, A. J. (2010). Applied Linguistics in its Disciplinary Context. *Australian Review of Applied Linguistics*, 33(2): 14.1–14.17.

Palmer, C. L. (2001). Work at the Boundaries of Science: Information and the Interdisciplinary Research Process. Dordrecht: Kluwer Academic Publishers.

Repko, A. F. (2008). *Interdisciplinary Research: Process and Theory*. Los Angeles, London, New Delhi, Singapore: Sage.

Richards J. C., and Rodgers, T. S. (1986). *Approaches and Methods in Language Teaching*. Cambridge: Cambridge University Press.

Spolsky, B. (2000). Language Motivation Revisited. *Applied Linguistics*, 21(2): 157–169.

Tobi, H., and Kampen, J. K. (2018). Research Design: The Methodology for Interdisciplinary Research Framework. *Quality & Quantity. International Journal of Methodology*, 52(3): 1209–1225.

Tucker, G. R. (2022). Linguistic Society of America. Homepage. https://www.linguisticsociety.org/resource/applied-linguistics [accessed 190.01.2022].

Van Lier, L. (2004). *The Ecology and Semiotics of Language Learning: A Sociocultural Perspective*. Boston, Dordrecht, New York and London: Kluwer Academic Publishers.

Wernli, D., and Darbellay, F. (2016). Interdisciplinarity and the 21st Century Research-Intensive University. All LERU Publications. https://www.leru.org/files/Interdisciplinarity-and-the-21st-Century-Research-Intensive-University-Full-paper.pdf [accessed 19.01.2022].

Widdowson, H. G. (1980). Applied linguistics: The pursuit of relevance. In R. B. Kaplan (Ed.). *The Oxford Handbook of Applied Linguistics* (pp. 74–87). Oxford: Oxford University Press.

Widdowson, H. G. (2000a). On the limitations of linguistics applied. *Applied Linguistics*, 21: 3–25.

Widdowson, H. G. (2000b). Object Language and the Language Subject: On the Mediating Role of Applied Linguistics. *Annual Review of Applied Linguistics,* 20: 21–33.

Widdowson, H. G. (2005). Applied linguistics, interdisciplinarity, and disparate realities. In Bruthiaux, P., Atkinson, Eggington, W. G., Grabe, W., and Ramanathan, V. (Eds.). *Directions in Applied Linguistics* (pp. 12–25). Clevedon, UK: Multilingual Matters.

ABOUT THE AUTHOR

Hadrian Aleksander Lankiewicz is the holder of D. Litt. in applied linguistics and PhD in literary studies, and three MA diplomas (in history, English studies and Italian language and culture). He is currently an Associate Professor and the head of the Department of Applied Linguistics at the University of Gdańsk, Poland. His academic interests oscillate between history, American literature and applied linguistics, with the primary focus on language acquisition and foreign language teaching methodology. In recent years, his research has been inspired by the application of an ecological metaphor to the study of language and its learning. Drawing on the concept of multi-competence and political autonomy in the process of language learning, he concentrated on issues of marginalization, empowerment and legitimization in the use of English as a foreign language.

1

Building translation sub-competences of foreign language students in telecollaboration

Małgorzata Godlewska

ABSTRACT

This chapter discusses the main foundations of a collaborative learning strategy and offers a new methodological model built on this pedagogical approach, and enriched by the element of building shared expert knowledge in the field of translation. The main aim of the collaborative model it advances is to evaluate the effectiveness of its application in translation didactics at the higher education and professional training levels. The model is indebted to the socio-constructivist approach, cognitive psychology and discourse analysis. The chapter explores the synthesis of collaborative learning with the interpretation of collaborating utterances so as to expose the process of building translation sub-competences. The practical experiment involved the qualitative micro-analysis of data gathered from pre-activity scripts, recorded collaborative interactions and post-activity scripts. The proposed model constitutes a new version of an educational learning method which should appeal to the growing expectations of higher education and the professional translation sector in the area of expert competences and high social skills.

Keywords: translation competence, collaborative learning, teaching translation, online education

1.1. INTRODUCTION

The phenomenon of collaborative learning owes its enduring persistence to the contemporary imperative for networking, professional flexibility and to the increasing conception of learning as a social and cultural process. The proposal for the application of a collaborative learning strategy in on-line translation teaching leads to the attainment of educational goals on the levels of expert knowledge, practical skills and various social competences.

This research concentrates on the increased linguistic and non-linguistic translation competences (Małgorzewicz, 2014) activated as a group of students being trained in the area of translation studies collaborate. The didactic aim of the research is to establish one well-informed rendition of a literary text, while the methodological aim is to explore by means of micro-genesis the moments of increased "translation sub-competences" (PACTE, 2003, Hurtado Albir, 2017) during the negotiation of meanings in the students' discourse.

1.2. COLLABORATIVE LEARNING STRATEGY

1.2.1. Historical overview of main theories and concepts of collaborative learning

With their roots in pedagogical studies, the terms collaborative learning and cooperative learning have become prevalent across a variety of scientific disciplines, including cognitive psychology (Dillenbourg, 1999), business and management (Blundo, Simon, 2016; Loon, 2016), music and music education (Westerlund, 2013), information and communication technologies (Adams, 2005; Anastasiades, 2009; Dillenbourg, 1999; Dimarco, 2010) and healthcare (Croker, Smith, Fisher, 2016; Raney, Lasky, Scott, 2017). Collaborative and cooperative learning strategies can be detected in a vast number of current scientific theories which have emerged from pioneering works of the early and mid-20th century. George Jacobs and Peter Seow (2015: 28–29) have indicated the impact of scientific theories such as Sociocultural Theory, Social Interdependence Theory, Human Psychology, Social Constructivism and Multiple Intelligences Theory on the development of cooperative and collaborative learning, which the theories have been operationalizing for decades.

The terms "cooperative learning" and "collaborative learning" pertain to the same basic concept of group work and, due to this general association, are often regarded as two facets of the same educational problem (Johnson et al., 2013: 14–15), hence the terms tend to be used interchangeably. Nestor D. Roselli (2016) searches for the origins of collaborative learning in three major theories: socio-cognitive conflict theory, the intersubjectivity theory and the distributed cognition theory (2016: 254). He also argues that the origins of collaborative learning lie in the 1980s and early 90s, when advanced research into cooperative learning led to the rise of the new scientific field labelled "collaborative learning" (2016: 255). Collaborative learning, in turn, contributed to the development of another sub-discipline formed by its relation to the computer science and communications technology known as computer-supported collaborative learning or CSCL (2016: 261). Roselli also observes a general consensus on the key role of cooperative learning strategy in the application of computer technologies in education (Roselli, 2016: 261). All in all, the three scientific theories which Roselli addresses converge at one point, and given their significance for the understanding of collaborative learning, they foreground the importance of the process of negotiation and the construction of shared meaning (2016: 261).

The collaborative learning approach stems from Sociocultural Theory and its development is thoroughly indebted to the work of Lev Vygotsky (1978). Apart from the importance of social interaction, the Zone of Proximal Development and the significance of the didactic tools applied, such as various forms of scaffolding, it is the role of the historical and cultural contexts in the process of knowledge construction (Arvaja, 2007: 133) which continues to validate his research.

The origin of collaborative learning is often attributed to the work of Edwin Mason and the research of Sir James Britton (Jacobs & Seow, 2015: 15). Mason's vision of the education system is influenced by his perception of people as "processes in a system of energy exchange" (1973: 91). For Britton, educational goals should be achieved through the freedom of group interactions between students and, sometimes, teachers, and originate from student dialogues (Britton, 1990, after Jacobs & Seow, 2015: 15).

In the 1990s, Kenneth Bruffee advanced research into collaborative learning. In his view, both collaborative and cooperative learning strategies coincide with regard to shared educational activities and the significance of human interactions as a means to successful educational goals (1999: 83). It was proposed that cooperative learning could realize educational goals at the early stages of primary school education, with collaborative learning complementing this phase at the university level (Bruffee, 1999: 87). Bruffee's approach subscribes into the broader discipline of social constructivism and social psychology of knowledge where knowledge, and teaching likewise, is understood as "a process of negotiation or joint construction of meanings" (Roselli, 2016: 256).

One of the main differences between the collaborative and cooperative learning types rests in the distance between learners and teachers, or in the degree of the collaborative autonomy achieved. Cooperative learning is marked by a high degree of teacher intervention in group work activities, while collaborative learning rejects these interventions and expects more independence and decidedness from its learners (Myskow et al. 2018: 365). Collaborative learning should be preceded by cooperative learning at the initial stages of a group task to provide students with suitable procedures to be employed in interactive activities (2018: 366). Collaborating students are expected to possess various social skills prior to their interactions and to be ready to use them in shared activities (Mathews et al. 1995: 40).

Murphey and Jacobs explore the relationship between collaborative learning and learner autonomy while underscoring the emphasis of cognitive psychologists on the role of learners and the learning process (2008: 2). They believe that students are able to construct their own knowledge in the learning process but also to participate in the construction of the learning environment (ibid.). This assumption about a significant change in the perception of the learning process allows them to observe a link between learner-centredness, learner autonomy and collaboration.

Murphey and Jacobs recognize collaboration as a result of successful cooperative learning achieved through a set of strategies (2008: 4). Their definition of collaboration incorporates key concepts of the cooperative learning indicated by Johnson et al. (1994), namely positive interdependence and individual accountability, as well as collaborative skills, such as "disagreeing politely, checking if others understand, and listening attentively" (2008: 4–5). Collaboration grounded in the principles of cooperative learning is capable of supporting learner autonomy. Firmly entrenched in Vygotsky's sociocultural theory, their research accentuates the role played by the discourse of others in the construction of understandings tied-in with prior knowledge (2008: 7).

Pierre Dillenbourg defines collaborative learning as a type of a social contract which determines the conditions for specific interactions (1999: 5), and specifies a set of four categories whose determination should guarantee the production of these interactions: setting up initial conditions; the over-specification of the "collaboration" contract with a scenario based on roles; the scaffolding of productive interactions by encompassing interaction rules in the medium; and monitoring and regulating the interactions (1999: 5–6).

Dillenbourg argues that the theory of collaborative learning should consider the criteria for defining the situation, interactions, processes, and effects (1999: 13). The first of these, situation, acquires a collaborative quality if the peers involved in the activity are at a similar level, perform the same action or share the same goal (Dillenbourg, 1999: 7). Dillenbourg argues that the situation and interactions should be determined by three categories, "symmetry of action", "symmetry of knowledge" and "symmetry of status" (1999: 7). Symmetry of action designates the degree of similarity in the distribution of actions among individual group members. Symmetry of knowledge (also known as symmetry of skills or development) refers to the degree of similarity between individual members' knowledge levels, and symmetry of status to the degree of similarity between each member's status in a given community (1999: 7).

Common goals constitute the second significant feature of a collaborative situation, which may be only partially shared in the initial phase of the task. These goals need to be subjected to constant negotiation and revision during the realization of the project. These group processes may succeed in producing group awareness of their mutual goals (Dillenbourg, 1999: 8).

Interactions, the second concept which underlies collaborative learning, must be viewed through the prism of three criteria: interactivity, synchronicity and negotiability. The interactivity of a collaborative situation depends on the quality of interactions and on their potential to exert an impact on the group members' cognitive processes (1999: 8). Synchronicity, the second criterion underlying collaborative interactions, stands in contrast to the asynchronous quality of cooperative learning (1999: 8). Lastly, collaborative interactions must be negotiable, in that they must reject any authority imposed on peers and, instead, encourage dialogue and argumentation (1999: 9).

The final component of Dillenbourg's collaborative learning model concerns its effects, which, it is suggested, are to be analysed in relation to the particular category of the interactions which triggered them. Furthermore, as opposed to the general trend to evaluate the effects of collaborative learning by "individual task performance measures", Dillenbourg argues for a more credible method of evaluation – the evaluation of group performance (1999: 12).

One vital alteration in the development of the collaborative learning theory is related to the transfer of the focus of interest away from the products and onto the process of collaboration (Hämäläinen & Arvaja, 2009: 1). In addition, more attention is given to the potential outcomes of the integration of collaborative learning in the area of computer technology under the common term of Computer-Supported Collaborative Learning, and to the ways in which these two areas of research may foster learning (2009: 1). One of the weaknesses of virtual learning environments is the infrequency of high-level collaboration induced by collaborative activities (Hämäläinen & Arvaja, 2009: 2). Other obstacles in the studies devoted to CSCL may involve mounting disagreements among group members, free riding behaviour, and "discussions that lack depth, high-quality reasoning, and argumentation" (Janssen & Bodemer 2013: 1).

The difficulty of accomplishing shared knowledge provides another problematic issue in collaborative learning, and indeed one of the utmost significance in computer-supported collaborative learning. Hämäläinen and Arvaja observe the clash between the optimistic expectations raised by the virtual learning environment and the realities of life, which confront learners with interruptions, unpredictable events or irritation. Furthermore, despite the views on the naturalness of interactions offered by collaborative work, research proves that collaboration hardly ever results from spontaneous and uncontrolled group activities (Arvaja et al., 2003; Järvelä & Häkkinen, 2002, after Hämäläinen & Arvaja, 2009: 2). The achievement of high-quality collaborative outcome is barely feasible and collaborative learning is hence often regarded as an "ideal" form of group work (Vass & Littleton, 2009; Arvaja, 2007; Hämäläinen, 2012).

The application of collaboration scripts is proposed as a method to elevate the quality of collaborative work (Dillenbourg & Jermann 2006; Hämäläinen, 2012: 604). A variety of pre- and post-structuring activities can be added to the learning process in order to introduce increased control and structure into the collaborative work, and enhance its effectiveness. Scripting is believed to lead to "higher-level cognitive processing" and increased collaborative learning effectiveness (Hämäläinen & Arvaja, 2009: 2–3). Micro-scripts provide detailed guidance for group interactions, while macro-scripts offer more general instructions on group performance, thus opening the way for creativity on the part of group members (Hämäläinen, 2012: 605).

Recent research into computer-supported collaborative learning has emphasized the necessity for exploration into the process of shared knowledge construction through the study of the interdependence between group members, as reflected in two dialogical spaces, "the content space" and "the relational space of collaboration" (Janssen & Bodemer, 2013: 41). The goal of the interactions in the content space is to expand knowledge in a scientific domain with the aid of collaborative activities, whereas the goal of the interactions within the relational space is to construct and maintain shared understanding in the collaborative group (2013: 41).

The coordination of the collaborative work within the two interactive spaces presupposes the possession of "awareness information" in the collaborating team: members must be conscious of the group's behavioural activities, knowledge and skills (Janssen et al., 2011; Janssen & Bodemer, 2013: 42). Group awareness, specifically the knowledge which the group members possess about their individual contribution to the collaborative activities and the distribution of knowledge among the group members, constitutes an underlying condition of successful CSCL (2013: 42).

The role of the group awareness concept and its performance in computer-supported collaborative learning can be substantiated by means of the cognitive load theory (Janssen & Bodemer, 2013; Janssen & Kirschner, 2020). Expanded with the concepts of mutual cognitive interdependence, collective working memory and transactive activities, the cognitive load theory gives prominence to collective learning processes over individualistic ones (Kirschner et al. 2018, after Janssen & Kirschner, 2020: 784). Collaborative learning, exemplifying primary knowledge, is assumed to assist in the acquisition of "biologically secondary skills", that is, those obtained during a conscious process of learning (Kirschner et al. 2018: 3).

The processes of collaboration pose a challenge for measurement and usually rely on subjective measures, as Janssen and Kirschner argue (2020: 795). The latest research, however, offers a more pragmatic means to measure the effectiveness of collaborative processes by relying on physiological information obtained from heartbeat, skin temperature, or electro-dermal activity (2020: 795). The examination of group members' individual discourse is a more common assessment method, for instance, through the content analysis of verbal protocols (2020: 795).

The study of social interactions through the analysis of discourse rather than mental processes has evolved from the sociocultural approach, as in the research of Raija Hämäläinen and Maarit Arvaja. Arvaja (2007) proposes a methodological model of investigation in the process of computer-supported collaborative learning which relies on the study of discourse and its contexts. Arvaja argues against the study of individual knowledge construction in isolation from the context. Instead, she proposes an exploration of knowledge construction as being dependent upon the social, cultural and material environment of its occurrence (Arvaja, 2007: 134).

Collaboration is predominantly a multidimensional phenomenon which can be explored from a variety of perspectives, ranging from team cognition, knowledge construction, through structures and problem-solving processes and up to team norms and interpersonal skills (Newell & Bain, 2018: 60). The basic components central to collaboration in higher education, which have been re-iterated in research papers of the last decade, encompass the following issues: a basic number of two or more participants; the autonomous and voluntary nature of the process; consensual participation in the process; its role in approaching an understanding of the domain studied; the shared process of decision-making; and the group's acting towards a common goal (Newell & Bain, 2018: 60). The collaborative component of interdependence, accompanied by joint contributions, pervades all phases of collaborative actions in various disciplines (Newell & Bain, 2018: 61).

1.2.2. The conception of collaborative learning strategy applied to the translation sub-competence model

In this research, collaborative learning strategy is viewed as a social contract, and the group discourse triggered through this learning, as the interpretative source of interactions which imitate professional relations in the translation market. Murphey and Jacobs (2008) assert that collaborative learning fosters autonomous learning and facilitates critical evaluative abilities among team members. The on-line form of collaborative learning, or "telecollaboration", is believed to increase students' translation sub-competences, and consequently their employability on the translation job market, which are recognized as highly valued skills (Krajka & Marczak, 2017: 375).

The methodological framework for this research is founded, primarily, on the socio-constructivist approach (Stahl, 2004; Hämäläinen, 2012; Hämäläinen & Arvaja, 2009; Arvaja, 2007; Myskow et al., 2018; Kumpulainen & Mutanen, 1999) by focusing on the process of learning on a group level in a semi-authentic professional context. Furthermore, this methodology draws on the social psychology of knowledge (Dillenbourg, 1999; Janssen & Bodemer, 2013) by exploring the process of constructing collective knowledge through collaborative negotiations of meaning.

The basic frame of collaborative learning theory applied in this chapter acknowledges the perspective of Myskow et al. (2018), who stress the unbreakable relationship between cooperative learning and collaborative learning which should be applied successively in the process of learning, with cooperative learning principles serving as an introduction to a more autonomous collaborative learning type. Collaborative learning may constitute a beneficial strategy to stimulate students' autonomous and critical thinking.

The collaborative interactions of this research will be structured by means of pre- and post- collaborative scripts, as suggested by Myskow et al. (2018) and Hämäläinen and Arvaja (2009). Macro-scripting supports the participants' natural interactions and stimulates creativity and autonomous decision-making. However, no specific roles or detailed tasks will be assigned to any group member. Ideally, the collaborative learning strategy should limit the teacher's role to the organization and facilitation of team interactions. The process of learning is intended to recreate the semblance of a natural professional environment and, for this reason, the teacher should assist students in their activities as an equal partner (Rutherford, 2014: viii) in a didactic zone stripped of hierarchical structures.

In addition, this methodology adopts Pierre Dillenbourg's structure of collaborative learning activities which identifies the components of situation, interactions, processes and effects, as well as the symmetries of action, knowledge and status (1999). Consequently, collaborative interactions will be discussed with respect to their three features of interactivity, synchronicity and negotiability (Dillenbourg, 1999).

1.2.3. Building collective knowledge through the analysis of discourse

The focal point of this research is on the process of collaborative learning towards shared knowledge construction, as understood in terms of the development of expert knowledge, specifically translation sub-competences. The central aspect of this methodology lies in the conviction that collaborative learning contributes to "building collective knowledge" (Scardamalia & Bereiter, 1996: 270; Stahl, 2004). It is argued after Gerry Stahl that collaborative learning leads to the construction of meaning and that group members participate in this process by offering "a new degree of understanding" about the issue in question (2004: 2). Groups create these new meanings, share them during collaboration and learn to interpret them (2004: 20). Hence, group discourse triggers the formation of a whole network of meanings. Meaning must be interpreted by each group member and then shared among the participants in "the collaborative interpretive process" (2004: 23). This process involves ongoing shifts between tacit and explicit knowing. The role of discourse is to transform the tacit into the explicit by expressing it in words (2004: 23), or in the succinct words of Stahl, "discourse is interpretation" (2004: 22).

The meaning constructed in the discourse originates from the network of participant interactions, rather than from any individual member's utterances. In the discourse, members share their views, present various possibilities of interpreting meaning and select a particular interpretation which arose in any group member's previous utterance. This interpretation becomes reactivated as the meaning in the discourse (Stahl, 2004: 26). Thus, collaborative learning might be perceived as a manner of extending the group's knowing through the ongoing process of social interactions, with discourse at its core (2004: 32).

Stahl identifies a number of constituent elements which will be applied to this research: artifacts, situation, meaning, interpretation, perspectives, tacit knowing, explicit knowing and negotiation. It is also possible to identify symbolic, linguistic, physical or artificial artifacts. The term "cognitive artifacts" designates those which result from the process of the internalization of meaning and refer to mental phenomena (2004: 26). Stahl's concept of situation pertains to the network of interrelations which occur during group discourse. Meaning is grounded in a particular situation which must be interpreted from the participants' perspectives during the negotiation of meaning (2004: 24). In discourses, group meanings, as well as various individual interpretive perspectives, interconnect and lead to the formation of new degrees of interpretation of meanings which emerge from the common negotiations. This process can stimulate the internalization of the constructed cognitive artifacts in the participants' minds (2004: 30).

1.2.4. The components of the collaborative translation sub-competence model

1.2.4.1. *Translation sub-competences as the goal of collaborative activities*

This methodology adopts the model of translation competence proposed by the PACTE Group (PACTE, 2003; Hurtado Albir, 2017), which is derived from the research of Orozco and Hurtado Albir, as it represents a multicomponent approach to the issue of translation competence best explored through empirical studies (Krajka & Marczak, 2017: 367). The PACTE translation competence model differs from other existing models (e.g. Pym, 2003, Kiraly, 2013) in proposing a hierarchical structure of its components (Krajka & Marczak 2017: 365). PACTE researchers emphasize the underlying difference between the competence (the system of knowledge and performance) that is translation (2003: 3). They equate translation competence with expert knowledge in the sense of a combination of declarative knowledge and the predominant procedural knowledge (PACTE, 2003: 3).

This methodology will apply the PACTE translation model, which consists of five interconnected sub-competences and psycho-physiological components which underlie all the others. The five sub-competences cover: (1) bilingual competence, a procedural type of knowledge of two languages comprising "pragmatic, sociolinguistic, textual, grammatical and lexical knowledge" in the languages operated in translation; (2) extralingual sub-competence, which relies on declarative knowledge, and refers to encyclopaedic knowledge and subject knowledge; (3) knowledge of translation sub-competence, also declarative and further split into two subtypes of knowledge: one referring to methods of translation, e.g. translation units, the processes involved, the translation strategies, methods and procedures applied, and the second to "professional translation practice"; (4) instrumental sub-competence, which corresponds to the translator's use of communication technologies and various information resources, such as reference books and search engines; (5) strategic sub-competence, another component which relies mostly on procedural knowledge and constitutes the central sub-competence which influences the others. It is responsible for global efficiency in the translation process by interconnecting the components of the TC model. Among its functions are the initial planning of the translation process, differentiating between translation problems and adopting a method appropriate for the type of a problem, assessing the whole process of translation and stimulating the other sub-competences. The psycho-physiological components of the model encompass cognitive components, such as "memory, perception, attention and emotion", as well as the so-called attitudinal aspects – the translators' confidence, intellectual curiosity and motivation, as well as abilities such as "creativity, logical reasoning, analysis and synthesis" (Hurtado Albir, 2017: 40).

1.2.4.2. Translation problems and Rich Points in the analysis of translation sub-competences

This methodology applies the PACTE Group's model of translation sub-competences, together with its premise on the potential of translation competences, in order to overcome translation problems (2017: 10). These are defined as various objectively observed linguistic and non-linguistic obstacles detected by every translator, no matter the level of translation competence (Hurtado Albir, 2017: 11). The ability to solve problems is directly related to the capacity of the central strategic sub-competence, a skill at the heart of all decision-making processes and the entire translation process (2017: 10). This is the perspective adopted in this chapter.

The analysis of translation problems in the students' discourses will rely on Alves's assumption about the multidimensional character of translation problems, which can be placed under five main, but often overlapping, categories: "linguistic translation problems", which include the problems of "comprehension and/or reformulation" at the lexical and morphological text level; "textual translation problems", which address the problem of comprehension and/or reformulation on the levels of cohesion, style and genre of a translated text; "extralinguistic translation problems", which investigate source cultural phenomena and encyclopaedic issues; translation problems with the "intentionality" of a translated text, namely questions about the information conveyed by the source text through, for instance, "intertextuality, speech acts, presuppositions, and implicatures", and, finally, problems originating from "the translation brief and/or the characteristics of the target reader" and which exert an impact on the process of text reformulation (Hurtado Albir, 2017: 11).

Selected textual units which contain the translation problems outlined above will be defined as Rich Points (Nord, 1994, after Hurtado Albir, 2017: 11) and subjected to micro-analysis. The choice of Rich Points is determined by the study of collaborating students and their discourse, as well as the identification of features which signal the presence of a translation problem. The observation will consider the markers of translation problems suggested by Hurtado Albir, such as hesitation, omissions and corrections (2017: 10). The occurrence of pauses in the collaborative discourse should be of a few seconds' duration in order to be recognized as hesitation.

1.2.4.3. Specification of three informative perspectives in the analytical model

The analysis of collaborative activities will consider three aspects of the students' utterances: the type of communicative functions they exemplify, the contextual knowledge resources addressed and the Bloom's taxonomy thinking levels which they represent. The data from the network of negotiating utterances will be confronted with the translation sub-competences which they are intended to activate. The resulting information should lead to conclusions about the interdependency between the effectiveness of the team's collaborative activity and the increase in translation sub-competences.

The method of analysing group utterances through an investigation of their communicative functions and their knowledge resources was inspired by Arvaja (2007) and Hämäläinen (2012). The categorization of language functions to be used in the interpretation of collaborating discourses borrows from Kristiina Kumpulainen and Mika Mutanen's research (1999: 456). However, the categorization was completed with other communicative functions of sentences expected to occur during the experiment, and these include: informative, reasoning, evaluative, interrogative, responsive, organizational (i.e. controlling behaviour), judgemental positive and judgemental negative, argumentational (e.g. justifying one's views), suggestive, exemplifying and justifying.

Knowledge resources, the second source of data about the collaborative discourses are taken from Per Linell's perception of discourse as inserted into various contexts (Linell, 1998: 128), and indebted to Arvaja's research on the relationship between context and collaborative knowledge construction (2007). The present research is influenced by Linell's prior definition of "contextual resources" activated during speakers' dialogical interactions (1998: 128).

The basic distinction of knowledge resources applied by translators while solving a translation problem might be drawn between internal, or cognitive, resources, and external ones (Alves, 2005: 97). Linell classifies contextual resources into three types: co-textual (discursive) resources, situational resources and background assumption resources. The first refers to abstract phenomena rather than real life situations, and pertains to the prior part of the discourse in conjunction with the events which preceded the utterances. Co-text, the term proposed by Linell, might involve non-verbal elements of discourse (1998: 128–129). The second subtype of contextual resources encompasses "the surrounding concrete situations" with real life people, objects and physical spaces (Linell, 1998: 129).

The third class of contextual resources consists of abstract phenomena which might be divided into a number of subcategories. These partially interlocking categories comprise: "a model of discourse-in-context", namely the assumptions and beliefs which speakers have about the issues raised in a discussion; speakers' knowledge and assumptions about other speakers in the discussion; "the frame" or the definition of the abstract situation which the speakers participate in; "the organizational context" related to working conditions or regulations relevant in a given professional setting; knowledge of language and communication appropriate for a given culture; and general background knowledge about the world (Linell, 1998: 128–131).

The final aspect of this methodology is related to the revised version of Bloom's taxonomy thinking levels. It is argued after Magas et al. (2017) and Saputra et al. (2019) that Bloom's levels of thinking can be categorized into two levels – low-level thinking, which addresses the processes of remembering, understanding and applying, and high-level thinking, which encompasses processes such as analysing, evaluating, creating (Magas et al., 2017, after Saputra et al. 2019: 1079). This two-fold categorization of thinking models will support an investigation into the collaborating students' discourses and help in assessing the validity of their negotiations of meaning.

1.3. THE METHOD OF INVESTIGATION APPLIED TO THE COLLABORATIVE TRANSLATION SUB-COMPETENCE EXPERIMENT

1.3.1. Background information about the experiment

The practical project in question took place at the University of Gdańsk, Poland and involved a group of eight 1st year students on an Applied Linguistics Master's degree course. The project consisted of six 90-minute on-line meetings from December 2020 to January 2021, plus one extra on-line meeting after task completion.

Data for the collaborative translation project comes from three main sources: 1. A pre-activity Introductory Questionnaire with details about the participants gathered via the Microsoft Forms application; 2. A series of six recorded on-line meetings with the collaborating students and supervised by the teacher. The meetings include observation of student interactions during the translation task, their presentations of a pre-activity script, Jigsaw puzzle, and the students' mind maps with translation issues uploaded to the MS Teams platform; 3. Post-activity scripts: a. Two Student Satisfaction Questionnaires – A and B, conducted on-line via MS Teams Forms and discussed with the group on-line; b. a translation problem list, created from student feedback sent individually by email; c. The main goal of the project was a collaborative translation of the literary text, "Joy" by Zadie Smith (2013).

1.3.2. Phase 1 of the collaborative translation sub-competence experiment: analysis of three symmetries of the collaborative activities

The situations created by the students' collaborative utterances manifest the three types of symmetry indicated by Dillenbourg (1999: 22): symmetry of status (team members all from the same university community), symmetry of action (each team member's responsibility for a similar workload) and partially the symmetry of knowledge of the participating team.

Symmetry of status was assessed on the basis of data collected from the Introductory Questionnaire. It was observed that the collaborating group is homogeneous with respect to the criteria of age, gender and social status. The group includes seven female students at the age of 22–24 and one 25-year-old, who had all either graduated from the University of Gdańsk and obtained a B.A. degree in Applied Linguistics in 2019 (three students) or in 2020 (five students).

The symmetry of knowledge in this group is assessed as partial. The data necessary to verify this aspect of the collaboration was gathered from the Introductory Questionnaire, which consisted of thirteen multiple choice questions conducted via MS Teams. Subsequently, the data from the Introductory Questionnaire was compared against (1) the programmes of studies for the B.A. degree in Applied Linguistics, one for the years 2016–2019, and the other for 2017–2020, as well as (2) the programme of studies for the first semester of the M.A. degree in Applied Linguistics, which all of the group members were pursuing at the time of the project. According to the B.A. and M.A. programmes of studies, the whole group had participated in academic courses devoted to the theory and practice of literary and functional translations. The three 2019 graduates stated that they had attended between 60–120 class hours of translation, while the five 2020 graduates had attended more than 120 class hours. Thus, the group's theoretical knowledge in the field of translation studies varies.

Another issue with the group's symmetry of knowledge relates to their expertise in practical translation activities. Only three of the group members, all 2019 graduates, had participated in on-the-job training in a translation office: one student for between 20–60 hours, and two for over 60 hours. This divergence in professional translation practice stems from the university requirements to participate in forty hours of on-the-job training in a translator's office or international company. As a result, half the group members had not experienced work in a professional translation environment. Nevertheless, all confessed to doing some translations as a hobby, four members – occasionally, the other four – hardly ever.

The final question in the Introductory Questionnaire, on the group's experience with collaborative learning, showed that only three students had participated in a collaborative team on a few occasions, three others regarded collaborative learning as a common university practice, while the remaining two claimed to have never experienced a collaborative learning method.

Thus, the collaborating group is marked by partial symmetry of knowledge. All had obtained a degree of practice, as well as basic theoretical knowledge in translation studies in general. Nevertheless, the levels of knowledge in the field of translation and collaborative learning methods differ between the 2019 graduates and 2020 graduates.

Symmetry of action, which pertains to sharing common goals in collaboration, can be evaluated positively. In this project, each team member contributed equally towards a single common translation of the extract from Zadie Smith's essay during on-line meetings. The translation of the same source text constituted the ultimate goal of the whole collaborating team, and of each group member.

1.3.3. Phase 2 in the collaborative translation project: Pre-activity scripts

During the first on-line meeting, the students were acquainted with the source text by Zadie Smith, "Joy", which they were asked to translate during six on-line classes. The first paragraph of the original essay was used as a model to demonstrate how students might negotiate various meanings in collaboration during the whole project.

Due to the observed gaps in the students' declarative and procedural knowledge in the field of literary translation, the teacher decided to revise the common translation problems expected to occur in the source text by means of an initial collaborative task in pairs. The students were allowed to choose their partner for a short joint presentation on one of the following topics: 1. Translation techniques applied to metaphors; 2. Types of metaphor and problems in their translation; 3. The translation of idioms and set phrases, and 4. Techniques applied to the translation of cultural elements. At the start of the second on-line meeting, the student pairs demonstrated the results of their collaboration in short oral presentations on the translation problems selected. The mind maps of their summarized translation presentations were placed on the platform so as to serve as co-texts for the collaborative translation experiment. The pre-activity script, in the form of the Jigsaw puzzle, can be said to have successfully rehearsed the collaborative skills in pairs and acquainted the group with the use of on-line communication, video conferencing, chat or sharing files on the MS Teams platform.

1.3.4. Phase 3: interpretation of students' collaborative discourse

Five on-line meetings were devoted to the observation and video recording of the students' collaborating interactions during the translation of the literary text. The technique of macro-scripting applied to the collaborative experiment added a degree of authenticity to the situation, as well as eliminating the initial didactic hierarchy and restructuring classroom relations. The teacher's role in the collaborative task was restrained, and intrusions into the students' discussions were intended solely to generate interactivity, synchronicity and negotiability.

The selection of the situations to be interpreted was determined by the students' translation problem list and confronted with the moments of breakdown observed in the interactions (signalled by long pauses and text omissions). The transcripts of video recorded situations include the indication of pauses longer than a few seconds, student and teacher utterances and non-verbal signals transcribed in block letters. The students' translations are back translated into English and provided in square brackets.

The situations analysed revolve around three main groups of translation problems inserted in their Rich Points: textual, extralinguistic and linguistic. The analysis also includes an observation of translation problems with textual intentionality, though this is discussed in relation to the first three types of translation problems as an overlapping category.

1.3.4.1. Textual translation problems

Rich Point 1: "A lot of people seem to feel that joy is only the most intense version of pleasure..." (Smith, 2013, 1).

Situation 1

Pause

1. Student MB: *Dużo ludzi sądzi, że ...* Back translation: [lots of people think that ...]

    Pause

2. Student MK: Maybe, *wielu osobom...* [for many people ...]
3. Teacher: *Wielu osobom ...*
4. MK: Or – *wielu sądzi, że ...* [many think that ...]

    Pause

5. Teacher: OK, what do you think about that? Which version do you prefer?

    Pause

6. MB: OK, this version *wielu sądzi* sounds more natural.
7. AD, AB: (NOD)
8. ZC: Mhm.

    Pause over 4 seconds

The first transcript from the recorded video conversation demonstrates the opening exchange of perspectives among a few team members and the teacher. The occurrence of the translation problem is manifested by the long hesitation before the discussion (about 6 seconds), the inclusion of the problem into the translation problem list and the omission of the verb seem. The translation problem is both linguistic and textual in nature and concerns the reformulation of the source unit on the lexical, stylistic and sentence structure levels.

The collaborative situation results from the exchange of two students' perspectives, MB and MK. MB's suggestive utterance 1 enters into the process of meaning negotiation by relying on her background assumption knowledge, expressing her tacit understanding of the text. Her interpretation of the linguistic artifact reveals a capacity for high-level thinking and addresses the translation sub-competences of the bilingual and strategic types.

The first moment of collaborative negotiation of meaning occurs after MK's expression of two translation variants (utterances 2, 4) provoked by her interpretation of MB's first utterance. A relevant step in the negotiation of meaning is made by MB's utterance 6 which relies on the co-text established by MK's utterance 4. This exchange of meanings influences the other students' perspectives (7, 8) and results in a collective agreement rooted in the group's extended co-texts. The participants' developing translation sub-competences were seemingly impacted on various levels: the bilingual, as the students are notified of other possibilities of meaning interpretation; the level of knowledge of translation, once the participants recognize the techniques of reduction and structural modification applied; the strategic level, due to witnessing the evaluation and selection of the translation solution (utterance 6). Furthermore, the psycho-physiological component of the translation sub-competence model is activated during this introductory exchange: the engagement of the first two participants influences the attitudes of the other group members, who had initially been passive regarding the collaborative task. The negotiation of meanings between MK and MB is responsible for enriching the group's awareness and simultaneously extending their co-text. This outcome of their exchange, as well as the active attitudes of two students towards to the task, sparked the group's intellectual curiosity and influenced their motivation to join in the collaborative discourse.

Situation 2

1. MK: *...że radość to tylko bardziej intensywna przyjemność.* [that joy is just more intense pleasure]
   Pause
2. AN: I have a different proposal, if I may. *Wielu ludzi postrzega radość jako intensywniejszą formę przyjemności.* [Many people perceive joy as a more intense form of pleasure]
3. AD, MB: (NOD)
4. ZC: Personally, I like AN's version, with this verb *perceive*. I could accept it, really. (Pause) The second part of the source sentence seems rather metaphorical, so ... the beginning doesn't need to be so literal.
5. MK: Personally, I like AN's version too.
   Pause
6. Teacher: Are you withdrawing yours?
7. MK: She renders this unit pretty well.
8. Teacher: Your version is also very good. It is not incorrect. Why do you think the verb *postrzega* fits better here?
9. ZC: The verb *sądzić, że* doesn't fit in the first version. I would suggest here: *Wielu osobom wydaje się, że* [many people seem...]. A bit more gently. But I don't know...
10. Teacher: Why do you reject *sądzić, że* ?
11. AN: Well, I see it that way. This text is about different ways of seeing things. One person can see it this way, another a different way. If you begin the text with the verb such as *sądzi* [to judge, think], it is like giving a verdict, if I may call it that. And, simply, for me the case is closed.

This network of utterances demonstrates the group's efforts to deal with the textual translation problem of style and cohesion. The negotiation of meaning is initiated by the long pause after the suggestive utterance 1, which marks the group's hesitation on the discovery of the translation problem. Utterances 1 and 2, with two translation variants, represent a suggestive communicative function at the high-thinking level since the students demonstrate their creative abilities. This exchange of perspectives effects the bilingual translation sub-competence because it engages the linguistic abilities grounded in procedural knowledge. Furthermore, the students address their background assumption resources in order to formulate their translation variants.

After the second pause, the group members negotiate the degrees of meaning related to the co-text created by utterances 1 and 2. ZC's utterance 4 is evaluative, judgemental positive and reasoning, as it draws attention to the metaphorical level of the translation unit. It is the first step in the collective process of interpreting the source implicatures and identifying the translation problem. The utterance derives from background assumption resources, and the organizational context in particular, as it detects the literary device in the source language.

Furthermore, ZC's perspective 4 begins the process of evaluation of the co-text activated by AN's suggestion 2. As a result of the negotiation of meanings, MK (5) alters her perspective and accepts AN's translated unit and ZC's justification 4. The discussion related to this Rich Point encourages group members ZC (utterances 9, 4,), MK (7) and AN (11) to justify their views rather than simply agree with the new translation versions, as is the case with the less active, though equally attentive group members, who accept AN's perspective by nodding. AN's utterance 11, indicative of evaluative, reasoning and argumentational communicative functions, also participates in the collaborative process of building shared translation sub-competences, both bilingual and strategic.

Situation 3

1. MB: What if we wanted to include the meaning of the original verb *seem*, it would be like, *Wiele osób wydaje się postrzegać* [many people seem to perceive]? Like that?
2. T: What do you think about this option of literal translation?
3. MB: Maybe, *wiele osób postrzega*? [many people perceive]
4. ZC: And if we were to use both verbs, *wydawać się* [seem] and *postrzegać* [perceive], I would change the sentence structure in the first part. I mean, *wydaje się, że wiele osób postrzega* [it seems that many people perceive]. But I am not sure if that would not change the sense? But stylistically, it would be much better than the literally literal one.
5. T: So what is your priority – the literal, formal translation or the more dynamic one?
6. ZC: I think in a text with many translation problems, the style matters more, I think..., because with metaphors, the literal one may sound awkward... And this text seems to be like that, metaphorical, a bit...
7. T: Your decision: *wydaje się, że wielu ludzi postrzega* ... or without *wydaje się*?
8. AN: I opt for the shorter version. The longer one is, just, too much fuss around all this perceiving... I'd just use the shorter one.

9. AD: Me, too.
10. MB: Yeah, me, too.

The negotiation presented above on the textual problem of sentence structure predominantly engages students MB and ZC, who build their utterances on the co-texts created in the previous part of the discourse. MB's utterance 1 is built on the co-text of ZC's prior translation variant in situation 2, while ZC (4) builds her own perspective on the co-text of MB's utterance 3. MB suggests two different translation versions of the source unit (1, 3), thus demonstrating creativity and high-level thinking. ZC (4) addresses the concepts from MB's perspective and suggests a third version of the translation unit, considering the stylistics of the target text. ZC evaluates the previous utterances, proving her analytical skills and selection of translation options, which generate strategic translation sub-competence. It should be stressed that ZC contradicts the ideas proposed by MB and suggests her own translation solution with reference to the co-text of the previous utterance.

AN builds her perspective (8) on the co-text of the previous discourse of the two active students and evaluates their solutions, which elicits tacit approval from the other two students, AD (9) and MB (10). Thus, it can be concluded that the proposals from the first student, MB, triggered a network of utterances with suggestive, evaluative and judgemental functions constructed on the co-texts of the collaborating perspectives, a process which led to the final decision to approve the translation solution (8, 9, 10). The gradually developing collective discourse can therefore be credited with activating the group's strategic sub-competences.

1.3.4.2. Extralinguistic translation problems

Rich point 2: "An egg sandwich from one of those grimy food vans on Washington Square has the genuine power to turn my day around" (Smith, 2013, 1).

Situation 1

1. T: Which of the elements of this translation unit might be most problematic for you?
2. MB: I'm wondering about this Washington Square and I'd say *nieopodal* [nearby] *Washington Square in English.*
3. AN: For me, *turn my day around* sounds difficult to translate.
4. T: First, a cultural element and an idiomatic expression.
5. MB: I'll paste my proposal into the chat with Washington Square: *Jedna kanapka z jajkiem przygotowana w umorusanym food tracku nieopodal Washington Square potrafi niesłychanie poprawić humor.* [One egg sandwich in a begrimed food van in Washington Square can incredibly improve my mood.]
6. T: Your opinions?
      Pause

7. T: Has anyone read about these translation problems?
8. ZC: We did with MB. With cultural translation problems, you can either leave the source unit in the original language or find its equivalent in the target language.
9. T: We should find out if this element is translated into Polish. Have you checked that, anyone? MB left it untranslated.
10. ZC: Yes, let's leave it like that.
11. AN: I think that in Polish, it is also called Washington Square.
12. ZC: But I also found it translated as *Plac Waszyngtona*.
13. T: Will the reader know which Washington Square is referred to here?
14. ZC: I think that *Washington Square* gives the reader more information than *Plac Waszyngtona*. Because this text in translation contains cultural elements, so... *Washington Square* says which culture it comes from. And *Plac Waszyngtona* – someone would need to check where it is.
15. T: Would you know where Washington Square is, and that it is the one in NYC?
16. ZC: I would guess that. But with the English name, I would know immediately.
17. AN: But is it really that important, this Washington Square? More than the fact that it is from a *food van* on *Washington Square*? If you really want to know that, you can search the net to find out.
18. ZC, MB, KK, AN: (LAUGH)
19. AN: In my translation, I'd leave the English name.
20. KK, KH: Me, too.

Situation 1 concerns the extralinguistic translation problem suggested in the students' translation problem list – the rendition of the source geographical term. The teacher refers to the students' Jigsaw puzzle related to the cultural translation problem and to the associated mind map, accessible on the MS Teams platform to be adopted by the group as their contextual resources. ZC refers to these two contexts (8) by summarizing the data from the presentation she prepared with MB. As a result, the two students' collaborative work is upgraded to the level of the whole group's co-text activated in the subsequent group discourse.

The exchange of perspectives in this situation concerns the validity of translation variants of the proper noun. ZC (10) and AN (11) opt for the transference of the source term into the Polish target text. Nevertheless, ZC (12) expresses uncertainty over the discovery in on-line databases of two possible translation solutions to the problem. Her analysis of the translation solution is grounded in her contextual resources and extended by means of the Jigsaw puzzle and by an additional on-line search. Utterance 14 reveals her perception of the translation unit through the prism of her contextual resources and by means of her own evaluative and reasoning abilities, which confirms high-level thinking. Besides this, the observation shows the student's awareness of the particular extralinguistic translation problem. Her well-informed contribution impacts on two members' decisions (19, 20) to transfer the source geographical term into the Polish translation.

AN's utterance 17 contradicts ZC's perspective by highlighting the significance of another translation problem found in the cultural element, *food van*. Utterance 17, with its judgemental negative, interrogative and exemplifying communicative functions, can be assumed to have triggered the group's decision-taking process and to have contributed to their final acceptance of the translation solution. The two students' network of utterances activates the entire group's strategic competences, since they succeed in differentiating translation problems, suggesting solutions and assessing the whole process of meaning negotiation.

Situation 2

1. ZC: I haven't noticed the word *food truck*. How do you write it in Polish? Now I'm thinking, isn't it a linguistic calque?
2. KH: A borrowing...
3. ZC: But it functions also in the Polish language.
4. T: But you said *food truck*, not a *food van*? There is another word for it, *furgonetka* in Polish. (Pause) And how should we write it? Has anyone checked it?
5. MK, MB: Yeah, I checked that.
6. T: So as one word or separately, with a small or capital letter?
7. MK: I checked that. It is spelled as two words, without a hyphen, inflected as *food tracki*.
8. MB: Not always separately, sometimes together.
9. KH: I found this word spelled as two words, with a small letter in front. In the Online Dictionary of Polish Language.
10. MB: OK, I see, as two words then.

Situation 3 illustrates the students' collaborative efforts to establish a final rendition of the source compound noun, *food van*. The translation problem, both linguistic and extralinguistic, concerns a borrowing from the English-speaking world. The presence of the translation problem is signalled by ZC after the group's agreement on the translation variant for the pre-modifying adjective *grimy*. This short exchange of student observations reflects increasing collaborative skills: utterances 1 and 2 exchange information rooted in the individual background assumption resources established during the course of their studies.

The first two students' negotiations concern the source compound *food van*, though it is referred to in the discussion as *food truck*, the term the students applied in the target text. This moment of confusion is corrected by the teacher, though without any significant reaction from the students. Moreover, the teacher suggests another translation variant for the source noun found in the Polish dictionary. Nevertheless, the students ignore this intrusion into their negotiations, which might be symptomatic of their prior tacit acceptance of the borrowing from the English language as the only acceptable rendition of the compound noun. Besides, the situation confirms the teacher's increasingly equal status in the discussion. Utterances 7, 8 and 9 demonstrate the group's growing instrumental sub-competences as students become more confident at working on-line via MS Teams and succeed in sharing their knowledge resources on the platform during the task. The exchange of perspectives on the translation unit shows the group's increasing translation strategic sub-competence, manifested by their ability to assess the translation problem and evaluate potential solutions.

1.3.4.3. Linguistic translation problems

Rich point 2

Situation 1

Pause

1. ZC: I have a problem with this *grimy* translated as *umorusany* [begrimed]. I don't know what adjective to add and I thought of *obskurny* [raggedy], but now I think it's too strong. Just an idea…
2. MB: I was thinking about *zapyziały* [sleazy].
3. ALL LAUGH
4. T: Why *zapyziały*? As a synonym of *grimy*?
5. AN: It would add this degree of informality. We are talking about an egg sandwich only.
6. Pause
7. T: So, what could accentuate this informal character?
8. AN: I was thinking this *zapyziały* [sleazy] could.
9. T: Do you all know this word?
10. ZC: Yes. But I think I like *zapyziały*.
11. T: And the other one, *umorusany*?
12. MB: When I think about it now, this *umorusany* means dirty outside, and *zapyziały* rather something more than dirty, I think …
13. AN: Yeah, I wouldn't use this word to refer to a building either. I could say that my dog is *umorusany* after a walk, but not a food track.
14. T: Which translation do you prefer then? Let's check the meaning of *grimy* in an English-English dictionary. How many meanings have you found?
15. KK: Just one, dirty. In the Cambridge dictionary.
16. AD: Yeah, "covered with dirt".
17. T: Look at your translation options and check if they mean covered with dirt.

18. AN: *Obskurny*, I would argue about that. It is about the interior, connected with austerity perhaps… Or old furniture… And we are talking about the external looks so *obskurny* doesn't work here.
19. T: Are you sure? Don't you think it indicates neglect?
20. AN: Yeah, but about the inside, not the outside.
21. ZC: But to say that *grimy* is just *brudny* [dirty], is not enough…
22. T: What's your decision?
23. KH: I'd use a different word *niechlujny* [slummy]. It shows that it's not really clean there.
24. AD: The definition in the Polish-Polish dictionary says *niechlujny* means untidy, sloppy.
25. MB: *Niechlujny* is a stronger expression, and *zapyziały* a bit of a humorous, tongue-in-cheek one. I like *zapyziały*.
26. ALL LAUGH
27. AN: Yeah, I like that, too.
28. ZC, KK, AD: Yeah, me, too.
29. KK: If you say *niechlujny*, you think the food is badly prepared, and *zapyziały* – it's just about the food truck, not the food.

The initial exchange of perspectives 1 and 2 revolves around two translation variants analysed with respect to their formality level and textual intentionality. ZC rejects the first translation variant *umorusany* proposed by MB in the previous situation, proposing instead the option *obskurny*. She critically evaluates her own perspective at the very moment it is made explicit, leading to a shift in MB's perspective 2 as well. AN's positively assesses MB's translation solution (2) with a justifying and reasoning comment – utterance 5. In this part of the group discourse, AN's perspective rests on the co-text created by MB's utterance 2.

Utterance 12 evaluates MB's own translation option critically by contrasting the first variant *umorusany* with the second, *zapyziały,* advocated by AN and ZC. As a result of her explicit comparison of the two synonyms, she selects the second variant and justifies her decision (12). AN (13, 18) defends her favoured translation option *zapyziały* by contrasting it with MB's translation solution (12), and demonstrates her perspective (18), expressing criticism towards the other two translation variants. The negotiation involves new contextual resources in the form of on-line dictionaries. At the teacher's suggestion, two students verify the meaning of *grimy* in an English-English dictionary (utterances 15, 16). Nevertheless, the subsequent discourse indicates that the students tend to rely on their own ideas and the co-texts of the previous utterances rather than on other contextual resources. Utterances 18, 20, 21, 23, 25, each from a different student, indicate that group members can negotiate degrees of meaning by discussing the associations evoked by the Polish adjectives. In this network, utterances 18, 21, 23, 25, by expressing evaluative and justifying communicative functions, can activate bilingual and extralingual translation sub-competences, since students share personal interpretations of meaning rooted in individual contextual resources.

Situation 2

Pause

1. ZC: *...to turn my day around...* what about *odwraca dzień do góry nogami?* [turns the day upside down]
2. KH: or *ma prawdziwą moc by zmienić mój dzień ...* [it has a real power to change my day] perhaps...
3. Pause
4. KH: Not really like that...
5. ZC: Well, actually not, when I'm reading it...
6. MB: I'll paste mine: *potrafi niesłychanie poprawić mi humor* [it can incredibly improve my mood].
7. KH: About this humour that it can improve my mood. I'd add that it has this power to change something ... *ma moc aby zmienić...*
8. MB: I'm wondering whether this *egg sandwich* always changes my day for better or ... Because I chose *it can incredibly improve my mood* and the original text says *to turn my day around*, which does not always mean that this day gets better.
9. AN: Well, it does and it talks about the satisfaction you get from food.
10. KH: And the next sentence includes a phrase will *get a five-star review*.
11. T: So the meaning of the phrase is positive, it is about improving your day, right? Pleasure you get from eating a sandwich. What shall we do with this phrase then?
12. MB: What about this, *ma prawdziwą moc by odmienić mój dzień* [it has the real power to transform my day]? Just like that?
13. T: You mean to have the *power* to do something?
14. MK: Or we could combine both versions: MB suggested *it can incredibly improve my mood* and connect it with *it can incredibly change my day*? Something like that? Or *diametrically...*
15. MB: I like that. I got used to *this improve my mood* ... but I like this *diametrically change my day* as well.
16. T: So you want to add *my day...*
17. MB: Yes, exactly.
18. Pause
19. AD: I like that too. I thought of *improve* but this *change my day* sounds great.
20. KH, ZC: NOD

Situation 2 involves interactions between five students over the linguistic translation issue of rendering an idiomatic phrase. The network was created during the previous on-line meeting when the relationships between group members intensified. Introduced by a pause of a few seconds, the negotiation begins with the presentation of three translation variants by ZC (1), KH (2) and MB (6). ZC's proposal demonstrates a tendency towards literal translation and stands in contrast to the other, more dynamic translation versions. The situation shows the students' growing translation sub-competences, as indicated by the increased number of interactions on the high-thinking level.

Furthermore, the students succeed in evaluating their own translation versions after their explicit presentations to the rest of the group. KH assesses her translation proposal critically immediately after hearing it in utterance 4. This triggers ZC's judgement of KH's proposal (5). This exchange shows the intensification of interactions among the group members and their increasing confidence at assessing translation procedures applied by themselves or by the other team members. MB (8) evaluates her own proposal just as KH in utterance 4 and 7.

Utterances 8–11 introduce a shift in the process of meaning negotiation since they refer to the background assumption resources and the organize context formed by reference books and on-line dictionaries. MB (8) evaluates her translation solution by addressing the lexical translation problem of the source idiom. The communicative functions of the utterance range from suggestive, judgemental negative to informative because the utterance manifests the student's ability to assess her own idea, criticize it and interpret the source meaning of the idiom. Her perspective is confronted with the other students' interpretations of the source idiom (9 and 10). This negotiation of meanings is accepted by MB (12), who creates another translation variant based largely on KH's prior perspective (2).

The translation solution found in MK's utterance 14 exemplifies the result of collaborative meaning negotiation built on the students' collective co-text. This process may arguably contribute to the development of the group's bilingual and strategic translation sub-competences. MK's final translation variant (14) from the group's negotiation of interpretations of the source idiom is acknowledged enthusiastically by the other group members (15, 19, 20). The translation solution results from the collaborative interpretation of the source meaning, which engaged the students' low-level thinking in the initial process of understanding the source idiom, and which activated high-level thinking in the collaborative evaluation and creation of degrees of meaning. To conclude, the co-text built by the group's conflicting perspectives underlies the successful process of constructing collective expert knowledge and translation competence on various dimensions.

1.3.5. Phase 4 – The interpretation of post-activity scripts

The final component of the collaborative translation task involves the analysis of the answers students provided in two on-line Student Satisfaction Questionnaires A and B, and their confrontation with the students' opinions, as expressed during the post-activity group meeting.

The results of questionnaire A, rated on Likert's scale, indicate the group's general positive, though not unanimously so, assessment of the collaborative translation project. The first part of the questionnaire measures satisfaction from the collaborative learning and consists of the following points graded by participants: 1. It was acceptable but I prefer working individually – three students; 2. I enjoyed it a lot. It was better than individual translating activities – two students; 3. I don't know. It's hard to tell – two students; 4. I didn't like it. I prefer individual training – one student. The results indicate divided opinion on their satisfaction with the collaborative learning experiment. Nevertheless, during the final semi-formal meeting, they expressed a generally positive evaluation of the project. The one negative response found in the questionnaire was justified voluntarily by a student as her initial scepticism over group activities in general.

The second part of the questionnaire enumerates various aspects of the experiment from a purely positive perspective and ranks them by multiple answer questions. The aspects rated as highest include the following categories (with the number of respondents in brackets): 1. the idea of learning translation techniques (five); 2. the possibility to compare many versions of translation of the same text unit (five); 3. friendly and more personal atmosphere (five); improving my translation skills in a team (five); the possibility to try something new, such as collaborative learning (four); the teacher's role as a partner, rather than a mentor (four); extending my knowledge on translation theory and typical translation problems (four); searching for additional information on translation practice (four); lack of conflict with students (three); easy use of MS Teams including chat and sharing information on-line (three); working together rather than individually (3); more chances to speak (1); improving my social abilities on how to act in a team (2).

The third part of the questionnaire evaluates the same aspects of the experiment, though from the negative perspective by means of multiple answer questions. The results indicate one central concern of participants, "stress and fear of sharing ideas with others", selected by four group members. The other negative aspects of the project listed in the questionnaire were selected by from one to three respondents: working together rather than individually (three); not improving my translation skills in a group (two); trouble with using MS Teams, chat, video and sharing information on the platform (two); looking for additional information concerning the appointed task on translation problems (one); the idea of studying on-line (one); the possibility to compare many versions of translation of the same text unit (one).

Part 2 and 3 of the questionnaire asked about students' attitudes to the same aspects of the collaborative translation project, though from different perspectives. It is significant that part 2, indicative of the positive aspects of the task, attracted the majority of student responses. The highest score was attributed to the central goal of the collaborative project, namely the group's development in the field of translation studies in theory and practice. In addition, the students appreciated the friendly atmosphere created during the project, despite the obstacle of on-line, rather than personal, communication. Additionally, as they admitted during the on-line meeting, the group's appraisal of the chance to compare other students' translation versions and to discuss them together without conflict underlies the principles of cooperative and collaborative learning strategies, such as group interdependence and mutual accountability.

The main problem manifested by the questionnaire responses pertains to the psychological and social aspects of collaborative activities. Four students admitted to an increased level of fear and stress during collaborative learning, as opposed to individual learning activities. The post-activity discussion with the group revealed that this trepidation was caused by the sense of the unknown, as they had little experience at collaborative tasks, in particular those related to translation activities. Furthermore, some of their concerns were provoked by the social aspect inherent in the collaborative project. The students expressed initial reservations about cooperating with group members with whom they were barely familiar. As a result, the students, though regarded as partially equal in terms of translation sub-competence levels, felt unease and anxiety during the first on-line meetings. They justified their apprehension by their initial conviction about the potential of the evaluative utterances resulting from collaborative interactions to provoke conflicts among group members.

Finally, the group confessed to a rather basic preparation for on-line activities via MS Teams, despite the compulsory IT training provided for all University of Gdańsk students. The group admitted to a fear of on-line learning caused by low IT competence. This problem, as the group admits, was gradually reduced as they became accustomed to the use of the MS Teams application.

Student Satisfaction Questionnaire B was designed to reflect the team's collaborative achievement level as regards the development of translation sub-competence. The questionnaire includes six points, each referring to a different translation sub-competence. The respondents were requested to rate their sense of individual development within every sub-competence. The rating scale ranges from 1, indicative of the lowest increase in a sub-competence, up to 5 points, for the highest increase. The final point was descriptive, respondents being invited to choose those aspects of the psycho-physiological components which they perceived to be highly activated during the collaborative project. The respondents decided on one to three components from the following list based on the PACTE Group's categories (Hurtado Albir,

2017): memory, perception, attention; intellectual curiosity, perseverance, critical spirit, knowledge of and confidence in one's own abilities, the ability to measure one's own abilities, motivation; creativity, logical reasoning, analysis and synthesis.

The results of questionnaire B revealed that the students did indeed observe the highest increase in their strategic translation sub-competence (two students – 5 points; four – 4 points; two – 3 points) in the psycho-physiological components (six students – 4 points; two – 5 points) and in the bilingual sub-competence (five – 4 points; two – 3 points; one – 5 points). The students graded the other sub-competences as follows: extralingual sub-competence (three – 3 points; four – 4 points; one – 5 points); knowledge of translation sub-competence (three – 3 points; three – 4 points; two – 5 points), and finally instrumental sub-competence (four – 2 points; three – 3 points; one – 4 points). Components of the psycho-physiological dimension of the translation competence model which the group marked as significantly activated during the experiment include intellectual curiosity (six students), the ability of analysis and synthesis (four), creativity (three), critical spirit (two), perception (two), attention (two), motivation (two).

1.4. CONCLUSIONS OF THE RESEARCH INTO THE COLLABORATIVE TRANSLATION SUB-COMPETENCE MODEL

The research presented in this chapter was inspired by the difficult situation arising from the global pandemic of 2020–21, where on-line learning was recommended as the only feasible form of education. Telecollaboration, the application of collaborative learning in an on-line environment, can be promoted as an educational method with the potential to activate the processes of building group competences and expert knowledge in various fields, including the professional practice of translation. The proposed model of collaborative learning is advocated as an advantageous educational practice which can successfully bridge the gap between the demands of higher education and the expectations of the professional business sector.

This chapter highlights the collaborative learning strategy and, most notably, its positive impact on the development of expert knowledge, specifically on the process of forming translation sub-competences. The author of this chapter reinforces the perception of collaboration as a global strategy which can be employed in diverse processes of meaning negotiation, and as a multidisciplinary phenomenon with the capacity to be operationalized by various scientific theories and fields of study, such as social constructivism, cognitive psychology and, in particular, discourse analysis. This chapter interrogates the multidisciplinary aspect of collaboration in the domain of applied linguistics, specifically translation teaching, to validate telecollaboration in the higher education of future translation experts.

The research findings substantiated by the interpretation of the group members' interactions, as well as the pre- and post-activity student questionnaires, authenticate the effectiveness of its collaborative learning model in fostering the development of participants' translation sub-competences. The detailed analysis of the situations, established by the students' utterances around selected translation problems, reveals instances of breakdown in group discourses, and illustrates the students' interactions while tackling translation obstacles on the textual, extralinguistic and linguistic levels. The disruption of collaborative activities, signalled primarily by pauses and text omission, activated the students' motivation and resulted in networks of utterances with translation solutions. This regular discursive practice advanced the process of negotiation of meanings among group members, and the clashes of verbalized perspectives created the foundation for the group's collective co-texts, which functioned in the subsequent exchanges as the group's main sources of knowledge.

Successful collaborative exchanges of meanings, i.e. those which generated optimal and collectively accepted translation solutions, relied predominantly on the group's co-texts, rather than on individual background assumption resources, inclusive of reference books or teacher's guidance. As these co-texts were established from the group members' verbalizations of their tacit knowledge, this observation validates the role of collaborative interactions in the educational context, as well as in the area of professional training, and accentuates the need for further investigation into collectively constructed discourses and sub-competences.

Furthermore, the project outcomes imply that successful moments of collaborative learning, that is moments when the co-texts were established and when they generated a new degree of meaning which was explicitly verbalized during the situation, are constructed by those utterances on the high-thinking level. These, in turn, pertain mostly to the evaluative, judgemental, suggestive and justifying communicative functions observed during the group's collaborative negotiations of translation options.

The data collected during all phases of the research project lead to the final conclusions about the correspondence between the level of activation of the collaborative strategy of learning and the development of the translation sub-competences in the process of shared expert knowledge building. The analysis of the Student Satisfaction Questionnaires supports the results of the investigation into students' interactions by underscoring the most significant impact of the collaborative activities on stimulating strategic and bilingual translation sub-competence, as well as on activating the psycho-physiological components. The Student Satisfaction Questionnaires indicate correspondents' awareness of their individual development on the three main dimensions of the translation sub-competence model mentioned above.

One aspect of the research which merits emphasis is the development of the psycho-physiological components of the translation sub-competence model during the collaboration process. The participants indicated an increase in their processes of analysis and synthesis, creative and critical thinking, intellectual thinking and in their perceptive abilities. These group observations, in conjunction with the positive aspects of the project indicated in questionnaire A – the possibility to work in a friendly and more personal environment, the chance to compare individual ideas with other group members' perspectives, and the general sense of improvement of one's practical skills applied to translation – affirm the favourable assessment of the group's collaborative efforts.

The interpretation of the data collected from the group project resulted in several suggestions to enhance the effectiveness of future collaborative models. In order to activate a successful process of collective knowledge building, it is essential to confirm a high degree of "awareness information" about the collaborating team members (Janssen & Bodemer, 2013: 42). The omission of this factor might have led to the initial sense of apprehension mentioned by students. The fear of potential conflict and timidity towards the other participants might be attributed to the lack of sufficient information about each group member collected at the outset of the task.

In addition, the number of collaborating members should be suited to a particular collaborating task in order to limit or increase the number of possible paths of interactions. As the project shows, the exchange of collaborating perspectives between three or four students may exclude shy participants from simultaneous interactions. On the other hand, a higher number of perspectives on a given situation may delay the development of the translation project. In other words, a collaborative task engaging an inappropriate number of students increases the possible "transactive" (Kirschner et al., 2018: 11) or "cognitive costs of collaboration" (Mende et al., 2020: 3).

Nevertheless, the second type of collaborative transactive costs (the fear and anxiety of on-line collaboration mentioned by the group members) led to the development of psycho-physiological abilities, as all students admitted. The results of the collaborative translation project should be traced within two interactive spaces of every collaborative work (Janssen & Bodemer, 2013: 41). The positive outcomes of the students' interactions within the content space of the project encompass a newfound awareness of translation problems, and of various degrees of meanings concealed in the source text, as well as a growing ability to evaluate multiple translation options. Nevertheless, the true asset of the collaborative learning project can be detected within its relational space, i.e. in the group's increasing confidence in dealing with conflicts and negotiating the validity of their perspectives, as well as in their awakened intellectual curiosity and creativity, all faculties highly valued in the translation profession but dangerously undermined by the impersonal on-line communication reinforced by education in a pandemic.

REFERENCES

Adams, D., and Hamm, M. (2005). *Redefining Education in the Twenty-First Century: Shaping Collaborative Learning in the Age of Information.* Springfield, Illinois: Charles Thomas.

Alves, F. (ed.). (2005). *Triangulating Translation: Perspectives in Process Oriented Research.* Amsterdam: John Benjamins Publishing.

Anastasiades, P. (2009). *Interactive Videoconferencing and Collaborative distance Learning for K-12 Students and Teachers: Theory and Practice.* New York: Nova Science Publishers Inc.

Arvaja, M. (2007). Contextual Perspective in Analysing Collaborative Knowledge Construction of two Small Groups in Web-Based Discussion. *Computer-Supported Collaborative Learning.* Springer. 2: 133–158. DOI 10.1007/s11412-007-9013-5 [accessed 5 November 2020].

Arvaja, M., Rasku-Puttonen, H., Häkkinen, P., and Eteläpelto A. (2003). Constructing Knowledge through a Role-Play in a Web-Based Learning Environment. *Journal of Educational Computing Research*, 28(4): 319–341.

Blundo, R., and Simon, J. (2016). *Solution-Focused Case Management.* New York: Springer Publishing Company.

Britton, J. (1990). Research currents: Second Thoughts on Learning. In Brubacher, M., Payne R., and Richett K. (eds.). *Perspectives on Small Group Learning: Theory and practice* (pp. 3–11). Oakville, Ontario: Rubicon.

Brubacher, M., Payne, R., and Richett, K. (eds.). (1990). *Perspectives on Small Group Learning: Theory and Practice.* Oakville, Ontario: Rubicon.

Bruffee K. A. (1999). *Collaborative Learning. Higher Education, Interdependence, and the Authority of Knowledge.* Baltimore, London: John Hopkins University Press.

Croker A., Smith, T., and Fisher, K. (2016). *Educators' Interprofessional Collaborative Relationships: Helping Pharmacy Students Learn to Work with Other Professions.* Australia/ Oceania: MDPI AG.

Dillenbourg, P. (ed.) (1999). *Collaborative-Learning: Cognitive and Computational Approaches.* Oxford: Elsevier.

Dillenbourg, P., and Jermann, P. (2006). Designing Integrative Scripts. In Fischer, F, Mandl, H., Haake, J., Kollar, I. (eds.). *Scripting Computer-Supported Collaborative Learning: Cognitive, Computational and Educational Perspectives* (pp. 275–301). New York, NY: Springer.

DiMarco, G., and Luzatto, E. (eds.) (2010). *Collaborative Learning. Methodology, Types of Interactions and Techniques.* New York: Nova Science Publishers Inc.

Fischer, F., Mandl, H., Haake J., and Kollar, I. (eds.) (2006). *Scripting Computer-Supported Collaborative Learning: Cognitive, Computational and Educational Perspectives.* New York, NY: Springer.

Gouadec, D. (ed.) (2007). *Quelles qualifications pour les traducteurs?* Paris: La maison du dictionnaire.

Hämäläinen, R. (2012). Methodological Reflections: Designing and Understanding Computer-Supported Collaborative Learning. *Teaching in Higher Education*, 17(5): 603–614. DOI:10.1080/13562517.2012.658556 [accessed 12 December 2020].

Hämäläinen, R., and Arvaja, M. (2009). Scripted Collaboration and Group-Based Variations in a Higher Education CSCL Context. *Scandinavian Journal of Education Research*, 53(1): 1–16. DOI: 10.1080/00313830802628281. [accessed 6 November 2020].

Hurtado Albir, A. (ed.). (2017). *Researching Translation Competence by PACTE Group*. Amsterdam, Philadelphia: John Benjamins Publishing.

Jacobs, G., and Seow, P. (2015). Cooperative Learning Principles Enhance Online Interaction. *Journal of International and Comparative Education*, 4(1): 28–38.

Janssen J., Erkens, G., and Kirschner, P. A. (2011). Group Awareness Tools: It's What you do with it that Matters. *Computers in Human Behaviour*, 27: 1046–1058.

Janssen, J., and Bodemer, D. (2013). Coordinated Computer-Supported Collaborative Learning: Awareness and Awareness Tools, *Educational Psychologist*, 48(1): 40–55, DOI: 10.1080/00461520.2012.749153 [accessed 6 November 2020].

Janssen, J., and Kirschner, P. (2020). Applying Collaborative Cognitive Load Theory to Computer-Supported Collaborative Learning: towards a Research Agenda. *Educational Technology Research and Development*, 68 (2): 783–805. https://doi.org/10.1007/s11423-019-09729-5 [accessed 5 November 2020].

Johnson, D. W., Johnson, R., and Johnson Holubek, E. (1994). *The Nuts and Bolts of Cooperative Learning*. Edina, Minn.: Interaction Book Company.

Johnson, D. W., Johnson, R., and Smith, K. (2013). The State of Cooperative Learning in Postsecondary and Professional Settings. *Educational Psychology Review*, 19: 15–29.

Järvelä, S., and Häkkinen, P. (2002). Web-Based Cases in Teaching and Learning: The Quality of Discussion and a Stage of Perspective Taking in Asynchronous Communication. *Interactive Learning Environments*, 10(1): 1–22.

Kiraly, D. C. (2013). Towards a View of Translator Competence as an Emergent Phenomenon. Thinking outside box(es) in Translator Education. In Kiraly, D. C. Hansen-Schirra, S., and Maksymsk, K. (eds.), *New Prospects and Perspectives for Educating Language Mediators* (Translationswissenschaft) (pp. 197–224). Tubingen: Narr Verlag,

Kiraly, D. C., Hansen-Schirra, S., and Maksymsk K. (eds.). (2013). *New Prospects and Perspectives for Educating Language Mediators* (Translationswissenschaft). Tubingen: Narr Verlag.

Kirschner. P. A., et al. (2018). From Cognitive Load Theory to Collaborative Cognitive Load Theory. *Intern. J. Comput.-Support. Collab. Learn.* 13: 213–233. https://doi.org/10.oo7/s11412-018-9277-y [accessed 5 November 2020].

Koschmann, T. (ed.). (1996). *CSCL: Theory and Practice of an Emerging Paradigm*. Hillsdale, NJ: Lawrence Erlbaum Associates.

Krajka, J., and Marczak, M. (2017). Telecollaboration Projects in Translator Education – Design, Implementation and Evaluation. In Smyrnova-Trybulska, E. (ed.) *Effective Development of Teacher's Skills in the Area of ICT and E-Learning* (pp. 365–388). Cieszyn: University of Silesia – NOA.

Kumpulainen, K., and Mutanen, M. (1999). The Situated Dynamics of Peer Group Interaction: An Introduction to an Analytic Framework. *Learning and Instruction*, 9 (5): 449–473. https://doi.org/10.1016/S0959-4752(98)00038-3 [accessed 12 November 2020].

Kumpulainen, K., Hmelo-Silver, C., and Cesar, M. (eds.). (2009). *Investigating Classroom Interaction. Theories in Action*. Rotterdam: Sense.

Linell, P. (1998). *Approaching Dialogue. Talk, Interaction, and Contexts in Dialogical Perspectives*. Amsterdam: John Benjamins.

Loon, M. (2016). *Professional Practice in Learning and Development: How to Design and Deliver Plans for the Workplace*. London: Kogan Page.

Magas, C. P., Gruppen L. D., Barrett, M., Dedhia, P. H., and Sandhu, G. (2017). Intraoperative Questioning to Advance Higher-Order Thinking. *American Journal of Surgery*, 213(2): 222–226. http://doi.org/10.1016/j.amjsurg.2016.08.027 [accessed 22 November 2020].

Małgorzewicz, A. (2014). Językowe i niejęzykowe kompetencje tłumacza. Próba zdefiniowania celów translodydaktyki akademickiej [Linguistic and Non-linguistic Competence of the Translator. An Attempt to Define the Goals of Academic Translodidactics]. *Lingwistka Stosowana*. Uniwersytet Wrocławski. 11: 1–10. https://portal.uw.edu.pl/documents/7276721/12447778/Lingwistyka+Stosowana+11+Anna+Malgorzewicz [accessed 21 November 2020].

Mathews, R. S., Cooper J. L., Davidson N., and Hawkes, P. (1995). Building Bridges Between Cooperative and Collaborative Learning. *Change*, 27(4): 34–40.

Mende, S., Proske, A., and Narciss, S. (2020). Individual Preparation for Collaborative Learning: Systematic Review and Synthesis. *Educational Psychologist*. https://doi.org/10.80/00461520.2020.1828086 [accessed 12 December 2020].

Murphey, T., and Jacobs G. M. (2008). Encouraging Critical Collaborative Autonomy. *JALT Journal*, 22: 220–244.

Myskow, G., Bennett, P. A., Yoshimura, H., Gruendel, K., Marutani, T., Hano, K., and Li, T. Fostering Collaborative Autonomy: The Roles of Cooperative and Collaborative Learning. (2018). *Relay Journal*, 1(2): 360–381.

Newell, C., and Bain, A. (2018). *Team-Building Collaboration in Higher Education Learning and Teaching: A Review of the Literature*. Singapore: Springer.

Nord, C. (1994). It's Tea Time in Wonderland. Culture-Markers in Fictional Texts. Purschel, H. (ed.). *Intercultural Communication*: proceedings of the 17th International L.A.U.D. Symposium Duisburg, 23–27 March. (pp. 523–538). Frankfurt am Mein: Peter Lang.

PACTE. (2003). Building a Translation Competence Model. In Alves, F. (ed.). *Triangulating Translation: Perspectives in Process Oriented Research* (pp. 43–66). Amsterdam: John Benjamins,

PACTE. (2007). Une recherche empirique expérimentale sur la compétence de traduction. In Gouadec, D. (ed.). *Quelles qualifications pour les traducteurs?* Paris: La maison du dictionnaire.

Pym, A. (2003). Redefining Translation Competence: Conceptual and Methodological Issues. Ubersetzungskompetenz. *Meta*, 50(2): 609–619.

Raney, L., Lasky, G., and Scott, C. (2017). *Integrated Care: A Guide for Effective Implementation*. Arlington, Virginia: American Psychiatric Association Publishing.

Roselli, N. (2016). Collaborative Learning: Theoretical Foundations and Applicable Strategies to University. *Propósitos y Representaciones*, 4(1): 219–280. http://dx.doi.org/10.20511/pyr2016.v4n1.90 [accessed 24 November 2020].

Rutherford, S. (2014). *Collaborative Learning: Theory, Strategies and Educational Benefits*. New York: Nova Science Publishers Inc.

Saputra, M. D., Joyoatmojo, S., Wardani, D. K., and Sangka, K. B. (2019). Developing Critical Thinking Skills through the Collaboration of Jigsaw Model with Problem-Based Learning Model. *International Journal of Instruction*, 12(1): 1077–1094. https://doi.org/10.29333/iji.2019.12169a [accessed 4 December 2020].

Scardamalia, M., and Bereiter, C. (1996). Computer Support for Knowledge-Building Communities. In Koschmann, T. (ed.) *CSCL: Theory and Practice of an Emerging Paradigm* (pp. 249–268). Hillsdale, NJ: Lawrence Erlbaum Associates,

Smith, Z. (2013). Joy. *The New York Review of Books*. Jan. 10. https://www.nybooks.com/articles/archives/2013/jan/10/joy/?page1 [accessed 3 November 2020].

Smyrnova-Trybulska, E. (ed.). (2017). *Effective Development of Teacher's Skills in the Area of ICT and E-Learning*. Cieszyn: University of Silesia.

Stahl, G. (2004). Building Collaborative Knowing. Elements of a Social Theory of CSCL. In Strijbos, J. W. Kirschner, P. A., and Martens, R. L (vol eds.). *Computer-Supported Collaborative Learning*, vol. 3. *What We Know About CSCL ... and Implementing it in Higher Education* (pp. 53–85). Boston, MA: Kluwer Academic Publishers,

Strijbos, J. W., Kirschner, P. A., and Martens, R. L. (eds.). (2004). *Computer-Supported Collaborative Learning*, vol. 3. *What We Know About CSCL...and Implementing it in Higher Education*. Boston, MA: Kluwer Academic Publishers.

Vass, E., and Littleton, K. (2009). Analyzing Role Distribution in Children's Computer-Mediated Collaborative Creative Writing. In Kumpulainen, K., Hmelo-Silver, C., and Cesar, M. (eds.). *Investigating Classroom Interaction. Theories in Action* (pp. 99–120). Rotterdam: Sense.

Vygotsky, L. (1978). *Mind in Society: Development of Higher Psychological Processes*. Harvard: Harvard University Press.

Westerlund, H., and Gaunt, H. (2013). *Collaborative Learning in Higher Music Education*. Burlington: Routledge.

ABOUT THE AUTHOR

Małgorzata Godlewska has a PhD in literary studies and works as an Assistant Professor in the Department of Applied Linguistics at the University of Gdańsk, Poland. Her scientific interests encompass contemporary literature, with a particular focus on dialogism and intertextuality. She is currently conducting research on literary and audio-visual translation from the perspectives of the translation competence model and translation acquisition model. Her work reflects her attempts to create an interdisciplinary research model which would apply literary and linguistic tools in the analysis of multimodal texts in the field of translation studies.

2

How does language become a skill? Analysing languaging in a problem-solving activity using a multimodal methodological framework

Grzegorz Grzegorczyk

ABSTRACT

Thinking and language emerge through interactivity, or sense-saturated coordination (Steffensen, 2013) that couples agents to their social and physical environments. The term "languaging" directs attention to the fact that bodily and situational processes in the here-and-now and their organization across different spatial and temporal scales are fundamental in communication and sense-making (e.g. Love, 2017). In order to illustrate these claims, we analyse a video recording of the board game "Codenames" played by a group of six students. By applying elements of Norris' Multimodal Analysis, Linell's idea of Communicative Project and the notion of Recurrent Languaging Activity (Newgarden and Zeng, 2016) we zoom in on the linguistic contingencies players deploy in their dialogical exchanges, as they realize their goals and strategies in the game, and use the Jeffersonian coding system to present the linguistic interactions observed in selected fragments of the recording. We hope that the combination of these tools will enable us to address the micro-scale of dialogical interactional dynamics exhibited by participants cooperating in a problem space. Our interest will be in the way the players as languaging agents orientate to verbal patterns or "repeatables" which organize their interactivity (sense-saturated coordination) as they move along dialogically towards the desired results. In this way we aim to interrogate the claim that "linguistic knowledge should be conceived of as practical knowledge – or knowing-how – rather than theoretical knowledge – or know-ing-that" (Herik et al., 2019: 60). On a more theoretical level, this should find echo in Mulcaster's 500-year-old insight that "languaging enables us to under-stand" and, in so doing, enables us as humans to engage actively with each other.

Keywords: dialogicity, languaging, interactivity, game playing, language as a skill

2.1. INTRODUCTION

When humans confront a problem and decide to solve it together, they invite each other to what Linell, drawing on Bakhtin, terms "dialogicality" or the ability and practice to interact and make sense together (Linell, 2020). Conversing agents establish interdependent relationships with their environment and each other as they apply social norms of communication. They exhibit activities (languaging) and resort to resources and knowledge "systems" (language) which help them establish specific strategies and bring them closer to achieving their goals. When observing people involved in a type of "guess-the-word" game, we find that they exhibit dialogical practices which help them to find ways of resolving the problems they face on the way to winning the game. Examining what the players say and how they act during the game should present an interesting opportunity to observe what happens when two or more people converse on the subject of words and their meanings. Likewise, this should be a chance to say something about language when people interact in a problem space, specifically about the contingencies they depend on as they strive to address their communicative goals. We predict that the players will attempt to reach a consensus, to negotiate and establish meanings together by drawing on their understanding of words and concepts. In doing so, they will probably exhibit many different types of linguistic behaviour that should provide us with sufficient evidence to disclose the ways in which linguistic know-how supersedes linguistic "know-that". Our view of language emphasizes its biological, embodied, dialogical, sociocultural and situated nature. Human speech is contingent on these dimensions, as we realize values and enact our lives in coordination with others.

The work of Clark (e.g. 1996, 2008, 2012) and Hutchins (e.g. 1995, 2010) paved the way for looking at human communication and interaction in a novel way. The distributed approach they took to research on mind and cognition offers a solid foundation for more in-depth analysis of human communication, particularly talk-in-interaction. Convinced by their arguments, we employ in this text the distributed approach to language (as in Cowley, 2011; Thibault, 2011, Linell, 2013, Steffensen, 2015), a philosophy which stresses the "centrality of co-acting agents who extend their worlds and their own agency through embodied, embedded processes of languaging behaviour rather than uses of an abstract language system" (Thibault, 2011: 211). The integration of language with thought and action places us in the realm of biosemiotics and calls for research methods which go beyond those well-nested in traditional linguistics. There is some rationale behind this. First of all, academic research on language is boldly adopting multiple disciplines (biology, cognitive psychology, neuroscience, anthropology) and their backgrounds to explore the nature and mechanics of language. The proposition to invert the traditional ontological order of language by saying that it is a "system applied in practice by its users" is gaining adherents. "Third-wave linguistics" offers such a reverse view: "dynamics first and symbols afterwards" (Cowley, 2011: 11). Such an approach requires a much broader perspective, embracing not only the behavioural, biological and the sociocultural but also the semiotic aspect. Finally, language in face-to-face interaction (prototypical aspect preceding written forms) is multimodal in that it involves speaking, hearing, gesturing, gazing, postural swaying, facial expression, mimicry, etc. For example, two interacting persons may coordinatively engage in manual activities, like painting a wall together, which entail hands and vision. In doing so, they are able to communicate by means of the auditory/phonetic qualities of speech.

The contributions from Rączaszek-Leonardi et al. (2018), Deacon and Rączaszek-Leonardi (2019), Li, Steffensen and Huang (2020), Jensen (2014), Goldin-Meadow (2014), Özyürek (2014), Skipper (2014) and others have opened new ways in which Applied Linguists and Ecolinguists can design and develop their research. For this reason, in the case of our microgenetic study of a video recording of six people playing the game *Codenames*, we test an alternative method in an attempt to uncover the ways in which the players as languaging agents organize their interactivity (sense-saturated coordination) and how languaging and language facilitates the social and communicative strategies in the game. In order to do so, our study, as opposed to the game itself, emphasizes the participant's efficiency over their effectiveness, approaching language from the social and dialogical perspective. We predict that due to the unique social, spatial and communicational setting constituted by the rules of the game, the range and type of communicative activities displayed by the players will lead them to create patterns of interactional flow different from what we would see in typical conversational interactions. These differences recall such moments as an ecological niche where players engage their languaging skills to solve problems and manage social space.

We intend to broaden the scope of our analysis here beyond the language-as-a-code paradigm in order to signal that language and verbal interaction cannot be separated from the remaining aspects of human life. "Interactional script" (in conversationally-analytical terms) proves its significance in analysing talk-in-interaction by providing the scaffolding and constraints on the possibilities of actions and interpretation in any dialogue. Just like linguistic symbols (e.g. categories, deictic markers, verb tense etc.), these "script" structures lend themselves as efficient tools for profiling and navigating a joint attentional space. They are also necessary to safeguard the organization and ultimate effectiveness of any case of talk-in-interaction. It is part of the skills of the interacting individuals to use them in order to accomplish goals in communicational tasks. In this chapter we address two questions: 1) How are linguistic activities and practices distributed in the group of six players? 2) How do players co-ordinate and manage their interaction in the problem space through languaging? Ultimately, we hope to be able to test the claim that "language is a skill" (Herik et al., 2019).

Apart from wordings, individuals who intend to communicate with each other in most cases employ material symbols in their interaction, for instance, when regulating social relations, coordinating complex actions or solving problems (cf. Clark, 1996; Vygotsky, 1978; Fusaroli & Tylén, 2016; Pickering & Garrod, 2004). In line with Fusaroli et al. (2014), we claim that in such interpersonal communicative contexts "language enables skilful intersubjective engagement" in which the coordination of individual cognitive systems contributes to the emergence of more complex units which transcend the potential capabilities of their constituent parts. Dialogue then becomes a shared human activity embedded in linguistic practices and undoubtedly goes beyond mere turn-taking ritual or an exchange of cues. The means for individuals to co-orchestrate their speech is language as an interactional, coordinative and multimodal activity. It is "a particular kind of engaged activity, constituted by practice and skilful coordination, and not just as a set of variously organised material symbols, or even the mere storage or a transfer of information via material symbols" (Fusaroli et al., 2014: 33). As Cowley asserts, "language is a dialogical activity that prompts people to develop linguistic skills" (Cowley, 2015: 125). But what lies behind the assertion that "language is a skill"?

Herik understands "skills as those activities we perform that are subject to correction by others. This correction in turn is possible because there is a conventional way in which the activity is performed" (Herik et al., 2019: 61–62). In other words, convention guides performance. Following Millikan (1998), Herik understands conventions as emergent, relatively stable patterns of behaviour. These patterns occur as recognizable and repeatable forms of linguistic behaviour which is content- and context-sensitive. Such sensitivity involves observation and sense-making as occurring together with languaging in a circular manner. In other words, utterances take on a particular sense as a languaging human's activity evokes wordings characterized by multiple subtle distinctions. However, before one learns to recognize patterns one needs to grasp "a repeatable in use" (Herik, 2017: 25). Then, when the need arises, one is ready to activate this potential as a reflexive linguistic skill. Herik notes that linguistic behaviour "is skilful because it is subject to correction.

This correction is based in the (dis)similarities perceived between current and previous utterances based on metalinguistic experience, as well as criterial relations to which people attune through metalinguistic practices" (Herik, 2017: 26). Therefore language is conceived in action-orientated terms, as an exercise of skills, rather than in terms of knowledge of an abstract system. This means that in order to target Herik's claim, we should investigate the languaging behaviour exhibited by the interacting agents in its totality, with special focus on what happens between them rather than what can be seen from the turn-to-turn perspective. Such a strategy brings us closer to analysing linguistic events rather than just wordings, gestures or facial expression because "humans link linguistic patterns with affect, artifacts and social skills" in communicative events (Cowley, 2012: 13). The languaging activity they display at such moments is multimodal in nature and managed under material and cultural constraints (cf. "skilled linguistic action" in Cowley, 2012), involving regular patterns of interactional behaviour, which yield relatively predictable effects in the other participants of a social situation (Krebs, 1984). In doing so, humans connect their speech with pico-scale events so as to interactively engage in sense-making activity. In order to trace these processes and acknowledge their multimodality, we need an accurate and precise tool. Some inspiration can be found in a group of methods, otherwise referred to as Multimodal Analysis, Multimodal Semiotics or Multimodal Studies, an approach rooted in Michael Halliday's social semiotic theory (Halliday, 1978; 1994). If, as Cowley (2015) suggests, all human activity can be described as semiosis, then so too can languaging, since, as we clarify below, language spreads in space and time both during talk and when human individuals engage with other individuals, texts, objects or technology. These are the extensions which allow our sense-making by languaging when we orientate ourselves either to social (and verbal) routines or to one-off events (Cowley, 2015: 126).

2.2. LANGUAGING AND INTERACTIVITY

Before embarking on the choice of research method and performing an analysis, we intend to present the philosophical underpinnings of our approach. Since modern man relies on texts, static or moving pictures, computers, mobile phones and calculators (Linell, 2020) in social and linguistic interactions, we can observe an increasing reliance during talk-in-interaction on the presence and exploitation of these extra-bodily artefacts and objects (third parameter). The central objects in games will be all the paraphernalia which constitutes a suitable and essential environment for the players. In the case of the game, we observe dialoguing players resorting to artefacts such as the cards with printed images and words, the table on which they are laid out and the chairs on which the participants are sitting. Although not every game requires such material artefacts, in *Codenames* they constitute a vital element of what we in this text call a "problem space". Finally, the fourth parameter which characterizes dialogue as skilful interpersonal engagement is individual agency, or the ways interactants co-ordinate with each other. Routines and automatic conversational behaviours play a vital part here, a fact which emphasizes the importance of learned and practised ways of engagement in talk. What makes the players progress in their communicative tasks and projects is the fact that some aspects of action and utterance meaning are due to active and conscious mental planning. Nevertheless, these still become a product of a dialogical process with contexts and interlocutors (cf. Linell, 2010).

In dialogue, as in all social happenings, the human participants co-ordinate their actions and actively construct sense together. In the video recording of six students playing the game we can observe humans who are situationally conjoined in the activity of solving a cognitive task dialogically. What makes their talk on words and concepts possible and effective is the "species-specific capability for sense-making" (Linell, 2009). In other words, "a conversation is a kind of social cognition" (Linell, 2019) that, it may be added, is saturated with sense and occurs in specific spatio-temporal surroundings. This view clearly draws on Bakhtin's insight that "all real and integral understanding is actively responsive" (Bakhtin, 1986: 69) and can be treated as foundational to the concept of languaging and the closely related play of interactivity.

Language (or languaging) seems to have a constitutive role in an evolving social meshwork that enables people to self-fabricate meanings and reports about them. This statement abandons the instrumental perspective on language in which individual thought processes are scaffolded by internalized verbal instruction, inner speech (e.g. Vygotsky, 1986) or the manipulation of material symbols (Clark, 2006; Roepstorff, 2008). Rather, we consider the role of language as a phenomenon mediating minds and in this way facilitating human interactions. While languaging we make and interpret linguistic signs, becoming in this way engaged in "a real-time, contextually determined process of investing behaviour or the products of behaviour (vocal, gestural or other) with semiotic significance" (Love, 2004: 530). Consequently, language can be seen as "a heterogeneous set of physical, cognitive and social activities that unfold in real time on many time-scales. It arises as we adjust to each other and coordinate our life worlds (using a Husserlian expression) with each other, behaviorally and cognitively" (Steffensen, 2009: 684). This echoes Pennycook's "experience of social practices" (Pennycook, 2016) and/or in "realizing" a social semiotic (see Halliday and Matthiesen, 2006). Experiments performed by Tylén et al. (2013) demonstrate that language can be conceived of as a process of contextually sensitive reciprocal adaptation, to the point that the dynamics of the engagement evolve and shape words and other expressive behaviours. It then becomes evident that linguistic interaction is more than a mere exchange of words but an activity consisting of the skilful deployment of resources such as talk, gestures, sounds, gaze or material artefacts which serve sense-making purposes.

Real-time coordinated activity is referred to as first-order languaging (emphasizing the fact that language is activity). Cowley sees languaging as "a form of communication bound up with attention, perception, action and learning. Languaging gives rise to selections that make up an individual's lived world" (Cowley, 2015: 126).

Thibault clarifies that "[f]irst-order languaging is an experiential flow that is enacted, maintained, and changed by the real-time activity of participants" (Thibault, 2017). Love (2017: 115) adds to this, saying that languaging identifies "activities involving language: speaking, hearing (listening), writing, reading, 'signing' and interpreting sign language. ... activities that can be united by a specific superordinate verb." It permeates experience and, despite its unquestionable instrumental/communicative role, precedes linguistic form, thereby assuming a position "intrinsic to being human in any historically shaped socio-cultural domain" (Cowley, 2019: 484). These linguistic behaviours co-occur with what speakers hear, or second-order patterns of language. Like visible first-order languaging, verbal patterns become salient to speakers of a language, which explains their persistent dominance in current theories of language. However, in first-order languaging, the verbal often serves merely to orientate affect and attention to a common focus. At such moments, for Cowley (2015: 133), wordings direct (often) subtle actional and perceptual moves. The actual occurrence of verbal patterns relies on an individual's phenomenological experience of other utterances, i.e. the words and sentences that we think he/she hears. Such patterns arise only for those who are adequately familiar with actual ways of speaking in order to be able to (re)produce utterances with some accuracy.

2.3. THE REQUIREMENTS OF THE METHOD

We argue here that languaging is a dialogical activity contingent on human biology (brains mirroring the actions of perceived others (Barsalou, 2013), the vocal, auditory and visual systems, etc.) and social practices. Implicitly, languaging involves sense-saturated coordination (Steffensen, 2012) and as such provides interacting agents with the means to cooperate, collaborate and co-act in ways which allow them to accomplish situational goals. As Steffensen observes "[b]ecause we live together and act together – and because we can take a language stance – we find ourselves living in an historically derived meshwork of interactivity-based co-adaptivity, co-agency, and co-regulation" (Steffensen, 2012: 521). Being part of a language community connects us to a socioculture upon which we rely for engaging in interactions with other humans. With this said, we find that our analytical tool should allow us to pursue languaging events rather than "turns", "themes", "movements", "tools", etc. An example of a languaging event is given by Newgarden and Zheng (2016: 279):

> Imagine two or more kids building with Lego blocks together. As they build, they move a Lego block to present a new thought or express a color or shape preference to each other, they manipulate the Lego to take a perspective, they move their body to interpret the space etc., all of which are necessary actions in the process of languaging. In theoretical terms, they negotiate, coordinate, co-act with gaze, with body, with the Lego (a material artifact), and with language.

The above example aligns with experiments performed, amongst others, by Shockley et al. (2003), Clark and Krych (2004), Shockley et al. (2007) or Fowler et al. (2008) and Richardson et al. (2008), which have all proved the value and significance of "patterns" in human co-languaging. Their findings reveal a tight-knit relationship between discourse, visual attention and bodily control. In other words, they suggest (as in the case of playing with Lego) that agents, when interacting, in conjunction with speech patterns, make use of the rich expressive qualities of bodily gestures, eye gaze etc. Our aim in the research method will be to capture these. In our study we follow a constructive problem-solving process where group interaction links verbal patterns, linguistic embodiment and game cards as a cognitive resource. In the analysis we aim to focus on recurrent regularities and to combine this with attention to players' experience based on pico-scale effects. Being ever-forward progressive, human interaction derives its force from sequentiality. Enfield asserts that

> [t]his conception of social interaction entails a dynamic relation between a communicative action and the response it elicits. And, in turn, such a reaction may in itself be a communicative action, engendering, in response, a further communicative action (see below). Moreover, any sequence "communicative action and subsequent response" is a unit, not a conjunct
>
> (Enfield, 2011: 286)

As a sign each response has the potential to evoke another response. In this way, every interaction may unfold as a sequence of pivoting sign-response relations (Enfield, 2011: 287). Enfield refers to the causal-conditional trajectory of relevance relations as enchrony (Enfield, 2009: 10). Like experience, talk uses an enchronic scale (Enfield, 2014) and is arguably best illustrated by a moment-to-moment analysis of unfolding events. We find that turning towards microgenetic methods which examine change as it occurs should be appropriate to capture the micro-scale dynamics of the interaction between players. Hence, we should be able to observe and interpret the moment-to-moment interactions between them. We hope to see how participants language together and, by repeating and reiterating patterns of linguistic behaviour, form a problem-solving process, the unfolding of which culminates in the team guessing (or not guessing) the word.

As the present study is based on a broad ecological paradigm, we initially have to reject any approaches that pare the complexity of person-to-person communication down to a single perspective. Unfortunately, most research methods reduce human talk and interaction to the domain of the social order and external representations of structures. We intend to go beyond this reductionist tendency by observing that human interaction is a bio-cognitive phenomenon facilitated by both biomechanics and the social order constructed through local coordination. Therefore, in order to choose or design a useful method for the purposes of our study, we need to take account of the nature of the empirical material, so that the tools we apply cater for all its aspects. In so claiming, we refer, for example, to Cowley (2011), Thibault (2011) and Steffensen (2013), for whom joint interactional activity means flexible adaptive behaviour in which language combines with cognition. The emphasis in their research is on the embodied character of cognitive dynamics and linguistic utterances, which is precisely what we need for the present study. As it becomes increasingly evident that our research questions cannot be fully answered by the application of any single analytical method within linguistics, or interaction analysis, we employ a combination of methods and notions with the purpose of reconnecting the micro- and macro- scale observations. Here we take the distributed perspective on language. In this paradigm, languaging is a first-order activity prior to a symbol system, which as such is understood as a second-order language. Consequently, first-order languaging constrained by second-order, societally and culturally defined practices may be defined as metabolic activity (Cowley, 2012). Hence languaging is the primary activity for any communicative event, in which, "[m]eaning is created, enacted and shared in conversation and meaningful language learning is, therefore embedded in conversation" (van Lier, 2004: 145).

The research method required for the present purposes should enable us to reveal a dynamic pattern of languaging between social agents. Just as Baldry and Thibault use the term "periodicity" to refer to "structures that repeat themselves in a patterned way and that allow variation within a fixed framework" (Baldry & Thibault, 2006: 26), so we turn to the vocal and gestural features which arise as players cooperate or compete in the flow of interactivity. Since we must not turn a blind eye to work done by experts in other disciplines which apply multimodal analytical methods (e.g. film, fine arts, advertising, webpage design, etc.), we admit that our approach is predominantly rooted in language and social semiotics, meaning that our predicted observations will safely remain in the linguistic (Hallidayan) framework. With variables pertinent to the nonverbal aspects of language and some elements of participants' environment, we will subsume them under the label of language to account for its distributed character.

2.4. MULTIMODAL APPROACHES TO INTERACTION ANALYSIS

Multimodality in our understanding includes not only the aspects and elements of speakers' environment but also their own personal characteristics, such as sensory modalities (gaze, hearing, motion, etc.). Multimodal Discourse Analysis is one of the methods that allows us to delve into these aspects on the micro-level, as it orientates researcher's attention towards the intersemiosis of language, gesture and material artefacts (e.g. Royce, 2006; O'Halloran, 2007; O'Halloran & Lim, 2014). Part of the value of MMDA for our research is also in its interest in how multimodal phenomena are resemioticized across place and time and in "how meaning making shifts from context to context, from practice to practice, or from stage of a practice to the next" (Iedema, 2003: 41). In other words, resemioticization is a dynamic process which accentuates "the material and historicised dimensions of representation" (Iedema, 2003: 50). In MMDA, language is but one among multiple means available for meaning making.

Much as the MMDA approach goes beyond text, it still leans towards a single speaker with the interactional aspect of talk relegated to the margin. In contrast, the Multimodal Interaction analysis proposed by Norris (2004) not only integrates the verbal with the nonverbal, but also links them with material objects and the environment as they are used by individuals acting and interacting in the world. Norris asserts that every action an individual undertakes in orientating him/herself towards the environment is in fact interaction. This methodology is grounded in Scollon's mediated discourse analysis, Goffman's interactional sociolinguistics and van Leeuwen's multimodal analysis. As a result, it integrates the worlds of research into sociology, education, psychology, anthropology and linguistics. MMIA tends towards the mediation of cultural tools in human (inter)actions, asserting that social actors cannot act without these tools and vice versa, i.e. that cultural tools would not exist without the social actors who employ them in daily communicative occurrences (Norris, 2011). Norris understands modality as a way of theorizing heuristically about the world of social actors performing social actions. She sees modes, the entities produced, learned or acquired in use by social actors, on a continuum of systems of mediated action from the concrete (material) to the abstract (conceptual).

The objective of MMIA is to describe the events occurring in a given interaction and to "gain a better understanding of how modes (language, gesture, movement) play together in human (inter)action" (Norris, 2013: 280). As a unit of analysis Norris proposes "mediated action", which is a social actor seen as acting with and/or through mediational means or a cultural tool. The action is performed at the "site of engagement", which includes space together with the temporal, physical and affective aspects of the action. Actions build up in a tier-like system from lower-level (smallest meaning unit, e.g. an utterance in the language mode) to higher-level actions (a number of chained lower-level actions in different modes). Both types of actions mutually organize each other in (inter)action. The socio-behavioural stance is clearly evident in her philosophy, a fact which may perhaps explain why her understanding of language is limited to a "mode" of interaction as a semiotic system similar to gesture or posture. In this way she denies language its embodied character, calling it instead "an abstract system of representation" in contrast to drawing, running or swimming, for instance. Since each system of representation in her methodology of data analysis is governed by rules and regularities, the same applies to language in an apparent echo of Herik's concept of "repeatables", Cowley's "verbal patterns" and Rączaszek-Leonardi's "replicable constraints". The "rules and regularities" are embedded in syntax, semantics, etc., which for Norris appear to be manifestations of cultural tools/mediational means. It transpires then that in order for a social actor to perform action "with" language he/she needs to "use" syntax, semantics or phonology as mediational means. Such a view is against our understanding of language as a two-order phenomenon and significantly limits the scope of application of her method in our study. Norris ignores the first-order linguistic activity understood by Love as "making and interpreting of linguistic signs, which in turn is a real-time, contextually determined process of investing behaviour or the products of behaviour (vocal, gestural or other) with semiotic significance" (Love, 2004: 530).

To our minds, the concept of levels of analysis is a definite asset and valuable resource in this context, as it permits well-organized and systematic work along the trajectory of actors' actions and practices. It also ensures clarity and relative precision in pinpointing the focal issues. The "levels" correspond in some degree with the concept of a "cognitive event" (Steffensen and Trasmundi, 2018), which is also orientated towards observing human interaction on a trajectory of behaviour. What makes Norris's MMIA incomplete from our perspective is that it overlooks the fact that language is inseparable from human interactivity, or sense-saturated coordination (Steffensen, 2013). What we observe in dialogical interactions is, apart from the use of linguistic "forms", the integration of past experiences with the present moment, interbodily movements and new actions emerging from previous actions. This constant experiential flow is enacted, maintained and altered by participants' real-time activity. If we reduce these processes to talking agents creating sequences of abstract forms, then we radically misconstrue what it is that humans do in their languaging. In line with our philosophy, this analysis sets out to integrate the ecological, social, cultural, biological, material, and bodily dimensions because language or first-order languaging is "a form of whole-body behaviour or whole-body sense making" (Thibault, 2011: 211). Norris believes that "the view which unquestionably positions language at the center limits our understanding of the complexity of interaction" (Norris, 2004: 2). We maintain that it is quite the opposite.

2.5. UNIT OF ANALYSIS

By emphasizing language, or, more precisely, languaging (and recurrent languaging events), as the underlying explanatory concept behind human dialogicality and interactivity, we find the unit of analysis to be multifaceted and therefore strategically important to address. MMIA assumes action to be its unit of analysis (Norris, 2013; Norris & Pirini, 2017), and Norris models her understanding of action on Scollon, Wertsch and Vygotsky. In this approach a social actor is seen acting with and/or through a mediational means. She postulates a focus on the "constant tension that is created through the social actors using various and always multiple mediational means as they perform the action." By acknowledging the mediating role of cultural tools, such as language, furniture, mobile phones or various technologies, her methodology assumes an ecological stance. The mediated action as an analytical unit has higher and lower dimensions, the lower comprising the smallest interactional meaning units, such as gesture or utterance, depending on the "mode" of interaction, and the higher level constituting a chain formed by a sequence of lower-level actions with a clear opening and closing, such as a conversation. The difficulty with this division is that Norris does not provide tools for a more detailed analysis of the internal structure of lower-level units. Likewise, with higher-level units, the difficulty lies in demarcating the border between one action and another. Besides, the concept of mediation may blur the analysis if the researcher focuses excessively on the role of the mediational means and the actor's interaction with them instead of the human interactivity or sense-saturated coordination (cf. Steffensen, 2013).

One interesting theory we find applicable for our purposes in that it integrates the social, behavioural and linguistic aspect is Linell's Communicative Project Theory, which adopts the interactional perspective of focusing on the 'what's-going-on-between-speakers'. Some instances of such inter-speaker action include solving communication-based problems, information sharing, or meaning making (Linell, 2009: 211). The concept of communicative activity connects linguistics (language use) with social psychology (joint activity), cognitive psychology (the concept of mind) and sociology (sociocultural institutions). As such it fulfils the postulate of interdisciplinarity in designing a relevant unit of analysis for situated interaction (Zittoun, Gillespie, Cornish & Psaltis, 2007). Linell argues that his communicative project (e.g. opening a conversation) can be applicable in the analysis of different activity types with possible ensuing "nesting" patterns. For example, within the activity type of a patient seeking a diagnosis, there would be the activity sub-types of making an appointment and waiting in the waiting room. Communicative projects will move along the trajectory of opening, clarifying the issue, asking and answering questions, and closing the conversation. By applying the idea of nesting patterns in the analysis, each element is rendered a separate unit and permitted to combine into a homogeneous analytical unit of contextually situated thought and interaction.

Linell proposes the "communicative project" (CP) as a unit of analysis, thus acknowledging the sociocultural factors in human-to-human linguistic interaction. CPs involve a specification of the significance of verbal actions and interactions, and can be analysed by breaking down more extensive projects into the more detailed projects subsumed within them. Contrary to Conversation Analysis which partially ignores the relations between communicative interactions (by focusing on turn-to-turn perspective and "next turn proof of procedure"), subsequent interactions evidence the transformative consequences of an interaction. For Linell "situation transcending phenomena" (e.g.: minds, selves, various discourses and narratives, artefacts, institutions, etc.) as incrementally transformed through speakers' interaction come prior to any interaction. As Linell (2009: 188) asserts, "[t]alking is not just coordination, cooperation, control, truth-telling etc.; these are only means to [...] solving local (and global) communicative projects". In each CP, conversing and/or action centres on a task that requires the coordination of two or more individuals (Linell, 2009: 178). Projects are linked and therefore, "[d]iscourse may be seen as a flow of projects, varying in size and partly overlapping and nested into each other" (Linell, 2009: 188). This perspective is used to define how conversations are parsed for analysis and suggests that lines of chat or utterances may simultaneously be coded as part of several nested communicative projects.

The overall event of playing the game *Codenames* includes larger patterns of actions and interactions, what Linell labels "Communicative Activity Types". Drawing on Levinson's (1979) notion of "activity type", Linell sees these activities as subject to habit (routines, norms, rules), physically and socially constrained, affected by intentions (such as conscious decision-making), or a range of occasional features. In this way, activity types allow the researcher to perspectivize a setting from the vantage point of its participants, i.e. it "defines the situation for the actors" (Linell, 1998: 235). When intertwined, they influence each other to create *hybrid* activity types (see Linell, 2009; Sarangi, 2016). CATs are settings that assign contextual roles to their participants, generating different types of social interaction between them, as for example, in seminars, meetings, games, interviews, etc. In the case of game activities performed by the players of *Codenames*, these shift, according to situational demands, between talking about game problems (e.g. speculating on word meanings) and game-organizing issues. For this reason, both types should be addressed as integral parts of a gameplay interactional episode. What connects these settings is that social and situational roles in each are naturally assigned to participants. This creates the potential for some types of interactions to arise while others decrease in significance. Each time, such settings (understood as activity types) impose goal-defined roles on social actors, limiting events through their constraints (as in Levinson 1979: 69) and regulating the patterns of actors' actions. Settings define the situation for the actors (Linell, 1998: 235) and as such are categorized through the way participants see them. Linell's emphasis on the communicative aspect of activity types (e.g. Linell, 2010) has its roots in Bakhtin's (2006 [1986]) dialogical view on interaction. One consequence is that Linell develops traditionally monological perceptions of discourse which highlight the role of CAT as contextually and socially related. A CAT, then, usually combines "transactional and social-relational talk" (Linell, 2009: 211) which seems to link its mechanics to the tenets of Conversation Analysis and by its dialogical stance supplies the missing element of "togetherness" and "betweenness". In other words, the dialogical foundations in the concept of CP allow us to focus on interaction between speakers rather than on a "turn-to-turn" basis, as is true in CA.

Within a single CAT, different CPs can be distinguished as being nested in each other. An example might be the CAT of a business presentation constructed of a number of CPs, such as greetings, presenting an agenda, establishing points for discussion, answering questions, concluding and closing the meeting. The main goal of a Communicative Project is to resolve a communicative task. Christensson (2020) lists three main features of a CP:

1. dependence on participants' interactions – a CP emerges from and reaches its end through their communicative co-orchestrated activities;
2. complexity and multifunctionality – a CP can be both the process and the final result (even a whole encounter can be described as a CP);
3. dialogicality – a CP involves more than speaker in interaction with another/other participant/s.

These points will help us in orientating towards isolating specific CP for the purposes of our analysis.

2.6. THE METHOD

We follow a constructive problem-solving process where group interaction links verbal patterns, linguistic embodiment and game cards as a cognitive resource. In this analysis, we aim to focus on a combination of recurrent regularities and players' experience based on pico-scale effects. As human interaction is ever-forward progressive, it derives its force from sequentiality. Enfield asserts that:

> This conception of social interaction entails a dynamic relation between a communicative action and the response it elicits. And, in turn, such a reaction may in itself be a communicative action, engendering, in response, a further communicative action (see below). Moreover, any sequence "communicative action and subsequent response" is a unit, not a conjunct

(Enfield, 2011: 286)

As a sign, each response has the potential to bring about another response. In this way every interaction may unfold as a sequence of pivoting sign-response relations (Enfield, 2011: 287), this causal-conditional trajectory of relevance relations being referred to by Enfield as enchrony (2009: 10). Similarly to experience, talk uses the enchronic scale (Enfield, 2014) and seems to be best illustrated by a moment-to-moment analysis of unfolding events. We believe that microgenetic methods which examine change as it occurs should be appropriate tools to capture the micro-scale dynamics of interaction between players. In this way we should be able to observe and interpret the moment-to-moment interactions between players, as well as the ways in which the patterns of linguistic behaviour shape the problem-solving process.

With the above in mind, we feel that there is no ready-made method which would be more suited to our needs. This is because languaging is a primary activity for many different types of social occurrences, playing games being merely one example. In the ecological perspective, a speaker's activity makes his/her linguistic information relevant and available for further action. The domain of research into the mechanics of human communicative interaction has to date been occupied by conversation analysts who focus on the organizational aspects of conversation. However, if we intend to delve into the mechanics of the ways in which humans interact linguistically in daily situations, this method seems inadequate. The distributed stance invites the researcher to take a more comprehensive look at how people communicate, e.g. when solving problems or playing games, due to the emphasis placed on dialogicality and interactivity. The engagement of other individuals requires the researcher to look beyond turn-taking and towards the space where languaging is co-constructed. Therefore, the researcher's attention should not only be directed at the wordings but also gestures, body movements, gaze, postural arrangements and facial expressions, in order to expose what occurs between speakers rather than in turn-to-turn transactional rounds. In the last decade, the design of a suitable research method has been focused on how trajectories of action change in different problem-solving settings. For example in Steffensen (2013), Steffensen et al. (2016) and Steffensen and Trasmundi (2018) we find early descriptions and then developments of Cognitive Event Analysis which are used to pursue cases of fine-grained interactivity and to hypothesize on the role of insight in problem-solving. The value of this method lies in its anti-mentalist and distributed approach, however, as it centres on cognitive aspects of interaction, it does not offer adequate research measures for our current needs.

We have no hesitation in categorizing the 50-minute recorded episode of the game *Codenames* as a Communicative Activity Type. As in Linell's description, it qualifies as "a comprehensive communicative project tied to a social situation type" (Linell, 2009: 201). Furthermore, a CAT is characterized by a sequence-realized action agenda and can be clearly divided into opening, main and closing activities. Since CATs are usually samples of "transactional and social-relational talk" (Linell, 2009: 211), this will also be true of *Codenames* as a language-based group interaction. Each distinguished dialogical unit is a type of social situation and, in Linell's terms (Linell, 2009: 201) can be tied to separate comprehensive CPs. We chose two CPs (the first two rounds of the game) and illustrated them with relevant transcription and photo stills as samples of lived language and action. In each CP, dialogical and/or action is task-orientated and requires the coordination of two or more players, which also influences the manner in which our analysis is organized. Typically, when playing games, players either refer to the problem intrinsic to the game itself or organize the game environment, such as establishing tactics, negotiating leadership or referring to topics beyond the game. This suggests that all types of projects should be recognized as pertinent elements of the gameplay episode. Interestingly, in the study by Newgarden et al. (2015) statistical evidence is presented to demonstrate that players' multimodal languaging impacted on the quality of communicative projects. This makes some elements of their methodology particularly attractive in our case. Additionally, we will loosely draw on Newgarden and Zheng's (2016) systematicity to design our own three-step analytical procedure.

Firstly, in Step 1, we distinguish Communicative Projects which constitute the ways in which players connect speech and action within the Communicative Activity Type (the game). Then we identify Languaging Modes (wordings, gestures, posture, gaze, use of material objects, etc.) as Step 2 and explore each with the aim of tracing the "repeatables" (replicable constraints/verbal patterns) that help players to orientate themselves to the game tasks and to operate in the problem space. Such cases of prototypical interactions in the game are Step 3 of the analysis under the label of Recurrent Languaging Activities, (cf. Newgarden and Zheng, 2016). We predict that different recurrent languaging activities will afford different communicative activities within each CP and draw on multiple modalities, thus facilitating gameplay. RLAs signal players' attitudes, social stances and interactional strategies. By observing and registering their occurrence and deployment by individual speakers, it should be possible to distinguish how they demonstrate their languaging abilities through enacting a variety of communicative activities that are inherent and recurrent in a group play. We relate the notions of Communicative Project, modes of interaction and recurrent languaging activities to establishing the ways in which players co-ordinate the game linguistically and therefore exhibit a skill.

Findings on linguistic aspects, intersubjectivity or use of discourse strategies have hitherto been based almost exclusively on transcripts. We too, in order to register the vocal aspect of the interaction, use a CA-type approach based on a standardized Jeffersonian transcription (Jefferson, 2004). For the more detailed multimodal actions, Mondada's (2016) and Norris's (2004; 2011) conventions for multimodal transcription were adapted by simplifying and orientating them towards our research goal. Constant developments in, and novel applications of this notation system (e.g. in computer-mediated interaction, efficacy of psychotherapeutic methods or in forensic linguistics) make it, in our opinion, a satisfactory tool to register and document the trajectory of the events occurring in the video-recorded situation. Indeed, descriptions based on turn-taking norms go against our interests in observing what goes on "between" speakers rather than in a turn-to-turn routine. To compensate for this, we will treat each consecutive turn as evidence of the dynamics of the interaction. Technically, with regard to our research question (Is language a skill?), CA-inspired transcription will allow us to highlight regularities of "language use". One line in the transcript refers to the entire speech unit and may in reality encompass more than one line of printed text. A speaker's verbal turn is synchronized with a number of variables, such as prosody, gestural and facial "expression", body movements, body alignment, posture, gaze, etc. and is treated as one unit. This said, in highly charged interactional linguistic events (e.g. moments of concentrated activity by players) transcription alone may be insufficient to illustrate some important elements of micro-scale dynamics. To account for such other instances of participant activity coordinated with each other, or with other aspects of the situation, we will at times provide relevant still images for greater precision of the presentation of our insights. As a technical analytical tool we chose Elan 5.8 software as it permits zooming in on significant or pivotal moments of interaction, the combination of which yields results in terms of players performing game tasks. The transcriptions we presented tend to feature interactional details so we refrain from entering the field of conversation analysis. Nevertheless, due to its social and interactional orientation, some influence of CA is inevitable in the description of dialogical exchange events. Since the players in the recording use Polish as their native tongue, we provide literal English translations. Still, we wish to emphasize the approximate and non-literal character of these, as our primary purpose was simply to enable the non-Polish-speaking reader to understand the content of the recording.

2.7. TRANSCRIPT AND EVENTS PRESENTATION

There are two teams in *Codenames*, each composed of a "code master" and two or three "operatives". In the game recording analysed here there are two teams of three players. In one Artur is the codemaster for Tomasz and Matylda, while Patrycja assumes the same role for operatives Patryk and Agnieszka in the other. The teams compete to score points by attempting to identify the words their code masters have concealed amongst other words written on the cards laid out on the table in front of them. The code masters may only give hints in the form of category terms relating to the specific generic one-word nouns printed on the cards. Together with the hint, the spymaster provides a number which indicates how many nouns are linked to the hidden word. The operatives then have to point to the words best related to the hint word. They can confer before making their choice of specific card. In this way, the game becomes a rich communicative environment in which players interact by discussing words and their meanings. In order to meet the objectives of the game, the participants are obliged to talk about words and concepts. They are supposed to guess the connection between the categories proposed by team leaders and the words on the cards. Both the categories and the inscriptions become "material anchors" or linguistic artefacts which for each individual hide some meanings. We are interested here in how the speakers interact in the game in order to talk about meanings, how they relate to one another and, most importantly, how they language about the problem to be solved.

We use the following abbreviations to denote each participant: PK for Patryk, PA for Patrycja, AG for Agnieszka, AR for Artur, M for Matylda and T for Tomasz. In the script we will use additional annotations (e.g. **AG-**, **-T**, **PK-**, etc.) to register the trajectories of speaker's modes of interaction other than vocalizations. For example, **AG-** signifies the beginning of Agnieszka's bodily action and **-AG** its end. Table 2.1 will help us systematize the transcription and supply comments regarding modes (gestures, gaze, posture, etc. and elements of the environment) and Recurrent Languaging Activities, together with relevant commentary. Since the players communicate in Polish, a translation into English will be given. Its main objective will be to reflect the sequence of lexical components of each utterance, which may detract from their naturalness in English. Some of the events will be illustrated with relevant stills from the recording to provide the reader with a more comprehensive understanding of what is actually going at a particular moment. Unfortunately, the poor camera angle means that Matylda's body movements cannot be seen fully, so our comments in this respect will be significantly reduced and focused more on her RLAs.

Table 2.1 Communicative Project 1: Agnieszka and Patryk are solving their task

	Vocalizations in Polish and English (below in italics)	Languaging Mode (LM) with commentary	Recurrent Languaging Activities (RLAs)
1	PA	`Dobra. ghghgh (6.5) Za: granica:: [1.0]>trzy<` `OK. ghghgh (6.5) A:broad:: [1.0]>three<`	Patrycja is leaning on the table	
2	PK	`(3.4)No dobrze` `(3.4)Well OK`	Before uttering his cue, Patryk rests his chin on his hand; as he starts speaking he folds his arms on the table and leans on the table, overtly signalling that he is considering the problem.	Patryk is preparing for the game and opens dialogical interaction: interactional opening ("no dobrze" / well OK). RLA: conversation maintenance
3	AG	`To PK- Nowy Jork -PK AG-(.) jest za granica= -AG` `Then PK- New York -PK AG-(.) is abroad= -AGFig`	Agnieszka starts by turning her head towards Patryk on finishing her cue. By doing so, she emphasizes her point. Patryk glances at Agnieszka and then at the cards on the table once more. He silently accepts Agnieszka's argument.	Agnieszka responds to the invitation immediately, taking the initiative in providing solutions: "To" (Then). RLA: argumentation, control

(*Continued*)

Table 2.1 (*Continued*)

	vocalizations in Polish and English (below in italics)	Languaging Mode (LM) with commentary	Recurrent Languaging Activities (RLAs)

4 PK	`AG-=TAK jest. -AG Em: Nowy Jo:rk e:::m: PK-[po`
	 `  kolei]-PK`
	 `AG-=THAT'S correct. -AG Em: New Yo:rk e:::m:`
	 `PK-[one by one]-PK`
		Agnieszka turns her head back to look at the table.
		
		 Patryk still looks at the cards while biting his lips and tilting his head to the right, away from Agnieszka – he is at his wit's end.
			Patryk readily agrees with Agnieszka
			 "tak jest" (that's correct).
			
			 RLA: agreement
			
			 Then he reveals hesitation, unable to come up with another idea.
			
			 RLA:
			 uncertainty, hesitation

5 AG	`T-[Jeszcze jest]-T Australia=` *`T-[There's also]-T Australia=`*	Agnieszka keeps looking at the cards. Tomasz takes a quick and discreet glance at her.	Agnieszka continues searching for solutions. "Jeszcze" functionally corresponds with "To" in line 3 RLA: argumentation leadership
6 T	`=A może wios:°<na>°↑T--T` *`=Or maybe spr:°<ing>°↑T--T`*	Tomasz looks at cards as he delivers his cue. On finishing, he turns his head to the right to look at Agnieszka and gently tilts forward.	Tomasz deliberately offers an absurd solution attempting to provoke "a może" (maybe). RLA: provocative remark

	vocalizations in Polish and English (below in italics)	Languaging Mode (LM) with commentary	Recurrent Languaging Activities (RLAs)
7 AG	(1.0) AG- eh:::m= *(1.0) AG- eh:::m=*	Agnieszka laughs then smiles, as Tomasz clarifies his argument, all the time looking at the cards. Patryk smiles about 1 second after Agnieszka starts laughing.	The one-second pause signals that Agnieszka seems unsure what to do about Tomasz's cue ("em"). RLA: uncertainty, hesitation
8 T	=bo T- inna pora roku -T PK- °może być° -AG (1.9) T- -T (nb°) sierpień: T na przykład. -PK *=because T- a different season -T PK- °may be°* *-AG (1.9) T- -T (nb°) August: T for example.* *-PK*	Tomasz makes two consecutive clarifying and argumentative movements with his left arm gesture. Patryk tilts his head to the right and then smiles until the end of Tomasz's cue; Agnieszka stops smiling but Patryk continues to do so. She seemingly begins to think of her next cue.	Tomasz's tentative "może być" (maybe) is in fact a strategically provocative remark. RLA: provocative remark
9 AG	Co do tego się AG- zgadzamy takt (.) że Nowy Jork -AG i Aust[ralia]. *As for this AG- we agree don't wet (.) that New* *York -AG and Aust[ralia].*		Agnieszka takes responsibility and displays leadership by referring to their previous ideas "co do tego [...], tak?" (As for this [...], don't we). RLA: leadership, affirmation
10 PK	[Tak. I] co mamy jeszcze::? PK- um:yhm= -PK um:yhm= -PK *[Yes. And] what else have we got::? PK-*		Patryk initiates another round ("I co mamy jeszcze" What else have we got), only in social terms, as in line 2. RLA: conversation maintenance

(Continued)

Table 2.1 (*Continued*)

	vocalizations in Polish and English (below in italics)	Languaging Mode (LM) with commentary	Recurrent Languaging Activities (RLAs)

11 PA	`=Ale ( )  PA- moga jakby co zrezygnować (1.0)`
	`AR- nie? Jakby z trzeciego -AR (0.5) jak nie`
	`wiedzą-PA`
	`=But ( )  PA- they may if anything give up(1.0)`
	`AR- not? For example the third one -AR (0.5) if`
	`they don't know!-PA`
		Patrycja makes a downward left forearm movement as she's resting on her left elbow. Artur turns his head towards Patrycja and then returns to looking at the cards on the table.	

12 AR	`Moga: zrezygnowa:ć` `They may: give: up`		

13 AG	`Um::: Wiesz co PK- >mi się wydaje że pingwin<`
	`AG- może być za granica. (1.0) Bo u [nas nie`
	`ma] -PK`
	`Um::: You know what PK- >I think that a`
	`penguin< AG- may be abroad. (1.0) Because [we`
	`don't have any] -PK`
		Patryk strokes his check and looks at the cards, probably uncertain what to do next. Agnieszka raises her head and looks at Patrycja (the group's codemaster).
		
		Patryk, on hearing Agnieszka, strokes the bottom of his chin and then moves his right hand to the back of his neck as if to show insecurity.
			Agnieszka takes the lead again by directing her question to Patrycja, ignoring Patryk as her partner in solution seeking:
			"wiesz co" (you know what).
			
			RLA: initiative taking, leadership

14 PK	`[Uhm](0.6) AG- tak je:st.` `[Uhm](0.6) AG- that's righ:t.`	Agnieszka starts turning her head towards Patryk after his pause.	Patryk nevertheless intends to mark his presence in the game interaction: "tak jest" (that's correct). RLA: agreement

vocalizations in Polish and English (below in italics)	Languaging Mode (LM) with commentary	Recurrent Languaging Activities (RLAs)

15 AG `Tak? -AG- [0.2] ·hhhDobra (.) to AG- może >po`
`prostu< PK- zaznaczymy to czego jesteśmy pewni`
`[a pote:m] -AG -PK`
`Yes? -AG [0.2] ·hhhOK (.) then AG- maybe >just<`
`PK- we will mark what we are sure of [and`
`the:n] -AG -PK`
	Agnieszka stops turning her head and looks at the cards on the table.
	
	Agnieszka makes circular hand movements right above the edge of the table as if preparing her hand for the next move.
	
	As soon as she does so, Patryk folds his hands and rests his body on the table in a more relaxed manner, as if relieved that Agnieszka has made a decision.
		Agnieszka takes the initiative after an audible inhale. She seems to be shouldering responsibility here, marked by some uncertainty: "Dobra to może najpierw, po prostu" (OK then maybe first we just...).
		
		RLA: initiative taking, leadership
		RLA: tentative guess

16 PK `[>DOBrze<]. Czyli Nowy Jork.` `[>Ok<]. Then New York`		Patryk sums up and agrees again ("Dobrze"/OK).
17 AG `AG- Nowy Jork↑` `AG- New York↑`	Agnieszka looks at Patrycja and, while maintaining eye contact, pats the relevant cards with her forefinger then reaches to the pile of cards in front of her.	RLA: agreement
18 PA `Tak:` `Yes:`	nods her head.	

(Continued)

Table 2.1 *(Continued)*

vocalizations in Polish and English (below in italics)	Languaging Mode (LM) with commentary	Recurrent Languaging Activities (RLAs)
19 PK ZAZnaczamy. (2.0) ·hhhAUSTralia (0.9) *We are MARking. (2.0) ·hhhAUSTralia (0.9)*		The decision does not come from him but from Agnieszka and is then affirmed by Patrycja. Patryk only agrees with their moves by a decisive "zaznaczamy" (we're marking) This is an echo of "tak jest" from line 4 and "dobrze" (OK) from line 16.
		RLA: agreement
20 PA **AG--AG** Tak. **AG--AG** Yes.	Agnieszka makes the patting movement and then gives Patrycja a prolonged exploratory look. Patrycja gently nods her head in agreement. Agnieszka's interaction with Patrycja makes her move forward in the problem space more effectively than her cooperation with Patryk.	
21 PK °zaznaczamy° (0.5)i teraz zastanówmy się co **PK-** nam zostało.-**PK** °*we are marking*° (0.5)*and now let's think what* **PK-** *we are left with.* -**PK**	Agnieszka pats the card on the table and places another card on the table. Patryk brings his left hand to his chin as if considering another move but the tone of his voice is decisive as if he intended to cover his passiveness in solving the problem.	Patryk ostensibly takes over the initiative from Agnieszka ("I teraz zastanówmy się" – And now let's think) but again, as in line 2 and 10, he only keeps the conversation going rather than contributing to solution finding. RLA: conversation maintenance

	vocalizations in Polish and English (below in italics)	Languaging Mode (LM) with commentary	Recurrent Languaging Activities (RLAs)
22 AG	(5.4) Może być baobab ale nie wiem AG- czy w Polsce rośnie.-AG *(5.4) Maybe baobab but I don't know AG- if it grows in Poland.-AG*	Agnieszka turns her gaze to Patrycja. Then she blinks a few times as if demonstrating uncertainty.	Agnieszka's *"może być"* is again directed towards Patrycja, not Patryk. This suggests her independence in making decisions, despite the hesitation expressed ("ale nie wiem, czy w Polsce rośnie." But I don't know if it grows in Poland).
			RLA: tentative guess
23 PA	Tsch:: *Tsch::*	Patrycja snorts, Agnieszka responds by smiling;	RLA: initiative taking, leadership The snort is in fact a non-word yet still a vocalization of a "no".
24 T	AG- PA- Może połączenie. -AG -PA *AG- PA- Maybe connection. -AG -PA*	Agnieszka and Patrycja look at Tomasz and return their gaze to the starting point in the same sequence.	Tomasz uses *"może"* (maybe) not to offer another solution (as a tentative guess) but again as an intentionally misleading clue-giving.
25 AG	[( )]		RLA: provocative remark
26 T	[( )]		
27 AG	Na przykład CO? *For example WHAT?*		Agnieszka shows leadership by challenging Tomasz. RLA: initiative taking, leadership

(Continued)

Table 2.1 (*Continued*)

	vocalizations in Polish and English (below in italics)	Languaging Mode (LM) with commentary	Recurrent Languaging Activities (RLAs)
28 PK	(4.2) Najbardziej pasuje **PK-** ten <u>pingwin</u>= *(4.2) The best match is* **PK-** *this* <u>*penguin*</u>=	Patryk's bodily work contrasts to his words and signals hesitation, as he pinches his check and holds this position for 3 seconds.	Patryk ignores Tomasz's clue and finally his initiative ("najbardziej pasuje" the best match is). RLA: initiative taking, leadership
29 AG	=No:: też bym [1.0] zaryzykowała. **AG--AG -PK** *=Yeah:: I would also [1.0] risk it.* **AG--AG -PK**	Agnieszka accepts Patryk's idea, touches the card and looks at Patrycja, whose facial expression informs her that she has made a bad guess; Patryk realizes this and expresses his disappointment by stroking his chin.	Agnieszka follows Patryk ("No też bym zaryzykowała" – I would also risk it) but expresses uncertainty. RLA: agreement
30 PA	**AG-** Nie↓ **AG-** *No↓*	Begins to remove her hand from above the card.	RLA: tentative guess
31 AG	Nie? **-AG** *No?* **-AG**	Agnieszka brings her hand to her chest and forms a fist; she feels unsure.	
32 PA	Niebieski *Blue*		
33 AG	·hhhhh	Lowers her hand and hides it under the table in disappointment.	Agnieszka's vocalization aligned with her bodily action communicate the realization of failure and embarrassment. RLA: failure/embarrassment

vocalizations in Polish and English (below in italics)	Languaging Mode (LM) with commentary	Recurrent Languaging Activities (RLAs)
34 AR Dziękujemy *Thank you*		
Communicative Project 2: Matylda and Tomasz are guessing words		
35 AR y::::: No to w takim razie (.) zwierzęta T- dwa -T *y::::: Well in that case (.) animals T- two -T*	Tomasz leans forward towards the table.	
36 T To może ślimak? T--T *Then maybe snail? T-T*		Tomasz makes contact – "to może" (then maybe)? taking the lead although in a tentative manner. RLA: tentative guess and taking initiative
37 M No::: ale jest M- też dzięcioł i robak -M *Yeah::: but there is M- also woodpecker and worm -M*	Matylda places the tip of her index finger delicately on the table next to the cards; all the time leaning away from the table in contrast to Tomasz, whose body is slightly tilted towards the table surface and whose right arm is resting on it. We might infer that he is more engaged in risk-taking.	"No ale" (Yeah but) is argumentative and contributive; aligned with the finger-tap, it constitutes a gentle suggestion to broaden Tomasz's perspective. RLA: expressing argument

(Continued)

Table 2.1 (*Continued*)

	vocalizations in Polish and English (below in italics)	Languaging Mode (LM) with commentary	Recurrent Languaging Activities (RLAs)
38 T	Ale T- robak to nie jest zwierze hhhhh· ·hhhhh hhhhh· ·hhhhh -T *But T- a worm is not an animal hhhhh· ·hhhhh hhhhh· ·hhhhh -T*	Tomasz turns his head towards Marylda and starts laughing. All other participants follow suit.	By using "ale", "to nie jest", Tomasz takes a strong assertive stance and positions himself as an expert, dismissing Marylda's contribution as worthless. RLA: expressing argument Marylda lacks further argument and gives in.
39 M	-T Kurcze *-T Blimey*		RLA: failure/embarrassment
40 T	hhhhh ·hhhhh hhhhh ·hhhhh		By laughing, Tomasz reinforces his position as the leader in this CP.
41 M	Dobrze (.) ok. *Good (.) ok.*		Marylda tries to cover her embarrassment by agreeing with Tomasz. RLA: concession

	vocalizations in Polish and English (below in italics)	Languaging Mode (LM) with commentary	Recurrent Languaging Activities (RLAs)
42 T	£Nie wydaje mi się(.)żeby robak był zwierzęciem(.)no **T- -T** *£I Don't think(.)worm is an animal (.) yes **T- -T***	Tomasz turns his head towards Matylda and shrugs his shoulders.	"Nie wydaje mi się" [I don't think] corresponds to a dismissive shrugging gesture. In this way Tomasz keeps arguing his point. RLA: expressing argument
43 M	No nie wiem. £No dobra↓ **M--M** hhhhh [·hhhhh] *Well I'm not sure. £well OK↓ **M--M** hhhhh [·hhhhh]*	Downward hand, points at the cards while touching the table.	Matylda continues to retract her idea and concludes with a self-deprecating laughing sound. RLA: concession
44 T	[hhhhh]·hhhh		Tomasz concludes this stage of their CP by affirming his stance. RLA: tentative guess and initiative taking

(Continued)

Table 2.1 (*Continued*)

	vocalizations in Polish and English (below in italics)	Languaging Mode (LM) with commentary	Recurrent Languaging Activities (RLAs)
45 M	Ale na M- pewno dzieciol nie?= *But surely M- woodpecker isn't it?=*	Marylda repeatedly makes a patting movement in the air close to the table as if securing the cards.	Marylda aims to compensate for her failure in the previous stage and continues making suggestions. Despite "na pewno" (surely), she seeks Tomasz's approval, RLA: concession
46 T	T- =Dzieciol na pewno= -T *T- =Woodpecker for sure= -T*		RLA: approval seeking "na pewno" (surely) adds to Tomasz's position as leader
47 M	=Na sto procent↑ -M *=One hundred per cent↑ -M*	Only at this point does Marylda end her patting.	RLA: tentative guess and taking initiative Marylda's "certainty" is secured by Tomasz's "na pewno in line 46. RLA: concession

vocalizations in Polish and English (below in italics)	Languaging Mode (LM) with commentary	Recurrent Languaging Activities (RLAs)
48 PK Jest jeszcze **PK**- Feniks -**PK** *There's also **PK**- Phoenix -**PK***	Patryk points to the card.	"Jest jeszcze" echoes Tomasz's tactics from line 8 and 24. RLA: provocative remark
49 T No Feniks ale Feniks to raczej nie= *Well Phoenix but Phoenix rather not=*	Glances at Agnieszka after which both manipulate their clothing at the neck as if uncertain.	Tomasz suspects "raczej" (rather) as an expression of tentativeness. RLA: tentative guess
50 AG =**M**- Feniks jest [( )] =**M**- *Phoenix is [( )]*	Puts her hand to her pendant and starts fiddling with it.	
51 T [bo to jes::t] **T**- (0.2) [*because this is::] **T**- (0.2)* mitologia -**M** *mythology -**M***	Tomasz loosens his turtleneck collar; only now does Marylda finish her "pendant" action.	Tomasz argues against Patryk's point, trying to dismiss it but there is some hesitation in his voice and body work. RLA: expressing argument
52 PT Tak *Yes*		
53 T Więc to odpada -**T** ·h[Wtedy będzie] *So that's out -**T** ·h[Then it will be]*		Tomasz has made a decision for them both. RLA: taking initiative

(Continued)

Table 2.1 (*Continued*)

vocalizations in Polish and English (below in italics)	Languaging Mode (LM) with commentary	Recurrent Languaging Activities (RLAs)
54 M [To wtedy:] ślimak i:::: *[Then:] snail and::::*		Matylda echoes Tomasz's words and returns to his first proposal.
55 T (1.0) [Zaznacz] *(1.0) [Mark it]*		RLA: concession Tomasz gives instructions.
56 M [i co?] *[and what?]*		RLA: leadership Matylda gives in and needs precise instructions from Tomasz.
57 T dzieciola najpierw *woodpecker first*		RLA: instruction seeking Tomasz continues to give instructions.
58 M M-M	Touches the card with his index finger and covers it with another card.	RLA: leadership
59 AR AR- Dobrze -AR (0.7) dzieciol jest nasz *AR- Good -AR (0.7) woodpecker is ours*	Artur nods his head.	
60 M M- -M [inaudible]	Matylda uncovers a card from the pile and places it on top of one of those already laid out.	

	vocalizations in Polish and English (below in italics)	Languaging Mode (LM) with commentary	Recurrent Languaging Activities (RLAs)
61 T	[No i co (.) ślimak?] °£No nie M- no bo no -M nie wiem, mi się tak jakoś T- nie kojarzy° no ale= *[Well what (.) snail?] °£Well no M- because -M I don't know, it doesn't really T- remind me of° well but=*	Tomasz turns his head towards Marylda. On hearing Tomasz's "nie", Marylda touches her pendant as if to defuse the tension of embarrassment.	Tomasz undertakes a self-dialogue, excluding Marylda from the interaction.
			RLA: leadership
62 M	=Też się zastanawiam nad tym -T *=I'm also thinking about that -T*		Marylda joins in but does not add any new argument, which again expresses her conservative and secure stance. ("Też")
			RLA:
			concession
63 T	(1.2)No::: T--T Dobrz:: *(1.2)No::: T--T Dobrz::*	Tomasz moves his jaw, looking at the cards, apparently uncertain what to do.	The prolonged "o" in "No" and consonantal sound in "dobrze" correspond with jaw movements; both are repeatable signalling indecision.
			RLA:
			tentative guess

(Continued)

Table 2.1 (*Continued*)

vocalizations in Polish and English (below in italics)	Languaging Mode (LM) with commentary	Recurrent Languaging Activities (RLAs)
64 M No: no dobrz:: T- To ruszamy [( )] *So: so then:: T- So let's go [( )]*	Tomasz nods a few times.	Marylda's initiative is built on. Tomasz's licence from line 62. It is also interesting to see how they depend on each other's RLAs when they reiterate them "No dobrze" (so then) RLA: taking initiative, leadership
65 T Śli:mak -T *Snai:l -T*	Then he turns his head away from the table, smiles and leans back in the chair.	The prolonged vowel sound signals certainty and complacency. RLA: certainty
66 M M—M	Marylda points at a card on the table.	
67 AR AR- Dobrze↓ -AR *AR- Good↓ -AR*		

2.8. ANALYSIS

In this section we focus on the most active players, i.e. the two involved in guessing the words and, potentially, any other participant who affects the course of interaction. The players use the cards and the table as major material artefacts to mediate their interactivity and languaging practices. They perform most of their body work, by leaning on the table, moving closer to or further away from it, enhancing their vocalizations and signalling their interactive and cognitive engagement. As the solutions are hidden among them, the cards become a natural point of reference, so the players' gaze is predominantly directed at the table. Some cards are also manipulated towards the end of each round to conclude the message about partial or full task completion. The game situation promotes cooperation which is driven ultimately by competitiveness, rather than understanding and communication. Here, they do not talk about language but about the concepts which they think the team player "has in mind". However, the inventory of resources comprises language and other semiotic tools. By finding, probing and communicating solutions (not meanings!), they have to language about their linguistic experience.

In Communicative Project 1, Patryk (PK) takes on the task but it is Agnieszka (AG) who actually proposes the first suggestion for a solution. Patryk tries to keep up with her by accentuating his agreement. Agnieszka takes the lead in speculating about a possible solution but she seems to be certain. Her posture is distanced from the table. In the opening fragments of CP1, Patryk readily acknowledges Agnieszka's ideas and his own contribution is limited to accepting what his teammate says, e.g. in line 10 he shows some degree of hesitation. He does so by asking a problem-orientated question as a conversational filler and a form of self-presentation as an initiative-taking team member. In fact, he is observed to be locked in a problem space (hand stroking chin), assuming the role of a quasi-conversational mirror and an additional – apart from language – mediator of Agnieszka's understanding of the words on the cards. His bodily activity compensates for the lack of dialogical initiative. Although Patryk's posture might communicate greater engagement than Agnieszka's, it is she who actually takes leadership and control of their problem solving by probing and proposing solutions. This can also be seen in the cue she actually delivers to Patrycja, not Patryk ("Wiesz co, mi się wydaje że pingwin może być za granicą"). Tomasz (T) clearly adopts the role of a disturbing factor when he provokes his opponents into considering his solution. In order to reinforce his message, he tilts and turns his body towards Agnieszka and moves his arms to emphasize his point and clarify his proposal. Agnieszka's response is to ignore this remark. She chooses not to respond verbally and displays unruffled equanimity by keeping her eyes on the cards, with her body still and delivering a line unrelated to Tomasz's turn. Agnieszka's reaction suggests that languaging in conversation is an emergent process of selecting the resources which best realize the goals of the speakers.

Although Tomasz does not greatly affect her solution-probing, he constitutes a vital participant in the ecology of this conversation. Then Agnieszka makes another guess at the last word, expressing, however, doubt about its appropriateness. Tomasz probably spots her hesitation and comes up with another suggestion, which is comparable to throwing a ball for her to catch. This she returns, by asking a question which Tomasz does not answer. His move activates Patryk, who comes back to the original idea ("penguin"). Tomasz's role is again that of propelling the interactivity between Agnieszka, Patryk and Patrycja. Agnieszka agrees with Patryk, however, albeit not without reservations. This constant flow of verbal and bodily interaction is the axis along which their Communicative Project develops.

Communicative Project 2 consists of Matylda and Tomasz. In the opening stage Matylda welcomes Tomasz's idea with some reservation, which she reinforces by challenging his proposal. She supports her argument by pointing at the cards which become a material extension of her verbal activity. In the ensuing sequences of CP2 we can observe her resorting to this strategy again. In this particular case, the gesture and the cards not only constitute the means to redirect Tomasz's thinking towards another solution but also become a form of disagreement. Matylda repeats this "disagreement" pattern (line 37 and 45) and lacks conviction when she submits to Tomasz's argumentative and authoritative stance (e.g. in lines 38, 42, 52, 54, 56). Her RLAs seem to be expressions of a face-saving ploy after her solution proposal was mocked by Tomasz. Also the concessive gestures she uses to reinforce her conversational strategy suggest that, instead of proving her point, she finds conceding more important than coming up with an alternative solution. This becomes even more evident in line 45 ("Ale na pewno dzięcioł nie?"/"But surely not a woodpecker?"), which again brings her back to the concessive domain rather than a proactive direction-setting position. By contrast, Tomasz openly affirms his opinions, as he does when addressing Patryk's deliberate misguidance. Although at first he picks up Patryk's "Feniks" argument after discussing it for a while, he ultimately rejects it as out of line with his thinking.

In CP1, the players display the following dominant modes: Agnieszka – gaze and voice, Patryk – gaze, hand, Tomasz – gaze, voice. The Recurrent Languaging Categories the main actors in this interaction present belong to these prototypical categories: Agnieszka – leadership and argumentation, Patryk conciliation and following. In CP 2, Matylda communicates in a more concessive way, whereas Tomasz's languaging is argumentative (even authoritative at times) and leadership-orientated. The distribution of modes of interaction corresponds with specific RLAs (as indicated in the table above) and harmoniously supplements them. Players take on their roles in the game and fulfil them in order to achieve not only the objects of the game but the values characteristic of each role. They do so by skilful intersubjective engagement. By exhibiting specific forms of behaviour, employing space and particular verbal patterns, the players adopt the roles which make them proceed with their tasks to their conclusion. The appearance of Recursive Languaging Activities in conjunction with other repeatable modes of interaction prove that language (in distributed perspective) is a system of repeatable constraints, or "repeatables". If we adopt Herick's philosophy, then the players do indeed exhibit considerable skill in constructing the trajectory of their interaction in the game dialogically by resorting to wordings. These wordings fall under specific communicatively functional categories which are grouped here under the label of Recurrent Languaging Activities.

The alignment of RLAs with prosodies, gestures, gaze etc. permits the assumption that language is an activity where wordings and other semiotic resources, such as hand gestures, gaze, facial expression and body alignment, play a vital role, all ultimately contributing to the manner in which players interact and achieve results in the problem space. Taking linguistic forms into account, we can notice how the game participants' individual experience of symbolic forms meshes and affects their dialogical activities. They skilfully manipulate these forms, which allows each of them to assume the position of a decision-making languaging agent, for whom the presence of others becomes mere assistance rather than partnership. The players clearly understand what the game requires them to do (talk about words, negotiate meanings, report solutions, etc.), and in order to meet this objective, they intuitively establish their own mode of language-based interaction. They engage in dialogical mutual interaction, albeit while demonstrating distinct strategies. For example, while Agnieszka builds her position as leader-initiator by minimally relating with Patryk, Tomasz is more orientated towards Matylda's utterances (in a critical way). Although the two pairs use different communicative strategies in their solution seeking, solution-probing and solution-finding, they all orientate themselves towards linguistic patterns in the same way.

2.9. DISCUSSION OF THE METHOD'S APPLICABILITY

The fieldwork of our study is grounded in observational research, specifically video-observation. Such a design allows us to pay attention to both the micro and macro scale of interactivity in a gameplay setting. The study's focus is on the micro time-scale, including what happens in real time, by the use of video-observation. Video-observation, as a framework for holistic analysis of interaction which entails more than just pure verbal utterances (e.g. Streeck et al., 2011; Goodwin, 2002, 2007), has some obvious advantages. It delivers data information as a reliable source for documenting interactional details; it also allows for a comprehensive analysis and unlimited review of events, and facilitates results based on actual evidence, as opposed to researcher's recall. Naturalistic descriptions based on recorded data have been proven to be of higher scientific value, in that they prevent potential and (often) inevitable cognitive biases in the ways a researcher reconstructs past events based purely on recollection. One amongst many of the promising features of our methodological framework is its openness to other analytical methods and theoretical perspectives which can be integrated into the analysis. An instance of such an extension can be found in Pedersen (2012), who in order to investigate aspects of human interactivity, broadens her study by integrating concepts such as "voiced others", sense-making, values realization, direct perception and affordances.

We have demonstrated that communicating individuals organize interaction in which their bodily co-actions precede the words they use. The methodological paradigm chosen proves its suitability and effectiveness in that it provides us with the relevant tools to observe, in micro-scale, cases of "a first-order activity" of making and interpreting linguistic signs. By following the details of linguistic events, we can now state that, unless the events are labelled as "non-linguistic", they show that human language transgresses the mechanical "use" of verbal patterns, becoming instead a "cognitive trajectory to a viable solution [which] is thus self-organized, unplanned, and on the edge of chaos" (Steffensen, 2013: 195). All moments of solution-probing and solution-finding in the interactions under study draw on interactivity, dialogicality and languaging. To trace rapid dynamics of interactivity, our methodological attempt, as an interdisciplinary framework, opens the way to presenting how interaction is built on complementary interactional movements on the part of the agents involved.

Much as our study is fragmentary and sketchy, we feel that the strength of the framework we present here lies in its multifacetedness and indiscriminate attitude to the notion of language. By drawing on synergies from various domains, it opens the path to investigating the linguistic aspect of human interaction. The analytical tools we employ also permit defensible explanations of how organizational culture and norms of conversation serve the local purposes of interacting individuals. Any endeavour to describe such cases by purely investigating the events and what happens within them would seem insufficient. Rather, we are convinced that an applied linguist should be orientated towards human bodily and verbal behaviour which co-regulates the ways in which people manage to do things together when engaged in conversation. Our intention was to incorporate such an orientation in our methodological framework in order to fuse the standards of academic research with analytical precision and consistency.

As the interbodily dynamics, included in the analysis as a contribution to the overall picture of talk-in-interaction, occur in a very brief timescale, which often escapes our phenomenological experience, they can only be systematically captured in digital recordings. While the number of studies using video-ethnography is constantly on the increase, video-data is still insufficiently employed in many cases, particularly given its potential. Although the volume of studies using video-observation is rising, research into moment-to-moment interaction based on video-recordings of real-life is still relatively scarce. To trace the unpredictable dynamics of interactivity, we propose a methodological framework that moves beyond turn-taking or bodily movement analysis towards the dynamics of languaging and dialogical between-ness. Traditionally, analysts have been interested in the ways interacting agents construct their own perspective and reality through that particular perception and action. The ethnomethodological approach focuses attention to how humans "do things", particularly through language use (Seale, 2012: 247). In contrast, our interactivity-based framework pursues a more naturalized view of language events. While the ethnomethodological approach is concerned with the reality people construct, we propose here a method of observing the multiple gradations which account for interactivity, i.e. we intend to design tools to register the complexities of interaction, including what speakers say, think, do, feel, etc. As a starting point, we work from the enchronic timescale (Enfield, 2014) and define a nested communicative task within the overall gameplay. By so doing, we are in a position to identify the relevant event foci, transition points and other significant moments in interaction in a way that illuminates the main points of our study. On a micro-level, our method investigates how players pursue and achieve the results posed by the rules of the game and by themselves. On a macro scale, the method proves effective in investigating the structural and cultural organization of social events and their results.

2.10. CONCLUSIONS

On a more abstract level of observation, we assert that the game participants display a set of linguistic practices in moment-to-moment cognitive and communicative (inter)activities. What makes these practices happen is their use of structured symbols (wordings) as constraining, normalizing and stabilizing elements in their first-order languaging (e.g. prosody, gestures, posture, facial expression, gaze and material artefacts). These symbols allow them to structure their sense-making and conversational activities and propel their work in the problem space. As they language in the problem space about individual words and concepts, they seek, find and eventually probe solutions, in each case remaining in a dialogical framework, although each of them does so within a different range of interactional strategies. In this way, they demonstrate their natural practical skill ("knowing how") rather than theoretical knowledge ("knowing that").

When playing the game, the participants become involved in a situated cognitive and communicative project which is based on languaging. In realizing their game objectives, they orientate to language, primarily as an activity. The Communicative Projects players open and conclude are instances of languaging in which, by tight bodily coordination and synchronization, they manage their verbal interaction. Recurrent Languaging Activities allow players to enact the kinds of pragmatic activities which lead to goal attainment. By employing prototypical interactional categories as verbalized repeatables, they carry on the conversation along the rules of the game. The orchestration of speech, gesture body alignment and material artefacts renders their interactions symbiotic and dynamic, therefore the players are able to cooperate strategically and shape events during the game. The systematic repeated emergence of verbal patterns, rather than their use by the players, encourages us to think of language as a skill ("knowing how"), than knowledge ("knowing that").

The methodological approach proposed here allows the communicative activities and events to be systematized and coded into three categories. The three-tier description of the approach to analysing the interaction illustrates the moments which prove strategic for the unfolding flow of linguistic interaction between players in the game. Thus we were able to demonstrate some of the Recurrent Languaging Activities that, in turn, afforded the variety of communicative activities performed as players pursue different game goals. Such RLAs can allow players to exploit their linguistic skills when performing actions that have immediate outcomes applicable to gameplay, particularly in finding a solution to the task. Our analytical framework has the potential to reveal how speakers indeed enact Recurrent Languaging Activities. By changing the local situation in the environment of the game (e.g. in CP2 where Tomasz dominates Agnieszka's attempts to challenge his ideas), they change the way they exercise their abilities in future actions in the game.

By applying our research framework, we have managed to prove some claims of "third-wave linguistics" about how language happens in real-life situations. Consequently, we confirm what others have noted as characteristic features of language:

1. language is a two-order phenomenon: an activity and a system – by languaging about words in the mechanics of a conversation, participants use their dialogic competence as social actors (e.g. Love, 2017; Thibault, 2011);
2. language is social: the most important things in human lives happen between persons, rather than within or without them (cf. Sidorkin, 1999: 11);
3. language is distributed, in that it constitutes a set of behaviours contributing to human interaction (e.g. Cowley, 2011).

Finally, the empirical investigations performed through the application of our methodology orientate us towards theoretical insights which may assist in the development of other new methods for exploring human linguistic interaction. Building on the results of this study, we hypothesize that an interdisciplinary framework of human interactivity may bring a positive qualitative change in Applied Linguistics research since, in contrast to most existing models, it provides a relatively high degree of explanatory power regarding human sense-making and result-achieving processes in linguistic interactions.

REFERENCES

Bakhtin, M. (1986). *Speech Genres and Other Late Essays*. Austin, TX: University of Texas Press.

Bakhtin, M. M. (1986/2006). The Problem of Speech Genres. In Jaworski, A. and Coupland, N. (eds.). *The Discourse Reader*. New York: Routledge.

Baldry, A., and Thibault, P. J. (2006). *Multimodal Transcription and Text Analysis: A Multimedia Toolkit and Coursebook*. London: Equinox.

Barsalou, L. W. (2013). Mirroring as Pattern Completion Inferences within Situated Conceptualizations. *Cortex*, 49(10): 2951–2953.

Christensson, J. (2020). Interactional Role Shift as Communicative Project in Student Teachers' Oral Presentations, *Multimodal Communication*, 9(2): 497–516.

Clark, H. H. (1996). *Using Language*. Cambridge: Cambridge University Press.

Clark, A. (2006). Language, Embodiment, and the Cognitive Niche. *Trends in Cognitive Sciences*, 10(8): 370–374.

Clark, H. H. (2008). Talking as if. *Proceedings of the 3rd ACM/IEEE International Conference on Human Robot Interaction*. New York NY: ACM.

Clark, H. H. (2012). Spoken Discourse and its Emergence. In Spivey, M., McRae, K. and Joanisse, M. (eds.). *Cambridge Handbook of Psycholinguistics* (pp. 541–557). Cambridge: Cambridge University Press.

Clark, H. H., and Krych, M. A. (2004) Speaking while Monitoring Addressees for Understanding. *Journal of Memory and Language*, 50: 62–81.

Cowley, S. J. (2011). *Distributed Language*. Amsterdam: John Benjamins.

Cowley, S. J. (2012) Cognitive Dynamics: Language as Values Realizing Activity. In Kravchenko, A. (ed.). *Cognitive dynamics and Linguistic Interactions* (pp. 1–32). Newcastle upon Tyne: Cambridge Scholars Press.

Cowley, S. J. (2015). Verbal Patterns: Taming Cognitive Biology. In Velmezova, E., Kull, K., and Cowley, S. (eds.). *Biosemiotic Perspectives on Language and Linguistics. Biosemiotics*, 13 (pp. 123–150). Cham: Springer.

Cowley, S. J. (2019). The Return of Languaging: Toward a New Ecolinguistics. *Chinese Semiotic Studies*, 15(4): 483–512.

Deacon, T., and Rączaszek-Leonardi, J. (2019). Abandoning the Code Metaphor is Compatible with Semiotic Process. *Behavioral and Brain Sciences*, 42. http://yoksis.bilkent.edu.tr/pdf/files/14400.pdf [accessed 23.01.2022].

Enfield, N. J. (2009). *The Anatomy of Meaning: Speech, Gesture, and Composite Utterances*. Cambridge: Cambridge University Press.

Enfield, N. (2011). Sources of Asymmetry in Human Interaction: Enchrony, status, Knowledge and Agency. In Stivers, T., Mondada, L., and Steensig, J. (eds.). *The Morality of Knowledge in Conversation Studies in Interactional Sociolinguistics* (pp. 285–312). Cambridge: Cambridge University Press.

Enfield, N. P. (2014). Causal Dynamics of Language. In Enfield, N. J., Kockelman, P. and Sidnell, J. (eds). *Cambridge Handbook for Linguistic Anthropology* (pp. 319–335). Cambridge: Cambridge University Press.

Fowler, C. A., Richardson, M. J., Marsh, K. L., and Shockley, K. (2008). Language Use, Coordination, and the Emergence of Cooperative Action. In Fuchs, A. J., and Jirsa, V. (eds). *Coordination: Neural, Behavioral and Social Dynamics* (pp. 261–279). Dordrecht: Springer.

Fusaroli, R., Gangopadhyay, N., and Tylén, K. (2014). The Dialogically Extended Mind: Language as Skilful Intersubjective Engagement. *Cognitive Systems Research*, 29: 31–39.

Fusaroli, R., and Tylén, K. (2016). Investigating Conversational Dynamics: Interactive Alignment, Interpersonal Synergy, and Collective Task Performance. *Cognitive science*, 40(1): 145–171.

Goldin-Meadow, S. (2014). Widening the Lens: What the Manual Modality Reveals about Language, Learning and Cognition. *Philosophical Transactions of the Royal Society B: Biological Sciences,* 369(1651): 20130295. https://royalsocietypublishing.org/doi/pdf/10.1098/rstb.2013.0295 [accessed 23.01.2022].

Goodwin, M. H. (2002). Exclusion in Girls' Peer Groups: Ethnographic Analysis of Language Practices on the Playground. *Human Development*, 45(6): 392–415.

Goodwin, C. (2007). Environmentally Coupled Gestures. In Duncan, S., Cassell, J., and Levy, E. (eds.). *Gesture and the Dynamic Dimension of Language* (pp. 195–212). Amsterdam, The Netherlands: John Benjamins.

Halliday, M. A. K. (1978). *Language as Social Semiotic: The Social Interpretation of Language and Meaning*. London: Edward Arnold.

Halliday, M. A. K. (1985/1994). *An Introduction to Functional Grammar*. London: Arnold.

Halliday, M. A. K., and Matthiessen, C. (2006). *Construing Experience Through Meaning: A Language-Based Approach to Cognition*. London: Cassell.

Herik, J. C., Muller, F. A., and Vromen, J. J. (2019). *Talking about Talking: An Ecological-Enactive Perspective on Language*. Rotterdam: Erasmus University Rotterdam.

Herik, J. C. (2017). Linguistic Know-How and the Orders of Language. *Language Sciences*, 61: 17–27.

Hutchins, E. (1995). How a Cockpit Remembers its Speeds. *Cognitive Science*, 19(3): 265–88.

Hutchins, E. (2010). Cognitive Ecology. *Topics in Cognitive Science*, 2: 705–15.

Iedema, R. (2003), Multimodality, Resemioticization: Extending the Analysis of Discourse as a Multisemiotic Practice. *Visual Communication*, 2(1): 2957.

Jefferson, G. (2004). Glossary of Transcript Symbols with an Introduction. In Lerner, G. H. (ed.). *Conversation Analysis: Studies From the First Generation* (pp. 13–31). Amsterdam: John Benjamins.

Jensen, T. (2014). Emotion in Languaging: Languaging as Affective, Adaptive, and Flexible Behavior in Social Interaction. *Frontiers in Psychology*, 5 https://www.frontiersin.org/articles/10.3389/fpsyg.2014.00720/full [accessed 23.01.2022].

Krebs, J. R. (1984). Animal Signals: Mindreading and Manipulation. In Krebs, J. R., and Davies, N. B. (eds.). *Behavioural Ecology: An Evolutionary Approach*, 2nd ed.) (pp. 380–402). Blackwell Scientific Publications, Oxford.

Levinson, S. C. (1979). Activity Types and Language. *Linguistics*, 17: 365–399.

Li, J., Steffensen, S. V., and Huang, G. (2020). Rethinking Ecolinguistics from a Distributed Language Perspective. *Language Sciences*, 80, https://doi.org/10.1016/j.langsci.2020.101277 [accessed 23.01.2022].

Linell, P. (1998). *Approaching Dialogue: Talk, Interaction and Contexts in Dialogical Perspectives*. Amsterdam: John Benjamins Publishing.

Linell, P. (2009). *Rethinking Language, Mind, and World Dialogically: Interactional and Contextual Theories of Human Sense-making*. Information Age Publishing, Charlotte, NC.

Linell, P. (2010). Communicative Activity Types as Organisations in Discourses and Discourses in Organisations. In Tanskanen, S-K, Helasvuo, M-L, Johansson, M., and Raitaniemi, M. (eds.) *Discourses in Interaction* (pp. 33–59). Amsterdam: John Benjamins.

Linell, P. (2013). Distributed Language Theory, With or Without Dialogue. *Language Sciences*, 40: 168–173.

Linell, P. (2019). Dialogical Tensions: On Rommetveitian Themes of Minds, Meanings, Monologues, and Languages. *Mind, Culture, and Activity: An International Journal* (pp. 219–229). Psychology Press.

Linell, P. (2020). Extending Theories of Dialogue. In Howes, C; Dobnik, S., and Breitholtz, E. (eds.). *CLASP Papers in Computational Linguistics* (pp. 61–67). University of Gothenburg. https://gupea.ub.gu.se/bitstream/2077/63998/4/gupea_2077_63998_4.pdf [accessed 23.01.2020].

Love, N. (2004). Cognition and the Language Myth. *Language Sciences*, 26(6): 525–544.

Love, N. (2017). On Languaging and Languages. *Language Sciences*, 61: 113–147.

Millikan, R. G. (1998). Language Conventions Made Simple. *The Journal of Philosophy*, XCV(4): 161–180.

Mondada, L. (2016). *Conventions for Multimodal Transcription* (v. 3.0. 6). https://franzoesistik.philhist.unibas.ch/fileadmin/user_upload/franzoesistik/mondada_multimodal_conventions.pdf [accessed 31.01.2022].

Newgarden, K., Zheng, D., and Liu, M. (2015). An Eco-dialogical Study of Second Language Learners' World of Warcraft (WoW) gameplay. *Language Sciences*, 48: 22–41.

Newgarden, K., and Zheng, D. (2016). Recurrent Languaging Activities in World of Warcraft: Skilled Linguistic Action meets the Common European Framework of Reference. *ReCALL*, 28: 274–304.

Norris, S. (2004). *Analyzing Multimodal Interaction. a Methodological Framework*. London: Routledge.

Norris, S. (2011). *Identity in (Inter)action. Introducing Multimodal (Inter)action Analysis*. Berlin: De Gruyter.

Norris, S. (2013). Multimodal (inter) Action Analysis: An Integrative Methodology. In Müller, C., Cienki, A., Ladewig, S., McNeill, D., and Teßendorf, S. (eds.). *Body–Language–Communication: An International Handbook on Multimodality in Human Interaction*, vol. 1 (pp. 275–286). Berlin: de Gruyter Mouton.

Norris, S., and Pirini, J. (2017). Communicating Knowledge, Getting Attention, and Negotiating Disagreement via Videoconferencing Technology: A Multimodal Analysis. *Journal of Organizational Knowledge Communication*, 3(1): 23–48.

O'Halloran, K. L. (2007). Systemic Functional Multimodal Discourse Analysis (SF-MDA) Approach to Mathematics, Grammar And Literacy. In McCabe, A. (ed.). *Advances in Language and Education* (pp. 75–100). London: Continuum.

O'Halloran, K. L., and Lim, F. V. (2014). Systemic Functional Multimodal Discourse Analysis. In Norris, S., and Maier, C. (eds.). *Texts, Images and Interactions: A Reader in Multimodality* (pp. 135–154). Berlin: De Gruyter.

Özyürek, A. (2014). Hearing and Seeing Meaning in Speech and Gesture: Insights from Brain and Behaviour. *Philosophical Transactions of the Royal Society B: Biological Sciences*, 369 (1651). https://royalsocietypublishing.org/doi/pdf/10.1098/rstb.2013.0296 [accessed 23.01.2022].

Pedersen, S. B. (2012). Interactivity in Health Care: Bodies, Values and Dynamics. *Language Sciences*, 34 (5): 532–542

Pennycook, A. (2016). Language Policy and Local Practices. In García, O., Flores. N., and Spotti, M. (eds). *The Oxford Handbook of Language and Society* (pp. 125–140). Oxford: Oxford University Press.

Pickering, M. J., and Garrod, S. (2004). Toward a Mechanistic Psychology of Dialogue. *Behavioral and Brain Sciences*, 27(2): 169–190.

Rączaszek-Leonardi, J. Nomikou, I. Rohlfing, K., and Deacon, T. (2018). Language Development from an Ecological Perspective: Ecologically Valid Ways to Abstract Symbols. *Ecological Psychology*, 30: 39–73.

Richardson, D., Dale, R., and Shockley, K. (2008). Synchrony and Swing in Conversation: Coordination, Temporal Dynamics, and Communication. In Wachsmuth, I., Lenzen, M., Knoblich, G. (eds). *Embodied Communication* (pp: 75–93). Oxford University Press, Oxford.

Roepstorff, A. (2008). Things to Think With: Words and Objects as Material Symbols. *Philosophical Transactions of the Royal Society B: Biological Sciences*, 363(1499): 2049–2054.

Royce, T. (2006). Intersemiotic Complementarity: A Framework for Multimodal Discourse Analysis. In Royce, T., and Bowcher, W. L. (eds). *New Directions in the Analysis of Multimodal Discourse* (pp: 63–109). Mahwah, NJ: Lawrence Erlbaum.

Sarangi, S. (2016). Activity Types, Discourse Types and Role Types: Interactional Hybridity in Professional-Client Encounters. In Miller, D. R., and Bayley, P. (eds.). *Hybridity in Systemic Functional Linguistics. Grammar, Text and Discursive Content* (pp. 154–177). Equinox Publishing,

Seale, C. (2012). *Researching Society and Culture*. London: Sage.

Shockley, K., Santana, M. V., and Fowler, C. A. (2003). Mutual Interpersonal Postural Constraints are Involved in Cooperative Conversation. *Journal of Experimental Psychology: Human Perception and Performance*, 29: 326–32.

Shockley, K., Baker, A. A., Richardson, M. J., and Fowler, C. A. (2007). Articulatory Constraints on Interpersonal Postural Coordination. *Journal of Experimental Psychology: Human Perception and Performance*, 33: 201–8

Sidorkin, A. M. (1999). *Beyond Discourse: Education, the Self, and Dialogue*. New York: State University of New York.

Skipper, J. I. (2014). Echoes of the Spoken Past: How Auditory Cortex Hears Context During Speech Perception. *Philosophical Transactions of the Royal Society B: Biological Sciences*, 369 (1651), https://royalsocietypublishing.org/doi/pdf/10.1098/rstb.2013.0297 [accessed 23.01.2022].

Steffensen, S. V. (2009). Language, Languaging, and the Extended Mind Hypothesis. *Pragmatics & Cognition*, 17: 677–697.

Steffensen, S. V. (2012). Care and Conversing in Dialogical Systems. *Language Sciences*, 34(5): 513–531.

Steffensen, S. V. (2013). Human Interactivity: Problem-Solving, Solution-Probing, and Verbal Patterns in the Wild. In Cowley, S. J., and Vallée-Tourangeau, F. (eds.). *Cognition Beyond the Brain: Computation, Interactivity and Human Artifice* (pp. 195–221). Dordrecht: Springer,

Steffensen, S. V. (2015). Distributed Language and Dialogism: Notes on Non-Locality, Sense-Making and Interactivity. *Language Sciences*, 50: 105–119.

Steffensen, S. V., and Trasmundi, S. B. (2018). Cognitive Event Analysis: A Method for Studying Cognitive Processes in Embodied, Multimodal Interaction. Paper presented at 4th Copenhagen Multimodality Day, Copenhagen, Denmark.

Streeck, J., Goodwin, C., and LeBaron, C. (2011). *Embodied Interaction: Language and Body in the Material World.* Cambridge: Cambridge University Press.

Thibault, P. J. (2011). First-Order Languaging Dynamics and Second-Order Language: The Distributed Language View. *Ecological Psychology*, 23(3): 210–245.

Thibault, P. J. (2017). The Reflexivity of Human Languaging and Nigel Love's Two Orders of Language. *Language Sciences*, 61: 74–85.

Tylén, K., Fusaroli, R., Bundgaard, P. F., and Østergaard, S. (2013). Making Sense Together: A Dynamical Account of Linguistic Meaning-Making. *Semiotica*, 194: 39–62.

van Lier, L. (2004). *The Ecology and Semiotics of Language Learning: A Sociocultural Perspective.* Norwell, MA: Kluwer Academic Publishers.

Vygotsky, L. S. (1978). *Mind and Society.* Cambridge, MA: Harvard University Press.

Vygotsky, L. S. (1986). *Thought and Language* (rev. edn.). Cambridge, MA: Massachusetts Institute of Technology.

Zittoun, T., Gillespie, A., Cornish, F., and Psaltis, C. (2007). The Metaphor of the Triangle in Theories of Human Development. *Human Development*, 50(4): 208–229.

ABOUT THE AUTHOR

Grzegorz Grzegorczyk has a PhD in linguistics and currently occupies a position of an Assistant Professor at the Department of Applied Linguistics at the University of Gdańsk, Poland. His scientific interests focus on interactivity, dialogicality and languaging as emerging in educational, therapeutic and coaching conversations. His current research is in two domains, dialogically constructed learning spaces in academic tutoring and agency and linguistic interactivity in coaching. He chooses video ethnographic methods to collect data for multimodal analysis where he observes how interbodily dynamics and languaging contribute to speakers co-ordinate in their communicative and sense-making activities. Inspired by Love's concept of two orders of language, Steffensen's understanding of interactivity and Cowley's distributed approach to language he concentrates on pico-scale events in interpersonal synergies which constitute talk.

3

Integrating duoethnography with ethnolinguistics in an endeavour to reconstruct the profiles of education in the discourse of third-year students of applied linguistics: A case study

Magdalena Grabowska

ABSTRACT

In the current paper, I try to elucidate the notion of education and how it is conceived by those whom it most concerns, i.e. students. I look at duoethnographic conversations as sites in which the participants share with a partner their views, opinions and experiences of education. While revealing conceptions and beliefs, they ponder what this notion means to them personally. Interacting with partners of difference they may confront their own views with those held by that partner. These varying definitional nuances will be depicted in the form of semantic profiles which are subjective variants of how we conceptualise a given notion. It is worth noting that the adopted methodology originates from social sciences, in particular health and educational research. Here, however, it will be coupled with linguistics to yield a more interdisciplinary result.

Keywords: education, duoethnographic study, education beliefs, semantic study

3.1. INTRODUCTION

Duoethnography, as an interpretative, dialogic method of data collection whose purpose consists of enabling insights into people's understanding of notions, but also evoking transformative reflections, will serve here as a tool to help collect and demonstrate how students of Applied Linguistics and their interlocutors view the issue of education. Through reconstructing the commonsensical, discourse-based understanding of concepts, we not only study the language-entrenched interpretation of reality, but also, and more importantly for the current endeavour, we discover the epistemological (interpretive) nature of language which is not limited to what is "fossilised" or closed as a "structure" but which paves the way for a more dynamic and open understanding of it (Bartmiński, 2009: 24).

By integrating the duoethnographic method with ethnolinguistics, we will consider the concepts of profile and profiling which are assigned to the idea of linguistic worldview. To put it simply, profiling may be depicted as a linguo-conceptual operation in which an object of attention is shaped according to a set of aspects pertaining to its nature. What is more, this process depends upon knowledge of the world, the system of values and point of view of the speaking subject (Bartmiński, 2009). For instance, a chair can be profiled according to such criteria as, for instance, a piece of furniture or a work of art, whereas an apple will be characterised as a fruit or a symbol of life. Each time the object of interest will require a different set of definitional criteria.

For the present study we try to find places which enable cooperation and mutual penetration of the two approaches. The meeting points which first come to the fore seem to be a turn towards the experiential and commonsensical, definitional basis but also the integration of theory and life. Both these approaches embrace the role of personal experiences and beliefs, the speaking subject and how he or she perceives a given notion.

3.2. DUOETHNOGRAPHY AS A DIALOGIC AND NARRATIVE RESEARCH METHOD

Duoethnography was developed in 2003 as a qualitative research genre (Norris, Sawyer & Lund, 2012). It is a considerably new qualitative research method which draws its original inspirations from ethnography, curriculum study (Pinar, 2004) and narrative studies. Pinar's concept of *currere*, "understanding self", according to Sawyer and Norris (2016) is a critical form of autobiography and curriculum studies whose main thrust is everyday life. *Currere* offers the means of re-examining the formation and socialisations of one's beliefs and actions through a historical lens

(Sawyer & Norris, 2016). Duoethnography's contribution to curriculum studies is the contingent and relational nature of meaning and knowledge formation, since by "regarding one's life as a curriculum, one can reconceptualize oneself" (Sawyer & Norris, 2016: 7). It draws from the heritage of Levinas's (1984) concept of the Other and the dialogism of Bakhtin (1981). "It invites the other to assist in the reconceptualization of perceptions of self and society, making all duoethnographies pedagogic" (Sawyer & Norris, 2016: 7).

The distinctive characteristic of duoethnography is a collaborative approach in which two or more researchers representing opposing views focus on their biographies to provide multiple understandings of the world (Norris, 2008; Norris & Sawyer, 2004; Sawyer & Norris, 2009). Duoethnographic researchers nurture a belief that the meanings people give to their lived experiences are not fixed once and for all but transform through the research act. In addition, researchers are perceived as active meaning makers in the process of narrative exposure and reconceptualisation of beliefs held (Pinar, 1975). Duoethnography has the following aims:

- to learn about oneself from the Other.
- to explore and articulate personal and collective narratives of resistance in relation to dominant discourses and metanarratives.
- to use one's self as a site for inquiry into sociocultural socialisation and inscription.
- to articulate emergent thinking and changes in perception to their readers in the form of dialogic storytelling (Reason & Hawkins, 1988, after Norris, Sawyer & Lund, 2012: 10).

Its intent is to evoke transformative reflections, both in the researchers who are active participants in the dialogue and the readers. "The result is not a new set of essences or theories that claim universal understanding; rather, the intent is for emergent meanings and meaning making to become dialogic within the text and between the text and the reader, problematizing reader (and inquirer) alignment with implicit metanarratives" (Norris, Sawyer & Lund, 2012: 10).

Duoethnographic conversation is, therefore, not an interview with open-ended and focused questions. On the contrary, it takes the shape of a natural, informal, polyvocal and provocative exchange of views between equals, which serves as a threshold to past experiences with which the Other can connect.

> A dialogic context in duoethnography is a conversation – not only between people but also between people and their perceptions of cultural artifacts (such as photos) – that generates new meanings
>
> (Sawyer & Norris, 2013: 2).

In duoethnographic conversations people tell stories to evoke other familiar ones. Some are easily forgotten and emerge as a detail when triggered by the story of the Other. Unlike autoethnography, in duoethnographic methodology the researcher does not rely on memory, but by listening to relevant stories retold by the Other manages to elicit their own ones. It seems crucial to add that the essence of duoethnography resides in its communal character (Norris, Sawyer & Lund, 2012). In the words of Reason & Hawkins (1988), storytelling changes how researchers ask questions, explore sense making and how they tell what they know. It also changes how experience is gathered.

It should be underlined that duoethnography is premised on postmodern notions of identity, which are in turn viewed as "culturally layered, contradictory, socioculturally based, and not stage bound" (Norris, Sawyer & Lund, 2012: 41). It is also perceived as constantly changing with some of its parts resonating within larger national or international metanarratives.

Norris, Sawyer, and Lund (2012) provide the main tenets of duoethnographic research strategy which include:

- focus on one's life as a curriculum.
- polyvocality and dialogue.
- disruption of the metanarrative found in solitary practice.
- differences not seeking resolution.
- questioning meanings held about the past, inviting reconceptualisation.
- not seeking universal truths but relying on subjectivity and intersubjectivity to provide a polyocular perspective on a phenomenon.
- theoretical and practical application in many spheres of life, not only in science.
- trust between participants (Norris, Sawyer & Lund, 2012: 12–23).

3.3. ETHNOLINGUISTICS

Duoethnographic, reflective exchange is conducive not only to rethinking one's views and perceptions, but also to gaining new insights and discovering new meanings. Thus, it is justifiable to relate this method to cultural linguistics, where meanings are studied in the context of the experiences lived by people sharing a common cultural and social background. Although ethnolinguistics (*ethno-* relating to the study of different societies and cultures, *Cambridge Dictionary of English*) grew and garnered attention in America together with an interest in micro-languages and micro-cultures, its origins are in European, primarily German, scholarship. In the final decades of the twentieth century, the Sapir–Whorf hypothesis received renewed attention, which gave rise to research into language as a cultural phenomenon (Bartmiński, 2009).

This conception relates language to a subject, a community of speakers but also culture. Thus, due to its interest with the last, it functions under various names. Apart from *ethnolinguistics,* there is *cultural linguistics, anthropological linguistics, linguo-culturology, anthropological-cultural linguistics* or *linguistic anthropology* (Bartmiński, 2009: 7).

Thanks to the Moscow school of Nikita I. Tolstoy, ethnolinguistics also won recognition in Slavic linguistics. There, it was defined as a branch of linguistics studying the links between language and culture, but also, more broadly, as a complex discipline focused not only on culture but also folk psychology and mythology, thus becoming an interdisciplinary field of research (Bartmiński, 2009).

The key notions which constitute the ethnolinguistic apparatus are:

- linguistic worldview.
- values and stereotypes which form the worldview.
- cognitive, commonsensical definition as a method of describing stereotypes.
- viewpoint and perspective.
- profiling.
- conceptualising and profiling subject (Bartmiński, 2009: 19).

3.4. DEFINING CONCEPTS BASED ON COMMONSENSICAL CRITERIA

When people share views in informal conversations, they make commonsensical, often stereotypical judgements. They reflect on an idealised picture of the world, one which is not free from subjective opinions and views. They reveal a more colloquial manner of defining concepts not based on academic, rigorous reasoning but rather on how these notions are perceived by the subject (Zinken, 2009). The mode of defining concepts in which answers are elicited based on commonsensical data has been termed "cognitive", a term which Bartmiński (2007) defines in the following way:

> Definicja kognitywna za cel główny przyjmuje zdanie sprawy ze sposobu pojmowania przedmiotu przez mówiących danym językiem, tj. ze sposobu utrwalonej społecznie i dającej się poznać poprzez język i użycie języka wiedzy o świecie, kategoryzacji jego zjawisk, ich charakterystyki i wartościowania. [The aim of cognitive definition is to present the way speakers of a language perceive an object, i.e. the way it is categorised, characterised and evaluated in the language they speak.]

> (Bartmiński, 2007: 42)

As Zinken indicates, "it is the job of the ethnolinguist to reconstruct the linguistically entrenched interpretation of the world by a subject in terms that are meaningful for that subject" (Zinken, 2009: 2). He further specifies that the explication of meaning should be based on the speakers' sociocultural situatedness, since the cognitive definition should reflect the point of view and perspective of the envisaged person. This approach to semantics assumes an examination of the main aspects of meaning, which later lead to the emergence of a subject-bound conceptual profile, and which is often contrasted with a taxonomic approach to word meaning.

Furthermore, cognitive definition assumes that language interprets and classifies culture. It is a conglomerate composed of elements of the worldview as well as a culturally based cognitive system. Thus, a cognitive definition should consolidate numerous sources of knowledge (Smyk, 2008). What is more, in this approach the borderline between semantics and pragmatics is obliterated.

3.5. PROFILING AND THE SUBJECT-ORIENTED INTERPRETATION OF THE WORLD

The concept of profiling foregrounds ideas encapsulated in the concept of cognitive definition, namely that the meaning of a word is a resultant of semantic content plus construal (image) (Langacker, 2008).

The sources propose two basic ways in which the notion of profiling can be viewed in semantics. One application has its roots in American cognitivism (Langacker, 1991, 2000), whereas the other can be traced to the writings of Anna Wierzbicka (1985), among others. In the former, profiling equals a cognitive domain, or a frame (Langacker, 2000). In the latter, it relates to a more anthropological stance which considers the speaking subject who is composed of rationality, knowledge about the world, system of values, subject-oriented viewpoint plus the worldview motivated by this viewpoint (Bartmiński, 2009). In this conception, meaning is linked through "a network of relationships to a certain background: the situation, a wider conceptual structure, or the 'subject's circumstances'" (Bartmiński, 2009: 88).

Grzegorczykowa (1998) notes that profiling, for Bartmiński, operates on available conceptual data, while for Langacker it is already active on the preconceptual level and, by highlighting certain elements, leads to the formation of a concept.

The experiential basis against which profiling operates is formed based on culture-based criteria such as beliefs, values, emotions, and the like (Bartmiński, 1993). In turn, the preconceptual frame is linked to the working of visually perceived and later conceptually processed cognitive data (Langacker, 1995).

In its most intuitive dimension, the noun "profile" evokes associations which the *Cambridge Dictionary* online defines as: "1. short description of someone's life, work, interests, etc. on a social networking website; 2. a side view of a person's face". In turn, in *Słownik Języka Polskiego* (online version) a profile is understood as a "contour (outline), sketch, shape of something", which seems to accurately depict the idea.

Bartmiński depicts profiling as:

> (...) a subjective (i.e. performed by the speaking subject) linguo-conceptual operation, which consists in shaping the picture of the object in terms of certain aspects (subcategories, facets) of that object: e.g. its origin, features, appearance, functions, experiences, events connected with them, etc., within a certain type of knowledge and in accordance with the requirements of a given viewpoint
>
> (Bartmiński, 2009: 89)

Profile and profiling form part of a set of notions, which include viewpoint, aspect, experiential frame and scene. On a more general level, all these notions are assigned to that of the linguistic worldview, in which the human being acts as an interpreter and "organizer of the scene" (Tokarski, 1991: 137). An aspect or facet is understood as a bundle of judgements which form the explication. What Bartmiński calls a facet, Langacker (2000: 4–7) and his followers name a domain.

One question which agitates scholars is whether facets emerge from the empirical data under scrutiny or are superimposed upon the material, enabling easy comparison between dictionary entries (Bartmiński & Niebrzegowska, 1998). According to Anna Wierzbicka, lexical groups can be assigned certain universal schemata. In other words, for the scholar taxonomic, functional, patronymic and collective concepts can be ascribed independent of definitional structures. For instance, the definition of a cup should include information about the material, purpose, appearance, size and use (Bartmiński & Niebrzegowska, 1998). However, the claim that certain universal definitional schemata exist is difficult to maintain because, as Bartmiński (1994) remarks, research on national stereotypes regarding Germans and Russians showed that the former were interpreted by Poles in national terms, the latter more ideologically.

Apart from facets, Bartmiński draws our attention to two other elements that participate in the process of profiling, namely categorisation and object characteristics which correspond with the facet (2007). Hence, profiling assumes object categorisation, selection of facets and object description with respect to these facets. This is a process which results in the emergence of a profile.

Bartmiński (1993, cited in Bartmiński, 2009: 92) underlines that profiles function within meanings and differentiate the image of a prototype by shaping its base content. Essentially, the value of a profile depends on the choice of categorising factor. For instance, "cornflower" can be categorised as a plant, flower, herb or weed, each time receiving a different set of facets and different content within the set.

3.6. PROFILING THE NOTION OF EDUCATION: A DUOETHNOGRAPHIC PERSPECTIVE

> Curriculum, from the learner's standpoint, ordinarily represents little more than an arrangement of subjects, a structure of socially prescribed knowledge, or a complex system of meanings which may or may not fall within his grasp. Rarely does it signify possibility for him as an existing person, mainly concerned with making sense of his own life-world. Rarely does it promise occasions for ordering the materials of that world, for imposing "configurations" by means of experiences and perspectives made available for personally conducted cognitive action
>
> (Sawyer and Norris, 2016: 1)

Sawyer and Norris (2016) draw attention to the standpoint of a learner, his or her sense of purpose and the significance of the educational programme (curriculum) which they are expected to fulfil at an institution. The authors put forward certain problematic aspects which may evoke disappointment or at least lack of motivation, i.e. arrangement of subjects, prescribed knowledge, system of meanings which learners may or may not grasp. On the other hand, they note deficiencies from the institution of school itself in assisting learners' personal development, stimulating sense making practices or supporting an experience-based approach.

That said, let us now consider how their own education is viewed by the research participants whose duoethnographic interviews are the focus of attention in the present study, and whether this picture has evolved during their dialogic practice with peers.

Shared knowledge and experiences lead us to believe that people applying for university are driven by the necessity to obtain a degree, which is intended to pave the way to the world of professionalism and expertise. In turn, it is difficult to escape the feeling that there is also a deeper motivational factor behind the decision to apply for university – the sheer drive for self-development. Still, education, as we know it, recalls associations closer to a systemic endeavour which may or may not be inner driven. Nevertheless, irrespective of whether people feel motivated by the perspective of obtaining a degree or by the fact that learning makes them happy and fulfilled, they, one way or the other, become part of a greater system which sooner or later oozes into their lives, shaping their worldviews and discourses.

Duoethnography as a research method is predicated on several assumptions, among others, on a dialogic, collaborative sense making of experience. Its intent is to provoke transformative reflections in its immediate participants and in those whom it reaches, i.e. the readers. The essence of duoethnography resides in its communal character (Norris, Sawyer & Lund 2012), thus, by listening to a relevant story retold by the Other, we feel encouraged to elicit our own.

The current endeavour to discover how education is viewed by those whom it concerns, i.e. students of linguistics, draws from two conceptions, namely the qualitative, social science method and the linguistic one premised on the assumption that language is a culture-driven phenomenon which encourages its users to interpret the world in a specific way. Essentially, the analytical assumptions should also embrace the institution as a crucial factor in shaping the general educational experience and learners' discourse. The notion of discourse, Brünner and Graefen (1993, cited in Wodak, 1997: 5) define as a totality of interactions in a domain, depicted as units and forms of speech which penetrate everyday linguistic behaviour but also appear in an institutional context, such as the school. Furthermore, discourse reveals a behavioural aspect and is a form of social practice. This account implies that there is a "relationship between a particular discursive event and the situation, institution and social structure that frame it: the discursive event is shaped by them, but it also shapes them" (Wodak, 1996: 17).

3.7. RESEARCH OBJECTIVES

In studying a linguistic worldview, we take into consideration two aspects, namely that language reveals a certain interpretation of the world and that this in turn enables its users to form judgements about the reality around them. This interpretation, though shared, is nuanced and varied, reflecting subjective and experience-based ways of understanding a notion. It illustrates the idea that the judgements people make about a notion are formed based on different categorising factors and thus give rise to varying profiles of the object in question.

Duoethnography as a critical research method may enhance the recognition of hidden aims or even yearnings. According to Norris and Sawyer (2013), a duoethnographic dialogue serves as a mediating device which aids reflection upon the frames which people use to situate meaning. This dialogue is polyvocal and through transaction leads to the emergence of a text (Norris & Sawyer, 2013).

Hence, the present paper aims to take a closer look at how Polish students perceive their own educational experiences and what meanings they attach to these. In addition, the study may offer insights into the role of the shared social and cultural background in shaping the worldview on education in Poland. It may demonstrate to what extent the participants are eager to reflect upon their experiences and past beliefs through dialogic and collaborative experience and what results this effort can bring.

3.8. PARTICIPANTS AND THEIR ROLES IN THE RESEARCH

The participants (n=7) were Polish-speaking, female undergraduate seminar students of Applied Linguistics at the University of Gdańsk whom I decided to introduce to duoethnographic methodology. Following Sawyer, Dekker and Rasmor (2016), I intended to evoke a situation in which theoretical framework will mix with lived experiences, as the curriculum theory sees no special boundary between theory and life (Sawyer, Dekker & Rasmor, 2016). Although my class was rather theoretical, primarily focused on mentoring undergraduates in the process of completing their theses, the introduction of duoethnographic methodology was a transformative moment. Its biographical character called for sincerity and openness, as students felt encouraged to reflect upon their own beliefs and experiences in an institutional context. This was an unusual, intimate situation, one which seldom occurs in the classroom. What is more, studying in an institution does not present opportunities for reflecting about the purpose and significance of what one is expected to complete. Quite the reverse, the entire focus is on what is supposed to be done and not what is considered important for development and well-being. In other words, students seem to have little influence on what they learn or master, or how this is achieved. Their attention is chiefly centred on acquiring the prescribed knowledge and skills and, more importantly, on demonstrating the effects and progress once a semester ends.

I decided to introduce the idea of duoethnographic methodology to the students beforehand. Only then did I present the idea of the project and its outline, as well as explaining the details. I also sought approval of the conditions of the research. Afterwards, I asked the participants to find an interlocutor for whom education is equally important, with the proviso that he or she should be known to represent a different opinion than the research participant initiating the conversation. Eventually, there were 12 participants and not 14 as may be expected, because two seminar students decided to interview each other. The task was to share views and opinions about education stimulated by, but not limited to open-ended questions such as: "What does education mean to you?", "How important is it for you?", etc. There was one, crucial condition: the dialogues should take the form of sincere, one-on-one and face-to-face conversations rather than the typical interview format with set questions and predetermined structure.

3.9. DATA COLLECTION METHODS

The data was collected through dialogic and audio recorded conversations. The participants could choose the language of conversation, i.e. Polish or English, and the majority opted for the former, with just one person doing it in English. Transcription of the recorded text followed. Then, both the recording and the rendered transcription was submitted to the supervisor and the author of the relevant text. Eventually, all the research participants and their mentor met and had an audio recorded group talk about their findings and research experiences. The students were also asked to read the completed text to verify the validity of the findings and conclusions drawn.

3.10. STAGES OF THE RESEARCH

Students received the following instruction:

Before the conversation

1. Find a person with whom you would like to have a conversation about education. The person you look for should represent an opinion, point of view or understanding of what education is which is different from yours.
2. Ask the person for permission to carry out a short, audio recorded conversation.
3. During the talk, focus on the meaning of education in life. Share your opinions about education too. Remember to record it.

After the conversation

4. Transcribe the recorded material.
5. Analyse what you said about education and write down your reflections.
6. Analyse what the other person said and write down your reflections.
7. Submit the recording, transcription and your reflections to the supervisor.
8. Share your reflections with other members of the seminar group.[1]

---

1   See Werbińska, D. (2018). Wykorzystanie duoetnografii jako innowacyjnego podejścia w rozwijaniu refleksji przyszłych nauczycieli języka obcego. *Neofilolog,* 51(1): 59–73.

3.11. DATA ANALYSIS

The research material was collected with the intention of studying if and how duoethnographic methodology played a role, namely whether its application was effective and helped to create the appropriate dialogic atmosphere to evoke reflective and transformative results. During conversations, participants were engaged in discussing the meaning of education. Unlike the structured form of an interview, this method paved the way for a more open and sincere exchange between people who know each other well. For this reason, the material which emerges is all the more valuable.

Inspired by Werbińska's (2018) dueothnographic project, also completed among students of foreign languages, I followed a similar route. Having received the transcripts, I quickly read through them. After some time, I approached the material for the second and third time in order to analyse it more closely, paying attention to the thematic content of these conversations. In the meantime, I listened to the recordings received from the research participants with the aim of noting any extra, non-verbal cues. I succeeded in selecting the dominant tendencies in which education was depicted in the conversations. I also noted moments of hesitation, deeper reflection or even a modification in how the concept was viewed. I also examined the post-research, student reflections and the recorded conversation which occurred in the university classroom, with seminar students (i.e. the conversation initiators) at the end of the data collection process. This proved a valuable moment because we (including myself) shared our experiences related to education. I, for instance, am a mother of two children and in that situation, felt encouraged to talk about education from the point of view of a parent. Interestingly, many participants referred to moments in the past when their notion of education was gradually formed. Many of us mentioned negative school experiences or alluded to the role of teachers. Some were even eager to talk about the then current situation at university or even to express criticism towards the system and the process of education there. Some admitted to having reformulated the way they perceived school or education after the duoethnographic experience.

In the following phase, I looked at specific tendencies in conceptualising education in the discourse analysed. To do so, I employed the conception of profiling derived from ethnolinguistic methodology. Based on available material, I extracted the dominant tendencies in viewing the concept and plotted them against the facets (domains). To mark these relations, I used the following system of notations:

"+"   when meaning components are in a positive relation
"++"   when meaning components are in a strong positive relation
"+/–"   when meaning components are neutral to each other
"–"   when the relation between the meaning components does not apply (system based on Pietrucha, 2003, cited in Grabowska, 2014: 1).

3.12. DATA INTERPRETATION

3.12.1. Education in dictionary definitions

A quick glance at available dictionary definitions of education may be juxtaposed with the original meaning of the word. In the *Online Etymology Dictionary* we read that the English *educaten* was used for the first time in the mid-15th century to mean "bring up (children), to train", derived from the Latin *educates* meaning "bring up, rear, educate". In contemporary usage the word refers to "the process of teaching or learning, especially in a school or college, or the knowledge that you get from it" (*Cambridge Dictionary* online). *Merriam Webster* online adds that the word may also be used with reference to "the knowledge and development resulting from the process of being educated; the field of study that deals mainly with methods of teaching and learning in schools". Słownik Języka Polskiego PWN (online edition) relates this notion to the idea of raising and bringing up. Słownik Współczesnego Języka Polskiego (Dunaj, 1996) presents education in terms of a process of gaining knowledge and skills, as part of a curriculum, but also as learning or bringing up.

It follows from the above that words such as *teaching*, *learning*, *school*, *knowledge*, *development*, *studying* and *upbringing* form the set of essential, definitional components of education. This will be later compared with the emergent profiles which, as Bartmiński (2007) posits, do not change the denotation of an object but rather introduce new ways of organising the semantic content within the available definitions.

3.12.2. Education in semantic profiles

The conversations bring to light various aspects of how education can be understood and differ in terms of emotional involvement from the participants, which may have some impact on the results. Nevertheless, they all share one component, namely that each openly evaluates education and attaches importance to it. We may conclude that three different ways emerge in which the vitality of education is presented. The following are selected and essentially paraphrased opinions expressed by participants which illustrate the emerging trends in how research participants conceptualise education. These have been termed *development*, *relations* and *basis*.

> **Profile 1. Development**
> Education offers opportunities for self-development.
> It is a process which is measured by progress.
> We should develop ourselves all the time.
> Thanks to education, we know more and feel happier.
> Education should offer some practical skills.
> It enables access to a better social position.

Profile 2. Relations

At school there are opportunities to meet new people and make friends. Teachers are a very important part of this process because they may encourage or discourage students.

Profile 3. Basis

School subjects offer a basic knowledge which everyone can gain. Education is a basis which enables further growth and development.

The profiles correspond with facets whose choice depends upon the dictionary-based denotations of the word *education*. The list of essential definitional components contains the following, *teaching, learning, school, knowledge, skills and studying*. However, based on students' material, it transpires that the range of facets should be extended to include *life, interests, usefulness and practicality, choice, opportunities, profession* and *social status*.

In the table the emergent profiles have been plotted against the facets in order to chart the correspondence of meaning with profile.

	Semantic Profiles		
Facet	DEVELOPMENT	RELATIONS	BASIS
Teaching	+	++	−/+
Learning	+	+	+
School	−/+	++	++
Knowledge and skills	++	+	+
Studying	++	+	−/+
Life	++	++	++
Interests	++	+	+
Usefulness and Practicality	+	−/+	++
Choice	+	−/+	+
Opportunities	++	+	−/+
Profession	+	−	++
Social status	+	++	−

The system of notations is explained in section 3.11.

The emergent profiles present education as a complex and multifaceted notion, the range and dimension of which exceed dictionary definitions. It transpires that education is perceived not only through the prism of teaching and learning but also as development and relations. Nevertheless, school and teachers occupy a prominent position in this picture.

The "development" profile is linked to almost all the facets in a positive or very positive relation. In just one case, school, is the relationship neutral.

Research participants very often present education in terms of developing and discovering interests and opportunities. Furthermore, it is strongly associated with acquiring knowledge and skills, hence it is naturally linked with educational institutions. Education as development becomes an important part of life, a mission, and a permanent component.

This tendency in depicting education comes to the fore in the following fragment:

> Na ten moment edukacja dla mnie jest czymś potrzebnym na pewno i może nie do końca w takiej sferze, że trzeba dużo wiedzieć, że trzeba mieć dużo informacji, ale bardziej tak żeby rozwijać swój umysł. Ja bym bardziej powiedziała, że jest po prostu rozwój umysłu [...] i uważam, że edukacja trwa całe życie. [Right now, education is an important thing for me but not in the sense that you must know a lot but more importantly as something which stimulates us. For me education is associated with cognitive stimulation and I believe it is a lifelong project].

What is more, education is linked with the opportunities of attaining a professional career in the future. Thanks to education, we know more and can eventually climb the social ladder. One participant expressed the following thought:

> Edukacja jest dla mnie czymś, co może mnie doprowadzić do przyszłego stanowiska. Umożliwia kształcenie się, a przy okazji mam możliwość poznawania nowych rzeczy. [Education is a thing which can lead me to a future position. Along the way, it allows me to learn and get to know new things].

Development is positively associated with teaching and learning, which means that participants relate education with a process of instruction and acquisition. However, they do not ascribe a positive evaluation to education as understood in such terms. Quite the opposite, participants often indicate that they separate what they consider to be true learning from what they perceive as systemic and imposed. One participant claimed the following:

> Jakby oddzielić edukację of faktycznej nauki to dla mnie edukacja na ten moment byłabym tematem takim trochę yyy nie wiem, jak to powiedzieć ładnie. Chodzi mi o to, że takie to jest ważne w cudzysłowie, ale koniec końców jest to prowadzone w taki bardzo sztywny sposób, czyli ta edukacja byłaby czymś bardzo sztywnym, bo właśnie taka typowa

edukacja to tak samo jak system edukacyjny, jest to coś sformułowanego przez kogoś innego i nam narzuconego z góry. [If we separated education from the actual learning, I would say that the former is something stiff, formulated by other people and imposed on us].

Moreover, they acknowledge the presence of teachers in this process. For instance, in one conversation the words "teacher" or "teachers" occur in as many as 31 results. The participants eagerly elaborated on their school-time experiences, and the positive and negative role of teachers in this context. They theorised on the reasons why certain teachers do not really care about making students understand, while others do. One participant noted that there are teachers who simply do not care to explain because they probably do not like their profession. Another, however, commented that they act like this because they feel they are not suitably remunerated.

Many participants underlined the necessity to introduce a more practical approach in Polish schools because the one they know is too theoretical. In the words of one participant:

[...] chciałabym, żeby ta edukacja również odnosiła się do sfer życia osobistego oraz umiejętności praktycznego korzystania ze zdobytej wiedzy, a nie jedynie do posiadania dużej ilości informacji. [I would like education to relate to personal life and offer practical skills and not only encourage the possession of information].

Some participants remarked on the necessity to make Polish schools a fair and equal place for all. At the same time, they believed that the lesson of tolerance is not learned at school, but at home, and from parents. For that reason, even if they brought up this problem in conversations, they did not tend to blame the school. They automatically saw that the reason for intolerance lies in the home.

Another issue raised was the question of choice. This appeared in the context of compulsory school subjects but also in relation to future profession. Research participants link education with the possibility to choose what one wants to learn and do in the future. The following exchange illustrates this approach:

G: Yea I think. So you are trying to say that people should choose much earlier what they wanna do?

M: Yes.

On the other hand, the opinion was voiced that people should not be given a choice at the beginning in this respect because, and this aspect brings us closer to the basis profile, everyone should possess a basic, general knowledge acquired at primary school.

Education viewed in terms of relations offers a picture in which this notion is associated with the presence of other people. Relations strongly come to the fore when research participants discuss not only the role of teachers, school and parents but also social status. It is vital to add that relations seen through the prism of people do not always receive a positive evaluation. On the one hand, participants highlight the opportunity to meet people and make friends at school. One remarked:

> [...] postrzegam edukację jako coś, co pozwoliło mi poznać znajomych
> [I perceive education as something that enabled me to make friends].

On the other, they often draw attention to the negative impact of teachers, who are a predominant component in this picture. Some of the participants portray them in neutral or even negative terms. They are viewed as either a source of students' low self-esteem or as busy people who cannot devote their time to building positive relations with students, for example:

> [...] myślę, że teraz jestem bardziej świadoma tego, że jest dużo takich ludzi, którzy nie są na odpowiednim miejscu, wybierając ten zawód [I think I am now more aware of the fact that there are people who shouldn't be teachers].

In another conversation teachers are presented as people who think they can easily earn money in this profession:

> I think, they sometimes want to be teachers because it is an easy way to get money, somehow.

These quotations put the teaching profession in a very negative light and reveal the gravity of the situation. In presenting such opinions, the participants seemed truly concerned and an unspoken reaction could be sensed that could be termed "a sigh of resignation".

Interestingly, relations turned out to be positively linked with knowledge and skills, studying, interests and opportunities, one participant stating that education offers opportunities to hold interesting and inspiring conversations and to defend arguments. The participants also linked this profile with the learning which they received as young children at home. In this context the emphasis is on parents as the people who initiate education, as understood in terms of rules on social interactions.

However, with one exception, the relations profile does not seem to demonstrate many connections with usefulness and practicality. Some participants linked parents with a practical approach, remarking that parents are responsible for the practical preparation of their children for adulthood. What is more, some seemed eager to reinforce awareness of the necessity for sex education, which should also be taught at home rather than at school. There were, however, opposing voices which communicated the necessity to introduce sex education in schools. One participant specifically referred to the problem of psychosexual orientation and tolerance. She believes that school as a public institution should support young people in discovering their sexuality:

> No ale nie wszyscy mają w domu na tyle otwartych rodziców, którzy nie boją się takich ciężkich tematów. Moi rodzice rozmawiali na te tematy ze mną dopiero jak zapytałam. [Not everyone has parents who are ready to deal with such hard topics. My parents did not talk about it as long as I did not ask].

Choice is another underrepresented facet in the spectrum of relations. However, one participant was demonstrably willing to indicate that she had changed her attitude and perception: She had decided to abandon the restrictive schemas imposed at home, including stereotypical categorisation of other people or schematic behavioural patterns such as following the same daily routine. She admitted to having recognised this mechanism and to have changed. Hence, she communicated she had made a choice to alter herself.

The profile termed "basis" represents the idea whereby education is conceptualised as an essential, indispensable component in life but also as a sort of springboard to a future profession. One participant said the following:

> Po tej rozmowie przekonałam się do tego i patrzę w ten sposób na edukację, że to też podstawa będąca punktem wyjścia właśnie do późniejszego rozwoju dla osób, które chcą się edukować, a nie robią tego z przymusu [After this conversation I realised that education is a basis, a starting point for future development for people who want to educate themselves of their own free will].

In addition, education in this fragment is portrayed as an opportunity for development, which demonstrates the interconnectedness of profiles.

In general, when participants conceptualised education as some sort of basis, they often placed it in the period of elementary schooling. One participant captured this idea in the following way:

Każdy powinien zdobyć wiedzę na podstawowym poziomie, ale od gim-
nazjum, od liceum przedmioty powinny być stricte sprecyzowane i roz-
wijane w jedną stronę. [Everyone should acquire basic knowledge, but
from junior high school, from high school the subjects should be more
specified and developed in one direction].

Interestingly, this profile is underrepresented in the conversations in comparison
to the remaining ones, which may be indicative of the underlying, albeit not so explicitly stated, conviction that education is a complex phenomenon whose range
exceeds the limits of school. However, the participants suddenly noticed the relevance of compulsory schooling in the process of education after the research was
completed. In the post-research phase, some mentioned the beneficial role of institutional schooling which provides people with essential knowledge and skills. The
basis profile is predominantly characterised by domains such as school, life, usefulness and practicality, and profession. When put against the background of such facets, it evokes associations with concrete life decisions such as future job or practical
skills. As one participant stated:

Uważam jeszcze, że powinno być więcej szkół przygotowujących do za-
wodów, a to chyba jest w zaniku. Ludzie nie pieką chleba, a chcą być
youtuberami i zarabiać kupę pieniędzy. O to właśnie chodzi. Mamy de-
ficyt ludzi, którzy potrafią coś zrobić. [I also think there should be more
vocational schools, but they are dying out now. People do not bake bre-
ad but they want to become Youtubers and earn a lot of money. That's
the point. We are running short of people who can do something].

References to practicality occurred in a few conversations. In the fragment above
the participant is concerned about the future of education in Poland and expresses
a general criticism towards the contemporary Polish school system by pointing out
several of its shortcomings.

In turn, this profile evades immediate associations with studying, opportunities
and social status. It seems that these are presumably the criteria which typically pertain to education viewed as meticulously constructed lifelong project and not an essential, often compulsory process of acquiring basic knowledge and skills.

The utterances under study allow access to the metaphorical depictions participants employ in order to illustrate their points of view. To start with, education is
often conceptualised as being stiff and inflexible. This depiction brings forward the
idea in which the process of teaching and learning, especially set in the school context, is predominantly limited by external regulations. Evoking such an image in
this context clearly shows a negative evaluation of the phenomenon of education.

However, as previously mentioned, seeing education as stiff met with a certain appreciation because the participants realised that this prevents the school from functioning in a chaotic way.

For others, education in its contemporary form imposes limitations on pupils because it is sold like a ready-made product. The participant who expressed such an opinion sounds critical towards the country's lawmakers. For this person, Polish teachers are no longer intellectuals who perform their duties with passion and pleasure but an underpaid group of experts who have lost motivation.

In other metaphorical accounts, education is compared to a path on which one walks to reach the goal, whereas knowledge alone is a treasure.

3.13. DUOETHNOGRAPHIC REFLECTIONS FROM PARTICIPANTS

The research participants eagerly drew on their experiences, opinions and observations. Moreover, the research material recorded, as well as the post-research conversation in the classroom, testifies to moments of transformation through which students tended to reconsider their own understanding of education in order to endow it with new meanings.

One participant, for instance, reflected upon the conversation and realised that she had previously had a slightly different understanding of her own attitude towards the education system. She admitted that having exchanged views and experiences with the partner, she had come to recognise that although the Polish system is stiff and inflexible, it safeguards standards and protects against chaos. She also added that prior to the conversation she had not conceived of education as a fundament in life. What is more, she also added that she now distinguishes between education as a comprehensive development and as professional training in preparation for future employment.

An insightful remark was formulated by another participant who admitted that education should primarily be associated with a process of constant development, however, in her opinion, this does not guarantee success in future life. This statement highlights a pivotal issue which seems of concern to experts all over the world, namely, how to tailor education to the needs of its participants, while safeguarding the criterion of usefulness and practicality and, at the same time, providing some universals on which to rely in life.

Furthermore, the participants acknowledged modifications in their perspectives on the role of school in the process of education. They understood that, when thinking in the past about education, they had perceived it solely in relation to school, a natural link to make but one which nonetheless renders it a separate component in life. However, with time they began to view education not only as a duty associated with obligatory school, but rather as an all-encompassing and enriching process.

Another participant acknowledged that after the conversation with a partner, she realised something she had not considered before, i.e. that there are teachers who are not the most suitable for the job. An ideal teacher is a person who can create a relationship devoid of the attitude of superiority, a person who can listen and understand students, a guide or enabler who accompanies students in their academic endeavours and facilitates the discovery of their own strengths and weaknesses.

When thinking retrospectively about school-time experiences, some mention the role of relations which help to build a sense of identity. Being a part of a peer group is significant because of the safeguards it offers against social isolation. One participant revealed that she had experienced rejection and bullying on the grounds of her dual national identity. In turn, she linked this fact with the difficulty experienced while learning a variety of school subjects. However, as a student of linguistics, she currently feels much better and enjoys the knowledge and expertise she is acquiring.

Other reflections concern, for instance, the question of talents and strengths which pupils should be able to discover during school time, along with the role of parents in this regard.

During the meeting, one student made an interesting meta remark, by noting the difficulty in transforming one's own conception of education, becoming aware that her own notion of education was well-entrenched and solid, and thus resistant to evolution. Another participant added one extra benefit of education in her own life, namely the growth of brain potential while studying science and mathematics.

Education in all the participants' depictions is a process which begins in the home, where the norms of social coexistence and interaction are discovered. The picture of education emerging from the conversations is polyvocal, reflective and personal. Dueothnographic experiences proved illuminating because they unravelled conceptualisations which would probably otherwise have remained concealed and unspoken. This method enlivened or threw new light on memories from early years but also prompted participants to reconsider the notion in question.

3.14. CONCLUSIONS

A dialogical relationship with the other expands the possibilities for insight (Norris, Sawyer & Lund, 2012: 43). In other words, this experience is much more insightful than a solitary practice. Duoethnographic participants engage in the creation of narratives which do not serve as an organisational structure but rather as a communicative strategy where stories develop spontaneously and are subject to occasional unexpected turns (Norris, Sawyer & Lund, 2012).

Essentially, the duoethnographic method offers additional opportunities for self-development. According to Werbińska (2018), apart from reflexivity, duoethnography may stimulate students cognitively by enabling a more thorough understanding of one's own experiences and decisions or by increasing consciousness about the role of agency in life. Students may become more inquisitive about their own and their partner's convictions and beliefs, and in addition, develop socially and emotionally. By sharing experiences with a partner, they not only form deeper bonds, based on trust, but also learn how to tackle problems and weaknesses in life.

In their dialogues about education, the research participants drew on memories and forgotten details to elucidate on personal meanings and were eager to formulate commonsensical generalisations. At times, the interpretations offered showed signs of transformation and adjustment to the meanings evoked by the partner. Despite initial differences, the participants were eager to seek consensus and commonalities rather than maintaining opposing views.

Indeed, in seeking an answer to the question of how duoethnography as a dialogic method has affected the research participants and their notion of education, we may conclude that the majority have changed or at least modified their views and opinions, returning to past events related to education to reconsider their significance to the past and the present.

The idea of education emerging from the conversations reveals a process in which various components are present. These pertain to the broadly understood area of development, personal relations and the role of institutions which provide basic and essential opportunities. Most participants highlighted the role of other people in this process. They admitted that the main role of education is to enable growth. They eventually conceded that institutions such as school or university are crucial components of education. In other words, the participants cannot imagine education without them. However, they often mentioned the criterion of choice as a desired element in the school system. What is more, the system should enable recognition of individual strengths and weaknesses, hence, the idea of an institutionalised school as a body responsible for the fulfilment of certain goals, i.e. offering the basic and most essential knowledge and skills, teaching how to build rewarding relations and enabling development and choice recognition, is one of the key components of the image of education held by students of linguistics and their partners who took part in this research.

From the research material it emerges that the picture of education presented in the conversations studied exceeds the definitional scope to be found in dictionaries. The senses that the participants evoke seem to depict the notion as somewhat fluid and lacking clear-cut boundaries. Instead, meanings intertwine and interpenetrate. By being open to the dimension of personal experiences, the participants represent education as a nuanced phenomenon. Following the narration, we gain the opportunity to pry into what it means to learn, study or develop. We may see not only what it takes to educate but also what obstacles and difficulties this process entails.

Crucially, education as the topic of the conversations was naturally linked with the academic efforts being undertaken by the participants at the time. They were, and some remain, students of Applied Linguistics at the University of Gdańsk. Thus, the unravelled images have vividness, spontaneity and naturally transpose the reader to the world of academic endeavours. The narrations give access to study rituals, values and beliefs. They link the readers not only with how the research participants perceive education, but also how this notion is commonly conceptualised in Polish society. By looking through their narrations, we learn the biographies of concrete people living in a particular time and space, whose stories, however, are far from uniform. In these accounts we find contrasts such as freedom and oppression, fulfilment and dissatisfaction, true leadership and lack of direction. It is a multifarious mosaic where tiles of various shapes and sizes still fit together to form a unified composition.

REFERENCES

Bakhtin, M. M. (1981). *The Dialogic Imagination. Four Essays*. Austin, TX: The University of Texas Press.

Bartmiński, J. (1993). O profilowaniu pojęć w słowniku etnolingwistycznym [On Profiling Concepts in the Ethnolinguistic Dictionary]. *Philologia Slavica K 70 letiyu akademika N. I. Tolstogo* (pp. 12–17). Moskva: Nauka.

Bartmiński, J., (1994). Jak zmienia się stereotyp Niemca w Polsce? *Przegląd Humanistyczny*, 5: 81–101.

Bartmiński, J. (2007). *Językowe podstawy obrazu świata* [Linguistic Foundations of the World Image]. Lublin: Wydawnictwo UMCS.

Bartmiński, J. (2009). *Aspects of Cognitive Ethnolinguistics*, Zinken, J. (ed.), transl. A. Głaz. London, Oakville: Equinox.

Bartmiński, J. and Niebrzegowska, S. (1998). Profile a podmiotowa interpretacja świata [Profiles and the Subjective Interpretation of the World]. In Bartmiński, J., Tokarski, R. (eds.). *Profilowanie w języku i w tekście* [Profiling in Language and in Text] (pp. 211–225). Lublin: UMCS.

Brünner, G., Graefen G. (1993). Einleitung: zur Konzeption de funktionalen Pragmatik. In Brünner, G., Graefen, G. (eds.). *Texte und Diskurse* (pp. 7–24). Opladen: Westdeutscher Verlag.

Cambridge Dictionary https://dictionary.cambridge.org/ [accessed 11 February 2020].

Dunaj, B. (1996). *Słownik współczesnego języka polskiego* [Dictionary of the Contemporary Polish Language]. Warszawa: Wydawnictwo Wilga.

Grabowska, M. (2014). Profile obrazu pojęcia *wiara w Boga* w języku współczesnych Polaków w świetle badań ankietowych oraz wywiadów [Profiles of the Image of the Concept of Faith in God in the Language of Contemporary Poles in the Light of Surveys and Interviews]. *Język-Szkola-Religia*, 9(2): 7–20.

Grzegorczykowa, R. (1998). Profilowanie a inne pojęcia opisujące hierarchiczną strukturę znaczenia [Profiling and Other Concepts Describing the Hierarchical Structure of Meaning]. In Grzegorczykowa, R. (ed.). *Profilowanie w języku i tekście* [Profiling in Language and in Text] (pp. 9–17). Lublin: UMCS.

Langacker, R. W. (2000). *Grammar and Conceptualisation*. Berlin and New York: Mouton de Gruyter.

Langacker, R. W. (2008). *Cognitive Grammar. A Basic Introduction*. New York: Oxford University Press.

Langacker, R. W. (1991). *Concept, Image, and Symbol*. Berlin and New York: Mouton de Gruyter.

Langacker, R. W. (2000). *Grammar and Conceptualization*. Berlin and New York: Mouton de Gruyter.

Langacker, R. W. (1995). *Wykłady z gramatyki kognitywnej. Kazimierz nad Wisłą, grudzień 1993* [Cognitive Grammar Lectures. Kazimierz and Wisła, December 1993]. Kardela, H. (ed.), transl. J. Berej [et al.]. (pp. 7–17). Lublin: UMCS.

Levinas, E. (1984). Emmanuel Levinas. In R. Kearney (Ed.), *Dialogues with Contemporary Continental Thinkers* (pp. 47–70). Manchester: Manchester University Press.

Merriam-Webster Dictionary https://www.merriam-webster.com/ [accessed 12 February 2020].

Norris, J. (2008). Duoethnography. In L. M. Given (Ed.), *The Sage Encyclopedia of Qualitative Research Methods* (Vol. 1, pp. 233–236). Los Angeles, CA: Sage.

Norris, J., Sawyer, R. D. and Lund, D. (eds.). (2012). *Duoethnography. Dialogic Methods for Social, Health, and Educational Research*. Walnut Creek, CA: Left Coast Press Inc.

Pietrucha, M. (2003). Profile pojęcia demokracji we współczesnym języku polskim [Profiles of the Concept of Democracy in Contemporary Polish]. In Bartmiński, J. (ed.). *Język w kręgu wartości* [Language in the Circle of Values] (pp. 273–307). Lublin: Wydawnictwo UMCS.

Pinar, W. (1975). Currerere: Towards Reconceptualization. In Pinar, W. (ed.), *Curriculum Theorizing: The Reconceptualists* (pp. 396–414). Berkley, CA: McCutchan.

Pinar, W. (2004). *What is Curriculum Theory?* Mahwah, NJ, London: Lawrence Erlbaum Associates Publishers.

Reason, P., and Hawkins, P. (1988). *Storytelling as Inquiry*. In Reason, P. (ed.). *Human Inquiry in Action* (pp. 79–101). Newbury Park, CA: Sage.

Sawyer, R. D., and Norris, J. (2009). Duoethnography: Articulations/(re)creation of meaning in the making. In W. R. Gershon (Ed.), *The Collaborative Turn: Working Together in Qualitative Research* (pp. 127–140). Rotterdam: Sense.

Sawyer, R. D., and Norris, J. (2013). *Duoethnography. Understanding Qualitative Research*. New York: Oxford University Press.

Sawyer, R. D., Dekker, L. and Rasmor, M. (2016). Search of an Artistic Curriculum Identity. In Sawyer, R. D., and Norris, J. (eds.). *Interdisciplinary Reflective Practice through Duoethnography. Examples for Educators* (pp. 17–40). New York: Palgrave Macmillan,.

SJP PWN online https://sjp.pwn.pl/ [accessed 14 February 2020].

Smyk, K. (2009). *Językowo-kulturowy obraz bożonarodzeniowej choinki. Symbolika drzewka i ozdób* [Linguistic and Cultural Image of the Christmas Tree. Symbolism of the Tree and Ornaments]. Kraków: Universitas.

Tokarski, R. (1991). Człowiek w definicji znaczeniowej słowa [Man in the Meaning of the Word]. *Przegląd Humanistyczny* 3(4): 131–140.

Werbińska, D. (2018). Wykorzystanie duoetnografii jako innowacyjnego podejścia w rozwijaniu refleksji przyszłych nauczycieli języka obcego [Using Duoethnography as an Innovative Approach in Developing the Reflection of Future Foreign Language Teachers]. *Neofilolog* 51(1): 59–73.

Wierzbicka, A. (1985). *Lexicography and Conceptual Analysis*. Ann Arbor, MI: Karoma Publishers.

Wodak, R. (1996). *Disorders of Discourse.* London: Longman.

Wodak, R. (1997). Introduction: Some Important Issues in the Research of Gender and Discourse. In Wodak, R. (ed.). *Gender and Discourse* (pp. 1–20). London: Sage Publications.

Zinken, J. (2009). The Ethnolinguistic School of Lublin and Anglo-American Cognitive Linguistics. In Zinken, J. (ed.). *Aspects of Cognitive Linguistics,* transl. A. Głaz (pp. 1–5). London, Oakville: Equinox.

ABOUT THE AUTHOR

Magdalena Grabowska, having a PhD in linguistics, currently works as Assistant Professor and the deputy head in the Department of Applied Linguistics, University of Gdansk, Poland. Her interests focus on ethnographic linguistics, specifically on the study of sensitive issues which appeal for social heed, identity and religion being the case in point. Integrating ethnographic methodology into sociolinguistic research she is particularly interested in reconstructing commonsensical definitions, one with fuzzy categorial boundaries and experiential basis.

4

The four perspectives model for psychological/psychiatric case formulations in analysing the discourse of clinical-diagnostic case reporting

Magdalena Zabielska

ABSTRACT

Conceptually, the four perspectives approach is seen as a "common lore approach" (Bolton, 2014: 182) to case formulation, a micro-genre of case reporting as utilized in psychology/psychiatry. Its main aim is to detail the case, along with its precipitating factors and follow-up treatment, continuously emphasizing the uniqueness of the case (Sim, Gwee & Bateman, 2005: 290). In this chapter, this discipline-specific generic macro-scheme will be drawn upon as a tool to study the specialized discourse of clinical-diagnostic case reporting from an applied perspective. It will be shown that although the two micro-genres represent two conceptually different disciplines, the emphasis on the individual patient can be seen as a common ground and can be translated into particular linguistic resources, which may be of interest in the context of Language for Specific Purposes courses. This analysis is made possible thanks to a qualitative approach to the data, combined with some insights from a computer-aided analysis of the corpus, which consists of case reports derived from the prestigious Lancet journal.

Keywords: four perspectives model, medical case reporting, clinical-diagnostic case, linguistics qualitative research

4.1. INTRODUCTION

Studies in broadly understood healthcare communication draw on theories from neighbouring disciplines, such as the sociology of medicine, social psychology, philosophy of medicine, medical anthropology or medical ethics. Many of these studies have proven to be effective in tapping into the construction of professional and lay identities, as well as into the very nature of communication in this particularly sensitive context (Watts, 2008, 2010). In this chapter, the *four perspectives* model (henceforth four Ps) will be applied to the analysis of a corpus of case reports derived from the *Lancet*. Originally developed for streamlining the construction of case formulations in psychology and psychiatry, here it will be deployed as a tool to study the language of clinical-diagnostic case reporting from an applied perspective.

A case report is a written medical genre that discusses unknown diseases, their new aspects or anything novel about a specific treatment or drug use. Case formulations, by contrast, are psychological/psychiatric equivalents of clinical-diagnostic case reports. They involve "turning a patient's narrative and all the information derived from examinations, interviews with parents and teachers, and medical and school reports into a coherent and not necessarily lengthy story that will help to develop a treatment plan" (Henderson & Martin, 2015). The four perspectives model outlines four elements key to the complete description of a patient, their condition and subsequent treatment, namely *predisposing*, *precipitating*, *perpetuating* and *protecting* (Henderson & Martin, 2015). What lies at the heart of this approach is that it views psychological and social factors as integral elements of each case, thus emphasizing the differentiating features of psychology and psychiatry as disciplines. "[P]sychiatrists for the most part cannot use a stethoscope or the variety of tests (such as bloodwork, electrocardiograms and blood pressure readings) that other kinds of physicians routinely use as sources of information in making their diagnoses" (Berkenkotter, 2008: 2). Although primarily content-related in its original milieu, the model may be applied to the study of the discourse of clinical-diagnostic case reporting. Since the model features guidelines which help to discursively construct a complete case, not only from the biomedical (Wade & Halligan, 2004) but also from patient-centred (Balint et al., 1970) perspectives, it may provide for useful categories of information to be included in clinical-diagnostic case reports. It may also aid the identification or choice of the corresponding linguistic resources to express the information required and help to differentiate between these two viewpoints.

It will be demonstrated that texts written from a clinical-diagnostic perspective can be understood better and potentially constructed more effectively with reference to particular conceptualizations of various social and mental phenomena, as routinely utilized in psychology and psychiatry.

4.2. CASE REPORTING AS A COMMUNICATIVE EVENT

In specialized contexts, particular practices are accompanied by particular communicative activities realized by means of oral and written genres. One such group of practices, which belongs to the oldest communicative practices in medicine, is managing cases, from their recording to their representation. These forms can be oral and written and are referred to as *genres*. Genres are defined by Swales (1990) as a "communicative event" (1990: 58), "the patterned and recurring ways in which cultural members regularly accomplish elemental social activities" (Muntigl, 2006: 234).

The group of communicative activities used in managing cases can be referred to as a macro-genre (Martin, 1995), which stands for genres "which combine familial elemental genres" (Martin, 2000: 16). In the context of clinical-diagnostic medicine, *case-based* genres include, for example, case presentation, case notes, etc. In psychiatry and psychology, the focus of the current chapter, cases are constructed through so-called *case formulation*. In his introduction to an edited collection on the discursive and rhetorical aspects of cases across scientific areas, Asper (2020) follows Kuhn (1977), who viewed them as "shared examples", especially in "educative contexts of the natural sciences" (2020: 2). For Asper (2020), "cases are texts meant to impart or store knowledge" and they should be considered pragmatically bearing in mind their contextual and functional groundings, which will be considered below.

4.2.1. Case report vs. case formulation

While the communicative aim of both these micro-genres is to focus on an individual case of a disease or condition, these diseases/conditions belong to two different medical domains and thus their nature differs, which has a bearing on different aspects reported and different communicative foci. In the broadest sense, "[i]n its typical form, the *case report* records the course of a patient's disease from the onset of symptoms to the outcome, usually either recovery or death. The background and a commentary on the disease are also given, but their scope may vary. Often a limited review of the literature is added and the number of known cases stated" (Taavitsainen & Pahta, 2000: 60, italics added). In psychology/psychiatry, *case formulations* are "a process by which a set of hypotheses is generated about the etiology and factors that perpetuate a patient's presenting problems and translates the diagnosis into specific, individualized treatment interventions" (Winters, Hanson & Stoyanova, 2007: 111). The formulation should thus describe the patient's problem, taking into consideration not only what led to it, but also what should be done in this specific situation. Berkenkotter (2008) adds that "[t]his text, which becomes part of patient's medical record, is constructed from the patient's presentation – his or her narrative of the history of the present problem – as well as the patient's observable bodily symptoms" (Berkenkotter, 2008: 2).

The importance of this narrative aspect is aptly captured by Bolton (2014), who observes that case formulations should "minimally tell better stories, thicker stories", addressing the question of "how [...] we approach the problem or the patient in its uniqueness" (2014: 182). Since a narrative requires a particular structure (Labov, 1972), causality and chronology (Cohen, 2006; Rison, Kidd & Koch, 2013), also in case formulations, the plot, time reference, good structure and coherence of the "frame" should be attended to (Lewis, 2014: 195). In other words, the patient's health problem should be contextualized. This aspect leads to the other point of Bolton's view on case formulations, namely that the patient's uniqueness should be emphasized (see section 4.3). In Bolton's (2014) words, they should be seen as "unique, complex and situated" rather than simply a diagnostic type (Bolton, 2014: 181), which tallies with the above-cited conceptualizing of the difference between case reports and case formulations. Such a treatment is possible when the patient's case is viewed through a narrative lens. Of interest is also the fact that in such an approach, words should aid the construction of "the patient as a case rather than a type by revealing the dramatically different situations of individual patients" (Bolton, 2014: 182). In this sense, "case" stands for a particular patient's individuality and uniqueness, which contrasts with the reductionist clinical-diagnostic construction of a case. In this construction, what is important is a particular disease in a patient, who is just an insignificant secondary character. Since the ailment is decontextualized, the word "case" stands rather for the objectification, impersonality or even dehumanization. In other words, different areas the microgenres stem from, are translated into differences in both content and form. This is also aptly captured by Jellinek and McDermott (2004), who see diagnosis and case formulation respectively as the "science and art". Rzepa (2005), in her thorough analysis of the structure and character of case formulation vs clinical-diagnostic case report, observes that there has been a change in the perception of the case from an ailment to a person. This fact, according to Rzepa (2005), has helped the case formulation gain scientific status (2005: 28), since it clearly began to correlate particular events from the person's life with the logic of particular symptoms. In psychology and psychiatry, case formulations are treated as synonymous with life history, and the methodology of the presentation of the subject requires the reference to particular life events (2005: 27). What underlies this approach is Allport's contribution of an idiographic angle in the treatment of the personality, i.e., what is specific for a particular person (Hall, Lindzey & Campbell, 1997).

Yet, a number of shared areas can be pointed to as well. As Fernando, Cohen and Henskens (2012) observe, just as clinical disciplines make use of so-called *illness scripts* (Feltovich & Barrows, 1984) which serve as particular patterns to be recognized – as well as modus operandi to be applied in particular cases – a similar procedure may be used in psychiatric/psychological cases where given symptoms may also be indicative of certain conditions requiring particular action (2012: 122, see Schmidt, Norman & Boshuizen, 1990; Coderre et al., 2003). The four Ps model, utilized in formulating cases in psychology/psychiatry, may also be seen as a particular script for clinical-diagnostic cases, which will be discussed in section 4.4. In this way, it is possible to observe a dialogic relation between case reporting in these two seemingly different disciplines. Żelazowska-Sobczyk and Zabielska (2019a, 2019b) have compared case formulations with their clinical-diagnostic equivalents, concluding that they have a number of common features resulting from the fact that they belong to the same macro-genre. The difference, however, lies in the structure and the narrative element, with the latter allowing the author to focus more on the patient in question, which brings one back to the already discussed differences between case reports and case formulations stemming from the different nature of the phenomena they describe and the way their respective domains treat them.

4.2.2. Literature review

The literature on case reports and case formulations is rich and multifaceted, spanning different contexts, aspects and methods. Case reports have been examined with respect different foci, perspectives and methodologies. A strand particularly relevant to this chapter is the structural approach, with linguistic studies investigating generic features of case reports (Helán, 2012; Zabielska, 2014; Żelazowska-Sobczyk & Zabielska, 2016; Zabielska & Żelazowska-Sobczyk, 2017; Żelazowska-Sobczyk, 2019; Asper, 2020). There is also a body of publications of purely instructive character, detailing the required parts of case reports (Rison, Kidd & Koch, 2013 (emphasizing the patient's perspective); Shyam, 2013; Sun et al., 2013; Nguyen et al., 2014; Wardle & Roseen, 2014; Bavdekar & Save, 2015; Ivančević Otanjac & Milojević, 2015), with the last one specifically mentioning genre-specific rhetorical moves of academic argumentation (Swales, 1990) in case reporting, cf. similar studies for medical abstracts, e.g. Mureşan & Kic-Drgas (2019) and research articles – classic: Nwogu (1997), and more recent: Fryer (2012), Csongor (2013), Huang (2014), Davis (2015), with Uzun (2016) mentioning also the patient's perspective. More recently, certain guidelines have been proposed with a view to improving the quality of medical case reporting, both structure- and content-wise (McCulloch et al., 2009; Gagnier et al., 2013; Hirst et al., 2013; Agha et al., 2018), introducing particular models, e.g. the CARE (CAse REport) (Gagnier et al., 2013), the SCARE guidelines (Agha et al., 2018) and the

IDEAL framework (McCulloch et al., 2009; Hirst et al., 2013), with the last two referring exclusively to surgical case reports. Of interest are also studies which emphasize the patient's perspective as a contribution to the case report (Żelazowska & Zabielska, 2016; Zabielska, 2019b).

Regarding case formulations and contexts, Barrett (1988) focused on case formulations in Australia and Coker (2003) in Egypt, while Berkenkotter (2008) has written on English-language formulations from the historical perspective (see also Berkenkotter et al. (2015) for a study of twentieth-century case narratives). Case formulations as used in the treatment of anorexia were studied by Allen et al. (2016); Rogers, Reinecke and Curry (2005), as well Persons and Tompkin (2007) discussed their use in cognitive-behavioural therapy, while Mather and Jaffe (2011) centred on the context of psychology and special education; and Klos (1976) as well as Fernando, Cohen and Henskens (2012) on medical education. Baird et al. (2017) gave an account of their historical background as well as their status and role (cf. also Sim, Gwee & Bateman, 2005; Shahar & Poticelli, 2006; Flinn, 2015; and Johnstone, 2018); Andrade and Ugalde (2011) discussed the ethical issues involved in the process of case formulating. Regarding methods, in the aforementioned study by Berkenkotter (2008), the data was approached from a diachronic multimodal angle, while Alyami et al. (2015) showed the usefulness of visual metaphor in the study of case formulations.

Linguistic analyses of case formulations constitute a separate body of research (Hak & Boer, 1996; Antaki, Barnes & Leudar, 2005; Beckwith & Crichton, 2010; Korner et al., 2010; Fitzgerald & Leudar, 2012; Walsh, Cominos & Jureidini, 2016), where attention is paid to particular linguistic resources as utilized in the texts/ speech and how this knowledge can be used for instructive purposes. The aim of such studies is to sensitize professionals to the nature of psychiatric discourse. This group also includes Berkenkotter's abovementioned work, in which she juxtaposed written historical cases with more modern texts, complementing her analysis with interviews with their authors. There is also a group of articles offering guidelines as to the essentials of writing case formulations (Sperry, 1992; Aston, 2009; Flitcroft, Andrew & Freeston, 2007; Havighurst & Downey, 2009; Selzer & Ellen, 2014) as well as comprehensive handbooks (Eells, 2007; Sturmey, 2009; Ingram Lichner, 2012).

As has been demonstrated, although the research on case reports and case formulations is ample and multifaceted, this author knows of no study in which a linguistic analysis of a medical genre from the applied perspective – here, the case report – was enriched by structural and content contribution from a different medical area, sharing the patient's perspective.

4.3. THEORETICAL BACKGROUND FOR THE STUDY

The very character of the genre of case formulation reflects the recent changes that medical practice is continuing to undergo, i.e. the transition from the biomedical approach (Wade & Halligan, 2004) to patient-centred medicine (Laine & Davidoff, 1996; Mead & Bower, 2000). These can be seen as paradigms which guide our understanding of what disease is, what it means to be a patient, "the relation of mind and body, the meaning of diagnosis, the role of the physician, [and] the conduct of the doctor-patient relationship" (McWhinney, 2014), all of which are the consequence of the development of science – and thus thought-styles – and societal conditioning. With regard to the biomedical approach, this mode of reasoning has been present in medical sciences since the nineteenth century. From this angle, disease can be understood as a malfunction of the body-machine, as proposed by Descartes (1634, as cited in Foss, 2002: 37) and the patient as a passive undergoer of treatment. In other words, the patient may feel "reduced to a malfunctioning biological organism" (Toombs, 1992: 106). The approach thus is reductionist and exclusionist (Engel, 1977: 130), since disease is understood rather mono-aspectually, as a thing that could be easily "removed" from the body (McWhinney, 2014), while treatment does not seem to engage the patient in any way. The patient-centred approach, on the other hand, as the name suggests, has the patient at its core and entails three components: communication, partnership and health promotion (Constand et al., 2014). The first two components seem essential as, as has been already stated, diagnostic possibilities in psychiatry are less numerous and complex than in somatic medicine, and it is interaction that allows the clinician to tap into the patient's ailment and negotiate compliance (Savander et al., 2019: 211). Another building block of the approach was Engel's biopsychological contribution (Engel, 1977; cf. Smith & Strain, 2002; Smith, 2014: 24–25). In Smith and Strain's words:

> Engel claimed that the biopsychosocial model would enable the physician to extend application of the scientific method to aspects of everyday practice and patient care not previously deemed accessible to a scientific approach or even deemed worthy of examination, for example, inner feelings. [...] Engel's argument for the biopsychosocial model being a scientific one rested on his observation that the doctor's task is to find out how and what the patient is or has been feeling and experiencing, to formulate an explanation, and to engage the patient in further clinical and laboratory studies to test such hypotheses. The sole reliance on biophysical or somatic data was claimed to be insufficient and would lead to erroneous conclusions (2002: 459–460).

In general, what underlies this approach is the different understanding of the concept of disease and its diagnosis, as well as the role of the patient. The first component refers to the conviction that it is not the biological aspects of one's ailment but also psychological and social ones that are essential to correct diagnosis as well as the understanding of the disease. What is more, the patient cannot be seen as a passive recipient of treatment. This, in turn, is closely linked to the concept of the *unique individual* (Smith, 2014: 26). Western philosophy perceives the "Self" as a conscious entity who thinks, has a will and ability to experience things (Smith, 2014: 29) and is "able to entertain first-person thoughts" (Lowe, 2005: 806). Moreover, crucial to the understanding of the other person is the conceptualization of the self as something more than elements compiled into a whole, stressing the difficulty of adding this "more" element. In Aristotle's words, "totality is not, as it were, a mere heap, but the whole is something besides the parts" (Cohen, 2012). The authors also emphasize the existence and use of metaphor in the patient's accounts as a unique resource mediating this experience (Smith, 2014: 29). In this context, words should aid the construction of "the patient as a case rather than a type by revealing the dramatically different situations of individual patients", consequently, moving away from the abstraction of symptoms to the importance of "particulars" (McWhinney, 2014).

4.4. STRUCTURAL AND LINGUISTIC FEATURES OF CASE FORMULATION

On the conceptual level, the four Ps approach is seen as a "common lore approach" (Bolton, 2014: 182) to case formulation. What underlies it is the answer to the question: "Why does this patient suffer from this (these) problem(s) at this point in time?"" (Royal Australian & New Zealand College of Psychiatrists, 2012: 1), which entails not only a detailed description of the patient's condition but also the circumstances of this case and what can be done to remedy this situation, whilst continuously emphasizing the uniqueness of this case (Sim, Gwee & Bateman 2005: 290). What is more, all these elements need to be understood together, "highlighting the linkages between different aspects of the case" (Fernando, Cohen & Henskens, 2012: 121).

In this approach, the postulates of uniqueness and contextualization can be realized when considering the so-called four P-elements. Each of these is accompanied by a question and an explanation.

Element	Question	Explanation
Predisposing	*Why me?*	Genetic loading (biological)
		Immature defensive structure (psychological)
		Poverty and adversity (social)
Precipitating	*Why now?*	Iatrogenic reaction (biological)
		Poor response to medication (biological)
		Recent loss (psychological)
		School stressors (social)
Perpetuating	*Why does it continue?*	No support at school (psychological)
		Unable to attend therapy sessions because of parents' work schedule (social)
Protective	*What can I rely on?*	Family history of treatment response (biological)
		Insightful (psychological)
		Community and faith as sources of support (social)

(Henderson & Martin, 2015)

What is more, each element can be considered from three perspectives – biological, psychological and social (see above).

> The biological domain circumscribes neuropsychiatric, genetic and physiological issues, focusing on, but not limited to, the functional operations of the brain and what might be directly affecting it. The psychological dimension includes an evaluation of the child's psychological make-up, including strengths and vulnerabilities, and offers the opportunity to include psychodynamic principles like defense structures, consciously and unconsciously driven patterns of behavior, responses to trauma and conflict, transferences and counter-transferences. The social dimension situates the child in their communities, exploring relationships with family and friends, as well as larger collective cultural organizations like schools, religion, socioeconomic class and ethnicity.
>
> (Henderson & Martin, 2015: 3–5)

The questions centre around the individual, yet their consideration from the last two angles (psychological and social) offers a more holistic picture of the patient, which complements the typically reductionist angle of the case report (cf. the biomedical approach in section 4.3). The complementary information includes both the individual perspective (psychological), i.e. which events from one's experience or his/her psychological predispositions might be conducive to the development of an ailment, as well as social contributors to the condition, referring to one's environment. While the transfer of the particular questions into clinical-diagnostic case reports might be too detailed in their entirety, yet not impossible, the psychological and social angles offer a significant input into the biomedical perspective, which will be demonstrated in the examples analysed below.

In his article under the very telling title "Demystifying the psychiatric case formulation", Sperry (1992) discusses the structure of the genre with a view to streamlining the process of its creation among students and young professionals, emphasizing that "[t]he psychiatric formulation is the clinician's compass guiding treatment. It should accurately reflect the patient and his/her pattern of functioning as well as the precipitants, predisposing and perpetuating factors, and prognosis, while also being clear, concise and clinically useful" (1992: 12). He also observes that formulations orient towards three components: descriptive, etiological and treatment-prognostic, respectively answering the questions "What happened", "Why did it happen" and "What can be done about it and how?" (1992: 13). This way, the four Ps model introduces the aspects of chronology and etiology organizing the entire account (Henderson & Martin, 2015: 5–6) within the narrative frame (see section 4.2.1).

Linguistically, formulations are closer to scientific discourse with relatively simple sentence structure and high lexical density, i.e. a greater number of words per sentence as well as their complexity, e.g. nominalization. Impersonal features are used too, emphasizing internal states rather actions on the part of the patient (Korner et al., 2010: 217). This has been demonstrated in Francis and Kramer-Dahl's (2004) comparison of a literary text and a case report derived from neuropsychology. As the authors observe, although the latter text belongs to the genre of the case report (and in this way it is classified by the authors), the fact that it is derived from the area of neuropsychology may suggest at least partial similarities with case formulations. To confirm this claim, the authors point to the linguistic features identified in the case report in question, i.e. nominalized and abstracted themes, presentation of the patient as a goal, i.e. "done to" (2004: 178), whose responses are "appropriated" (2004: 201) by the author as well as relative textual distance via a disengaged researcher (2004: 178). Narrative aspects of the formulation are also emphasized, such as adding coherence and structure to human experience as well as use of metaphor, mediating its individual character (Korner et al., 2010: 217, cf. Smith, 2014, see section 4.2.1).

4.5. METHODOLOGICAL SOLUTIONS

As advocated in the current volume, interdisciplinarity is "any form of dialog or interaction between two or more disciplines" (Moran, 2010: 14, after Repko, 2008: 4) [which] emphasize combination "by which ideas, data and information, methods, tools, concepts, and/or theories from two or more disciplines are synthesized, connected, or blended" (Repko, 2008: 4). Consequently, this chapter attempts to combine methods, concepts and data. Methodologically, this analysis will be primarily qualitative, with a quantitative element. "[Q]ualitative researchers study things in their natural settings, attempting to make sense of, or interpret, phenomena in terms of the meanings people bring to them" (Denzin & Lincoln, 2011: 3) as well as "celebrat[ing] richness, depth, nuance, context, multi-dimensionality and complexity" of the data at hand (Mason, 2002: 2), and "striving for ecological validity" (Holmes & Hazen, 2014: 1). This is the case, because what is at the heart of both the case reports under investigation – as well the theoretical toolkit derived from the areas of psychology and psychiatry – is the individual and their experience of illness, albeit to different degrees. In the case of the former, although this case reporting variety belongs to clinical-diagnostic practice, it is still a genre that describes a case of a disease in a particular patient. Regarding the latter, the four Ps toolkit for the structuring of case formulations, the psychological/psychiatric equivalent of case reports, emphasizes the complex nature of the individual's condition even more, with a prominent narrative character to serve the purpose. It seems of particular importance, especially in light of the criticism levelled at contemporary case reports, whose impersonal and dehumanizing writing style is a textual manifestation of the biomedical approach (Helán, 2012; Zabielska, 2014; Zabielska, 2019a; Zabielska, 2019b).

In greater detail, the applied linguistic methods of investigation of specialized discourse, characteristics of one discipline will be supplemented with structural insights from a different medical field. In greater detail, it will be the combination of the genre analytic approach to studying a medical genre – as practiced for instance in applied linguistics, e.g., in the English for Academic and Special Purposes (EAP and ESP) frameworks, or, more specifically, English for Medical Purposes (EMP) (Maher, 1986), also Medical English as a Lingua Franca (MELF) in interlingual communication (Tweedie & Johnson, 2022) – and the strictly discipline-specific generic macro-scheme of the four Ps derived from psychiatry and psychology. In both cases, following Méndez-Cendón and López-Arroyo (2003: 247–248),

> [i]t is important to know how information is distributed in the English language in the expert-to-expert communicative setting. This information distribution never occurs at random; otherwise, experts would

have not only to identify the relevant information but also to understand its pragmatic function. Therefore, every textual pattern allows the experts to recognize the functions designated by the language from the way the phraseology is distributed.

This, in turn, derives from the assumptions behind EAP and ESP courses which are supposed to "provide learners with sufficient awareness of language, rhetoric and study skills to enable them to learn the subject content" (Dudley-Evans, 1998: 6). Additionally, the usefulness of the approaches in psychiatry/psychology is recognized.

Data-wise, two sets of discipline-specific texts (yet belonging to one macro-genre) will be compared: case reports and case formulations. In this way, the study addresses Swales' (1985) call to "look across" ESP contexts and its current rendition encouraging researchers to "connect with the culture of [the] chosen field" (Douglas, 2017: xvii). These recommendations underlie the current trends in ESP teaching (see, for instance, Franklin-Landi, 2017) where the discourse analytic approach is seen as one of the methodological options (Franklin-Landi, 2017: 155). In order to follow these recommendations, insights from computer-aided analysis of the corpus of the case reports will be provided, with the help of Sketch Engine', with the view to providing selected language patterns characteristic of the genre. This way, the qualitative approach will be supplemented by the elements of the quantitative one, "putting flesh on the bones" (Dörnyei, 2007: 45).

4.6. ANALYSIS

4.6.1. Data and methods

The data for the current analysis comes from the collection of case reports from the professional medical publishing outlet the *Lancet*, constituting the clinical-diagnostic type of the reports. The ten reports selected as examples were published between 2011 and 2013 and are derived from a larger corpus consisting of 866 texts published between 1996 and 2013. They were downloaded in electronic form from the journal's website. The analytical part consisted first of the application of the model for psychiatric/psychological case formulation of clinical-diagnostic case reports, which meant their careful reading, then identifying those elements of the model that were available in the texts, noting which were not present and considering their potential presence. Next, some insights were also derived from the computer-aided exploration of the corpus with the help of Sketch Engine®, in which keywords as well as frequencies of words and collocations were probed into. Additionally, the results were verified by a second reader, a practicing psychiatrist.

The analysis will focus specifically on the linguistic representation of the concept of the unique individual (Smith, 2014, see section 4.3), as well as the skill of pattern recognition (Fernando, Cohen & Henskens, 2012), which has bearing on the structuring of formulations and analogies with the clinical-diagnostic case reports. With regard to the first aspect, the analysis will follow the Conversational Model (Hobson, 1985; Meares, 2000, 2005) which sees conversations as "intersubjective, emphasizing that personal experience arises from interaction, particularly with the interpersonal environment". In the model, it is assumed that a formulation serves the function of bringing the patient's point of view closer in a structured way and of creating a story to be shared, possibly also with the patient (Korner et al., 2010: 218). In this context, the importance of language is stressed, both as a means used to convey as well as elicit relevant information (Korner et al., 2010: 215). As regards the first aspect, formulations help to tap into the individual situation whereas the latter, "is designed to use language to make sense of a presentation" (Korner et al., 2010: 215), "'talking to the other person' rather than of 'talking about the other'" (Korner et al., 2010: 218). Following this line of reasoning, as well as looking at the structural analogies between case formulations and clinical-diagnostic case reports, the linguistic aspects of the construction of cases will also be examined.

4.6.2. Results and discussion

4.6.2.1. The four Ps approach

In general, it is possible to identify equivalent information as required in the four Ps model in the clinical-diagnostic case reports. What follows are particular excerpts of clinical-diagnostic case reports reflecting the model in a different context.

Predisposing   *Why me?*

(a) She reported having had a non-productive cough without haemoptysis 1 month previously. The cough resolved, but a sore throat then developed (Miller, Zurflu & Jaipaul, 2011.)

(b) [...] a 37-year- old [...] woman presented to [a hospital] with a 2-year history of a slowly growing abdominal mass with associated dyspepsia, intermittent abdominal pain, anorexia, and weight loss. Her surgical history included four caesarean section deliveries and tubal ligation (Creighton et al., 2013).

(c) Although he denied any regular recreational sports activities, his new job as a delivery-van driver required a lot of climbing. He had no dietary restrictions. Elderly relatives of our patient had a history of osteoporosis and osteopenia (Yli-Kyyny et al., 2011).

(d) In May, 2004, a 44-year-old man presented to his primary-care physician having had severe left-sided headaches for 4 weeks (Salameh et al., 2011).

In case formulation, predisposing factors are "the constellation of features that render the [patient] vulnerable to the presenting symptoms such as family history, genetics, medical and psychiatric history, and chronic social stressors" (Henderson & Martin, 2015: 6). What is meant by predisposing in clinical-diagnostic reports is the previous history of a medical condition that is believed to have contributed to the current problem. That is why at this particular point in the report, usually at the beginning, the text goes back into the patient's history of illness in order to bring up this apparently relevant element. In example (a) the patient's cough is recalled which, consequently, led to a sore throat, a relevant factor in the subsequent diagnosis, similarly to the patient's history of illness in example (b), the activities and family's history in (c), or a previous visit to the doctor's, as in (d). Language-wise, this particular account in the global narrative of the report is given in flashback, signalled via past tense, time references (e.g. "1 month previously") and by means of such stock phrases as "having a history", thus bearing story-like features (Korner et al., 2010).

Precipitating   *Why now?*

(e) At the time she was assessed by her general practitioner and specialists in the emergency and otolaryngology departments, who diagnosed pharyngitis and recommended conservative management (Miller, Zurflu & Jaipaul, 2011).

(f) Several weeks before the onset of headaches he had had acute bronchitis with a severe non-productive cough. He also had a recent history of vertigo, hemianopsia, and scintillating scotoma (Salameh et al., 2011).

(g) In October, 2008, a 40-year-old man was referred to our hospital because of pain in his right groin, which had started a few days after he fell on his back at work 10 days earlier (Yli-Kyyny et al., 2011).

(h) In January, 2009, a 34-year-old man presented to our hospital with a 6-month history of four, well-defined, non-tender, erythematous plaques of area 1–3 cm² on his right hand (figure A) (Prasad et al., 2011).

Precipitating factors in psychology/psychiatry are defined as "current symptoms, diagnostic reasoning about the role of inciting events, and concurrent illness" (Henderson & Martin, 2015: 6). In clinical-diagnostic reporting, reference is made to previous events, but relatively recent ones, and which are in some way related to the current problem, unlike the definitely past events reported in the previous section. In (e) and (f) past diagnoses prior the current assessment are reported on, while in (g) and (h), the beginning of the current patients' complaints are the focus. In this way, in both cases emphasis is placed on the current problem as well as any triggers and accompanying conditions. Also, similarly to the "Predisposing" section, the use of past forms and time references can be observed.

Perpetuating   *Why does it continue?*

(i) Her odynophagia progressed until she was unable to eat solid foods, prompting her to present to our hospital (Miller, Zurflu & Jaipaul, 2011).

(j) A month after the onset of symptoms, the pain on weight bearing in the right groin had decreased but not resolved (Yli-Kyyny et al., 2011).

(k) 2 years later in April, 2007, our patient presented again to us with severe headaches, the same neurological symptoms, and a preceding history of severe bronchitis. Brain MRA showed a dissection of the left internal carotid artery at the craniocervical transition with 40% stenosis (Salameh et al., 2011).

(l) The pain often occurred after urination or defecation, and lasted from several minutes to several hours. She could not walk because of the severity of the pain, and had to lie supine with the affected thigh flexed to obtain some relief. Our patient had presented to emergency departments several times, receiving a diagnosis of psychogenic pain or osteoarthritis because of degenerative changes shown on hip radiographs (Toshihiko et al., 2011).

The "Perpetuating'" examples refer to the ongoing character of the current problem, which leads to more problematic consequences. In case formulations these are elements that "make the condition endure, such as the severity of the condition, compliance issues, and unresolved predisposing and precipitating factors" (Henderson & Martin, 2015: 6). In the above excerpts, these include an inability to eat, as in (i), and persistent pain in (j–l). From the patient's perspective exclusively, it is not only another symptom of the ailment, but rather its repercussions for their quality of life, e.g. affected ability to do particular things – examples (i), (j) and (l). Its signalling admittedly adds to the pronounced concern for the patient and their individual circumstances (see section 4.3).

Protective   *What can I rely on?*

(m) Therefore, physicians should consider laryngeal tuberculosis in the differential diagnosis of patients presenting with a persistent sore throat and odynophagia, especially in patients such as ours who also report weight loss. A chest radiograph should be considered before laryngoscopy to minimize unnecessary risk to healthcare providers (Miller, Zurflu & Jaipaul, 2011).

(n) Our patient's case should encourage the thorough investigation of severe headaches associated with neurological symptoms, particularly in regard to the cerebral vasculature (Salameh et al., 2011).

(o) In cases of primary spontaneous pneumothorax where there is a family history, and typical CT findings or disease recurrence after treatment, referral to respiratory specialists and for *FCLN* sequencing should be considered (Hopkins et al., 2011).

(p) Allergy to pork should be considered as a rare cause of BCNE in patients with porcine bioprostheses (Fournier et al., 2012).

(q) Although obturator hernia is a rare disease, it must be considered when any underweight woman, not only the elderly, complains of unexplained pain in the groin, thigh, knee, or hip (Toshihiko et al. 2011).

Case formulations conclude with the "Protective" section, where "a patient's strengths, resilience and supports" (Henderson & Martin, 2015: 6) are described, which refer to those character traits as well as any help offered that may contribute to the success of the therapy. In the context of the clinical-diagnostic case reports, however, regarding the question accompanying the Protective element, "What can I rely on" refers to the aspect that is brought on in the current report and recommended to be potentially sought by doctors, i.e. in a diagnosis of a particular condition. In other words, it may be paraphrased as what other potential patients may rely on with respect to the awareness on the part of doctors, who are sensitized to a particular reported problem. Linguistically, one common word used here is the verb "consider", in phrases such as something "should be considered" (o–p), "physicians should consider" as in (m), other verbs with the modal verb "should" (n) or a different modal verb, i.e. "must" (q).

As has been already observed, in case formulations each of the four Ps elements are considered from biological, psychological and social perspectives (see section 4.3.1). In the discussion of the literature on the topic, what was emphasized was not only the elements making up the formulation but also the connections among them (Fernando, Cohen & Henskens, 2012: 121). These "linkages" (Fernando, Cohen & Henskens, 2012: 121) can be identified at the level of language, i.e. resources demonstrating chronology and the resulting cause-and-effect relationship (Cohen, 2006; Rison, Kidd & Koch, 2013). These can be, e.g. "a few days after", indefinite time phrases, e.g. "at the time", "then", or definite, e.g. "1 month previously". Also, numerous phrases with the key element of clinical diagnosis, namely "history", e.g. "have/report/include/describe a history" or "with a unremarkable/ notable/suggestive/significant history of…".

4.6.2.2. *Unique individual*

The results of the examination also show that in the sample analysed what is primarily visible is the biological perspective. This can also be gleaned from the list of keywords of the corpus (vis-à-vis the English Web 2015 enTenTen15 reference corpus), in which those with the highest frequency are symbols for measurement units (e.g. mmol), various abbreviations (e.g. MRCP), or names for tests/diagnostic procedures (e.g. radiograph) or for tests parameters (e.g. creatinine). Only a few comments, however, appear to refer to the quality of patients' lives as affected by the condition described, e.g. (i), (j) or (l) above. Rarely, however, is an account made of the uniqueness of the individual reported on. In these clinical-diagnostic reports, examples of this are those fragments where the author emphasizes the uniqueness of the presented case, i.e. what the case can teach doctors as to what was particularly atypical for the set of symptoms associated with a given problem. In the examples below these are atypical features (r–t and v), less frequent procedures (u) or regimens (w). Yet, what is characteristic of clinical-diagnostic case reports is that the uniqueness tends to be presented as attributed to the case (an instance of occurrence, see section 4.2.1) rather to the patient, although the frequency of occurrence of the word "patient" is twice that of the "case".

(r)   However, our patient's fractures did not show features of such atypical fractures (Yli-Kyyny et al., 2011).

(s)   Our patient had very unusual manifestations of invasive aspergillosis extensively affecting the heart (Brooks et al., 2011).

(t)   Our patient had a rare case of relapsing and afebrile BCNE on porcine bioprostheses (Fournier et al., 2012).

(u)   Spontaneous dissections of cerebral arteries are rare events (23 per 100 000) (Salameh et al., 2011).

(v)   The clinical presentation may include coughing, odynophagia or dysphagia, cervical swelling, fever, and subcutaneous emphysema, or asymptomatic presentation as in our patient (Oliver et al., 2011).

(w)   Our patient received four porcine bioprostheses and various antibiotic regimens, which were prescribed after the diagnoses of BCNE and were unlikely to be the cause of the disease (Fournier et al., 2012).

Linguistically, the uniqueness is signalled, in general, by means of direct reference to the patient, also using the personal plural pronoun referring to the (team of) doctor(s), i.e. "our patient" (r). Adjectives are also used, such as:

- "atypical" (example (r) – which is also combined with "slightly" and modifying "presentation"),
- "unusual" (example (s) – also combined with "rather", "very" and modifying "nature", "presentation", "diagnosis", etc.),
- "rare" (examples (t–u), also combined with "very", "extremely" or "relatively" and modifying "cause", "condition", "presentation", "event", etc.), or
- "unlikely" (example (w), combined with "extremely", "very" and modifying "appearance", "diagnosis", etc.), signalling the uniqueness of the case (see also example (p) above).

In (v) the very use of the word "asymptomatic" signals the uniqueness of the course of the disease.

In the literature review earlier in the chapter, Francis and Kramer-Dahl's (2004) study was mentioned, in which a comparison between a literary text and a case report from neuropsychology was made, with the latter exhibiting similar linguistic features to case formulations. In this analysis, similar features of the presentation of the patient can be observed, such as a goal, i.e. "done to" (2004: 178), e.g. the patient was "treated", "managed", "discharged", "given", etc., and whose responses are "appropriated" (2004: 201) by the author, when the patient is referred to as "reporting", "describing", "admitting", "denying", "revealing", etc.

4.7. CONCLUSIONS

The literature on the topic of psychological/psychiatric case formulations advocates conceptual-structural recommendations for a well-formulated and informative report. These recommendations include not only elements essential to a complete description of the patient's problem but also their interrelations, which emphasize the cause-effect character of the symptoms. As has been demonstrated, in the clinical-diagnostic reports it is possible to determine similar conventions with reference to structure and content, although they deal with conditions of a different kind. This means that analogies can be found both in the way the conditions of the body, as well as of mental health are narrated about. What is more, some elements characteristic of psychiatric case formulations are also suggested as complementary elements to the regular case report, such as centring upon the concept of the unique individual, and thus emphasizing the individuality of the patient and their case. This shows that even in the face of the discipline-specific differences between clinical-diagnostic and psychiatric/psychological practice, the structural models for the two generic varieties belonging to these areas can be complementary, especially at the conceptual level of stressing the individual, which might actually be an instance of added value in the clinical-diagnostic variety, through linguistic emphasis of the patient's perspective. In other words, the unique individual approach may be said to add a more humane touch to its typically objective and impersonal style of case reporting stemming from the very focus on the body and disease manifestations in these reports. Case formulations, on the other hand, may benefit from the more rigid composition of clinical-diagnostic case reporting, adding structure and order to the accounts of mental health which may be seen as less structured and compartmentalized as well as prone to idiosyncratic modifications. The results are believed to constitute potentially instructional material to be used on, for example, Language for Specific Purposes courses where the genre-specific structural features of the clinical-diagnostic case report may be supplemented with insights from psychology and psychiatry, which adds a more patient-centred touch to the text. This is also possible since the current study constitutes a qualitative undertaking supplemented with some quantitative elements, i.e. findings from the computer-aided analysis of the corpus, thus offering observations on chosen linguistic patterns appearing in the genre.

REFERENCES

Agha, R. A., Borrelli, M. R., Farwana, R., Koshy, K., Fowler, A. J., Orgill, D. P. (2018). The SCARE 2018 Statement: Updating Consensus Surgical CAse REport (SCARE) Guidelines. *International Journal of Surgery*, 60: 132–136.

Allen, K. L., O'Hara, C. B., Bartholdy, S., Renwick, B., Keyes, A., Lose, A., Kenyon, M., De-Jong, H., Broadbent, H., Loomes, R., McClelland, J., Serpell, L., Richards, L., Johnson-Sabine, E., Boughton, N., Whitehead, L., Treasure, J., Wade, T., and Schmidt, U. (2016). Written Case Formulations in the Treatment of Anorexia Nervosa: Evidence for Therapeutic Benefits. *International Journal of Eating Disorders*, 49(9): 874–882.

Alyami, H., Sundram, F., Hill, A. G., Alyami, M., and Cheung, G. (2015). Visualizing Psychiatric Formulation. *Australasian Psychiatry*, 23(5): 575–580.

Andrade, B., and Ugalde, O. (2011). Ethical Self-Evidence and the Principle of Proportionality: Two Fundamental Ethical Principles Applied to a Psychiatric Case Report. *Ethical Human Psychology and Psychiatry*, 13(1): 29–46.

Antaki, C., Barnes, R., and Leudar, I. (2005). Diagnostic Formulations in Psychotherapy. *Discourse Studies*, 7(6): 627–647.

Asper, M. (2020). Introduction. In Markus, A. (ed.). *Thinking in Cases: Ancient Greek and Imperial Chinese Case Narratives* (pp. 1–7). Berlin: De Gruyter.

Aston, R. (2009). A Literature Review Exploring the Efficacy of Case Formulations in Clinical Practice. What are the Themes and Pertinent Issues? *The Cognitive Behaviour Therapist*, 2: 63–74.

Baird, J., Hyslop, A., Macfie, M., Stocks, R., and Van der Kleij, T. (2017). Clinical Formulation: Where It Came From, What It Is and Why It Matters. *British Journal of Psychiatry Advances*, 23: 95–103.

Balint, M., Hunt, J., Joyce, D., Marinker, M., and Woodcock, J. (1970). *Treatment or Diagnosis: A Study of Repeat Prescriptions in General Practice*. London: Tavistock.

Barrett, R. J. (1988). Clinical Writing and the Documentary Construction of Schizophrenia. *Culture, Medicine and Psychiatry*, 12: 265–299.

Bavdekar, S. B., and Save, S. (2015). Writing Case Reports: Contributing to Practice and Research. *Journal of the Association of Physicians of India*, 63(4): 44–48.

Beckwith, A., and Crichton, J. (2010). The Negotiation of the Problem Statement in Cognitive Behavioural Therapy. *Communication & Medicine*, 7(1): 23–32.

Berkenkotter, C. (2008). *Patient Tales: Case Histories and the Uses of Narrative in Psychiatry*. Columbia: University of South California Press.

Berkenkotter, C., Hanganu-Bresch, C., and Dreher, K. (2015). "Descriptive psychopathology" in asylum case histories: The case of John Horatio Baldwin. In Gotti, M., Maci, S. M., and Sala, M. (eds.). *The Language of Medicine: Science, Practice and Academia*. CERLIS Series Volume 5 (pp. 49–68). Bergamo: CELSB.

Bolton, J. W. (2014). Case Formulation after Engel – the 4P Model: A Philosophical Case Conference. *Philosophy, Psychiatry, & Psychology*, 21(3): 179–189.

Coderre, S., Mandin, H., Harasym, P. H., and Fick, G. H. (2003). Diagnostic Reasoning Strategies and Diagnostic Success. *Medical Education,* 37: 695–703.

Cohen, H. (2006). How to Write a Patient Case Report. *American Journal of Health-System Pharmacy*, 63(1): 1888–1892.

Cohen, S. M. (2012). Aristotle's Metaphysics (1045a8–10). In *The Stanford Encyclopedia of Philosophy*. http://plato.stanford.edu/archives/sum2012/entries/aristotle-metaphysics/ [accessed 24 June 2020].

Coker, E. M. (2003). Narrative Strategies in Medical Discourse: Constructing the Psychiatric "Case" in a Non-Western Setting. *Social Science & Medicine*, 57: 905–916.

Constand, M., Macdermid, J., Dal Bello-Haas, V., and Law, M. (2014). Scoping Review of Patient-Centered Care Approaches in Healthcare. *BMC Health Services Research*, 14(271). https://bmchealthservres.biomedcentral.com/track/pdf/10.1186/1472-6963-14-271.pdf [accessed 26 June 2020].

Csongor, A. (2013). Rhetorical Moves and Hedging in Medical Research Articles and Their Online Popularizations. Doctoral Dissertation. http://ltsp.etk.pte.hu/portal/wp/File/Doktoriiskola/Tezisfuzetek/CsongorA_dissz.pdf [accessed 2 December 2021].

Davis, R. H. (2015). A Genre Analysis of Medical Research Articles. Doctoral Dissertation. http://theses.gla.ac.uk/6724/1/2015DavisPhd.pdf [accessed 3 January 2021].

Denzin, N. K., and Lincoln, Y. S. (2011). Introduction: The Discipline and Practice of Qualitative Research. In Denzin, N. K., and Lincoln, Y. S. (eds.). *The SAGE Handbook of Qualitative Research* (4th edition) (pp. 1–19). Thousand Oaks, CA: Sage.

Dörnyei, Z. (2007). *Research Methods in Applied Linguistics*. Oxford: Oxford University Press.

Douglas, D. (2017). Foreword. In Sarre, C., and Whyte, S. (eds.). *New Development in ESP Teaching and Learning Research* (pp. xv–xvii). Voillans: Research-publishing.net.

Dudley-Evans, T. (1998). An overview of ESP in the 1990s. Presentation at the Japan Conference on English for Specific Purposes Proceedings (Aizuwakamatsu City, Fukushima, Japan, November 8, 1997). https://files.eric.ed.gov/fulltext/ED424775.pdf [accessed 7 January 2021].

Eells, T. D. (ed.). (2007). *Handbook of Psychotherapy Case Formulation*. New York: The Guilford Press.

Engel, G. L. (1977). The Need for a New Medical Model: A Challenge for Biomedicine. *Science*, 196: 129–136.

Feltovich, P. J., and Barrows, H. S. (1984). Issues of Generality in Medical Problem Solving. In Schmidt, H. G., and de Volder, M. L. (eds.). *Tutorials in Problem-based Learning: New Directions in Training for the Health Professions* (pp. 128–142). Assen, the Netherlands: Van Gorcum.

Fernando, I., Cohen, M., and Henskens, F. (2012). Pattern-Based Formulation: A Methodology for Psychiatric Case Formulation. *Australasian Psychiatry*, 20(2): 121–126.

Fitzgerald, P. E., and Leudar, I. (2012). On the Use of Formulations in Person-Centred, So-lution-Focused Short-Term Psychotherapy. *Communication & Medicine*, 9(1): 13–22.

Flinn, L., Braham, L. and das Nair, R. (2015). How Reliable Are Case Formulations? A Systematic Literature Review. *British Journal of Clinical Psychology*, 54: 266–290.

Flitcroft, A., James, I. A., and Freeston, M. (2007). Determining What is Important in a Good Formulation. *Behavioural and Cognitive Psychotherapy*, 35: 325–333.

Foss, L. (2002). *The End of Modern Medicine: Biomedical Science Under a Microscope*. State University of New York, Albany NY: SUNY Press.

Francis, G., and Kramer-Dahl, A. (2004). Grammar in the Construction of Medical Case Histories. In Coffin, C., Hewings, A., and O'Halloran, K. (eds.). *Applying English Grammar. Functional and Corpus Approaches* (pp. 172–190). London: Hodder Education.

Franklin-Landi, R. (2017). Identifying and Responding to Learner Needs at the Medical Faculty: The Use of Audio-visual Specialized Fiction (FASP). In Sarre, C., and Whyte, S. (eds.). *New Development in ESP Teaching and Learning Research* (pp. 153–170). Voillans: Research-publishing.net.

Fryer, D. L. (2012). Analysis of the Generic Discourse Features of the English-Language Medical Research Article: A Systemic-Functional Approach. *Functions of Language*, 19(1): 5–37.

Gagnier, J., Kienle, G., Altman, D., Moher, D., Sox, H., Riley, D., and the CARE Group. (2013). The CARE Guidelines: Consensus-Based Clinical Case Reporting Guideline Development. *Global Advances in Health and Medicine*, 2(5): 38–43.

Hak, T., and de Boer, F. (1996). Formulations in First Encounters. *Journal of Pragmatics*, 25: 83–99.

Hall, C. S., Lindzey, G., and Campbell, J. B. (1997). *Theories of Personality* (4th edition). New York: Wiley and Sons.

Havighurst, S. S., and Downey, L. (2009). Clinical Reasoning for Child and Adolescent Mental Health Practitioners: The Mindful Formulation. *Clinical Child Psychology and Psychiatry*, 14: 251–271.

Helán, R. (2012). Analysis of Published Medical Case Reports: Genre-based Study. Unpublished Doctoral Dissertation. Masaryk University, Brno.

Henderson, S. W., and Martin, A. (2015). Case Formulation and Integration of Information in Child and Adolescent Mental Health. In Rey, J. M. (ed.). *IACAPAP Textbook of Child and Adolescent Mental Health*. Geneva: International Association for Child and Adolescent Psychiatry and Allied Professions. https://dokumen.tips/reader/f/iacapap-textbook-of-child-and-adolescent-mental-health-case-formulation-a10 [accessed 26 June 2020].

Hirst, A., Agha, R. A., Rosin, D., and McCulloch, P. (2013). How Can We Improve Surgical Research and Innovation?: The IDEAL Framework for Action. *International Journal Surgery*, 11(10): 1038–1042.

Hobson, H. G. (1985). *Forms of Feeling*. London: Tavistock.

Holmes, J., and Hazen, K. (2014). Introduction. In Holmes, J., and Hazen, K. (eds.). *Research Methods in Sociolinguistics: A Practical Guide* (1st edition) (pp. 1–2). Malden, MA: John Wiley & Sons, Inc., Wiley Blackwell.

Huang, D. (2014). Genre Analysis of Moves in Medical Research Articles. *Stylus – A Journal of First Year Writing*, 5(1): 7–17.

Ingram Lichner, B. (2012). *Clinical Case Formulations. Matching the Integrative Treatment Plan to the Client*. Hoboken, NJ: John Wiley & Sons.

Ivančević Otanjac, M., and Milojević, I. (2015). Writing a Case Report in English. *Serbian Archives of Medicine*, 143(1–2): 116–118.

Jellinek, M. S., and McDermott, J. F. (2004). Formulation: Putting the Diagnosis into a Therapeutic Context and Treatment Plan. *Journal of American Academy of Child and Adolescent Psychiatry*, 43(4): 913–916.

Johnstone, L. (2018). Psychological Formulation as an Alternative to Psychiatric Diagnosis. *Journal of Humanistic Psychology*, 58: 1–17.

Klos, D. (1976). Students as Case Writers. *Teaching of Psychology*, 3: 63–66.

Korner, A., Bendit, N., Ptok, U., Tuckwell, K., and Butt, D. (2010). Formulation, Conversation and Therapeutic Engagement. *Australasian Psychiatry*, 18(3): 214–220.

Kuhn, T. S. (1977). *The Essential Tension: Selected Studies in Scientific Tradition and Change*. Chicago: University of Chicago Press.

Labov, W. (1972). The Transformation of Experience in Narrative Syntax. In Labov, W. (ed.). Language in the Inner City (pp. 354–396). Philadelphia: University of Pennsylvania Press.

Laine, C., and Davidoff, F. (1996). Patient-Centered Medicine. A Professional Evolution. *Journal of American Medical Association*, 275(2): 152–156.

Lewis, B. (2014). The Four Ps, Narrative Psychiatry, and the Story of George Engel. *Philosophy, Psychiatry & Psychology*, 21(3): 195–197.

Lowe, E. J. (2005). Self. In Honderich, T (ed.). *Oxford Companion to Philosophy* (2nd edition) (pp. 860). Oxford: Oxford University Press.

Maher, J. (1986). English for Medical Purposes. *Language Teaching*, 19(2): 112–145.

Martin, J. R. (1995). Text and Clause: Fractal Resonance. *Text*, 15(1): 5–42.

Martin, J. R. (2000). Analyzing Genre: Functional Parameters. In Frances, C., and Martin, J. R. (eds.). *Genres and Institutions: Social Processes in the Workplace and School* (pp. 3–39). London, Continuum.

Mason, J. (2002). *Qualitative Researching*. London: Sage.

Mather, N., and Jaffe, L. (2011). *Comprehensive Evaluations: Case Reports for Psychologists, Diagnosticians, and Special Educators*. New Jersey: John Wiley & Sons.

McCulloch, P., Altman, D. G., Campbell, W. B., Flum, D. R., Glasziou, P., Marshall, J. C. (2009). No Surgical Innovation Without Evaluation: The IDEAL Recommendations. *Lancet*, 9695 (374): 1105–1112.

McWhinney, I. R. (2014). The Evolution of Clinical Method. In Stewart, M., Brown, B., Weston, W. W., McWhinney, I. R., McWilliam, C. L., and Freeman, T. R. (eds.). *Patient-Centered Medicine – Transforming the Clinical Method*. London: Radcliffe Publishing.

Mead, N., and Bower, P. (2000). Patient-Centredness: A Conceptual Framework and Review of the Empirical Literature. *Social Science & Medicine*, 51: 1087–1110.

Meares, R. (2000). *Intimacy and Alienation*. London: Routledge.

Meares, R. (2005). *The Metaphor of Play* (3rd edition). London: Routledge.

Méndez-Cendón, B. and López-Arroyo, B. (2003). Intralinguistic Analysis of Medical Research Papers and Abstracts. Rhetorical and Phraseological Devices in Scientific Information. *Terminology*, 9(2): 247–268.

Moran, J. (2010). *Interdisciplinarity*. London: Routledge.

Muntigl, P. (2006). Macrogenre: A Multiperspectival and Multifunctional Approach to Social Interaction. *Linguistics and the Human Sciences*, 2(2): 57–80.

Mureşan, O., and Kic-Drgas, J. (2019). An Analysis of Abstracts in Medical and Economics Journals: Microstructure and Practical Applications. *Glottodidactica*, 46(1): 109–125.

Nguyen, J. T., Shahid, R., and Manera, R. (2014). Writing Case Reports: How to Enjoy the Journey. *Clinical Pediatrics*, 53(14): 1–5.

Nwogu, K. N. (1997). The Medical Research Paper: Structure and Functions. *English for Specific Purposes*, 16(2): 119–138.

Persons, J. B., and Tompkins, M. A. (2007). Cognitive-Behavioral Case Formulation. In Eells T. D. (ed.). *Handbook of Psychotherapy Case Formulation* (pp. 290–316). New York: Guilford.

Repko, A. F. (2008). *Interdisciplinary Research: Process and Theory*. Los Angeles: Sage.

Rison, R. A., Kidd, M. R., and Koch, C. A. (2013). The CARE (CAse REport) Guidelines and the Standardization of Case Reports. *Journal of Medical Case Reports*, 7(261).

Rogers, G. M., Reinecke, M. A., and Curry, J. F. (2005). Case Formulation in TADS CBT. *Cognitive and Behavioral Practice*, 12: 198–208.

Royal Australian and New Zealand College of Psychiatrists. (2012). *Formulation Guidelines for Candidates*. Melbourne: Royal Australian and New Zealand College of Psychiatrists.

Rzepa, T. (2005). *O studium przypadku i portrecie psychologicznym* [On the case formulation and the psychological portrait]. Szczecin: Print Group Daniel Krzanowski.

Savander, E., Pänkäläinen, M., Leiman, M., and Hintikka, J. (2019). Implementation of Dialogical Sequence Analysis as a Case Formulation for the Assessment of Patients at a Community Mental Health Centre: Randomized Controlled Pilot Study. *European Journal of Mental Health*, 14: 209–229.

Schmidt, H. G., Norman, G. R., and Boshuizen, H. P. A. (1990). Cognitive Perspective on Medical Expertise: Theory and Implications. *Academic Medicine*, 65: 611–621.

Selzer, R., and Ellen, S. (2014). Formulation for Beginners. *Australasian Psychiatry*, 4: 397–401.

Shahar, G., and Porcerelli, J. H. (2006). The Action Formulation: A Proposed Heuristic for Clinical Case Formulation. *Journal of Clinical Psychology*, 62(9): 1115–1127.

Shyam, A. (2013). How to Write a Case Report for Journal of Orthopaedic Case Reports – What Do Editor and Reviewer Want? *Journal of Orthopaedic Case Reports*, 3(4): 1–2.

Sim, K., Gwee, K. P., and Bateman, A. (2005). Case Formulation in Psychotherapy: Revitalizing Its Usefulness as a Clinical Tool. *Academic Psychiatry*, 29(3): 289–292.

Smith, G. C. (2014). Revisiting Formulation: Part 1. The Tasks of Formulation: Their Rationale and Philosophical Basis. *Australasian Psychiatry*, 22(1): 23–27.

Smith, G. C., and Strain, J. (2002). George Engel's Contribution to Clinical Psychiatry. *Australian and New Zealand Journal of Psychiatry*, 36: 458–466.

Sperry, L. (1992). Demystifying the Psychiatric Case Formulation. *Jefferson Journal of Psychiatry*, 10(2): 12–19.

Sturmey, P. (2009). *Clinical Case Formulation Varieties of Approaches*. Sussex: John Wiley & Sons.

Sun, G. H., Aliu, O., and Hayward, R. A. (2013). Open-Access Electronic Case Report Journals: The Rationale for Case Report Guidelines. *Journal of Clinical Epidemiology*, 66: 1065–1070.

Swales, J. (1985). *Episodes in ESP*. Oxford: Pergamon Press.

Swales, J. (1990). *Genre Analysis: English in Academic and Research Settings*. Cambridge: Cambridge University Press.

Taavitsainen, I., and Pahta, P. (2000). Conventions of Professional Writing. The Medical Case Report in a Historical Perspective. *Journal of English Linguistics*, 28(1): 60–76.

Toombs, S. K. (1992). *The Meaning of Illness. A Phenomenological Account of the Different Perspectives of Physician and Patient*. Norvell MA: Kluwer Academic.

Tweedie, M. G., and Johnson, R. C. (2022). *Medical English as a Lingua Franca*. Berlin: De Gruyter Mouton.

Uzun, K. (2016). A Genre Analysis of the Methodology Sections of Descriptive Medical – Surgical Nursing Articles. *Journal of Computer and Education Research*, 4(7): 65–81.

Wade, D. T., and Walligan, W. (2004). Do Biomedical Models of Illness Make for Good Healthcare Systems? *British Medical Journal*, 329: 1398–1401.

Walsh, J., Cominos, N., and Jureidini, J. (2016). How Language Shapes Psychiatric Case Formulation. *Communication & Medicine*, 13(1): 99–114.

Wardle, J., and Roseen, E. (2014). Integrative Medicine Case Reports: A Clinicians' Guide to Publication. *Advances in Integrative Medicine*, 1(3): 144–147.

Watts, J. H. (2008). Emotion, Empathy and Exit: Reflections on Doing Ethnographic Qualitative Research on Sensitive Topics. *Medical Sociology Online*, 3(2): 3–14.

Watts, J. H. (2010). Ethical and Practical Challenges of Participant Observation in Sensitive Health Research. *International Journal of Social Research Methodology*, 14(4): 301–312.

Winters, N. C., Hanson, G., and Stoyanova, V. (2007). The Case Formulation in Child and Adolescent Psychiatry. *Child and Adolescent Psychiatric Clinics of North America*, 16: 111–132.

Zabielska, M. (2014). *Searching for the Patient's Presence in Medical Case Reports*. Frankfurt am Main: Peter Lang.

Zabielska, M. (2019a). What a Difference a Case Makes. A Discourse Study of the Patient's Presence in Contemporary Medical Case Reports. *Tertium Linguistic Journal*, 4(1): 257–275.

Zabielska, M. (2019b). Reporting on Individual Experience: A Proposal of a Patient-Centred Model for the Medical Case Report. *Communication & Medicine*, 13(6): 292–303.

Żelazowska-Sobczyk, M., and Zabielska, M. (2016). Case Reporting as a Macro-Genre and Its Metadiscoursal Aspects – A Review of the Literature. *Language and Literary Studies of Warsaw*, 6: 77–108.

Zabielska, M,. and Żelazowska-Sobczyk, M. (2017). A New Variety of Medical Case Reporting as a Tool in ESP Teaching as well as in Medical Training and Professional Development. *Glottodidactica*, 1(44): 181–192.

Żelazowska-Sobczyk, M. (2019). *Polskie i angielskie opisy przypadków medycznych w ujęciu kontrastywnym* [Polish and English medical case reports in confrontative framing]. Warszawa: Wydawnictwo Naukowe Instytutu Komunikacji Specjalistycznej i Interkulturowej Uniwersytet Warszawski.

Żelazowska-Sobczyk, M., and Zabielska, M. (2019a). Polskojęzyczne opisy przypadku z zakresu psychiatrii i psychologii – model tekstowy czy wyjątek? Część I [Case reports in the field of psychiatry and psychology in Polish – a text model or an exception? Part I]. *Applied Linguistics Papers*, 26(1): 65–83.

Żelazowska-Sobczyk, M., and Zabielska, M. (2019b). Polskojęzyczne opisy przypadku z zakresu psychiatrii i psychologii – model tekstowy czy wyjątek? Część II [Case reports in the field of psychiatry and psychology in Polish – a text model or an exception? Part II]. *Applied Linguistics Papers*, 26(2): 1–19.

Publication examples discussed

Brooks, M., Royse, C., Eisen, D., Sparks, P., Bhagwat, K. and Royse, A. (2011). An Accidental Mass. *Lancet*, 377: 1806.

Creighton, Jr. F. X., Leeds, I. J., Master, A. V., and Srinivasan, J. K. (2013). Learning from Haiti. *Lancet*, 377: 205.

Fournier, P.-E., Thuny, F., Grisoli, D., Lepidi, H., and Vitte, J. (2012). A Deadly Aversion to Pork. *Lancet*, 377: 1542.

Hopkins, T. G., Maher, E. R., Reid, E., and Marciniak, S. J. (2011). Recurrent Pneumothorax. *Lancet*, 377: 1624.

Miller, P. E., Zurflu, E., and Jaipaul, C. K. (2011). Return of the Usual Suspect. *Lancet*, 377: 2150.

Oliver, M., Haag, S., Ulrich, S., and Naglatzki, R. (2011). A Loose Screw or Two. *Lancet*, 377: 782.

Prasad, N., Ghiya, B. C., Bumb, R. A., Kaushal, H., Saboskar, A. A., Lezama-Davila, C. M., Salotra, P., and Satoskar, A. R. (2011). Heat, Oriental Sore, and HIV. *Lancet*, 377: 610.

Salameh, A., Klein, M., Klein, N., Pfeiffer, D., Dähnert, I., and Dhein, S. (2011). Coughing into the Darkness. *Lancet*, 377: 1718.

Toshihiko, T., Ikusaka, M., Ohira, Y., Noda, K., and Tsukamoto, T. (2011). Paroxysmal Hip Pain. *Lancet*, 377: 1464.

Yli-Kyyny, T., Tamminen, I., Syri, J., Venesmaa, P., and Kröger, H. (2011). Bilateral Hip Pain. *Lancet*, 377: 2248.

ABOUT THE AUTHOR

Magdalena Zabielska, with a PhD in linguistics, is an Assistant Professor in the Department of Sociolinguistics and Discourse Studies at the Faculty of English at Adam Mickiewicz University in Poznań, Poland. She is particularly interested in the issue of the patient's presence in specialist medical publications in the context of the patient-centred approach to medical practice. She has published a number of papers regarding case-reporting genres.

5

The application of projective techniques to render linguistic repertoires of plurilingual language learners at the tertiary level

Emilia Wąsikiewicz-Firlej

ABSTRACT

The chapter takes a look at projective techniques and their application across disciplines. It goes back to the psychoanalytical foundations of the concept and traces its historical development. Various types of projective techniques are presented, followed by a critical discussion on the advantages and disadvantages of their employment in research. The very concept of "projection" is attributed to Sigmund Freud (Breuer & Freud, 1895). It involves transferring (projecting) unconscious and frequently suppressed beliefs to another person or object in order to protect one's ego. The term "projective techniques", advanced by Frank (1939), might be basically defined as questioning techniques "that depersonalize the question to the respondent thereby desensitizing the respondent to the answer they give and deactivating their conscious defences about the answer they give" (Das, 2018: 10) The first applications of the techniques took place within the field of clinical psychology, where they were mostly used in psychoanalysis or personality assessment. Within a decade they were adopted in management and marketing research. In fact, nowadays their usage in consumer and marketing communication research is in its heyday and is often considered to be superior to other research methods (cf. Kaczmarek et al., 2013). To some extent, projection techniques have been also adopted in linguistic research (e.g. Labov attitude research), however, contemporarily their use in this field is rather marginalised. This could be explained by certain controversies surrounding their application in psychometric testing as well as a massive paradigm shift towards the quantitative research approach in the last decades of the previous century. The main premise of this chapter, however, is that their use in the field of applied linguistics (as defined by Evensen, 2013) should be revisited, as they offer a unique potential for obtaining deep, meaningful responses from respondents. This is particularly valid in the case of research into sensitive issues such as, e.g. one's ethnic, cultural or family background. The full potential of projective techniques will be illustrated by a study on the language portraits (Busch, 2018; Kusters & Meulder, 2019) of plurilingual language learners at the tertiary level of education, in order to show how they can reduce social desirability bias and enhance reflection and self-expression through verbal and visual modes.

Keywords: projective techniques, language portrait, linguistic repertoire, plurilingualism, language awareness, language learning awareness

5.1. INTRODUCTION

The lion's share of previous studies on linguistic repertoires focused on individuals (mostly children) from multilingual families with migrant experience, or multilingual communities (e.g. Odeniyi & Lazar, 2020). The present study investigates the individual plurilingual repertoires of young adults – students of applied linguistics, who represent model European citizens in terms of the recommended command of at least two foreign languages. Their language competencies have not, however, been developed in the course of migrant experience or interaction with multilingual communities. All the respondents were raised in monolingual Poland, and their plurilingual repertoires were mostly developed through formal and informal learning at different stages of their lives. For this reason, the potential unevenness of their repertoires, or their "truncated" (Blommaert, 2010: 103) character might be assumed.

The aim of the research is not, however, to generate a list of the foreign languages mastered by the participants, specifying their proficiency level and order in which they were learned. The study takes into account the subjective aspects of language learning, emphasised by Kramsch (2009: 60): "[f]ar from being perceived as primarily a tool for communication and exchange of information, the foreign language is first and foremost experienced physically, linguistically, emotionally, artistically". Thus, the study focuses on language attitudes and emotional aspects of "lived experience of language" (Busch, 2018: 6). Additionally, it aims to uncover the often unconscious ideologies underlying language learning and use, represented by common stereotypes concerning perceived language "value" or "economy", ascribing to particular languages' various characteristics or the presumed advantages/disadvantages that might play a detrimental role in taking the decision to learn them (Council of

Europe, 2007: 12–13). The specific aims of the study investigating the multimodal (verbal-visual) representation of the individual plurilingual repertoires of young adults were translated into the following research questions (hereafter RQs):

> RQ1: How is an individual's linguistic repertoire represented in pictorial form?
> RQ2: How is an individual's linguistic repertoire represented in verbal form?
> RQ3: What values and emotions are associated with particular languages?

To obtain meaningful responses from the participants concerning their plurilingual repertoires, and to get an insight into their life experiences and the ideologies underlying them, as well as inspire reflection on language learning, the study revisits the application of projective techniques. Although widely applied in psychology and marketing research, projective techniques have attracted significant criticism. Thus, in order to take advantage of their benefits and overcome their limitations, the current paper advances a mixed-method/multimodal approach to study plurilingual repertoires that combines creative methods with a semi-structured interview, traditionally used in sociolinguistics. The language portrait (Busch, 2018) is used both as a data-elicitation tool and visual narrative. Special heed is paid to the potential of visual stimuli and a body silhouette to stimulate figurative language use by the respondents (see e.g. Coffey, 2015) to present their linguistic repertoires and articulate their embodied language experience. The metaphors verbalised in the interview are analysed quantitatively and qualitatively to uncover individual conceptualisations of the body and language vis-à-vis cultural conceptualisations (cf. Peters & Coetzee-Van Rooy, 2020).

The chapter is structured in the following way: section 5.2 discusses the notions of plurilingualism and linguistic repertoire, and situates plurilingualism in the context of language learning. Section 5.3 revisits projective techniques and overviews their application across disciplines with the aim of advancing methodological solutions to study plurilingual repertoires. In section 5.4, the methodological framework for the study is set forth, including the description of the research design, participants as well as data elicitation and analysis. Section 5.5 presents and discusses the qualitative and quantitative results of the multimodal analysis of language portraits and interview data. Section 5.6 reviews the applied methodological solution and examines its benefits and drawbacks. Conclusions are contained in section 5.7.

5.2. THEORETICAL FRAMEWORK FOR THE STUDY

Lifelong learning (LLL), one of the educational principles of the European Union, is nowadays seen as a must for individuals and organisations. It is defined as "all learning activity undertaken throughout life, with the aim of improving knowledge, skills and competences within a personal, civic, social and/or employment-related perspective" (Council of the European Union, 2002: 163–162). Language learning and communicating in foreign languages are among key skills for lifelong learning that need to be acquired to enhance EU citizens' educational and employment opportunities (European Commission, 2007; Council of Europe, 2007). According to the European Commission's recent recommendation (COM(2017)0673), advanced at the Social Summit held on 17 November 2017 in Gothenburg, by 2025 "in addition to one's mother tongue, speaking two other languages has become the norm" (European Commission, 2017). Apart from being an asset, leveraging individuals, plurilingual competencies also contribute to European integration by fostering political, economic and cultural cohesion. In the *Common European Framework of Reference for Languages,* plurilingualism is defined as:

> [t]he ability to use languages for the purposes of communication and to take part in intercultural interaction, where a person, viewed as a social agent, has proficiency of varying degrees, in several languages, and experience of several cultures. This is not seen as the superposition or juxtaposition of distinct competences, but rather as the existence of a complex or even composite competence on which the user may draw. (Council of Europe, 2001: 168)

The Council of Europe (2007), along with other researchers (e.g. Lüdi & Py, 2009; Marshall and Moore, 2013; Piccardo, 2013), differentiates between plurilingualism and multilingualism, where the former is seen as an individual characteristic and the latter a "societal phenomenon" (García & Otheguy, 2019: 5). In the guide for language education prepared by the Council of Europe (2007: 8) the two concepts are defined in the following way:

> – "multilingualism" refers to the presence in a geographical area, large or small, of more than one "variety of language" i.e. the mode of speaking of a social group whether it is formally recognised as a language or not; in such an area individuals may be monolingual speaking only their own variety.

> – "plurilingualism" refers to languages not as objects but from the point of view of those who speak them. It refers to the repertoire of varieties of language which many individuals use, and is therefore the opposite of monolingualism; it includes the language variety referred to as "mother tongue" or "first language" and any number of other languages or varieties. Thus in some multilingual areas some individuals

may be monolingual and some may be plurilingual. (Council of Europe, 2007: 8)

This distinction is also clearly explained by Marshall and Moore (2013: 474), who use the term "plurilingual(ism) to refer to the unique aspects of individual repertoires and agency, and multilingual(ism) to refer to broader social language context/contact(s) and the coexistence of several languages in a particular situation". Bearing in mind the criticism of the term *plurilingual(ism)*, mostly on the grounds of it being ideologically loaded and promoting a neoliberal agenda (see discussion in Marshall & More, 2018), it will be used throughout this paper in reference to individuals' linguistic repertoire and language competences.

5.2.1. The notion of linguistic repertoire

The concept of linguistic or verbal repertoire was originally developed by Gumperz (1965) who defined it as: "the totality of linguistic forms regularly employed within the community in the course of a socially significant interaction. Repertoires, in turn, can be regarded as consisting of speech varieties, each associated with particular kinds of social relationships" (Gumperz, 1965: 85). Accordingly, verbal repertoires are related to a given speech community, sharing a set of social norms and values concerning language use. Given the growing global mobility and the emergence of "super-diversity" (Vertovec, 2007), the concept needs to be revisited.

In response to these changes, Blommaert (2008) put forward the idea of a "polyglot repertoire", a new concept accounting for all the linguistic resources available to an individual, rather than discreet languages. Blommaert (2010) further argues that individuals are no longer members of a fixed community. Instead, they are characterised by mobility, which makes their cultural and linguistic backgrounds hard to predict. Accordingly, people's linguistic repertoires are not static but are affected by life and learning experiences. As Blommaert (2010: 170) suggests, a "polyglot repertoire (...) is not tied to any form of 'national' space, and neither to a national, stable regime of language. It is tied to an individual's life and it follows the peculiar trajectory of the speaker". Blommaert (2010: 103) also points to the fact that "[n]o one knows all of a language", which pertains both to our native language as well as "the other 'languages' we acquire in our lifetime". Taking into account the phenomena of globalisation and migration, Blommaert argues that multilingual repertoires of individuals with migration experiences, drawing on different languages, are "truncated", since parts of them "will be fairly developed, while others exist only at a very basic level" (Blommaert, 2010: 106). In this view, polyglot repertoires go beyond linguistic competence and might be interpreted as a set of unevenly deployed resources (Blommaert & Backus, 2011). Such truncated repertoires, "composed of specialized but partially and unevenly developed resources" (Blommaert, 2010: 23), account for various language resources that might be maximally, partially or minimally developed. Thus, depending on their life and learning experience, individuals might have different levels of proficiency in a given language and their truncated repertoires epitomise "a patchwork of skills" (Blommaert & Backus, 2012). The notion of truncated repertoires was, however, criticised by Canagarajah (2013: 10) who found it concomitant with deficient. Instead, the scholar emphasised translingual practice that enables individuals, especially with migration backgrounds, to enhance their communicative competence by employing all their available language resources. De Houwer (2009), for example, distinguishes between simultaneous bilinguals, who were raised in two languages, and consecutive bilinguals, who began as monolinguals but learned or acquired a second language at a later stage of their lives (De Houwer, 2009).

5.2.2. Plurilingualism and language learning

This paper, however, focuses on developing individual language repertoire through language learning, rather than acquisition. It must be emphasised that in this particular context, the concept of plurilingualism has indeed had a tangible impact on foreign language learning and teaching, and has led to the verification of traditional educational approaches. First of all, it swerved away from the dominant concept of "balanced bilingual competence" towards the appreciation of the role of the first language in learning foreign languages, as well as focusing on the individual's actual linguistic repertoire. Additionally, it brings extra value to education by its potential to contribute to the development of language awareness and tolerance (García and Otheguy, 2019: 6).

The process of language learning is perceived and experienced by individuals in different ways. As formulated by the Council of Europe (2007: 8): "[p]lurilingualism develops throughout life: individuals may acquire new languages and lose old ones at different points in their lives for different purposes and needs". Therefore, developing one's plurilingual repertoire is highly personalised, as it draws on life experiences and biographical trajectories (Blommaert & Backus, 2012). Throughout a lifetime, the plurilingual repertoire is affected by dynamically changing, often unpredictable, circumstances related to an individual's life choices and needs (Blommaert & Backus, 2012). For this reason, it does not remain stable but undergoes transformations, often dictated by altering placements, as well as professional, personal or family situations (Blommaert & Rampton, 2011). Repertoires, therefore, trace intricate paths of human life and, as such, they do not take a straightforward linear form (Blommaert & Backus, 2012: 9). The scholars (ibid., 24) also add that repertoires document "the trajectories followed by people throughout their lives: the opportunities, constraints and inequalities".

5.3. METHODOLOGICAL CONSIDERATIONS

5.3.1. The origins and development of projective techniques

Projective techniques are rooted in the concept of "projection", attributed to Sigmund Freud (Breuer & Freud, 1895). Projection involves transferring (projecting) unconscious and frequently suppressed beliefs, traits or desires to another person or object, to protect one's ego. The term "projective techniques", advanced by Frank (1939), might be defined as questioning techniques "that depersonalize the question to the respondent thereby desensitizing the respondent to the answer they give and deactivating their conscious defences about the answer they give" (Das, 2018: 10). In classical psychoanalysis, psychological projection involves attributing one's qualities, emotions or predispositions to others, often with an implication that those verbalised aspects are negated by the individual and the projection acts as a defensive, fear-suppressing mechanism (Reber & Reber, 2008: 583).

The application of projective techniques was initiated in clinical psychology for the purposes of personality assessment and psychoanalysis (Bellak, 1992). Its rise was underpinned by a hypothesis assuming that "research participants project aspects of their personalities in the process of disambiguating unstructured test stimuli" (Bond, Ramsey & Boddy, 2011: 3). In other words, projective techniques depersonalise questions and enable the respondent to distance themselves from their responses and disarm the process of their conscious defence (Boddy, 2005; Ramsey, Ibbotson & McCole, 2006).

Nowadays, they are mostly used in qualitative research in group or individual interviews, often as a supplementary or activating tool. Yet, it must be noted that their application raises certain controversies, and has both staunch advocates and opponents questioning the reliability and validity of projective research results (Boddy, 2005). The popularity of projective techniques peaked after WWII, along with their application in marketing and consumer research (e.g. Haire, 1950). Their popularity, however, was dramatically curbed in the 1970s by the development of computer technologies fostering the use of quantitative methods, along with the criticism voiced in some academic circles. At the end of the 20th century, however, a systematically growing interest in projective techniques, especially in marketing and consumer research, could be observed (Belk, 2006).

5.3.2. Types of projective techniques

The application of projective techniques, widely used in psychological and marketing research, involves providing stimuli in visual or textual form that is to be further interpreted by the research participant. In contrast to "objective" methods, projective techniques do not impose any restrictions on the research participant and enable them to give free responses (Wagner, 2008). Such an approach enhances the exposure of hidden desires, fears and complexes that an individual might not be aware of. Importantly, such techniques can be successfully used in research with both adults and children.

In psychology, the most widely applied, though often criticised, techniques embrace the Rorschach technique, also known as the "inkblot test", where the subjects are exposed to a defined set of blots of ink that are assumed to inspire the projection of their personalities (Graca & Whiddon, 1990). Apart from inkblots, projective techniques might draw on quite a range of unstructured stimuli such as vague and ambiguous visuals (e.g. pictures, drawings, photographs), language stimuli (e.g. word or phrases) or materials such as paper or modelling clay, which stimulate different manners of interpretation and types of responses or behaviours on the part of the informant. In this context, it seems well-substantiated to look at the classification advanced by Lindzey (1959) who has grouped a large variety of projective tools into five categories:

- **Associative techniques** in which a particular stimulus is used to elicit the first word, image or precept that comes to the subject's mind, exemplified by the Rorschach inkblot test (e.g. Rorschach, 1921).[1]
- **Completion techniques** in which the subject is required to finish incomplete sentences or drawings, such as the Washington University Sentence Completion Test (e.g. Loevinger, 1976).
- **Constructive techniques** in which the subject is required to produce something, e.g. a story, drawing, sculpture, such as the Thematic Apperception Test (e.g. Murray & Morgan, 1943).
- **Arrangement/selection techniques** in which the subject is required to make selections from a group, or to rank groups (of pictures, sentences, etc.) based on their perceived attractiveness or preference, such as the Szondi Test (e.g. Szondi, 1947).
- **Expressive techniques** in which, in response to particular stimuli, the subject is required to perform certain activities, such as expressive processes, like role-playing, psychodrama, dance, etc., exemplified by Projective puppet play (Woltmann, 1960) or the Luscher Color Test (Luscher & Scott, 1969).

The very classification of the techniques themselves illustrates core differences "in the ideation, activities and creations of research participants" (Belk, 2006: 145). Yet, as further noted by the scholar (ibid.), such methodological diversity might be both

---

1   The author is fully aware of the criticism targeted at the Rorschach inkblot test and its rejection in certain psychological circles. It is, however, mentioned in the historical context to illustrate the development of projective techniques and address controversies it might raise. Criticism of projective techniques is addressed in section 5.3.4.

a blessing and a curse. On the one hand, projective research draws on rich data that fosters nuanced analyses and gives insights into the respondent's opinions, beliefs, feelings and imaginations. Additionally, a variety of techniques facilitates triangulation. On the other hand, apart from the most recognised projective methods in psychology (e.g. the TAT, Rorschach or the Rosenzweig Picture-Frustration test) that have been profoundly examined and verified, other projective paradigms have not been subjected to sufficient scrutiny, which might be daunting for researchers.

5.3.3. Benefits and drawbacks of projective techniques

Irrespective of certain criticisms, projective techniques are successfully used across disciplines, for example, in psychology (Clark, 1995), consumer research (Chang, 2001), marketing (Chandler & Owen, 2002) or educational research (Catterall & Ibbotson, 2000). Since their first successful use in market research in the early 1950s (Haire, 1950), projective techniques have been particularly highly appreciated in this and other business-related fields of study (Boddy, 2005).

One of the key benefits offered by projective techniques is their potential to help respondents access their deeply held attitudes, beliefs or feelings, which might otherwise remain unrecognised, and verbalise them. This aspect corresponds with the Freudian concept of *primary motivations* stemming from basic urges and instincts (Freud, 1911). Owing to the ability of projective techniques to encourage the respondent to give "honest" answers and reveal their actual feelings and opinions, the data obtained is relatively unaffected by *social desirability bias* (Belk, 2006: 146).

Apart from fostering access to respondents' subconscious mental processes and their true opinions and beliefs, projective techniques are also appreciated for facilitating the elicitation of in-depth responses. By and large, they stimulate the elicitation of more emotional, imaginative or creative responses expressed in the respondent's behaviours, verbalisations or visualisations, ultimately generating data of a more symbolic, metaphorical or aesthetic value (Belk, 2006: 146). Compared to standard qualitative research instruments, the whole data-elicitation process may also be more stimulating and engaging for respondents, and thus increase their willingness to cooperate and provide valuable responses, opening new vistas for researchers. Additionally, most respondents have not been exposed to projective techniques and are naturally interested in the research purpose, their own and other's answers and their interpretation (cf. Das, 2018: 12).

A comprehensive list of benefits offered by projective techniques has been compiled by Springer (2013: 165–166) and presented below:

- identification of unconscious behaviours,
- identification of seemingly irrational decisions,
- reducing conformist behaviours,

- spurring creativity,
- overcoming the limitations of consumers' mental processes,
- recognising emotions accompanying consumers' cognitive processes,
- overcoming communication problems (especially those experienced by intro-verted respondents or respondents with low communicative competencies),
- reducing internal control (more tolerance for unrestricted behaviours, reduc-ing experienced shame),
- reducing the researcher's influence (due to an ambiguous research aim, lack of the "right" solution, difficulty in identifying the researcher's expectations),
- revealing thematically new content (Springer, 2013: 165–166; transl. EWF).

Taking into account the benefits offered by projective techniques, their use is par-ticularly recommended when the information elicited from respondents is sensitive, difficult to verbalise, or respondents find it difficult to be aware of their behaviour. Additionally, their application is also well-substantiated in the case of group re-search, as a means of stimulating the participants and diversifying their activity, as well as to minimise the effects of the group influence, such as group-think, group conformism or polarisation (cf. Belk, 2006: 146–150).

5.3.4. Criticism of projective techniques

Undoubtedly, projective techniques are an effective tool for eliciting data that pro-vide rich material for further analysis. This richness might be, however, a serious challenge to the researcher, who must often confront chaotic, unstructured data and find reliable methods to interpret them. Such analysis should always be guid-ed by the research questions posed and be subject to them. Data analysis skills re-quire not only psychological knowledge but are also developed through experience. In this context, it seems worth looking at Table 5.1, illustrating possible problems and consequences related to the application of projective methods that has been ad-vanced by Springer (2013: 167).

Apart from the aforementioned problems, major scepticism concerning projec-tive methods centres on their low reliability and validity, as well as failure to provide measurement norms (Belk, 2006: 151). Particularly harsh criticism has been voiced by Yoell (1974), who considers them "scientifically illegal" and questions their abil-ity to access the deep layers of the psyche that remain inaccessible in standard inter-viewing procedures, arguing that the responses obtained reflect cultural and social awareness rather than projecting unconscious thoughts and emotions. Paradoxical-ly, what Yoell and others (1974) found unacceptable a couple of decades earlier, is today considered desirable by consumer researchers. With the prevailing cultural turn in much consumer research, projective techniques are employed for what they

Table 5.1 Problems emerging at particular stages of the use of projective techniques

Stage	Problems	Consequences
Preparation	Use of ready-made or specially prepared, individual examples of tasks	An inappropriately prepared technique may not provide relevant information for solving the research problem
	Specific or general instructions for implementing the study	Instructions that are too detailed, limiting projections. Instructions that are too general – different people may understand the instructions differently, making it impossible to compare the results
Realisation	Lack of acceptance of this form of activity by participants (especially older people)	A sense of disregard, lack of trust and, as a consequence, a deep analysis – unwillingness to provide answers
	Low involvement of participants in the task	A small amount of material to analyse
	Misunderstanding or miscommunication	Low activity of participants
Interpretation	Attaching importance to each statement or looking for a recurring trend	Overgeneralisation – an individual characteristic is treated as a group characteristic
		Downplaying of individual statements – poor conclusions drawn
	Deep psychological interpretation	Too shallow an analysis – remaining at the level of behaviour
		Too deep an analysis – unauthorised conclusions, e.g. about personality traits

Source: Springer, 2013: 167 (transl. EWF)

can reveal about consumer products and brands as cultural symbols along with the myths that surround them (Durgee, 1988; Levy, 1994).

In order to ensure research validity and reliability, projective techniques are usually employed in combination with other quantitative and qualitative research techniques. Word association, sentence completion and bubble cartoons can be incorporated into interviewer-administered or self-completion questionnaires (Oppenheim, 1992). Other techniques, such as storytelling or personification techniques, are more appropriately employed in class discussions or focus groups. When projective techniques are introduced at an early stage in group discussions, the responses they generate can provide ideas and new perspectives for further discussion (Will et al., 1996). Clark (1995) suggested that they could be used in the counselling process for similar reasons.

5.3.5. Language portraits

The language portrait method, developed in Vienna by the group Spracherleben (Busch, 2016), qualifies as a projective technique. In language portrait research, participants are asked to choose a colour representing a language they know or that they are somehow connected with. Then they colour different languages inside a body silhouette by placing them in different parts of the body. The language portrait symbolically embodies one's linguistic repertoire and uncovers the socio-affective embedding of particular languages as well as the respondent's attitudes towards them (Busch, 2018; Soares et al., 2020: 2). As Busch (2018) explains:

> The silhouette suggests a structuring according to parts of the body, which may refer to common metaphors such as the head as the place of reason, the belly as the place of emotions, the heart as the location of intimacy and the hand as the site of social activity. Structuring is also frequently achieved with the help of spatial metaphors – internal/external as metaphors for familiar and unfamiliar, above/below, for example, for current and more remote, large/small surfaces for important and less important. In drawings iconic elements (such as arrow, lightning, heart), symbols (national flag) or ornaments are also frequently used. Colours, too, or different colour shades, are employed partly in the sense of common connotations (e.g. red for the emotional, blue as a "cool" colour, light for what has a positive, dark for what has a negative connotation), but also because they are associated with personal preferences (favourite colours) or aversions.
>
> (Busch, 2018: 10)

Language portrait research was initiated by Gogolin and Neumann (1991) who studied the language awareness of primary school children. Language portraits were also used in research investigating the relationship between language and identity in bi- and multilinguals in Europe (Krumm, 2013) and South Africa (e.g. Dressler, 2014; Prasad, 2014; Lau, 2016). In her classroom-situated research, Busch (2010, 2012, 2018) stimulated reflections on multilingualism in educational settings to raise language awareness and ultimately enhance language education policies in multilingual education in South Africa. Dressler (2014) points to the benefits of conducting language portraits activity in groups. In this context, the visual materials generated foster class discussion and enable students to express their linguistic identities and make them and the teacher aware of the diversity of linguistic repertoires in the classroom. Importantly, increasing the visibility of the whole repertoire of languages in the classroom legitimises them and leads to multilingual students' empowerment and open-mindedness (Hélot et al., 2018). The empowering potential of language portraits as a tool for expressing children's diverse linguistic identities, without constraining them to a particular language, was also noted by Prasad (2014).

The subsequent language portraits studies have been predominantly centred on children respondents in multilingual school settings. The novelty of the current study lies in the selection of plurilingual young adult participants, raised and educated in monolingual settings. Additionally, the research undertaken aims to contribute to a fledgling trend in language repertoires that focuses on the analysis of the metaphors generated by language portraits, and is represented by very few studies. For example, Coffey (2015) analyses language portraits produced by teacher candidates. Peters and Coetzee-Van Rooy (2020) employ a corpus approach to the study of metaphors generated by 105 South African multilingual students. The lived experiences of South African students were also studied by Botsis and Bradbury (2018). Similarly to Botsis and Bradbury (2018: 414), in the current paper, the visual portrait is not only treated as a stimulus for narration, but also as a trigger for shifting the participants into a creative modality that inspires figurative language use and equips participants with new lexical resources to verbalise their experiences.

5.4. RESEARCH DESIGN

In order to address the research questions posed (see Introduction), a concurrent mixed-method/multimodal approach was employed (Creswell, 2014). First, language portrait research was conducted to visualise the students' linguistic repertoires and explore their emotions, ideologies and attitudes associated with language(s) (Busch, 2018). After the completion of the previously mentioned task, semi-structured interviews were employed (Galletta and Cross, 2013). This kind of interview offers a compromise between the structured and unstructured interview format (Dörnyei, 2007: 135). Thus, they are "organized around a set of predetermined open-ended questions, with other questions emerging from the dialogue between interviewer and interviewee/s'" (DiCicco-Bloom & Crabtree, 2006: 315). The interview draws on a fixed protocol that is supplemented with follow-up questions, probes or comments that enable the interviewee to elaborate on particular issues (Dörnyei, ibid.). Semi-structured interviews are commonly used in qualitative research to gather open-ended data to explore participants' personal experiences, attitudes, perceptions, feeling and beliefs related to the topic under study, in order to "understand the world from the subjects' point of view, to unfold the meaning of peoples' experiences, to uncover their lived world prior to scientific explanations" (Kvale, 1996: 1). As this method typically takes the form of a conversation between the interviewer and interviewee (e.g. Hatch, 2002: 91), researchers often emphasise its relational character and see it as "a shared product of what two people – one the interviewer, the other the interviewee – talk about and how they talk together" (Josselson, 2013: 1).

Importantly, the visual portrait in this study is not treated merely as a stimulus for eliciting verbal data. Although it might act as a trigger activating the participant's creativity and alternative language resources to narrate an interpretive story on their language experiences for themselves and the interviewer (cf. Botsis & Bradbury: 2018: 414), the visual portraits and their verbalised descriptions are treated as complementary parts of the whole narration, following Riessman's (2008: 143) reflection that "just as oral and written narratives cannot speak for themselves, neither can images".

Additionally, the analysis of the multimodal, visual and discursive representations of linguistic repertoires, draws on the works of Lakoff and Johnson (1980, 1999) on the formation of metaphor. As the authors purport (1999), our language is permeated with metaphors that are rooted in "the flesh" – the bodily experience – and as such, they act as "a constituent of the bodily-sensory system of orientation" (Busch, 2018: 11). From this perspective, the language portrait is construed as a space constructed and customised by metaphors, providing data for the analysis at different "modes of understanding" (Lakoff & Johnson, 1999: 106). Thus, the language portraits are interpreted as the participants' embodied cultural-cognitive conceptualisations of their linguistic repertoires represented by the selection of colour and placements for particular languages on the body silhouette.

5.4.1. Participants

There were 19 participants in the wider study, all students or recent graduates of applied linguistics, with German and English as leading languages (n=19), five men and fourteen women, aged 21–23 (mean=22.1). All the respondents are Polish and speak Polish as their first language. This paper presents three cases, selected to represent three divergent visual and verbal representations of the plurilingual repertoires of individuals of seemingly similar sociolinguistic backgrounds, namely Edyta, Renata and Beata (pseudonyms) whose more detailed profiles will be presented in section 5.5.2.

5.4.2. Data collection procedure

The data were gathered by trained student research assistants in May 2020 who conducted interviews with volunteer participants. Due to the COVID-19 restrictions, all interviews were conducted online. The participants were informed about the aims of the study and expressed their consent to be audio-recorded. Before the interview, they were instructed by the research assistants to prepare their language

Figure 5.1 Stimulus material for the language portrait study. Source: Busch (2018: 9)

portraits, by colouring in the A-4 template of a body silhouette (Busch, 2010, 2012, 2018).

The participants were informed that they were free to choose how, in the self-portrait, they wanted to represent the language(s) that they speak, have been exposed to, or want to learn. It was emphasised that the self-portrait was not limited to languages in which the participants felt competent. The participants were also asked to create a caption and to designate or clarify the individual colour entries. The request to present the portrait normally results in a more, or less detailed spontaneous narrative, which could be supported by questions concerning the significance of a particular colour choice or location of particular elements in the picture (Busch, 2018: 7–9). Altogether, 19 portraits were gathered that were further digitised. They were audio-recorded and transcribed *verbatim*, following the transcription conventions put forward by Boje (1991) included in Appendix 1. Before the interview, the interviewees were informed that their identities would remain anonymous and research confidentiality would be ensured. The interviewees gave their informed oral consent to have their interviews recorded and transcribed. The length of the individual interviews differed, ranging in the whole corpus from 9.43 to 40.54 minutes (mean: 15.51). In the analysed case studies, the interviews lasted, respectively, 26.54 (Edyta), 40.54 (Renata) and 22.26 minutes (Beata).

5.4.3. Data analysis

The data were analysed in different stages. First, the whole corpus of data, including the portraits and interview audios transcripts, underwent close reading and listening. Second, the data from the language portrait were processed quantitatively, to illustrate the dominant trends in the visual representation (colour and body placement) of the respondents' key languages, i.e. Polish, English and German. Third, three case studies were selected from the corpus for a more detailed qualitative analysis that embraced a descriptive multimodal analysis of their visual and verbal contents. The verbal data were divided into themes and subjected to further metaphor analysis.

5.5. RESULTS AND DISCUSSION

5.5.1. Quantitative analysis: Language portraits

All of the participants were native speakers of Polish with knowledge of English and German at a comparable level, ranging from B2 to C1, as well as a less advanced competence in at least one more foreign language, in most cases a European one (e.g. Spanish, French, Russian, Norwegian, etc.). The participants marked between 4–7 languages on the portrait (mean=5.2) but the analysis will be only limited to Polish, English and German, as the languages shared by all participants.

It is clear from Table 5.2 that the visual representation of the three languages is not consistent, as the respondents used a palette of nine colours. One respondent used the national flags to represent each language. Nevertheless, almost half of the participants (n=9) coded the Polish language red. The other two languages were represented in a similar way either in blue or green.

As Table 5.2 illustrates, overall the most prominent placement of languages on the human body head, heart, hand and leg (cf. Coffey, 2015). For the purpose of the analysis, results for related areas on the silhouette (such as an arm or hand) will be presented together since participants refer to them interchangeably.

It is also clear from Table 5.2 that the representation of the three languages as parts of the body on the silhouette varies. The most prominent placement for Polish, the respondents' native language, is *head* (n=5) or *head and heart* (3) as well as the whole body (n=4). For both English and German, the most preferable location is on hands (n=10 and n=11, respectively). German also tends to be placed on

Table 5.2 Visual representations of plurilingual repertoires

Colour	Polish	English	German	Body part	Polish	English	German
Red	9	3	3	Head	5	3	5
Yellow	2	2		Heart	1	1	
Black	1		2	Head/heart	3	1	1
Brown	1			Torso	3		
Green	1	4	4	Right hand	1	5	6
Pink	1	1		Left hand		5	5
Blue	1	6	5	Right leg	1		1
None	2			Left leg		1	
Flag	1	1	1	Both legs	1	1	1
Silver		1	1	Neck		1	
Purple		1	3	Whole body	4		
				Mouth		1	
				None	2		

the silhouette's head (n=5) as frequently as Polish. This section only presents quantitative results for the analysed corpus of language portraits for further reference. Due to space restrictions, a detailed analysis of language portraits and the interview scripts will focus on three case studies discussed in the next section.

5.5.2. Qualitative data analysis: Case studies

The three participants, Edyta, Renata and Beata, have a very similar sociolinguistic profile. They are all 22-year-old females born and living in Poland since birth and raised in monolingual Polish-speaking families. Consequently, Polish is their first language, as well as the language of their education received in Poland. At the time of the data-gathering process, the young women were third-year undergraduate students of applied linguistics at a large university in Western Poland, with German and English as the main languages. They were all working on their BA theses in German. The respondents demonstrate great interest in and enthusiasm for learning foreign languages, which they perceive as a lifelong learning process, and plan to pursue a career in foreign languages. Apart from English and German, which they major in, the participants also learn additional languages. For example, Edyta has declared to have learned Spanish and French. Renata, a great enthusiast of German who participated in an Erasmus+ programme and spent one term at a university in Germany, has also learned Latin, Chinese and Swedish. Apart from German and English, during her studies, Beata also learned Italian.

5.5.2.1. Case 1: Edyta

Edyta's linguistic repertoire embraces five languages, i.e. Polish, English, German, French and Spanish. The portrait features two dominant colours: red for Polish (the native language) and silver for English (the first foreign language learned by the participant). Every part of the silhouette has been coloured in by the participant. The most significant languages have been placed in the area of the hand, head, chest and legs. Green represents German, the second foreign language that has been located on the silhouette's hand and a small part of the head. As far as the location of the remaining two languages is concerned, i.e. Spanish (symbolised by blue) and French (pink), they are respectively placed on the chest, close to the area associated with the heart. It can be observed, however, that some languages were scattered in different parts of the body to express their multiple functions and different language practices (Figure 5.2). The exact use of each language and its symbolism was clarified during the interview and will be discussed in the further part of the analysis.

During the interview, the languages were described in a particular order, beginning with the languages that take up the largest space in the picture. As it was later explained, the order of presenting particular languages reflected their rank from the highest to the lowest of their attained level. The interviewee elaborated on each

Figure 5.2 Edyta's language portrait

language, focusing on the three most important aspects: the process of learning the language, the emotional value attached to it, language usage and the interpretation of the language portrait.

Polish

The interviewee's first language takes up the space of the right leg, heart and a part of the head and is compared to a pillar:

> 9 (...) I kind of feel that I stand on this language so uhm I can may-
> be interpret it in like
> 10 different ways. So firstly, I stand on it, because it's my native lan-
> guage (...) so any other
> 11 knowledge I have about languages it all comes back to Polish [...].
> This is the language I
> 12 know the best, as it is my native language, so you know, it's the most
> understandable.

Edyta describes Polish as the foundation for constructing her knowledge about the world and acquiring languages. She draws on the capital of her mother tongue when learning foreign languages by referencing the rules of grammar and the use of Polish. The interviewee emphasises that she formulates her thoughts in Polish. Her native language has also been the medium of instruction at all levels of her education. Polish is, however, not only related to rational thinking, but also emotions. As the portrait shows, Polish is placed in the area commonly associated with the heart, which evokes connotations with emotions. This location symbolises the passion for languages that, according to the interviewee, started with Polish: "I do love our language and I think it's beautiful, and its complexity and ugh, and everything (...) so this is why it's in my heart and then it just goes up to my head" (23–24). As Edyta explains, she feels a sense of bonding with the Polish language that makes her perceive it in an emotional way. The selection of red to represent Polish was inspired by the colour of the Polish flag.

English

The second significant language in the picture is English, symbolised by silver. Similarly to Polish, it takes up the space of the leg and most of the head. The interviewee also describes it as a pillar she stands on in terms of learning languages and certain social situations. She explains that English became an important part of her life when she studied abroad and English was the basic tool for communication in that foreign country. Interestingly, English has been located in the area of the stomach, which symbolised becoming emotional: "When I get emotional, I would rather switch to English and the reason for that is that (...) to talk about emotions and feelings in Polish seems very serious to me (...). So whenever I don't really intend to sound so serious (...) ugh I (...) would rather express myself in English" (59–61). The placement of English in the area of the stomach was inspired by the English metaphorical expression "to have butterflies in one's stomach". Even though this phrase evokes rather negative connotations as it is typically used to signal emotions accompanying stressful situations, the interviewee associates it with overcoming difficulties when talking about her feelings. In her view, the use of English can be helpful in certain social situations and facilitate communication.

As the portrait shows, English was also placed in the area of the right hand, which often connotes work. Since Edyta plans to use English in her future profession, she placed it on her dominant hand. The symbolism of the silver colour for English plays a significant role here as well. It is associated with being talkative as conceptualised in the English proverb "speech is silver, but silence is golden" (91). Edyta also interprets the colour as the representation of her high level of proficiency in English. The interviewee positions Polish and English as the two dominant languages that she feels most comfortable with, in contrast to other languages pictured in the silhouette, i.e. German, Spanish and French.

German

German, symbolised by green, takes up a relatively small space compared to English and Polish. It is located on the left hand of the silhouette and a small part of the head. Similarly to English, the interviewee associates it with working:

112 (...) I plan on working with German [...]. Whatever I will do in
      the future, I think it will
113 be like tied with German. And this is my left hand because this is
      my weaker language
114 (...) I feel weaker in terms of my language skills in German, so this
      is why I chose this
115 weaker or supposedly weaker hand for this.

Despite the interviewee's daily use of German, mostly in academic settings, she expresses her concern that her German is not fluent enough and does not sound natural: "I always have this feeling that I sound very, I don't know, stiff in German, because my German is mostly academic German and this is why I think I'm definitely not that talkative in German as I am in English and Polish" (105–106). Edyta elaborates that due to the lack of interest in German pop culture, she does not know colloquial expressions, which in her view hinders communication. Since her use of German is limited to purely professional or academic settings, the respondent believes that she will take advantage of it in her future workplace. Her hopes related to the professional opportunities offered by the knowledge of German have been encapsulated in the symbolic use of the colour green to represent this language (130–132).

Other languages

Compared to other languages in her repertoire, the interviewee's competence in Spanish appears the lowest. Nevertheless, in the portrait, this language takes up a relatively large area of the silhouette's chest. As represented in the extract below, it is represented by blue and is placed in the lungs, symbolising freedom.

171 (...) Spanish was in my head supposed to be in my lung (...) It's
      also connected to why
172 it's blue, and it is blue because [...] I think that lungs and the blue
      colour, it's kind of a
173 sign of freedom in a way (...) and Spanish is a language I strong-
      ly connect with this
174 freedom.

Edyta also emphasises that she strongly embeds the Spanish language in the Spanish culture, especially the dance and music she is exposed to. Importantly, the respondent points to the fact that her Spanish was mostly acquired through exposure to the language in products of pop culture, such as song lyrics or films, rather than through formal instruction. For this reason, Spanish is seen by her as a language of entertainment, fun and artistic self-expression, as well as freedom and carelessness.

French takes up the smallest area in the silhouette compared to other languages. As the interviewee declares, she speaks French better than Spanish, but it is less significant to her. Edyta associates French with being emotional and therefore she placed it in the heart area:

194   (...) I think that French is kind of like (...) a very emotional language for [...], so this is

195   why it's close to my heart. Another reason for that would be that when I started learning

196   French, at first I hated it, and when I started to really put a lot of effort into it and started

197   learning it on my own, I kind of fell in love with this language. So this is why it's close

198   to my heart, it also has some personal connotations.

It can be easily noticed that French has been placed in the heart area along with Polish. However, it seems that French is rather associated with excessive emotionality or sentimentality that the interviewee does not identify herself with: "I'm not (...) necessarily a person that likes being emotional, too emotional, or like talking about emotions that much [...] So I think that's why I reduce that part that French took in my body to make it less emotional and less sensual, like to make me less sensitive in a way" (196–200).

The stereotypical emotionality of French is emphasised by the use of pink, which the respondent associates with the "sweetness" of French pronunciation (203–205). Edyta points out that, despite a certain scepticism towards French, she considers the possibility of developing her proficiency in this language in the future. This intention has been visualised by the pink line in the raised arm of the silhouette that stands for the interviewee's eagerness to make some effort to learn French that might come in handy in the future.

5.5.2.2. *Case 2: Renata*

The interviewee's language portrait depicts 7 languages, which include Polish (her native language), German, English, Spanish, Swedish, Latin and Chinese. Additionally, Renata separately pictured the Bavarian dialect of German, as well as the British English and American variety of English. As mentioned earlier, the participant was raised in a monolingual family. What is more, her parents do not share her passion for learning foreign languages and they only speak Polish (199). Polish and German are placed in the area at the top of the head and close to the heart. In addition, German is also found in the corners of the mouth. Polish is represented as green and German as orange. Each of these languages shares the same space in the two locations. The Bavarian dialect is pink and located in the upper part of the stomach. American English, represented as yellow, is located on the right hand, while British English is coded as brown and situated on the left hand. Spanish, designated as purple, is placed in the lower part of the stomach, under the Bavarian dialect, and in both feet.

86   ee of all dialects of German language, I like Bavarian the most and
      I think it's, it's really
87   great and it sounds incredible for me, and that's why I have also
      put it into like... into
88   place where I...where the (2.0) stomach is because when...ehhh...
      I associate with Bavary
89   also aaa Octoberfest eee yeah and some other food so that's why
      I put it into my stomach. [laughter]

Swedish is symbolised with a light blue colour and located in the mouth area, while Latin is represented by a deeper blue and placed on the right knee. Chinese is located on the left knee and its colour is a combination of green and orange. Importantly, in contrast to the previous respondent, the colours that were used to mark the languages have no special meaning to Renata. Only in the case of Swedish is light blue associated with the winter landscape in Sweden, and more specifically with the large amount of ice, glaciers and snow. The other colours were chosen randomly. On the body silhouette, some empty spaces symbolise the interviewee's openness to develop her language skills in the future or start learning more languages.

The proficiency levels of the languages presented in the portrait vary. The respondent has been learning German for 12 years and English for 16 years and she

Figure 5.3 Renata's language portrait

is fluent in both of them. She has had contact with them at every stage of education and is currently polishing her German and English in her studies of applied linguistics. Renata often speaks these languages either at the university or outside of it. Her portrait features both British and American English because she perceives the differences between these varieties and can easily recognise them while, for example, watching a film. The Bavarian dialect is the only language in her language portrait that Renata cannot speak. However, the respondent discerns characteristic features of the dialect and knows a lot of words in it. As regards Spanish, she has been learning it for two years in a course at university and has reached A2 level. In secondary school, she studied Latin, which was an obligatory course in her humanities-profiled class. Additionally, she attended a course in Chinese for a year, which was offered as an extracurricular subject at her school. Renata managed to attain a basic level in both languages. She ultimately gave up learning Chinese due to the lack of time, as well as the difficulty of the language. In Latin classes, she felt confident and did well. Recently, she has been studying Swedish for several months and has achieved a basic command of this language. In the future, the interviewee may continue to learn some of the languages from her language portrait.

Polish

The interviewee, as a citizen of Poland, emphasises her attachment to her mother tongue and the dominant position of Polish towards other languages. She assures that Polish has a special place in her heart. She loves being Polish and is proud of her country.

45   B: So Polish is in my head because I aaa I think in Polish so I... my thoughts are in

46   Polish, I would say, and in my heart because it's my mother tongue and I'm proud of

47   being Polish so I love my country. (laughter)

The interviewee thinks in Polish and finds her mother tongue beautiful. She is, however, aware that it may pose a real challenge to foreigners to learn, especially due to its particularly difficult pronunciation and grammar.

German

Yet, Polish is not the only language she feels attached to. In her linguistic repertoire, a special position is taken by German, as her favourite foreign language that plays an important role in her life at the moment. She uses German daily, essentially due to her study programme. The respondent believes that sometimes her German seems stronger than Polish, as in certain contexts she struggles to find Polish equivalents to some words. As one can see in the picture, German has been placed in the area of her head, heart and mouth.

102   B: Yeah, this could be a reason for it, that I have been in Germa-
       ny for a while, like for
103   one semester but eee...yeah... maybe it's also contributed to the
       fact that I, I started
104   thinking in German and that German has also place in my heart
       in some way, not so
105   much as Polish (laughter) to reckon it...but eee yeah, it's like I re-
       ally like German
106   language and Germany...

She treats this language as one of great importance, and her feelings towards German are comparable to those towards Polish. However, despite being emotionally attached to German, Polish remains the most important language to her: "German has also a place in my heart in some way, not so much as Polish" (104). In the interview, Renata admits that she is not completely sure which language is her "first language". She may feel connected with Polish because of her homeland, whereas German is "the love" she has acquired. She describes her love for the German language when she says that her "heart beats faster" when she speaks German. In the interview, Renata expresses her attachment to the German language and Germany on several occasions. Although the interviewee has not been learning German as long as English, she declares that her German is more advanced than her English. One of the breakthroughs in her language development was her stay in Germany within the Erasmus+ programme. During this exchange, she mostly communicated in German and developed her passion for the Bavarian dialect, which she finds particularly melodious and pleasant to the ear. Additionally, her emotional attitude to the Bavarian dialect emerges from her life trajectories and particularly pleasant life experiences at the time she was exposed to this language. Moreover, she associates the Bavarian dialect not only with the region but also with *Octoberfest* and Bavarian food. For this reason, the interviewee placed the Bavarian dialect in the silhouette's stomach.

English

The second foreign language mastered by the respondent is English. She has a very positive attitude towards English, especially British English. Nevertheless, her attachment to the language is not as strong as to German, which remains her most preferred language. Renata's attitude to English might be deemed rather "rational". Taking into account the long-standing commitment to learning English, Renata believes it would be rather unwise to give up excelling in her language skills. The interviewee appreciates the role of language investment (296–297) and perceives FL proficiency as capital for the future (Bourdieu, 1999).

Other languages

When it comes to languages such as Spanish or Swedish, the interviewee highlights how melodious these languages are. Renata was inspired to begin learning Swedish after listening to some Swedish songs. Yet, she admits that her feelings towards this language are rather mixed as Swedish simultaneously sounds strange and "a little bit creepy" (243) to her. Nevertheless, the respondent would be willing to continue learning this language in the future. Musical associations also come to the fore in the case of Spanish. Renata, however, does not intend to make any investment in learning Spanish as she is aware that it would involve too much effort to progress. The respondent also mentions several languages she started to learn at some point in her life but is not interested in making the effort with anymore. In the beginning, Renata treated learning Chinese as a challenge or extraordinary hobby that proved to be too difficult, demanding and time-consuming to persevere. This learning episode has, however, made her more sensitive to Chinese culture and gave her confidence that mastering Chinese would have been within her capacity if she had invested more time and effort in learning it. Latin, in contrast to Chinese, was not her choice, as it was an obligatory subject in her secondary school. Nevertheless, she found Latin classes interesting and admitted that it was "a little fun" (358). She liked her teacher and how the teacher praised her for making some translations and encouraged her to undertake studies in applied linguistics.

5.5.2.3. Case 3: Beata

The respondent used four different colours to visualise her linguistic repertoire that features Polish, English, German and Italian. The first language rendered in the picture is Polish, represented by green, which is interpreted as a colour of hope, and associated with calmness and serenity. The participant used green to outline the whole silhouette and fill in the head. Another colour that can be seen in the picture is red, which stands for German. Beata has chosen red to express the strong emotions this language evokes in her. Red has been placed in the middle of the body as well as inside the head area where it is surrounded by green. Yellow has been used to represent English since the author associates it with being natural, positive and common, because this language is considered the lingua franca in today's world. The area she covered with yellow also refers to perceiving English as a lingua franca since she associates legs metaphorically with the pillars for communication: "wherever you are, you can use English" (43). Purple hands represent the Italian language. In contrast to other languages, the colour was randomly selected in this case. The choice

Figure 5.4 Beata's language portrait

of hands, though, was dictated by the perceived dynamism of Italians as communicators, and their powerful use of gestures. In addition, the white space inside the silhouette also carries certain meanings as it symbolises the interviewee's openness to learn other languages in the future. Although at first no specific languages are mentioned, after a series of probing questions the respondent mentions Russian and her interest to find out more about the Cyrillic script. The participant underlines that she possibly knows some words in other languages that are not contained in the presented silhouette. Yet, she decided not to include them because they do not play any role in her life.

Polish

The interviewee sees Polish as the most important language, justifying this feeling by the fact that it is native to her so all her thoughts are in Polish. She underlines the importance of Polish in shaping her personality and determining her identity. However, Beata also admits that she managed to become aware of and appreciate the huge role of Polish in her life only through the experience of learning foreign languages. This experience also made her recognise the difficulty of her native language in comparison with other languages and look up to people who make the effort to learn it. Being a student of linguistics also helped her start paying more attention to language correctness in her native language and realise that she could always learn more. Apart from the special bond she has with Polish, as someone who professionally deals with languages, the interviewee feels close to all the languages she is learning. For example, she mentions that now German has started taking space in her mind and she sometimes thinks in this language, or that she enjoys listening to music in different languages. The plurilingual repertoire enabled the interviewee to develop a new perspective on language, including her native language.

This helped her to find the balance between all the languages she knows, and to see the positivity and usefulness in all of them.

German

As far as the verbal form of the representation is concerned, the respondent draws on complex metaphors to express her attitude towards the pictured languages that are used to express various associations. Metaphors are only created to visualise certain ideas and experiences, for example, certain events from the past that have influenced her view of a particular language. Beata's attitude towards German, associated with red and strength, is not always positive, due to the emotions that accompanied her during the challenging process of language learning: "I've struggled a lot with learning it" (12). On the other hand, this language evokes some positive emotions as well, since the participant associates it with her Erasmus experience and the people she met in Germany. This example presents a complex, metaphorical point of view that reflects an individual combination of discursive and visual forms.

The interviewee speaks openly about her emotions and, when asked to, she is willing to discuss them in more detail. While talking about the colours representing particular languages, Beata mentions the calmness and confidence that come with Polish as her native language and elaborates on the hope that she also relates with it. She is particularly open to sharing the immense emotions she feels towards German that evolved throughout the enduring and challenging process of learning it. Initially, under the influence of people in her surroundings considering German "ugly", her feelings for this language were negative. With time, however, her mindset changed and German became the respondent's strongest foreign language. Her bond with German was cemented after the one-term Erasmus exchange in Germany. Interestingly, Beata describes how easily she can associate specific words in German to the contexts in which she learned them. The interviewee considers her Erasmus stay in Germany and the people she met then as the key factors in shaping her positive attitude towards the language and facilitating the process of learning it.

English

As far as English is concerned, the interviewee points to its status as the lingua franca and its usefulness as a means of global communication. Despite taking a pragmatic approach to this language, Beata is overcome with negative emotions towards English. She looks back at the initial stages of learning it when she was still in kindergarten and reflects on being shy and intimidated. Although she perceives English as the most commonly used language, during the interview she does not make any further references to relations with English-speaking people or communicating with them, which may explain her rather pragmatic and unemotional attitude towards it.

Other languages

The interviewee has positive feelings for Italian, which probably originated in her four trips to Italy and her attitude towards this language. She associates her positive emotions with Italian people and their dynamic behaviour. She also mentions Italian culture and cuisine as important aspects of her perception of the language. Even the tone of the interviewee's voice changes when she speaks about Italian and reminisces about her trips to Italy. These narrations bring back happy memories that Beata is eager to elaborate on, and reveal her overwhelmingly positive emotions.

5.5.3. Metaphorical representation of linguistic repertoires: Discussion

Each portrait offered a unique multimodal representation of embodied plurilingual repertoires and a story of language learning that refers to "past experiences and future intentions" (Mossakowski & Busch, 2010: 166). Similarly to metaphors, the portrayals are "highly constrained both by the nature of our bodies and brains and by the reality of our daily interactions" (Lakoff & Johnson 1999: 96). Coffey (2015: 508) points to the dynamic character of one's embodied representations of plurilingualism that change over time as well as their dual deeply personal and social nature. On the one hand, the portrayals are idiosyncratic and give an insight into highly "personal inner worlds" (ibid.). On the other, they are simultaneously culturally shaped social constructs reflecting "public representations" (Gibbs, 1999: 160) that are comprehensible and open to interpretation, not only to the interviewer but also to wider circles of potential readers. In each case, the meaning of the visual metaphors is co-constructed in the interview with participants who verbalise and interpret their visual representations in narrative form.

5.5.3.1. Colour

In Kress and van Leeuwen's (2002: 355) view, colours are considered signifiers that offer "a set of affordances from which sign-makers and interpreters select according to their communicative needs and interests in a given context". As far as their meaning-making potential is concerned, Kress and van Leeuwen (2002, 2006) point to two distinct sources, i.e. association and distinctive features. Association pertains to the provenance of a particular colour, which might pertain, for example, to a specific object or place. Importantly, associations triggered by colours are socially embedded in terms of their symbolic and emotive value. Thus, a particular socio-cultural context provides certain frameworks for their creation and interpretation. The second affordance, i.e. the distinctive features of colour, designates values on various scales (e.g. the level of saturation) that not only help to differentiate the colours but also contribute to meaning-making through the analysis of specific arrangements of values on a particular scale unique for each colour (Kress & van Leeuwen, 2002). The selection of all affordances is regulated by individual interests, communicative needs and contextual determinants as well as socio-cultural constraints. At the individual level, the selection of colours manifests personal taste as well as represents "aesthetic attitudes and affective relations to language" (Botsis & Bradbury, 2018: 423). Thus, such interpretations might be constrained or free, depending only on an individual's creativity (Kress & van Leeuwen, 2002). The symbolic use of colours to manifest the respondents' (children's) emotions has been signalled in several studies (e.g. Burkitt, Barrett, & Davis, 2003; Soares et al., 2020).

The analysed cases seem to corroborate Kress and van Leeuwen's (2002) ideas since the participants present "embodied cultural-cognitive conceptualisations of languages" (Peters and Coetzee-Van Rooy, 2020: 586). Overall, the use of colours draws on commonly shared metaphorical associations. Only Renata states that her use of colour was random. The most common associations are based on the colours of national flags (e.g. Edyta's use of red for Polish). Pink is used by Edyta to signify the emotionality or sentimentality of the French language. To render her individual experience, Edyta uses the metaphorical representation of English as silver by employing the common proverb "speech is silver, but silence is golden" to illustrate her eagerness to speak English. In this case, new meaning is generated through the personal adaption of common cultural capital. The metaphor marks critical points in the narrative, exposing the implicit value of a given language in the plurilingual repertoire the respondent is often unaware of.

Another common association determining the selection of colour for a particular language are the landscape characteristics of the country a given language is spoken in. For example, Swedish is represented by light blue to render the winterlike characteristics of the northern scenery (e.g. Renata).

Beata's colour choices reflect certain clichéd associations, for example, green as a symbol of hope, calmness and serenity, or red rendering strong feelings, but their connection to particular languages is highly individualised. In her view, her second language German, coloured red, reflects her strong passionate feelings, while Polish, her native language, is rendered green. In the case of English, yellow represents naturalness and positivity. The same respondent, however, admits that the representation of Italian as purple in her portrait was completely random.

5.5.3.2. *Body*

The deliberate framing of linguistic portraits in the body silhouette stimulated reflection on the individual, embodied experience. According to Stein and Newfield (2007: 921), "[b]odies are repositories of knowledge, but these knowledges are not always knowable in and through language: they can be sensed, felt, performed, imagined, imaged, or dreamed". Botsis and Bradbury (2018: 425) point to the fact that the body simultaneously has a very personal as well as public dimension.

The expression of one's linguistic repertoire through colouring a silhouette shape draws on the HUMAN BODY AS CONTAINER OF LANGUAGES metaphor. In fact, all portraits in the corpus were limited by the boundaries of the body outline used as a stimulus and were positioned around the core organs such as the head and heart. As argued by Botsis and Bradbury (2018: 423), particular parts of the body have fixed cultural meanings, for example, THE HEART AS THE SITE OF LOVE, while others might carry numerous, sometimes opposing meanings. For instance, legs might represent either mobility or stability. In Edyta's portrait, English and Polish are allocated in the legs perceived as "pillars" of her identity.

As seen in the analysed corpus, as well as illustrated in the presented cases, the heart or head (or both at the same time) are used to represent the native language, illustrating the dichotomy between heart and reason. Accordingly, the heart stands for emotions, strong attachment, feelings and relations, while the head epitomises thinking. Some respondents consider beginning to think in a foreign language as a milestone, marking the transition to proficiency level. In the respondents' biographies, this transition appears to take place during longer stays abroad (e.g. Erasmus+ exchanges) that involve immersing oneself in the host country's language and culture, as well as interacting with native speakers. Such themes reverberate in all the analysed narrations.

Another frequent body trope is hands that stand for work, earning money or career. For this reason, the respondents who intend to become language professionals in the future, tend to place the languages they major in (i.e. English and German) in the area of their hands or arms. English especially, as a global lingua franca is associated with hands, as symbolic extensions to reach the world. Verbally, English is deemed "handy" to reflect its usefulness in work settings. Although the respondents show their strong emotional attachment to their mother tongue, as well as German, or even Spanish, they rarely position English in this way. What comes to the fore in their narrations is the practicality of English, leveraging their position on the job market. Thus, the narratives illustrate the global dominance and market value of English as a means to secure their employment and financial opportunities (Park & Wee, 2013). The respondents (e.g. Renata 296–297), see "years of learning" a language as an investment of time, effort and financial resources that motivates them to persevere and develop or at least maintain their competencies, especially in the case of "practical" languages.

In the eyes of plurilingual young adults, learning languages is overall presented as a pleasant activity or simply "fun" (e.g. Renata). Only occasionally the respondents mention some difficulties or challenges related to learning a particular language (e.g. Chinese in the case of Renata). The obstacles encountered at the beginning might, however, nurture ambition and motivate learners. Motivation for learning a particular language might also be provided by a particularly good or inspiring teacher. For example, based on her overwhelmingly positive experiences with learning Latin and positive feedback from her teacher who praised her translation skills, Renata was inspired to study applied linguistics and dedicate her future professional career to languages.

One of the most powerful metaphors emerging from the interviews is conceptualising LANGUAGE AS AN OBJECT OF LOVE. When referring to particular languages the respondents use the language expressing strong emotions, passion. In Renata's narration, the source domain for the metaphorical representation of languages is human romantic relations, which might be either fleeting or long-standing. In the extract below she deems her experiences with learning Latin and Chinese as "affairs":

461   A1: not so common languages like Latin and Chinese but they
        were only episodes
462   in your language like
463   B: it was like an affair only (laughter)
464   A1: yeas that's like an affair when we are talking /about love/
465   B: or relationship also
466   A1: yeah yeah exactly ... OK

Languages are also seen as the embodiment of culture. For example, Spanish, associated with dance and music, is placed on the hips. Renata mentions that she was motivated to study Swedish by music.

The respondents seem to realise that their linguistic repertoires are somehow "truncated" but emphasise that they are dynamic and prone to further change related to their future life trajectories. The respondents are open to learning new languages or improving their existing skills, which is sometimes symbolised by leaving empty, uncoloured space on the silhouette, as illustrated by Beata's words:

57   yeah, exactly so I've left this um free space, this white space, because (...) it
58   symbolise the space in my mind, and that is, um (2.0), free for other languages, which I
59   want to learn the future yeah so that's why

Thus, the respondents treat their current repertoires as "work in progress" that will evolve along with their life trajectories and emerging needs. This corresponds with Busch's assertion that:

[o]ur repertoire is not determined solely by the linguistic resources we have, but sometimes by those we do not have; these can become

> noticeable in a given situation as a gap, threat or a desire. (...) It not
> only points backward to the past of the language biography, which has
> left behind its traces and scars, but also forward, anticipating and pro-
> jecting the future situations and events we are preparing to face (Busch,
> 2017: 356).

Additionally, languages are not represented as separate entities but rather as elements that overlap each other and form a complex system. For example, in Beata's
portrait, Polish – represented by green – is not only placed in the silhouette's head
and heart, but also used to mark the outline of the whole body, which was explained
in the following way: "I used green on the outline of the body because um, I would
say it's, um, so /po-/ Polish language, uh, builds me somehow it defines who I am,
how I think and so on" (29–31).

Finally, the respondents demonstrated strong emotional attachment to particular languages as well as the language learning process. In the analysed portraits and
interview scripts, plurilingual repertoires are not only epitomised as linguistic capabilities, conceptualised as a mental activity but as the whole body experience (cf.
Kramsch, 2009; Coffey, 2015).

5.6. DISCUSSION OF THE METHOD'S APPLICABILITY

The employed mixed-method/multimodal approach has offered multiple benefits
to studying plurilingual repertoires of young adults. First of all, the combination of
the visual and verbal modes, as well as switching between the modes, enables the
participant to take a holistic look at their linguistic repertoires and develop a narrative that connects the dots between their life trajectories and their language and
identity. From the researcher's perspective, the multimodal approach helps to overcome the limitations of each separate mode and dismiss criticism concerning the
use of projective techniques. Additionally, such an approach, especially the use of
the semi-structured interview as a data-eliciting tool, provides rich, meaningful
data for analysis.

The current study has also provided evidence that the visual and verbal articula-
tions of linguistic repertoires "foreground language and languaging as a multimodal phenomenon, existing in different modalities" and "the narratives themselves are
a multimodal phenomenon, in that people become their portrait" (Kusters & de
Meulder, 2019: 65). Additionally, Salo and Dufva (2018: 427) assert that narrations articulated verbally "bring in dimensions that cannot be visually represented".
Thus, the integration of both modalities offers and added value and creates a syn-
ergistic effect.

Although the use of the multimodal approach has been reported in previous studies, most of the researchers asked the participants to submit written descriptions instead of interviewing them, especially in the case of plurilingual adults (e.g. Botsis & Bradbury, 2018; Bristowe, Oostendorp & Anthonissen, 2014; Busch, 2010; Coffey, 2015; Dressler, 2014; Melo-Pfeifer, 2015, 2017; Prasad, 2014).

The novelty of the applied method also lies in the focus on the figurative representation of plurilingual repertoires and the analysis of metaphors generated by the preparation of the portrait and the accompanying narration. The preparation of language portraits in the visual mode and conceptualising it as a body silhouette stimulates the use of figurative language and the formation of metaphors with the body as the source domain. This combination created a unique multimodal representation of an individual linguistic repertoire as an *embodied* experience of language use (cf. Busch, 2018). As noted by Salo and Dufva (2018: 442), language portraits provide a comprehensive description of an individual's language repertoire and experience due to the variety of employed "associative, metaphorical and symbolic elements". Indeed, in the study undertaken, the participants metaphorically interpreted parts of the body, such as hands signifying work or feet/legs representing roots or pillars. Additionally, as emphasised earlier, the language portrait, understood as space constructed and customised by metaphors, provides data for the analysis at different "modes of understanding" (Lakoff & Johnson, 1999: 06).

Another benefit of applying projective visual techniques for data collection is their potential to encourage the participant's deep reflection on the issue under study. Being engaged in the creative process of visualising one's linguistic repertoire makes individuals think about their linguistic practices, as well as language preferences and relations that are rarely consciously verbalised (cf. Soares et al., 2020: 17). The whole process of designing, articulating and interpreting the language portrait makes the respondents highly aware of their linguistic repertoires that might be revisited or revalidated (cf. Busch, 2018). In consequence, such reflection might translate into a conscious decision concerning language use or learning. In sum, employing the visual and verbal mode of representation reduced the risk of "reverting too rapidly to pre-established narrative patterns and responding to normative expectations" (Busch, 2018: 6).

Furthermore, by stimulating creative processes (Krumm, 2001), the respondents are provided with alternative affordances and language resources to articulate their experiences and emotions related to each language. Compared to regular narrative interviews (e.g. Wąsikiewicz-Firlej, 2020; Wąsikiewicz-Firlej et al., 2022), the use of projective techniques enhances the use of figurative language. Therefore, the stories shared by participants are not focused on the provision of detailed accounts of the language learning process and attained proficiency but might be treated as a form of languaging, offering insights into the subjective interpretation of the lived experience and identity (Wąsikiewicz-Firlej, 2014). As evidenced in the data, some participants focused on both positive and negative emotions concerning language use and learning. For example, Renata focused on the stress and anxiety accompanying the process of learning Chinese, but talked about joy and pleasure related to learning Latin. Despite certain rational arguments concerning language investment or practicality, the decisions concerning language learning are to a great extent taken on the grounds of a particular mindset. Contrary to migrant respondents whose emotions centre on "experiences related to migration, a minority position, discrimination and marginalization" (Salo & Dufva, 2018: 424), the plurilingual adults in our study mostly shared their aspirations and memories concerning their life and language biographies, positioning language learning as a positive and enjoyable experience and expressing their "love" for particular languages.

There is also a practical aspect of incorporating projective techniques in the researcher's methodological kit, especially when collecting sensitive data. In the undertaken study, most participants simply found preparing their linguistic portrait enjoyable and engaging. On the whole, the participation in the research project was considered quite pleasant and eye-opening, as it stimulated reflections on language and language learning. Importantly, language portraits triggered languaging and offered access to the whole pallet of emotions related to a particular language or language learning that could have been otherwise silenced (cf. Kusters and Meulder, 2019: 60). The interviewers, on the other hand, found the visual stimulus very useful to open and maintain the conversation. The portrait acted as a point of reference in the interviewer-interviewee interaction that facilitated the elicitation of data, which might be an issue in the case of intimidated or not very talkative participants. Additionally, projecting one's experiences and emotions on an anonymous body silhouette enables the participants to talk about personal issues without being emotionally overwhelmed. Drawing is also an alternative way of communicating for people who lack verbal resources or have problems with self-expression (e.g. children).

As far as the challenges are concerned, some adults, on the other hand, might be reluctant to draw because they consider such an activity childish, unpleasant or pointless. Although such arguments were not raised in our study, they were signalled by Kusters and de Meulder (2019: 61). When it comes to verbal expression, it is typically more effective for individuals with a higher metalinguistic awareness who can express themselves very well, which was exactly the case with our participants – plurilingual students of applied linguistics who intend to pursue careers in language-related professions. The effectiveness of verbal expression cannot be, however, taken for granted in the case of less-educated or mobile respondents. Another aspect that needs to be taken into account in future research is the selection of interviewees administering the portraits and interacting with participants. Due to the sensitivity of the collected data, they should be trustworthy, to encourage participants to share their life stories and talk about language-related emotions.

5.7. CONCLUSIONS

The current study aimed to contribute to understanding the plurilingual repertoires of young adults – students of applied linguists – who have been raised and educated in monolingual Poland and have not had any migration experiences. The application of a multimodal approach has made it possible to capture of the uniqueness of the profiles of a target group that has not been extensively studied before. From the methodological perspective, the combination of different methods of data collection and analysis provided rich, insightful data and enabled the researcher to triangulate findings.

When it comes to the visual representation of linguistic repertoires, it appears to be very subjective, rather than constituted by commonly accepted social patterns. Especially, the choice of the colour representing a particular language tends to be selected randomly, or dictated by unique personal experiences or associations rooted in individual biographies. The placements of particular languages in the silhouette outline also vary, but they are more conventionalised and inspired by verbal metaphors. Accordingly, the participants referred to common metaphorical conceptualisations of the head as a site for rational thinking versus the heart as the site for emotions. Both verbal and visual metaphors enabled the interviewees to render their attitudes and experiences in a figurative, creative way, which fostered reflexivity and contributed to the understanding of the complexity of plurilingual repertoires. As far as values and emotions are concerned, they are not attributed to all languages in the same way. The affection towards a given language does not typically coincide with the level of competence in a particular language but is related to positive emotions accompanying the process of learning or using a language. There is a whole spectrum of different social situations in which languages in the participants' repertoires may be used and be accordingly perceived rationally or emotionally. What comes to the fore, though, is the relational aspect of language. In other words, the participants' perception of particular languages in their repertoires tends to be affected by interactions and relations with users of a given language, as well as emotions accompanying these situations.

The portrayal that has emerged from the data depicts young plurilinguals open to new experiences, fascinated with languages and truly motivated to learn them. The respondents were fully aware that their plurilingual repertoires were somehow "truncated" but they perceived them as repertoires in-flux – being adapted, and evolving in response to changing life trajectories and emerging needs. At this stage of their lives, the respondents demonstrated their positive mindset towards the linguistic environment and readiness to face the challenges of a globalised world characterised by fluidity and instability. It must be, however, taken into account that the profile of participants in the study is not representative of society at large. The students demonstrate a particular interest in languages and find learning them not only practical but also pleasant and joyful. Additionally, the huge language investment must also be considered – not only in terms of time and effort, but also the financial costs incurred, mostly by their parents who pay for their extracurricular FL classes and courses. From this perspective, the participants might be seen as a privileged group.

The study has also had a pedagogical dimension. The participation in the research project and switching into the creative mode stimulated metaphor employment and reflexivity in the participants concerning their language practices and language learning, as well as attitudes towards particular languages. The multimodal approach helped students express their ideas and experiences in an alternative way and contribute to a better understanding of their plurilingualism that is "not dependent on monolingual and monoglossic ideologies" (Melo-Pfeifer, 2017: 54). In this sense, preparing language portraits and interpreting them appears to be a useful tool for language students and teachers for raising language awareness, particularly important in language-related professions.

REFERENCES

Belk, R. W. (ed.) (2006). *Handbook of Qualitative Research Methods in Marketing*. Cheltenham, UK: Edward Elgar.

Bellak, L. (1992). Projective Techniques in the Computer Age. *Journal of Personality Assessment*, 58(3): 445–453.

Blommaert, J. (2008). Language, Asylum, and the National Order. *Urban Language and Literacies*, 50: 2–21.

Blommaert, J. (2010). *The Sociolinguistics of Globalization*. Cambridge: Cambridge University Press.

Blommaert, J., and Backus, A. (2012). Superdiverse Repertoires and the Individual. In Saint-Jacques, I., and Weber, J.-J. (eds.). *Multimodality and Multilingualism: Current Challenges for Educational Studies* (pp. 1–31). Rotterdam: Sense Publishers.

Blommaert, J., and Rampton, B. (2011). Language and Superdiversity. *Diversities*, 13(2): 1–22.

Boddy, C. R. (2005). Projective Techniques in Market Research: Valueless Subjectivity or Insightful reality? A Look at the Evidence for the Usefulness, Reliability and Validity of Projective Techniques in Market Research. *International Journal of Market Research*, 47(3): 239–254.

Boje, D. M. (1991). The Storytelling Organization: A Study of Story Performance in an Office-Supply Firm. *Administrative Science Quarterly*, 36(1): 106–126.

Bond, D., Ramsey, E., and Boddy, C. R. (2011). *Projective Techniques: Are they a Victim of Clashing Paradigms?* MPR Paper No 33331. https://mpra.ub.uni-muenchen.de/33331/ [accessed 7 May 2023].

Botsis, H., and Bradury, J. (2018). Metaphorical Sense-Making: Visual-Narrative Language Portraits of South African Students. *Qualitative Research in Psychology*, 15(2): 412–430.

Bourdieu, P. (1999). *Language and Symbolic Power*. [transl. G. Raymond and M. Adamson]. Cambridge, MA: Harvard University Press.

Breuer, J., and Freud, S. (1895). *Studien ber Hysteria* [transl. Studies in Hysteria]. Vienna: GW.

Bristowe, A., Oostendorp, M., and Anthonissen, C. (2014). Language and Youth Identity in a Multilingual Setting: A Multimodal Repertoire Approach. *Southern African Linguistics and Applied Language Studies*, 32: 229–245.

Burkitt, E., Barrett, M., and Davis, A. (2003). Children's Colour Choices for Completing Drawings of Affectively Characterised Topics. *Journal of Child Psychology and Psychiatry*, 44(3): 445–455.

Busch, B. (2010). School Language Profiles: Valorizing Linguistic Resources in Heteroglossic Situations in South Africa. *Language and Education*, 24(4): 283–294.

Busch, B. (2012). The Linguistic Repertoire Revisited. *Applied Linguistics*, 33(5): 503–523.

Busch, B. (2016). Methodology in Biographical Approaches in Applied Linguistics. *Working Papers in Urban Language and Literacies*, 187: 1–12.

Busch, B. (2017). Expanding the Notion of the Linguistic Repertoire: On the Concept of Spracherleben – The Lived Experience of Language. *Applied Linguistics*, 38(3): 340–358.

Busch, B. (2018). The Language Portrait in Multilingualism Research: Theoretical and Methodological Considerations. *Working Papers in Urban Languages and Literacies*, 236: 1–13.

Canagarajah, S. (2013). *Translingual Practice: Global Englishes and Cosmopolitan Relations*. New York/ London: Routledge.

Catterall, M. and Ibbotson, P. (2000). Using Projective Techniques in Education Research. *British Educational Research Journal*, 26(2): 245–256.

Chandler, J., and Owen, M. (2002). *Developing Brands with Qualitative Market Research*. London: Sage

Chang, J. E. (2001). Special Session Summary the Revival of Projective Techniques: Past, Present, and Future Perspectives. In Gilly, M. C. and Meyers-Levy, J. (Eds.). *NA – Advances in Consumer Research* vol. 28 (pp. 253--54). Valdosta, GA: Association for Consumer Research.

Clark, A. J. (1995). Projective Techniques in the Counseling Process. *Journal of Counseling and Development*, 73(3): 311–316.

Coffey, S. (2015). Reframing Teachers' Language Knowledge through Metaphor Analysis of Language Portraits. *The Modern Language Journal*, 99(3): 500–514.

Council of Europe. (2001). *Common European Framework of Reference for Languages: Learning, Teaching, Assessment*. Cambridge: Cambridge University Press.

Council of Europe. (2007) *From Linguistic Diversity to Plurilingual Education: Guide for The Development of Language Education Policies in Europe. Executive Version*. https://rm.coe.int/16806a892c [Accessed 31 January 2021].

Council of The European Union. (2002). *Council Resolution of 27 June 2002 on Lifelong Learning*. Luxembourg: Official Journal of the European Communities.

Creswell, J. W. (2014). *Research Design: Qualitative, Quantitative, and Mixed Methods Approaches* (4th ed.). Los Angeles, CA: SAGE.

Das, G. (2018). A Review on Projective Techniques Applied on Social Science Research. *International Journal of Research in Business Studies and Management*, 5(3): 10–14.

De Houwer, A. (2009). *Bilingual First Language Acquisition*. Clevedon: Multilingual Matters.

Dicicco-Bloom, B., and Crabtree, B. F. (2006). The Qualitative Research Interview. *Med Educ*, 40: 314–21.

Dörnyei, Z. (2007). *Research Methods in Applied Linguistics*. Oxford: Oxford University Press.

Dressler, R. (2014). Exploring Linguistic Identity in Young Multilingual Learners. *TESL Canada Journal*, 32: 42–52.

Durgee, J. F. (1988). Interpreting Consumer Mythology: A Literary Criticism Approach to Odyssey Informant Stories. *Advances in Consumer Research*, 15: 531–536.

European Commission. (2007). *Key Competences for Lifelong Learning European Reference Framework*. Luxembourg: Official Journal of the European Communities.

European Commission. (2017). Communication from the Commission to The European Parliament, the Council, the European Economic and Social Committee and the Committee of the Regions-Strengthening European Identity Through Education and Culture: The European Commission's Contribution to the Leaders' Meeting in Gothenburg, 17 November 2017 (COM(2017)0673). https://ec.europa.eu/commission/sites/betapolitical/files/communication-strengtening-european-identity-education-culture_en.pdf [accessed 31 January 2021].

Evensen, L. S. (2013). *Applied Linguistics: Towards a New Integration?* London: Equinox.

Frank, L. (1939). Projective Methods for the Study of Personality. *Journal of Psychology*, 8: 389–413.

Freud, S. (1911/1956). Formulations on the two Principles of Mental Functioning. In Strachey, J., and Freud, A. (eds.). *The Standard Edition of the Complete Psychological Works of Sigmund Freud* (Vol. 12). London: Hoghart.

García, O., and Otheguy, R. (2019). Plurilingualism and Translanguaging: Commonalities and Divergences. *International Journal of Bilingual Education and Bilingualism*, 23(1): 1–19.

Galletta, A., and Cross, W. E. (2013). *Mastering the Semi-Structured Interview and Beyond: From Research Design to Analysis and Publication*. New York: NYU Press.

Gibbs, R. W., Jr. (1999). Taking Metaphor out of our Heads and Putting it into the Cultural World. In Gibbs, R. W. Jr., and Steen, G. J. (eds.). *Metaphor in Cognitive Linguistics* (pp. 145–166). Philadelphia/ Amsterdam: John Benjamins.

Gogolin, I., and Neumann, U. (1991). Sprache – Govor – Lingua – Language. Sprachliches Handeln in der Grundschule [Language. Linguistic Behaviour in the Elementary School]. *Die Grundschulzeitschrift* [The Elementary School Journal], 43: 6–13.

Graca, J., and Whiddon, M. F. (1990). Projections into Ambiguous Stimuli: Part II. Other than Inkblots. In Crumbaugh, J. C. (ed.). *A Primer of Projective Techniques of Psychological Assessment* (pp. 34–76). San Diego, CA: Libra Publishers Inc.

Gumperz, J. (1965). Linguistic Repertoires, Grammars and Second Language Instruction. *Monograph Series on Languages and Linguistics*, 18: 81–90.

Haire, M. (1950). Projective Techniques in Marketing Research. *Journal of Marketing*, 14(5): 649–659.

Hatch, J. A. (2002). *Doing Qualitative Research in Education Settings*. Albany, NY: Suny Press.

Hélot, C., Van Gorp, K., Frijns, C., and Sierens, S. (2018). Introduction: Towards Critical Multilingual Language Awareness for 21st Century Schools. In Hélot, C., Van Gorp, K., Frijns, C., and Sierens, S. (eds.). *Language Awareness in Multilingual Classrooms in Europe: From Theory to Practice* (pp. 1–20). Boston, MA: De Gruyter Mouton.

Josselson, R. (2013). *Interviewing for Qualitative Inquiry: A Relational Approach*. New York: Guilford Press.

Kaczmarek, M., Olejnik, I., and Springer, A. (2013). *Badania Jakościowe – Metody i Zastosowania*. Warszawa: CeDeWu.

Kramsch, C. (2009). *The Multilingual Subject*. Oxford: Oxford University Press.

Kress, G., and van Leeuwen, T. (2002). Colour as a Semiotic Mode: Notes for a Grammar of Colour. *Visual Communication*, 1(3): 343–368.

Kress, G., and van Leeuwen, T. (2006). *Reading Images: The Grammar of Visual Design*. London: Routledge.

Krumm, H. J. (2001). *Kinder und ihre Sprachen – lebendige Mehrsprachigkeit*. Vienna: Eviva.

Krumm, H-J. (2013). Multilingualism and Identity: What Linguistic Biographies of Migrants Can Tell Us. In Sigmund, P., Gogolin, I., Schulz, M. E., and Davydova, J. (eds.). *Multilingualism and Language Diversity in Urban Areas: Acquisition, Identities, Space, Education* (pp. 165–176). Amsterdam: John Benjamins.

Kusters, A., and De Meulder, M. (2019). Language Portraits: Investigating Embodied Multilingual and Multimodal Repertoires. *Forum: Qualitative Social Research*, 20(3), Art. 10.

Kvale, S. (1996). *Interviews*. Thousand Oaks: SAGE Publications.

Lakoff, G., and Johnson, M. (1999). *Philosophy in the Flesh: The Embodied Mind and Its Challenge to Western Thought*. New York: Basic Books.

Lakoff, G., and Johnson, M. (1980). *Metaphors We Live By*. Chicago: The University of Chicago Press.

Lau, S. M. C. (2016). Language, Identity, and Emotionality: Exploring the Potential of Language Portraits in Preparing Teachers for Diverse Learners. *The New Educator*, 12(2): 147–170.

Levy, S. (1994). Interpreting Consumer Mythology. *Marketing Management*, 2: 4–9

Lindzey, G. (1959). On the Classification of Projective Techniques. *Psychological Bulletin*, 56(2): 158–168.

Loevinger, J. (1976). *Ego Development: Conceptions and Theories*. San Francisco: Jossey-Bass.

Lüdi, G., and Py, B. (2009). To Be or Not to Be...a Plurilingual Speaker. *International Journal of Multilingualism*, 6(2): 154–167.

Luscher, M., and Scott, I. (1969). *The Luscher Color Test*. NY: Washington Square Press.

Marshall, S., and Moore, D. (2013). 2B or not 2B Plurilingual? Navigating Languages Literacies, and Plurilingual Competence in Postsecondary Education in Canada. *TESOL Quarterly*, 47(3): 472–499.

Marshall, S., and Moore, D. (2018). Plurilingualism amid the Panoply of Lingualisms: Addressing Critiques and Misconceptions in Education. *International Journal of Multilingualism*, 15(1): 19–34.

Melo-Pfeifer, S. (2015). Multilingual Awareness and Heritage Language Education: Children's Multimodal Representations of Their Multilingualism. *Language Awareness*, 24(3): 197–215.

Melo-Pfeifer, S. (2017). Drawing the Plurilingual Self: How Children Portray their Plurilingual Resources. *International Review of Applied Linguistics in Language Teaching*, 55(1): 41–60.

Mossakowski, J., and Busch, B. (2010). On Language Bio-Graphical Methods in Research and Education. In Arnesen, A.-L. (ed.). *Policies and Practices for Teaching Sociocultural Diversity: A Framework of Teacher Competences for Engaging with Diversity* (pp. 158–172). Strasbourg: Council of Europe Publishing.

Murray, H., and Morgan, C. (1943). *Thematic Apperception Test Manual*. Cambridge: Harvard University Printing Office.

Odeniyi, V,. and Lazar, G. (2020). Valuing the Multilingual Repertoires of Students from African Migrant Communities at a London University. *Language, Culture and Curriculum*, 33(2): 157–171.

Oppenheim, A. N. (1992). *Questionnaire Design and Attitude Measurement*. London: Pinter Publishers.

Park, J. S. Y., and Wee, L. (2013). *Markets of English: Linguistic Capital and Language Policy in a Globalizing World*. New York: Routledge.

Peters, A., and Coetzee-Van Rooy, S. (2020). Exploring the Interplay of Language and Body in South African youth: A Portrait-Corpus Study. *Cognitive Linguistics*, 31(4): 579–608.

Piccardo, E. (2013). Plurilingualism and Curriculum Design: Toward a Synergic Vision. *TESOL Quarterly*, 47(3): 600–614.

Prasad, G. (2014). Portraits of Plurilingualism in a French International School in Toronto: Exploring the Role of Visual Methods to Access Students' Representations of Their Linguistically Diverse Identities. *Canadian Journal of Applied Linguistics*, 17: 51–77.

Ramsey, E., Ibbotson, P., and McCole, P. (2006). Application of Projective Techniques in an E-Business Research Context. A Response to "Projective Techniques in Market Research – Valueless Subjectivity or Insightful Reality?" *International Journal of Market Research*, 48(5): 551–573.

Reber, A. S., and Reber, E. (2008). *Słownik psychologii* [Dictionary of Psychology]. Warszawa: Wydawnictwo Naukowe Scholar.

Riessman, C. K. (2008). *Narrative Methods for the Human Sciences*. Thousand Oaks, CA: Sage.

Rorschach, H. (1921). *Psychodiagnostics: A Diagnostic Test Based on Perception*. NY: Grune an Stratton.

Salo, N. and Dufva, H. (2018). Words and Images of Multilingualism: A Case Study of Two North Korean Refugees. *Applied Linguistics Review*, 9 (2–3): 421–448.

Soares, C. T., Duarte, J., and Günther-van der Meij, M. (2020): "Red is the Colour of the Heart": Making Young Children's Multilingualism Visible through Language Portraits. *Language and Education*. https://doi.org/10.1080/09500782.2020.1833911 [accessed 15 February, 2021].

Springer, A. (2013). Techniki projekcyjne [Projection Techniques]. In Kaczmarek, M., Ole-jnik, I., and A. Springer (eds.). *Badania jakościowe – metody i zastosowania* [Qualitative Research – Methods and Applications] (pp. 163–193). Warszawa: CeDeWu.

Stein, P., and Newfield, D. (2007). Multimodal Pedagogies, Representation and Identity: Perspectives from Post-Apartheid South Africa. In Cummins, J., and Davison, C. (eds.). *International Handbook of English Language Teaching*. Part 1 (pp. 919–930). New York, NY: Springer.

Szondi, L. (1947). *Experimentelle Triebsdiagnostik*. Bern: Verlag Hans Huber.

Vertovec, S. (2007). Super-Diversity and Its Implications. *Ethnic and Racial Studies*, 30(6): 1024–1054.

Wagner, E. E. (2008). Beyond "Objective" and "Projective": A Logical System, for Classi-fying Psychological Tests: Comment on Meyer and Kurtz (2006). *Journal of Personali-ty Assessment*, 90(4): 402–405.

Wąsikiewicz-Firlej, E. (2014). Constructing the Professional Identity of EFL Teachers through Languaging: A Narrative Inquiry. In Lankiewicz, H., and Wąsikiewicz-Firlej, E. (eds.). *Languaging Experiences: Learning and Teaching Revisited* (pp. 157–190). New-castle upon Tyne: Cambridge Scholars Publishing.

Wąsikiewicz-Firlej, E. (2020). Intercultural Experiences from the Perspective of Narrative Interviewing: Methodological Pitfalls and Challenges in the Eyes of the Student and the Teacher. *Neofilolog*, 55(2): 307–326.

Wąsikiewicz-Firlej, E., Szczepaniak-Kozak, A., and Lankiewicz, H. (2022). *Doświadczenie pobytu w Polsce w narracjach zagranicznych studentów*. Warszawa: Wydawnictwo FRSE.

Will, V., Eadie, D., and MacAskill, S. (1996). Projective and Enabling Techniques Explored. *Marketing Intelligence and Planning*, 14(6): 38–43.

Woltmann, A. G. (1960). Spontaneous Puppetry by Children as a Projective Method. In Rabin, A. I., and Haworth, M. R. (Eds.). *Projective Techniques with Children* (pp. 305–312). NY: Grune and Stratton.

Yoell, W. A. (1974). The Fallacy of Projective Techniques. *Journal of Advertising*, 3(1): 33–36.

ABOUT THE AUTHOR

Emilia Wąsikiewicz-Firlej, having D. Litt. in linguistics, PhD in applied linguis-tics and MA in English studies, holds a position of an Associate Professor in the De-partment of Ecolinguistics and Communicology at Adam Mickiewicz University in Poznań. Her research delves into applied linguistics and communication stud-ies, focusing on professional communication, intercultural communication and spe-cialised discourse. Emilia Wąsikiewicz-Firlej has published over 40 academic papers, including a monograph on corporate communication, journal articles, book chap-ters and edited collections. The scholar is a frequent presenter at national and in-ternational conferences. She has also delivered guest lectures abroad, e.g. in Italy, Portugal, Romania, Slovakia and Spain. Before joining academia, she worked as a marketing and public relations specialist.

APPENDIX 1: TRANSCRIPTION CONVENTIONS

//	Overlapping talk from the first to the last slash.
...	A pause of one second or less within an utterance.
(2.0)	A pause of more than one second within an utterance or between turns, the number indicates the length of the pause.
***	A deletion
[ ]	An explanatory insertion.
Italics	A word or part of a word emphasised by a speaker (Boje, 1991).

6

Deconstructing ethnic insults by means of dual character concepts: Finding evidence of newly emerging contemptuous meanings with recourse to philosophical concepts and corpus linguistics

Anna Szczepaniak-Kozak

ABSTRACT

This chapter applies the notion of dual character concepts, which were originally proposed by experimental philosophers and cognitive psychologists (Knobe et al., 2013; Del Pinal & Reuter, 2017; Reuter, 2019), to discuss how racist and xenophobic hate speech could be more easily identified, especially for the purpose of raising public awareness about it and its prosecution by law enforcement bodies. This type of research has not been developed extensively so far, apart from a few studies which delve into the reality of blacks who suffer from racism at the hand of white racists, e.g. Shelby (2002), Ikuenobe (2011; 2018).

Most terms and concepts are either descriptive or normative in character, but some terms and concepts are "part descriptive, part normative" and these parts are "related but independent" (Reuter, 2019: 1). Some of such combinatory concepts also contain the idealized social function which the person, object or notion is expected to feature (Leslie, 2015). Finally, when a normative term denotes human attributes, it often includes the component of "the commitment to fulfil the idealized function associated with that role" (Reuter, 2019: 4). What I intend to illustrate in this chapter is that individuals who spread hate speech argue that the offensive terms which they use should be treated as only descriptive in character, and thus they try to avoid judicial or social responsibility for propagating hate. This line of argumentation is substantiated using the example of the word Ukrainian and its negative synonym banderowiec. The latter is used by Poles who are prejudiced against Ukrainians, especially in social media, to offend Ukrainian migrants and refugees residing in Poland. When they are accused of insulting this national minority, they argue their innocence or ignorance, claiming that they are not aware of the value-ascribing potential which the hateful words bear. This way, they escape not only public contempt but also, what is worse, they are often acquitted in court. Studying hate speech slurs as dual character concepts may not only increase our knowledge and awareness of the essence of hate speech, but primarily could provide law enforcement personnel (police officers, judges) with a more precise terminological apparatus for their daily functioning, especially the argumentation in cases tried (Domselaar, 2018).

Keywords: hate speech, dual character concept, xenophobic prejudice, normative vs. descriptive meaning, insulting ethnonym, contempt expressed in words

6.1. INTRODUCTION

In 2015, Sarah-Jane Leslie published an article titled "'Hillary Clinton is the only man in the Obama administration': Dual character concepts, generics, and gender", which discussed the concept of *man* as used in the quote. Leslie argues that such a statement is offensive jointly to Hillary Clinton, male members of Obama's government and women in general. In her own words:

> The comment is primarily insulting to the male members of the administration – implying that they are weak, passive, and ineffectual – but is also insulting to Hillary Clinton, suggesting that she has taken on mannish characteristics to the point where she is no longer a woman. The comment further demeans women in general, associating them with undesirable features such as passivity and weakness – yet at the same time, it cautions women against rejecting these features, lest they end up like the mannish Hillary Clinton

(Leslie, 2015: 111).

In the commenter's mind, there are two separate but related concepts: 1) for a man: a descriptive concept based on physical features of a person, and 2) for a real man, which is an evaluative concept, related to gender-related behavioural portrait. These two concepts are related but only partially overlapping in connotation (Leslie, 2015: 112).

Following this line of reasoning, it is assumed in this chapter on hate speech targeting national or ethnic minorities that seemingly neutral terms may denote different concepts and that one can offend a person by using ethnic epithets in their less widespread meaning just like "it is possible to insult people by using gender terms in non-standard ways" (Leslie, 2015: 112). In fact, there are terms which denote a national or ethnic membership, whose dictionary definitions are neutral in sentiment, and which can be used by some speakers with their own specific categories in mind. In other words, a descriptive term becomes a folk concept, escaping catalogued definitions.

The reason why these non-standard cases of language use have become the subject of this text is because when a crime involving hate speech is tried in court, the defending counsel, and frequently the judge rely, in their accounts and interpretations of hate speech, on the dictionary meanings of words used in an incident, disregarding the contextual meanings involved. A frequent and lamentable consequence of such an approach is that not only the victim but also the judge and the public feel that the intention of a particular demeaning comment was to offend or express a prejudiced attitude, but it is difficult to find credible evidence for the presupposition rendered in the message. It is as if certain words led a double life, a neutral and negative/contemptible one.

A good example of such a practice can be the Polish word *Murzyn*. It is a common name for a dark-skinned person. It comes from Latin *Maurus*, which was borrowed by many European languages in the Middle Ages to denote a person from Africa. In this period, it started to be used to refer to dark-skinned figures in the Bible (Siuciak, 2004). For centuries its connotative meaning was considered to be neutral, as it was borrowed for referential use and not to stigmatize. And, indeed, in the majority of dictionaries of Polish, this word is not categorized as negative or offensive. This is in agreement with the perception of this word by Poles as well. According to an opinion poll conducted by the Public Opinion Research Centre in 2006, the majority of Poles, namely 81%, considered this word neutral and definitely not offensive (Feliksiak, 2007: 14).

The above arguments stand, however, in direct opposition to what black migrant communities in Poland perceive as neutral language use. They argue there are numerous proverbs in Polish in which *Murzyn* appears as a synonym and symbol of the primitive, the uneducated, the enslaved or the lazy. *Murzyn* constitutes the vehicle of such a meaning in proverbs such as:

- *sto lat za Murzynami* (Eng. literally: a hundred years behind the blacks, i.e. backward);
- *mieć swojego Murzyna* (Eng. literally: to have your own black, i.e. to have a servant);
- *nie chcę być Murzynem we własnym kraju* (Eng. literally: I do not want to be a black in my own country, i.e. I do not want to be a second-rate person in my own country).[1]

There is also a very vulgar expletive *w dupie u Murzyna* (Eng. literally: in a black's bottom, i.e. in a predicament/unpleasant situation). A popular Polish TV and radio presenter of Ghanaian descent, Brian Scott, says in an interview with Śmigulec-Odorczuk (2012): When I hear I am *Murzyn*, I do not feel needed in this company.[2] In a similar vein, Seydou Zan Diarra, an Afropole from Mali, considers offensive even the appreciative phrases that he hears at his daily veterinary doctor's practice, like: Since he was able to cure my dog, it does not matter whether he is *Murzyn* or not[3]. This is so, because such a comment indicates that the speaker did not expect much of a person who is black-skinned. Finally, in one of the interviews with victims of hate speech in Poland which I conducted for the purpose of another paper, there is evidence supporting the finding that the negative sentiment/connotation of the word *Murzyn* is known to Polish kindergarten children. One interviewee reports (Szczepaniak-Kozak et al., 2015, Interview 8)[4]:

> My child returned from kindergarten and said "Mummy, other kids do not want to play with me. They say they do not play with *Murzyn*". On this ground, I believe it must be a negative name as nobody says "I do not want to play with an African but they say not with *Murzyn*".

There is much truth in the saying that the word *Murzyn* disregards the fact that the people who are referred to by means of this negative epithet were born and brought up in different places, cultures and religions. In a sense, this is an example of a false origonym, i.e. a label implying commonality on false grounds, e.g. that they belong to a group spanning over nations and countries. Ohia (2013: 98–99) suggests that *Murzyn* is, in fact, demeaning on three metaphorical levels

---

1 This is an updated discussion of the same topic which was published in Adamczak-Krysztofowicz and Szczepaniak-Kozak (2017: 303).

2 All translations of Polish text into English included in this chapter were made by the author. Polish original words: *Jak słyszę o sobie 'Murzyn', to czuję, że jestem niepotrzebny w tym towarzystwie.*

3 *Skoro on wyleczył mojego psa, to co z tego, że Murzyn!*

4 *Moje dziecko przychodziło z przedszkola i mówiło „Mamusiu, dzieci nie chcą ze mną się bawić, bo powiedziały, że z Murzynami się nie bawią". Stąd też moje myślenie, że musi to być negatywne określenie, skoro nikt do niej nie mówi „Z Afrykanką nie chcę się bawić, tylko z Murzynem".*

(dirt, primitive backwardness and darkness) and suggests that this word should be treated as a pauloethnonym due to the implicit mechanism of negative evaluation which it triggers.

What I intend to illustrate in this chapter is that individuals who spread hate speech argue that the offensive terms which they use should be treated as only descriptive in character, and thus they attempt to avoid judicial or social responsibility for propagating hate. When they are accused of insulting a given national minority, they argue their innocence or ignorance, claiming that they are not aware of the value-ascribing potential which the hate-filled words bear. This way, they escape not only public contempt but also, what is worse; they are often acquitted (cf. Wodak, 2015). Studying hate speech slurs as dual character concepts may not only increase our knowledge and awareness of the essence of hate speech, but primarily could provide law enforcement personnel (police officers, judges) with a more precise terminological apparatus for their daily functioning, especially for the argumentation used in cases tried (Domselaar, 2018).

6.2. LITERATURE REVIEW

This chapter applies the notion of dual character concepts, which was originally proposed by experimental philosophers and cognitive psychologists (Knobe et al., 2013; Del Pinal and Reuter, 2017; Reuter, 2019) to discuss how racist and xenophobic hate speech could be more easily identified, especially for the purpose of raising public awareness about it and its prosecution by law enforcement bodies. This type of research has not been developed extensively to date, apart from a few studies which delve into the reality of blacks who suffer from racism at the hands of white racists, e.g. Shelby (2002), Ikuenobe (2011, 2018).

6.2.1. Dual character concepts defined

Most terms and concepts are either descriptive or normative in character. A descriptive word refers to something observable or experienced, whereas a normative one bears an evaluative content, that is, its meaning derives from norms or standards. In this sense, a cat is a descriptive term, while quality is a normative one. Although this seems a neat division, some terms and concepts do not fall easily into it. This is so, not only because norms and standards are socially agreed upon and dependent on individual features, e.g. one's background, intelligence, education or profession. In fact, the normative dimension very often represents certain abstract values associated with the corresponding descriptive elements (Knobe et al., 2013). This means that some terms and concepts are "part descriptive, part normative" and these parts are "related but independent" (Reuter, 2019: 1). Some such combinatory concepts also contain the idealized social function which the person, object or notion fulfils (Leslie, 2015). Finally, when a normative term denotes human attributes, it often includes the component of "the commitment to fulfil the idealized function associated with that role" (Reuter, 2019: 4).

The complex nature of dual character concepts can be exemplified by the word "mentor". This word denotes a colleague who assists a less experienced person in their job (the descriptive content). However, the social expectations which a mentor needs to fulfil are value- and norm-driven as well. For example, being somebody who leads the mentee through meanders of professional and personal development means that such a person should also be trustful, patient and supportive. Personal commitment is also expected – such a person should show emotional involvement in assisting the other to develop. All in all, a person can officially/descriptively be called a mentor, but if they do not conform to social expectations and professional standards, they are not true mentors and are not perceived as such.

Concepts like mentor are of a dual character, which means that "they encode not only a descriptive dimension but also an independent normative dimension for categorization" (Reuter, 2019: 1). There are certain ideals associated with being a real or true mentor, i.e. one "who exemplifies the ideals of" this role (Leslie, 2015: 117). It requires a certain degree of professional and contextual knowledge to differentiate between the descriptive and normative meanings of this, and many other words which have a dual character. Ideals involve certain salient properties "determined by widespread social agreement" (Leslie, 2015: 121) and roles attributed to such a group as typical, especially what is necessary to "successfully play such a role" (Leslie, 2015: 124). The properties associated with an ideal can be "undesirable", too. To clarify her idea, Leslie (2015: 125) proposes that:

> as a minimal condition of a kind having a dual character, there has to be a plausible characterization of the social role of that kind such that it can be successfully carried out by someone who does not meet the descriptive criterion for membership in the kind, and conversely, that meeting the descriptive criterion of the kind does not entail successfully carrying out the social role.

In Polish, the word *ciocia* (Eng. an aunt, diminutive in Polish) is a dual character concept. Although there is a descriptive plane to this word, specifying that *ciocia* is an older, senior woman in one's family, usually your mother's or father's sister, there are also some normative properties and roles that such a family member should play. An aunt is a caring and supportive woman with whom one has close relations. There are aunts who do not behave this way, meaning they are not "real" aunts. At the same time, there are women to whom one is not related, e.g. your parents' friends, whom one often sees and who takes care of you from time to time in your childhood. An emotional bond between you and them develops, and so such a woman may become a child's confidant and, despite her not being the child's blood-related family member, she is called *ciocia*. In this sense, such a person fulfils certain normative expectations which are held for "true" descriptively understood aunts. The normative properties which we associate with the social role which make us classify a given person as our aunt are called primary (Leslie, 2015: 125). In my example, this is a person who becomes our supporter and confidant when we are children. The fact of kinship is the secondary property.

Concepts which are dual in character could be considered from the lexical perspective as polysemous words. Leslie (2015: 116) posits that "dual character concepts give rise to lexical entries that have distinct, though related, senses – in this case a descriptive sense and a normative sense". The meanings can overlap or be separate, and what differentiates them is that "the subject term of normative generics is understood as involving the normatively loaded, not the flat descriptive, sense of the term" (Leslie, 2015: 135). The normative plane denotes whether "the subject succeeds (or fails) in living up to certain norms and ideals that apply to a group" described by a given word (Leslie, 2015: 135). The normative sense can be considered a conversational implicature which has been systematically communicated within a speech community, and thus the term has become polysemous (cf. Leslie, 2015: 137). The descriptive sense is, then, the conventional implicature, which is not truth-evaluable (Meibauer, 2021). In fact, Leslie aptly refers to Lakoff (1987), to substantiate her proposition: "Even if a particular phenomenon begins life as a pragmatic matter, the lexicon can evolve to assimilate it" (quoted after Leslie, 2015: 137).

According to Leslie (2015: 121, cf. Knobe et al., 2013), dual character concepts involve "social kinds" or categories. This is why Leslie uses them to explain gender and racial slurs, and I intend to apply them to hate speech motivated by xenophobia (see section 6.3).

6.2.2. Insults as a type of hate speech

In this writing, I adopt a wide definition of hate speech as the "expression of hate against persons or groups, in particular by the use of expressions serving their denigration" (Meibauer, 2013: 1, translated from German by the author[5]), jointly with a pragmatic one: "motivated, inherent and strategic linguistic impoliteness that deliberately [...] conveys hatred, contempt or aggression towards individuals" coming from groups different from that of the speaker (cf. Adamczak-Krysztofowicz &

---

5   Meibauer (2013: 1) considers only the verbal plane of hate speech.

Szczepaniak-Kozak, 2017: 288). In the context of hate speech motivated by xenophobic prejudice, it is worth mentioning that oftentimes it has a strategic aim, e.g. to pool people of the same extremist views together, to establish a hierarchy of difference among minorities or a relation between the majority and minority groups based on primary features, that is, traits which humans inherit and thus cannot change (national/ethnic descent, first language(s) spoken, characteristic physical features). The definition itself[6] is less important in the context of this paper, because any definition will be too general in order to help, say, prosecutors or judges differentiate an act of verbal abuse or impoliteness toward national/ethnic minorities or migrants, from an instance of hate speech. They do not explain what exactly should be understood by the term in its linguistic essence.

Hate speech can take many forms, implicit and explicit, straightforward or ironic. There already exists extensive research on it, indicating that it can be realized by phonetic, morphological, lexical, syntactic, non-verbal and multi-modal means. In this text, I am not going to delve into all of the possible facets of hate speech. Instead, I intend to focus on these types of hate speech which can be tried in court, or, to put it more precisely, to see whether it is possible to extend the repertoire of triable cases of hate speech by means of linguistic analysis supported by the dual concept approach. However, I purposefully put aside in this writing so-called hate speech messages calling for action, because they are relatively easy to account for and find convincing linguistic grounds to be tried. To illustrate, when a person says in Polish "let's get rid of this black shit" (Pol: *pozbądźmy się tego czarnego gówna*[7]), it is possible nowadays to convince the court that this is an ill-meaning threat targeting a dark-skinned person, which results in finding the author of this threat guilty. This is so because this comment calls for inflicting illegal action on the victim (forceful expulsion), which is punishable. What this chapter discusses are other instances of hate-filled communication – covert insults which stem from the xenophobic prejudice of their authors. The reason for my particular interest in such ethnic slurs comes from the fact that this article intends to clarify certain terms for legal prosecution of xenophobic hate communication based on my experience gathered from linguistic analyses of cases investigated by Polish prosecuting institutions.

Hate speech is not officially recognized in Polish criminal codices, and there is no straightforward relation between a word or phrase that is offensive and an actual offence, and each case/incident is to be considered individually on its own merits. Usually, the prosecutor or the judge investigates the reason for the attack, e.g. whether there was a reason, or perhaps if the reason was a trivial one, or if there was none at

---

6   There are many definitions available, the most well-known is that included in United Nations Strategy and plan of action on hate speech (2019).

7   Any offensive terms appearing in this chapter are included solely for the purpose of academic argumentation.

all. Some crimes involving or constituting offensive speech are persecuted as insults. Some insults are open racial slurs, e.g. *czarnuch* (Eng. *nigger*), but some are relatively vague words or expressions, which are interpreted as equally offensive or as menacing as overt slurs by the persons attacked. However, in numerous, infamous cases the offenders were acquitted because the judge, after seeking the informed opinion of a linguistic expert, passed sentence that the words concerned were not insulting. A well-known example is the word *pedał* (Eng. bicycle pedal), which is a common negative label for a male gay person in Polish. It is commonly used by Poles, yet, in a court case investigating an incident involving the physical and verbal abuse of a homosexual person, a famous Polish linguist claimed in his expert statement that the word's meaning is a bicycle part and was used accordingly in that case. In doing so, the linguist relied only on the descriptive meaning of the label which can be found in recognized dictionaries of Polish.

Such vague or indirect insults are frequent in political discourse as well, a good example of which is the expression "inner city families" as used in Donald Trump's speech. This phrase is seemingly neutral in sentiment, denoting somebody's place of residence in a densely populated urban area (the descriptive meaning). However, it can become synonymous for "poor blacks" in certain contexts. Khoo (2017), in his paper devoted to offensive words in political discourse, argues that this expression bears covert connotations of "poor, crime-ridden, African American neighbourhoods" when used in the following fragment of speech delivered by Donald Trump: "The American Dream will be in hock. The shining city on the hill will start to look like an inner-city wreck" (Trump, 2011: 4, after Khoo, 2017: 33). "Inner city" becomes a code word enabling passing racist remarks which can be easily denied. The same effect is achieved by the phrase "the flights from West Africa" (denoting undesirable African migrants) used in a tweeter entry by the same politician:

> I have been saying for weeks for President Obama to stop the flights from West Africa. So simple, but he refused. A TOTAL incompetent! (@realDonaldTrump, October 24, 2014) (example after Miceli and Castelfranchi, 2018: 209).

Khoo's take on why such signals are understood as racist, violating certain social norms of politeness and equality, but still being able to render the intended meaning precisely is:

> Someone using a code word exploits (intentionally or otherwise) their audience's stereotypical beliefs about what they are talking about, without explicitly communicating these beliefs. Thus, using a "code word" allows (or leads) the audience to draw additional inferences from the

> speech without it being clear that they are doing so – and this is what distinguishes coded speech from speech where the relevant stereotypical beliefs are explicitly asserted. In a slogan: code words don't work by being vehicles of implicit communication; they work by triggering inferences which they are not used to communicate (Khoo, 2017: 34).

Such code words enable winning over those audience members who do not want to pass as racist, but rather prefer to think of themselves, and to be thought of, as concerned simply about "the spread of crime and poverty" (Khoo, 2017: 36–37). To achieve this effect, code words tap into "pre-existing stereotypical beliefs" which are shared in a given society (Khoo, 2017: 56). This is why so-formulated statements are appealing and acceptable to a wider audience, but still convey a prejudiced and contemptuous attitude.

6.2.3. Contempt as the emotion underlying hate communication

In legal texts, an insult is often defined as a message whose function is to show contempt. Contempt is a negative emotion which is a result of comparing oneself with another person, and "evaluating the latter as much below one's own standard" (Miceli & Castelfranchi, 2018: 207). Such an evaluation focuses on a "trait which is remarkably negative and salient to the evaluator's standards. As a consequence, the negative evaluation elicits disrespect for the target […], and the typical attitude of 'looking down on' the contemned person" (original words by Miceli & Castelfranchi, 2018: 208). A contemptuous evaluation leads to the dislike of the other, considering them undeserving of interest and inferior on many levels. In extreme cases, this emotion may lead to neglecting the other, or to avoiding any contact with them. Some individuals prefer not to reveal their contempt openly and instead convey it by means of ridiculing or mocking messages. In some other people, the emotion is so strong that they want to rationalize their views based on faulty premises that they have "the right to pass judgments and influence other people's attitudes toward the person scorned; treating (verbally) a person worse than they deserve or worse than they should be treated" (Cegieła, 2012: 17).

Contempt is often linked with social hierarchy. As mentioned above, the source of contempt is the strong feeling of superiority and disapproval that the sender of the message has towards another person or a group of people. The sender despises and distances himself from these people because he believes them to be, for example, inferior, uneducated, uncivilized, backward or mentally ill. The people being the target of contempt are viewed by the commenter as having some (inborn) permanent disposition, e.g. being lazy. However, despite being considered a permanent feature, the person affected by it is expected to be willing to work on changing this disposition. Behaving in a particular "undesirable" manner is evaluated as a lack of effort and willingness to change – a type of stubborn persistence.

The feeling of superiority which some social groups have towards those who are considered a lower rank frequently underlies racism and xenophobia. In societies characterized by large differences in social position, and resulting (often hidden) privileges, such as better education, jobs and financial standing, they "are easily translated into differences in personal worth. Higher-rank people often view lower-rank ones as rough, mean, lacking in intellectual capacities as well as in refined feelings and tastes" (Kraus & Keltner, 2013, after Miceli & Castelfranchi, 2018: 213). Furthermore, "higher social class people are more likely than lower class people to believe that societal inequality is caused by genetic superiority or inferiority" (Kraus & Keltner, 2013, after Miceli & Castelfranchi, 2018: 213). This is why any form of bad treatment, especially social exclusion, marginalization, is easily recognized as the right treatment: the despised group is responsible for their (inborn) inferiority and they stubbornly persist in their unwillingness and inability to change. The group which is higher in social hierarchy feels absolved from remorse for mistreating the despised group because the targets are considered responsible for their "condition of inferiority" (Miceli & Castelfranchi, 2018: 214).

Contempt can be expressed in a variety of ways, both verbal and non-verbal ones. Miceli and Castelfanchi (2018: 209) list laughter or sneering, dismissing gestures (rolling one's eyes at another), plainly insincere compliments or ironic insults ("That was smart", when in fact the statement was not), name-calling (moron, loser) or (ethnic) jokes. The type which is of interest in this paper includes abusive words, insulting or ridiculing expressions, messages containing non-rationalized arguments that lack logical explanation or distorting the actual state of affairs. The speech or text is often constructed as a series of supposedly logical arguments. Such arguments tend to omit important arguments, distort others and make broad generalizations. The aim behind such messages is usually to justify amoral intentions towards the disadvantaged, e.g. social exclusion of the despised, harming them, including depriving them of respect, "deformation of someone's image through the use of discrediting destructive means that block independent, objective evaluation and positive emotions associated with the person discredited" (Cegieła, 2012: 18). Wojński (2011: 16) emphasizes that the recognition of words as insulting is determined by general moral norms. In detail, a linguistic phrase or gesture should be understood as it is accepted in a particular environment, even if the conventional but established meaning is significantly different from the dictionary meaning. Language, by definition, is a contractual code and not regulated by authorities or rules. Dictionaries therefore describe linguistic reality rather than constitute it.

Most of the existing body of research refers to contemptuous messages which include offensive epithets, e.g. objectifications, somatonyms, animalizations, militarionyms. However, there is dearth of studies on covert hate speech (Baider, 2020, 2022; Baider & Constantinou 2020). Anna Cegieła (2012: 18–19) lists the following means used by those who sow hatred and practice the rhetoric of contempt in a less straightforward manner:

- Invalidating disinformation – a procedure in which a portion of information concerning a despised person or group is subjected to selection. What is good about the group is usually passed over in silence or invalidated by diminishing its importance. However, those threads that serve to build a negative image are made known and exposed. Additionally, the selection of the material is carried out in a way that suggests that this is what the knowledgeable think, and only the ignorant think differently. Some such messages are supported by the statement of a person who is presented as an expert, who is one of the few who understands the gravity of the situation and whose knowledge guarantees understanding of phenomena, such as social and political, incomprehensible to the general public.

- Discrediting – is a statement containing mockery, derision, insult, understatement and/or attributing negative actions to people whom we want to harm. Discrediting can also consist in repeatedly recalling someone's mistake, to which great weight is given, which in the context of new selected information and the act of mockery or imputation strengthens the negative media image of the discredited person (or group). Discrediting has one goal – stigmatization leading to discrimination or isolation.

Discrediting can take different forms and types. Most often, the process of discrediting begins with categorizing the criticized person or group and attributing characteristics that particular individuals exhibit to the entire social group they belong to. This rhetorical strategy has been known since ancient times and is called metonymy. Metonymy consists in replacing the proper word with another one – related in meaning, which remains in a simplified relation to the proper one (cf. Korolko, 1998: 58–80). Metonymy is concrete, directly connected with what it refers to. Its understanding is based on the stereotypical processes of categorization and metonymy is one of the basic mechanisms which play a role in creating one's linguistic picture of the world. Interpretation of metonymy requires less intellectual potential than metaphor, so it is more understandable and reaches a wider audience. It can be a tool to hide shortcuts in argumentation and shallow thoughts. This is why copyrighters often prefer to rely on metonymy in commercials than on metaphor, because the former is easier to understand. It also draws the audience's attention to the connection between the object visible in the ad and the outside world, rather than presenting something new. An example of metonymy used in advertising could be a scene like this: the camera shows consecutive objects emerging from the darkness: a thick electric cable, a belt, a police truncheon, a leash, a riding crop, an iron and a poker. With each one, a calm voice asks the following questions: "Are you an electrician? A soldier? Maybe a policeman? Do you have a dog? Do you ride horses? Do you like ironed shirts? Do you heat your house with a stove?" The last image is the face of a crying child, in semi-darkness, and a voice: "What object is your child afraid of?" Only in the end do we learn that this is commercial for a social awareness campaign devoted to domestic abuse of children. It is suggestive because it uses metonymy. Instead of showing violence in the family, it shows ordinary objects used for violence (attributes of violence rather than a holistic phenomenon) (example taken from the lecture of Emilia Wąsikiewicz-Firlej, 11.12.2019).

In relation to the topic of this text, one type of metonymy – synecdoche – will be the most important. This rhetorical trope consists in using the name of a part of a set instead of the name of the whole, or vice versa. By means of this rhetorical trope the word used acquires a more general or more specific meaning. These considerations will be especially important when explaining the normative meaning of the word *banderowiec*.

Discrediting is also often constructed by rhetoric based on the contrast of us good/defenceless/peaceful vs. you bad/dangerous/hostile. Obviously, this contrast is detached from reality, or based on arguments that refer to a fraction of the discredited community. Anna Cegieła (2012: 22) emphasizes that this type of discrediting is used for a purpose: "a properly understood discrediting message should cause the recipient to understand why discredited people should be excluded, isolated or deprived of voting and/or other rights". Such rhetoric justifies exclusion and, if heard/read on many occasions/in different sources, makes it an obvious postulate after some time.

In order to obtain a clear and unambiguous image of the discredited persons or groups, the authors of such messages link "permanently certain traits or views to a given social group, here a national minority, and suggest that other traits and behaviours are also associated with these traits" (Cegieła, 2012: 20), such as a threat to the security of the state and its citizens, an economic or health hazard. In reality, these characteristics do not necessarily occur together or do not combine at all. Equally important, the threat from discredited individuals and groups is described as so significant that it is necessary to deprive the group of the right to vote, isolate them, exclude them or expel them from a particular territory. This image also presupposes the absence of individual characteristics of the individuals comprising the insulted group in question. Such a message, as a rule, is not rational, because it omits a whole range of facts on the way to generalization.

Having established the philosophical, psychological and linguistic mechanisms behind hate speech fuelled by xenophobic views and sentiments, in what follows, I intend to analyse two words which in Polish can function as dual character concepts, and due to this duality can overlap in meaning as ethnonyms.

6.3. AIMS OF THE RESEARCH AND METHODOLOGICAL SOLUTIONS

The words in focus in this analysis are *Ukrainiec* (Eng. a Ukrainian) and *banderowiec*, i.e. a historical term which was coined to refer to semi-legal partisans active during WW2. Their descriptive meanings are related but not synonymous, whereas the two became synonymous in the normative domain in contemporary Polish in specific communication contexts. More precisely, both of them, albeit descriptively having differing denotations (people living on the territory on Ukraine now/a historical Ukrainian paramilitary group), can be normatively used to evoke a negative sentiment, here contempt, for the same group – migrant or refugee Ukrainians living on the territory of Poland. In order to substantiate my reasoning, I will use corpus data of two types and selected data mining/analysis operations which are enabled by corpus linguistics algorithms, here these offered by Sketch Engine. To provide evidence for the dual character of these two words and the area in which they are overlapping in their normative reference, the analytical part of this chapter will be organized in line with the following research questions (RQ):

RQ 1: What is the descriptive meaning of the word *Ukrainiec*?

RQ 2: What is the normative meaning of the word *Ukrainiec*?

RQ 3: Can the word *Ukrainiec* be considered an expression of contempt, and if so, under what conditions?

RQ 4: What is the descriptive meaning of the term *banderowiec* historically and in contemporary Polish?

RQ 5: What is the normative meaning of the term *banderowiec*, taking into account the discourse of radical xenophobic circles in Poland today?

RQ 6: Can the term *banderowiec* be considered an expression of contempt, and if so, under what conditions?

RQ 7: Can the word *banderowiec* be considered a term that directly refers to the Ukrainian nationality, including synonyms or surrogates for the word *Ukrainians*, and if so, under what conditions?

6.3.1. Corpus linguistics as an analytical approach in this study

This piece's aim is to show how two particular nouns have become insulting words in their normative senses with the help of corpus data. Corpus data serves only as a source of useful attestations and not as a true methodological approach. This means that the dual character of the words will be evidenced with partial support from data mining and concordance analysis in order to demonstrate how the specific linguistic choices adopted by the authors of the hate messages reveal their contempt and prejudice. In a sense, the methodology applied is corpus-assisted critical discourse analysis (Aluthman, 2018; Mahmoud & Bahareh 2017; Partington, 2008; Taylor, 2008). This is in line with van Dijk's argument that "in CDA all methods of the cross-discipline of discourse studies, as well as other relevant methods in the humanities and social sciences, may be used" (2015: 466–467). The corpus methodology when applied in CDA primarily allows for a significant increase in the amount of data to be analysed, thus rejecting one of the arguments raised by its critics, regarding the lack of representativeness of the analysed texts (see among others Stubbs, 1997: 7; Orpin, 2005: 38; Cheng, 2013: 1; Wang, 2018). Advantages of using corpus linguistics techniques in CDA also include limiting the researcher subjectivity and selectivity as regards the analysed material, thanks to the use of transparent criteria for corpus selection (see Baker, 2006: 12; Breeze, 2011).

This combination of methods was initially applied by scholars such as Taylor (2008) to study the representation of migrants in the British and Italian press. Together with my colleague Katerina Strani, I used the same approach to investigate online reactions to the killing of Arkadiusz Józwik, a Polish migrant in Harrow, England, in 2016, which was initially portrayed in the media as an act of hate crime in the pre-Brexit period. The study revealed that hate speech patterns such as "us and them" distinctions, racialization, "deserving" and "undeserving" migrants, victimising the perpetrator's (dominant) group, or victim blaming, may not be relevant to the groups involved in the event but to socio-economic contexts (cf. Strani & Szczepaniak-Kozak, 2022).

Corpus linguistics presupposes drawing conclusions about linguistic processes on the basis of huge databases, usually covering texts of various origins or authors. These databases can be collections of authentic linguistic texts authored by different language users, spoken and written, representing different varieties, styles and types of texts which are composed in specific proportions, and which are collected as electronic files. These texts can be easily searched to find frequency lists or interconnections between lexical chunks and contexts. Algorithms designed for corpus linguistics computations also make it possible to understand how a given state of affairs is realized using linguistic resources in a given type of discourse, including how semantic/meaning processes and relations are generated. It is also possible to compare a given dataset with others. Most importantly, the person using a corpus can filter the search results, but as a rule, the selection of texts is beyond his/her discretion. Hence, corpus data is considered as an objective source of attestations about authentic language use.

The attestations derived from corpora can be of various types, however, for the analytical purpose of this study, collocations and their further analyses appear to be the most useful. Collocations are words that occur frequently together, combining into more or less fixed phraseological connections. Most often, we identify collocation within the words to the left and right of the word in focus. It is also possible to analyse the affinity of words within a given thematic field, for example, discourse about Ukrainians residing in Poland.

As already mentioned, the corpus analysis was conducted using Sketch Engine, a tool developed by Kilgarriff et al. (2014), which offers algorithms enabling text mining and analysis of authentic texts to identify what is typical in language and what is a rare, unusual or emerging usage. It enables access to annotated reference corpora in 30 languages, one of which was used in the present study. In Sketch Engine, it is possible to generate a Word Sketch visualization which presents a particular word's collocates and other words in its surroundings. It can be compared to a brief summary of "the word's grammatical and collocational behaviour" in the dataset. "The results are organized into categories, called grammatical relations, such as words that serve as an object of the verb, words that serve as a subject of the verb, words that modify the word etc." (Sketch Engine, 2021). Another useful analytical tool offered by Sketch Engine is its Word Sketch algorithm, designed to generate comparisons of two words' usages by contrasting their collocations found within a corpus or even corpora (Sketch Engine, 2021). In some cases, I also display word concordances which illustrate in which sentential co-text a particular word tends to appear.

6.3.2. Analysed data

In answering the research questions listed above, I will rely on attestations from two types of corpora: reference corpora, maintained by recognized bodies of experts in linguistics, and a tailor-made corpus compiled by a trained linguist. The reference corpora are listed below. They are the only voluminous open-access collections currently available which can be considered representative of contemporary everyday Polish:

- *The National Corpus of Polish* (PSEN) – covering texts written between 1945[8] and 2010 (Górski & Łaziński, 2012: 36). Most texts (80%) included in PSEN were written after 1990, 15% between 1945 and 1990 and only 5% before 1945. This dataset includes texts of fiction, daily and specialist press, recordings of conversations, ephemeral and online texts (Przepiórkowski et al., 2012). It covers over one and a half billion Polish words. Apart from diversity in terms of subject matter and genre of the texts, it has also been collected with attention to the representation of interlocutors of both genders, different ages and from different regions. Searching in it is facilitated by the PELCRA tool (http://www.nkjp.uni.lodz.pl/).

---

8   1945 marks the lower limit of contemporary Polish according to Zenon Klemensiewicz (1985).

- *The Polish Parliamentary Corpus* (PPC) (https://kdp.nlp.ipipan.waw.pl/over-view) – a collection of linguistically annotated texts from the plenary sessions of the Polish Parliament (Sejm and Senate of the Republic of Poland), parliamentary interpellations and questions, and committee meetings from 1919 to the present.
- *The Reference Corpus of the Polish Internet* (Polish Web, 2012), exact description: *Polish Web 2012, plTenTen12, RFTagger,* which is a part of an international collection of Internet corpora with the target size of +10 billion words. It contains various texts from the Internet and counts in total 7,715,835,214 words collected from 22 million documents. Sketch Engine currently provides access to and mining of this corpus in more than 30 languages. Similar to PELCRA, created for PSEN, it enables the compilation of grammatical and collocational behaviour of a word in a given context. It is particularly useful for this study because it comprises authentic online data downloaded by the SpiderLing program from the domain .pl without any preference filters set.

All these datasets are reference corpora because they have been developed in a balanced manner and thus can serve as a basis for comparison. However, the offensive words in focus are not very frequent there. Additionally, they are not entirely contemporary. Only the Polish Parliamentary Corpus (PPC) is regularly supplemented with new data. The National Corpus of Polish (PSEN) stopped being updated in 2010, and Polish Web 2012 was a corpus created from a huge amount of online texts available as of June 2012[9]. This is why, for the purpose of this study, in 2019 I also compiled an occasional/tailor-made subcorpus which included Polish texts in which *banderowiec* and *Ukrainiec* appeared. These are texts, comments and posts about Ukrainians living in Poland or about Polish-Ukrainian relations. This special dataset comprised 3,015 sentences, 106,361 words in total. I uploaded it to Sketch Engine under the name: *Ukrainiec and banderowiec.* It served as a source of information about these two words' usage and enabled studying their collocational behaviour (cf. Sketch Engine visualizations in Figures 6.1–6.5).

To provide evidence on the basis of more recent linguistic data, I will also refer to one more source, which is a corpus comprising 190 online texts (posts) that in 2020 Magdalena Jaszczyk-Grzyb collected and analysed under my co-supervision as part of her Ph.D. project (2021). Her corpus includes recent Internet posts and below the line comments characteristic of the discourse propagated by radical nationalist or xenophobic groups in Poland. They qualified for her study if the post itself,

---

9   A newer version of this corpus is available: Polish Web 2019, downloaded by SpiderLing in December 2019. At the time of writing this paper (Spring, 2021), the corpus was not accessible for Sketch Engine users.

or at least one of the comments or one of the replies, constituted an example of a hate message. Her corpus includes online texts which Poles uploaded to Facebook between January 2018 and January 2020 about four groups of foreigners: Muslims, Roma, Ukrainians and Jews. I will occasionally refer to her findings pertaining to the discourse about Ukrainians held in on the Polish Internet.

Since ethnonyms found in colloquial speech are highly variable, they seldom make it into traditional dictionaries, or are catalogued with some delay. Most often they cease to be used before lexicographers catalogue them and publish them in concise editions (Peisert, 1992: 219, cf. Niekrewicz, 2017: 53). They usually reflect the emotional tensions and moods of a particular time, so their ephemeral meanings do not find their way into dictionaries which appear in print because process of compiling dictionaries can sometimes take decades. According to Niekrewicz (2017: 56), "75 percent of the names of people by nationality and race recorded in community dictionaries do not appear in traditional lexicons. This is related to the smaller number of colloquial ethnonyms in dictionaries published in print". This is why the use of tailor-made corpora comprising online communication is necessary.

6.4. ANALYSIS OF *UKRAINIEC* AND *BANDEROWIEC* WITH VIEW TO THEIR DUAL CHARACTER

In order to provide evidence for the dual character of the words in focus, jointly with their potential to carry contemptuous sentiment, in what follows, first the research questions listed in section 6.3 will be answered and then a concluding discussion will be included (section 6.5). The analyses' starting points are visualizations generated by Sketch Engine algorithms (in Figures 6.1–6.5). On their basis, I draw inferences about situated meanings of the words in focus. Each collocate is displayed in a circled bubble, the size of which depends on its relative frequency in the entire corpus (the bigger the bubble, the bigger the frequency). The figures present word combinations in Polish and their translations into English are provided in the accompanying discussion. No changes or language corrections (including spelling) were made to the data.

RQ 1: What is the descriptive meaning of the word *Ukrainiec*?

Ukrainiec is a Polish ethnonym for a person from Ukraine. In the reference sources, representing more formal language (printed sources and parliamentary discourse), the word appears in word combinations which are mostly neutral. These include adjectives (as displayed in Figure 6.1): *odpowiedzialny* (responsible), *mądry* (wise), *greko-katolicki* (orthodox), *młody* (young) and *przeciętny* (average). It enters into

Figure 6.1 Word Sketch visualization for *Ukrainiec* in the tailor-made corpus: *Ukrainiec and banderowiec* (compiled on the basis of PSEN and PPC)

collocations with verbs as well: *żywić* (to feel), *wykształcić* (to educate) and *rozumieć* (to understand), *znać* (to know), *przyjeżdżać* (to come), *odjechać* (to leave), and *przyjmować* (to receive). There is only one word which can connote negatively: *napaść* (an/to attack), which comes from a hearing about an incident which took place during WW2.

RQ 2: What is the normative meaning of the word *Ukrainiec*?

The meaning of the same word appears to be slightly different when we analyse the informal texts compiled in the reference corpus for the Polish Internet, Polish Web 2012 (cf. Figure 6.2). There are only two (neutral) modifiers which appear in the Word Sketch visualization: *galicyjski* (from Galicia – a historical part of Poland) and *dwumetrowy* (two-meter). The verbs are more significant as the majority of them refer to hostile or unpleasant activities: *mordować, zamordować, wymordować* (to murder), *zabić* (to kill), *uzbroić* (to arm), *wysiedlić, wysiedlić* (to resettle), *napaść* (to attack) and *ostrzeliwać* (to shoot). The only neutral words are: *mieszkać* (to live) and *proklamować* (to declare e.g. independence). It is clear from these attestations that in informal online communication, the word appears in co-texts generating a

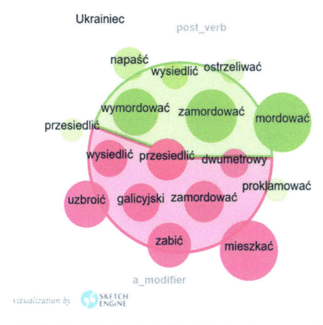

Figure 6.2 Word Sketch visualization for *Ukrainiec* in the reference corpus: *Polish Web 2012*

more negative sentiment. Ukrainians, as presented in the linguistic data downloaded from the Polish Internet, are associated with activities which may be evaluated as hostile (an enemy of Poles and Poland).

In a more recently compiled dataset (Jaszczyk-Grzyb, 2021), among 200 Facebook posts there are those which also suggest that Ukrainian men are lazy and do their job in a lackadaisical way, consequently they botch every job they take on. They are characterized as showing a demanding attitude and a tendency to abuse alcohol. Such posts are discrediting to Ukrainians in general[10]:

- Ukrainians come to Poland and they call us out because they don't like something
- I have a buddy who employed Ukrainian women and Ukrainians in his company (xxx) and he found out very quickly that the men/Banderites are total lazies and slobs! It was a bit better with the women – but they only worked

---

10   After Jaszczyk-Grzyb (2021):
      Przyjeżdżają Ukraince do Polski i nas tu WYZYWAJĄ bo im COŚ się nie podoba.
      Mam kumpla co zatrudniał w swoim przedsiębiorstwie Ukrainki i Ukraińców ... i stwierdził bardzo szybko, że faceci/banderowcy to totalne lenie i nieroby! Trochę lepiej było z kobietami – ale pracowały tylko żeby nakarmić swoich leniwych chłopów. Generalnie mówi, że nigdy więcej tej swołoczy.

to feed their lazy guys. Generally he says that never again [would he employ] this scum.

RQ 3: Can the word *Ukrainiec* be considered expression of contempt, and if so, under what conditions?

Assuming that vocabulary is the most expressive plane of language, through which the linguistic image of the world is manifested, we may conclude that the stereo-typical way Ukrainians are perceived by anonymous Poles is negative, sometimes escalating to contemptuous. The linguistic world picture is the knowledge about the world (i.e. the typical way of seeing reality, the relations and relationships in it, as well as certain values) fixed in the grammatical structure and meanings of words (especially the latter), as well as in the structure and meanings of texts. The processes of perception and thinking are inextricably linked with language. For instance, in Jaszczyk-Grzyb's (2021) corpus we may find the following sentences about Ukrainians[11]:

1. Animal filth, lots of them left for the regained territories. That's why it's so hard to live in western Poland.
2. WHO DO THESE COWS THINK THEY ARE … !!!!! DO WE POLES GO TO THIS SHITTY UKRAINE AND BEHAVE LIKE THEM IN POLAND….?

Furthermore, in the visualizations and examples presented above, Ukrainians are compared to cows (animalization), filth and scum (vulgar objectification), which are insulting epithets. Also in the PPC, we may find similar comparisons. In 1998, Aleksander Masiej, a minority activist, during discussions in a special committee for migrations uttered this belittling sentence: "an axe and a cow (Eng. literally cattle) equals an Ukrainian"[12] (https://kdp.nlp.ipipan.waw.pl/query_corpus/4/#).

RQ 4: What is the descriptive meaning of the term *banderowiec* historically and in contemporary Polish?

The meaning of the word *banderowiec* has evolved over years. In the past, the noun *banderowiec* referred exclusively to former members of the revolutionary faction

---

11 *Zwierzęce ścierwa, pełno tego wyjechało na ziemie odzyskane. Dlatego tak ciężko żyje się w zachodniej Polsce.*
   ZA KOGO TO BYDŁO SIĘ MA … !!!!! CZY MY POLACY JEŹDZIMY NA TA ZASRANĄ UKRAINĘ I TAK SIĘ ZACHOWUJEMY JAK ONI W POLSCE …?

12 *siekiera plus bydlę równa się Ukrainiec.*

operating within the Organisation of Ukrainian Nationalists (abbreviation in Polish OUN), called the Ukrainian Insurgent Army (abbreviation in Polish UPA). In the reference corpus for the Polish Internet, most of the examples of use of the word *banderowiec*, out of 4,863 results found in total, refer to a historical context in the past tense, thus describing members of the revolutionary faction of OUN-UPA or Ukrainians who took part in the genocide of Poles which took place during WWII in the region called Volhynia. In the majority of cases, this word occurs in co-text of verbs in the past tense. The pronouns used with them indicate deictic references (in a physical context) either to places and objects in Ukraine or to dead people. They also often refer to the massacre in Volhynia and former Polish provinces within present-day Ukraine.

For more than a dozen years, *banderowiec* has also been used to describe contemporary Ukrainian nationalists and sympathizers of strongly nationalist groups in Ukraine, who look up to questionable idols from the past, including the traditions of OUN and UPA. The two descriptive meanings of this word are historically linked. Collocations of the word, visualized as a Word Sketch, are shown in Figure 6.3. They indicate a military or hostile sentiment: *wróg* (an enemy), *faszysta* (a fascist), *maszerować* (to march), *równać* (to align with), *zbiorowy* (belonging to a group, here a paramilitary formation). All in all, the descriptive meaning of this word is

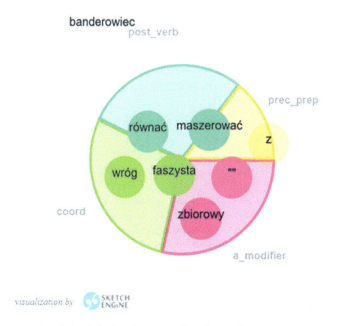

Figure 6.3 Word Sketch for *banderowiec* in the tailor-made corpus: *Ukrainiec and banderowiec*

negative because it refers to partisan groups that murdered Poles during World War II or groups of Ukrainian nationalists.

There are also other sources testifying to this descriptive meaning of the word *banderowiec*. For instance, PSEN provides a vivid evidence of the lexical presupposition of the word *banderowiec*[13]:

> In Gerhard's publications, the words *Ukrainian*, *upowiec* and *banderowiec* meant the same thing as a degenerate, bloody bandit. "His swarthy face never lightened up", he portrayed the figure of the sotnia commander. – "On narrow lips [...] cut by a scar from childhood, no one seems to have seen a smile. The grey eyes seemed to glare at everyone he talked to, and there were few people who would not feel uncomfortable under the weight of that gaze. Hryń did not recognize entertainment [...] he took part in traditional village fights, in which he distinguished himself with rare cruelty. During one such fight, he split his stepfather's head open with an axe. He bit until the body was damaged"
>
> (PSEN, text: 1303919981002, Pawel Smoleński, 1998-10-02).

RQ 5: What is the normative meaning of the term *banderowiec*, taking into account the discourse of radical xenophobic circles in Poland today?

In the years 2015–2022, before the Russian invasion on Ukraine, the number of Ukrainian citizens residing in Poland was steadily increasing[14], which was accompanied by anti-Ukrainian rhetoric in the Polish mass media and social media communications. *Banderowiec* acquired then another meaning (a normative one). It is now, in Polish, an allusion to the nationality of the people described in this way as illustrated in the titles of press articles, e.g.

---

13   *W publikacjach Gerharda słowa „Ukrainiec", „upowiec" i „banderowiec" znaczyły to samo, co zwyrodniały, krwawy bandyta. „Jego smagła twarz nie rozpogadzała się nigdy – portretował postać dowódcy sotni. – Na wąskich wargach [...] przeciętych od dzieciństwa blizną nikt chyba nie widział uśmiechu. Oczami o szarym połysku zdawał się świdrować każdego, z kim rozmawiał, i mało było ludzi, którzy pod ciężarem tego wzroku nie czuliby się nieswojo. Hryń nie uznawał rozrywek [...] brał udział w tradycyjnych wsiowych bójkach, w których wyróżniał się rzadkim okrucieństwem. W czasie jednej z takich bójek rozpłatał siekierą głowę swemu ojczymowi. Kąsał do uszkodzenia ciała.*

14   This text was written before more than three million Ukrainian refugees came to Poland in 2022.

- Today in Przemyśl "Ukrainians" and "bandera"[15] are synonyms (Smoleński, 2018)[16]
- For another suspect, "Ukrainian" means "Bandera" (Gorczyca, 2019)[17]

In some contexts, the word *banderowiec* is synonymous with the word *Ukrainian* in the general sense, especially for Ukrainian people residing on Polish territory. This is evident, for example, from more recent attestations from the tailor-made corpora. PSEN and PPC do not indicate this meaning, simply because they contain data from 2012 at the latest. On the other hand, in a more recent purpose-compiled corpus (Jaszczyk-Grzyb, 2021) covering the most current online texts of a hateful nature, the authors of contemptuous entries refer to Ukrainians in this way, e.g.

> Stupidity of some kind... Let the bandera get out of our country and that's it. Let them manage on their own or let Putin take them... there are eternal problems with them. Personally, it's starting to piss me off that I can hear their language all around me in my country!!! (Jaszczyk-Grzyb, 2021)[18].

Using *banderowiec* (here a derivative from *bandera*) to mean Ukrainians living in Poland illustrates the metonymy-based (synecdoche) inferencing mechanism discussed in section 6.2.3. The name of a fraction of a nation/society is used instead of the name that describes the whole nation/society. Such a word substitution is very easily accepted by the audience, as most people will find it logical (similar to the social awareness campaign message mentioned earlier). Entries of this type contain verbs in the present tense and refer to Polish reality. They also often suggest that people labelled as *banderowiec* should be expelled from Poland, which leads to a false and irrational conclusion that Ukrainian sympathizers of that partisan group and members of nationalistic groups live in Poland.

Jaszczyk-Grzyb's (2021) research also shows that, compared to hate messages targeting the other nationalities and ethnic groups she studied (Muslims, Jews, Roma), Ukrainians are ascribed a hostile character on the basis of non-rationalized lines of argumentation. In comments classified as hate discourse against Ukrainians in Polish, she observed an increased number of militarionyms, of which *banderowiec* is an example. A militarionym is a type of insulting epithet which functions as an

---

15 *Bandera* gave rise to the word *banderowiec*; Stepan Bandera was the leader of OUN UPA (the partisan group).

16 *Dzisiaj w Przemyślu „Ukrainiec" i „banderowiec" to synonimy.*

17 *Dla kolejnego przesłuchiwanego Ukrainiec znaczy banderowiec.*

18 *Głupota jakaś....Niech bandery robią wypad z naszego kraju i tyle. Niech sobie radzą sami albo niech ich Putin bierze....z nimi wieczne problemy. Osobiście mnie zaczyna wkurzać że w koło słyszę ich język w moim kraju!!*

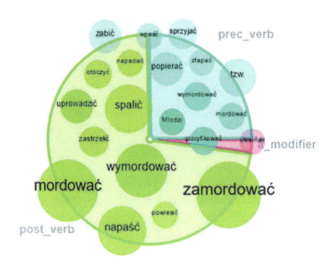

Figure 6.4 Word Sketch for *banderowiec* in the reference corpus *Polish Web 2012*

ethnonym/nationality name, which suggests (contains a lexical presupposition) that the national group denoted by it has an armed character and/or undertakes warlike and hostile actions. This negative normative meaning of *banderowiec* is confirmed by evidence coming from the contemporary Internet sources gathered in the reference corpus for the Polish Internet Polish Web 2012 (Figure 6.4). This word is accompanied by verbs which are rather negative in sentiment: *zabić* (to kill), *modować/wymordować/zamordować* (to murder), *powiesić* (to hang), *napadać/napaść* (to attack), *otoczyć* (to surround), *uprowadzić* (to abduct/kidnap), *spalić* (to burn down), *zastzelić* (to shoot), *złapać* (to capture), *gloryfikować* (to glorify). The only neutral in connotation words are: *młodzi* (the young), *sprzyjać* (to favour), *popierać* (to support) and *wpaść* (to fall into).

RQ 6: Can the term *banderowiec* be considered expression of contempt, and if so, under what conditions?

On the basis of analysis of the tailor-made corpora (e.g. Jaszczyk-Grzyb, 2021), we may posit that authors of hateful posts referring to Ukrainians by means of the word *banderowiec* attribute the following traits to them: stupidity (Example 1), hostility and home-/family-lessness (Example 2) or lack of human attributes due to being sent by the devil (Example 3). The contemptuous attitude towards Ukrainians is also evidenced by comparisons to distasteful objects or animals found in the dataset with vulgarisms in the co-text. In Example 1, it is also suggested that Ukrainians, in general, should be sent to Siberia, which in Polish is always associated with the Russian concentration camps where people die due to forced labour and harsh weather conditions. The overall sentiment in these examples is that Ukrainians, referred to by coinages created from *banderowiec* and *bandera*, are dangerous, hostile and deserve eternal condemnation. This way, these insulting posts reduce and/or pigeonhole individual Ukrainians to a single pattern, attributing to them characteristics which seemingly the entire Ukrainian people share (Jaszczyk-Grzyb, 2021)[19]:

1. Nice brainwashing at the banderas. The Russkies will have to run a new line to Siberia.
2. Get the hell out of Poland, you Bandera strays.
3. Qurvy banderowski SHIT FOR ETERNITY they are not people THEY ARE THE DEVIL'S SPAWN.

Calling someone *banderowiec*, especially someone unknown to us, who has not caused us any harm or other offence, can be considered an expression of contempt in Polish. Insulting someone by means of a militarionym attributes all Ukrainians with the features of a Ukrainian ultra-nationalist group, with radical views, which in the past or currently has shown a hostile attitude towards Poles. It is an act which is strongly emotionally charged and devoid of rational arguments. Furthermore, comparing a person to a member of a radical group, which is accused of criminality and active aggression, may involve the desire to arouse the strongest negative emotion (close to hostility) in the audience. It is therefore an act of insult by association with these groups. Perceiving people through the prism of (historical) crimes committed by some Ukrainians against Poles is also negative in its meaning, because it attributes "particularly negative traits" to the entire population of a given country. Such statements may cause feelings of strong dislike, or at least disapproval, of Ukrainians in general, or even fear in some of those who read such messages. Contemptuous words may convince some of the people reading them of the position expressed in the sentence and also of the acceptance of aggressive actions against this nationality. In the case of already radicalized people, on the other hand, these words maintain and intensify their negative attitudes or prejudices. According to the latest available research (cf. Gervais & Fessler, 2017; Winiewski et al., 2017), feeling contempt towards another person or social group triggers anger

---

19   *1: Ładna pralnia mózgu u banderowców. Ruskie będą musieli uruchomić nową linię na Syberię. 2: Won z Polski banderowskie znajdy. 3: Qurvy banderowskie PIEKŁO IM NA WIECZNOŚĆ to nie ludzie TO SZATAŃSKIE POMIOTY.*

and disgust, instead of compassion, guilt or shame, leading to desensitization to the group. The more contact people have with acts of discrimination in their environment, including hate speech, the more they are prone to becoming insensitive to it, become familiar with it and stop seeing it as a serious social problem. Hence, it is not surprising that some of the suspects see nothing offensive in certain messages they promulgate.

In addition, the word *banderowiec* itself, apart from referring to former or contemporary Ukrainian nationalists (i.e. a reference to a specific group of people), has a lexical presupposition. This is an element of a word's meaning that cannot be isolated from its constituent elements. The presupposition is a necessary and important element of a word's meaning, despite the absence of the element expressing it (Linde-Usiekniewicz, n.a.). The presupposition in the word *banderowiec* is the identification of a given person as one who harmed Poles in the past, who committed hostile acts against Poles, or who nowadays expresses negative opinions and has hostile intentions towards Poles. Associating an unknown person with such acts is an insult also in legal terms, because they are attributed with traits that "according to culturally determined and generally accepted evaluations constitute an expression of contempt for human beings" (Kulesza, 1984: 1, translation from Polish by the present author). In turn, the purpose of this statement is to arouse an eminently negative emotion and a negative attitude towards the persons concerned.

RQ 7: Can the word *banderowiec* be considered a term that directly refers to the Ukrainian nationality, including synonyms or surrogates for the word *Ukrainians*, and if so, under what conditions?

As already indicated, nowadays, some speakers of Polish treat the word *banderowiec* as a synonym for the word *Ukrainian*. It is a negative ethnonym, of the militarionym type. In a similar manner, people from Africa are recognized in communication on the basis of the somatonym *czarnuch* (Eng. Nigger, literary in Polish black), which implies dirtiness in Polish. By using these words, all Ukrainians are ascribed hostile intentions, just as all Africans are ascribed dirtiness, both of which are despicable features in the eyes of Poles.

Banderowiec is particularly often used to mean any person from Ukraine in the discourse conducted by radical xenophobic circles in Poland. Such a normative meaning of the word *banderowiec* is also adopted by non-nationalistic Poles, e.g. members of the Polish Parliament, which can be deduced from the Polish Parliamentary Corpus (PPC). For example, Tomasz Rzymkowski, MP, during a speech in the Polish Sejm on 21 January 2018, said[20] "For you banderowiec equals a Ukraini-

---

20   *Dla państwa* **banderowiec** *równa się Ukrainiec.*

an" (PPC, Label: 201519-sjm-ppxxx-00057-01). Earlier, another MP, Miron Sycz, argued that this was due to the fact that[21] "Kremlin propaganda has been hammering its citizens and the world for a long time that the entire Ukrainian people are a bunch of banderowiecs and fascists" (PPC, Sejm 23.04.2015, Label: 201115-sjm-ppxxx-00091-02).

Without trying to trace the sources and appropriateness of such widespread attitudes, most of the examples provided indicate that in some contexts *banderowiec* is used as a substitute for the word *Ukrainian*, and by analogy *banderowiec* means a Ukrainian. Such an interpretation of the meaning of this word is particularly viable when that it is accompanied by a verb in the present tense and when it appears in sentences not referring (e.g. by means of deictic expressions, including pronouns) to events in the history of Polish-Ukrainian relations, especially the period of 1942–1947, or to the activities of Ukrainian radical groups. Of these references, some will denote Ukrainian ultra-nationalists, but such references will appear in political contexts, often referring to (pseudo-) patriotic attitudes, issues happening in Ukraine and their reception in Poland. Texts in which *banderowiec* means a nationalistic Ukrainian will also include indexical expressions (pronouns and names) pointing to objects (e.g. monuments, symbols, people) representing ultra-nationalist ideologies. On the other hand, those of the contemporary references that deal with issues concerning social and economic relations in Poland, for example, the labour market, social welfare, contain expressions denoting the reality and people in Poland. In such instances, the word *banderowiec* is a negative militarionym substituting the predominantly neutral word *Ukrainian*.

The affirmative answer to the present research question, of whether the normative meaning of the word *banderowiec* overlaps with the descriptive meaning of the word *Ukrainiec,* can also be justified by means of CL findings. On the tailor-made corpus *Ukrainiec and banderowiec*[22], it was possible to generate a comparative visualization of their collocational behaviour: those collocations which are typical of each word separately and those which appear equally frequently with both (Figure 6.5). While various nationality names often appear with the word *Ukrainiec* in coordinate expressions/phrases, *Polak* (a Pole), *Żyd* (a Jew), *Białorusin* (a Byelorussian), *Anatolij* (a proper name typical of Ukrainian or Russian), the collocation typical of *banderowiec* is *faszysta* (a fascist). However, both words equally frequently appear in the co-text with the word *wróg* (an enemy).

---

21 *Propaganda kremlowska przez długi czas wbija swoim obywatelom i światu, że cały naród ukraiński to zbiorowy **banderowiec** i faszysta.*

22 The corpus was created of sentences including these two words which appear in PSEN and PPC.

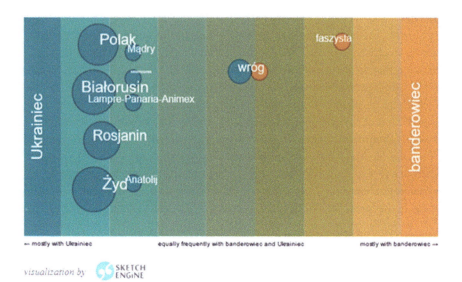

Figure 6.5 Word Sketch difference for *Ukrainiec* and *banderowiec* in the tailor-made corpus: *Ukrainiec and banderowiec*

6.5. DISCUSSION OF FINDINGS

The inspiration for the present study was the observation that hate messages may have implications for social actions on both the individual and collective level. It was my intention, then, to bring forward representative examples of such messages to enable readers to understand their full meaning, both in the descriptive and normative sense.

The analysis of the linguistic data by means of corpus linguistic tool enabled us to answer the research questions in an affirmative way, and alongside to provide evidence that in fact the two words in focus can be considered dual character concepts: they can have a descriptive and normative meaning which are related but which stand on their own. It is true that the nature of the words in focus can be explained by means of their lexical presupposition. However, thanks to presenting them as dual character concepts we provide forensic evidence to law enforcement officials that in some contextualised use both words on their own become ethnic militarionyms conveying xenophobic prejudice, rather than descriptive terms denoting a person's place of birth (*Ukrainiec*) or their belonging to a nationalistic paramilitary organization (*banderowiec*). For linguists it may seem self-explanatory, but when, for example, a case is tried at court, the presupposition may be too weak an argument. Saying that each word denotes two different concepts is more convincing than that a word has a hidden meaning which reveals itself at a closer look. In detail, for most everyday language use, it may be enough to consider that the ethnonyms simply feature some negative connotation when used to express a speaker's prejudice or emotion towards Ukrainians. However, this explanation, although perfectly logical and linguistically viable, is not enough for persecution and judicial trials. It is not possible for a judge simply to declare these words may become negative in sentiment. Persecutors and judges need evidence drawn from representative datasets that they have an independent negative meaning on their own. As I mention earlier in the chapter, hate mongers often defend themselves in court by saying that they are not aware of the value-ascribing potential which the hateful words bear and that such a meaning is not listed in a dictionary. Because it is difficult to find credible evidence for the presupposition rendered in, for example, a post uploaded to its author's social media account, my idea is that CL tools can help law enforcement officials argue that there are two different concepts which the word denote. This is what, in fact, this study indicates. CL data show that, for example, *Ukrainiec* when used to denote economic migrants or refugees living in Poland is a xenophobic slur, a code word enabling passing xenophobic remarks which can be easily denied. Such code words enable winning over those audience members who do not want to pass as nationalistic, but rather prefer to think of themselves, and to be thought of as concerned simply about the future of Poland and its prosperity. The same approach was used in the studies of verbal discrimination discussed earlier in this chapter (Shelby, 2002; Ikuenobe, 2011, 2018; Khoo, 2017). Finally, there is a clear advantage of conducting such an argumentation with the support of larger sets of data, generated from naturally recorded sources, produced by different members of a given community, spanning over a longer period of time. It can be considered not only grounded more in everyday language practices but also leading to more objective conclusions.

6.6. CONCLUSIONS

Language conveys and perpetuates certain stereotypes (i.e. fixed ideas about the world), creates "a community of thinking and feeling, and in a further way also influences our behaviour"[23] (Bartmiński, 2009: 25). As van Dijk (1995: 3) claims, hate can be socially learned, and language is essential to the process of its ideological production and reproduction. In his original words, hate speech:

---

23 *Język przekazuje i utrwala pewne stereotypy (czyli utrwalone wyobrażenia o świecie), wytwarza wspólnotę myślenia i odczuwania, a w dalszej kolejności wpływa poniekąd także na nasze zachowania.*

is not simply an innocent form of language use or a marginal type of verbal social interaction. Rather, it has a fundamental impact on the social cognitions of dominant group members, on the acquisition, confirmation, and uses of opinions, attitudes, and ideologies underlying social perceptions, actions, and structures (van Dijk, 1995: 3).

Equally importantly, language is also strongly connected to the system of values appreciated in a given group and resulting from the historical experience of the entire linguistic community. That is to say, people learn values by acquiring language and they express values through language. The processes of perception and thinking cannot be separated from language. Language is, therefore, a plentiful source of knowledge about the world which is fixed in the grammatical structure, meanings of words, clichéd texts (e.g. proverbs), but also of prior judgments, i.e. implied by linguistic forms, fixed at the level of social knowledge, beliefs, myths and rituals (Bartmiński, 2009: 12). This store of knowledge, including a system of values, is called the linguistic image of the world (Bartmiński, 2009: 25). People do not have a richer source of knowledge about other people. Finally, words constitute the most expressive level of language organization, by means of which the linguistic image of the world is revealed, i.e. the typical way of perceiving the reality, the relations and connections in it, all of which are underpinned by certain values. For instance, members of a given community learn what the normative and acceptable/expected behaviour typical of a particular national group is during their acculturation. In one interview which I conducted with Poles for a different study, there appeared a remark that a Polish woman learned as a child that *Ukrainiec* is a name for a troublemaker. She said: "we called any brat in our village Ukrainiec"[24] (Interview 8). Hearing such statements in their early years, children essentialise the social group. As Leslie (2015: 130) aptly posits, children begin to "view the members of the social group as sharing natural, inborn similarities" and continue to so throughout their lives. Furthermore, members of the group realize what properties are associated with their category and when confronted with other/antagonistic groups may perform in the way found typical, sometimes even against their values. For example, a hard-working and dedicated Ukrainian, having repeatedly heard stereotypical utterances or insulting epithets about Ukrainians may decide to adopt lower work ethics, in desperation coming to the conclusion that "one might 'feel the normative force' even if one thinks that in general one ought *not* to have the property in question" (Leslie, 2015: 130, emphasis in original). The opposite case is possible as well. When a person born Ukrainian does not have such properties, he or she is not called a true Ukrainian.

---

24   *Każdego gagatka w naszej wsi nazywaliśmy Ukrainiec.*

Hopefully, making the general public aware of the hidden meaning-making potential which some words carry may help us build a more open and less discriminatory society.

REFERENCES

Adamczak-Krysztofowicz, S., and Szczepaniak-Kozak, A. (2017). A Disturbing View of Intercultural Communication: Findings of a Study into Hate Speech in Polish. *Linguistica Silesiana*, 38: 285–310.

Aluthman, S. (2018). A Corpus-Assisted Critical Discourse Analysis of the Discursive Representation of Immigration in the EU Referendum Debate. *Arab World English Journal* (AWEJ) 9(4): 19–38. https://doi.org/10.24093/awej/vol9no4.2 [accessed 30.01.2019].

Baider, F. (2022). Covert Hate Speech, Conspiracy Theory and Anti-Semitism: Linguistic Analysis vs Legal Judgement. *International Journal of Semiotics and Law*. https://link.springer.com/article/10.1007/s11196-022-09882-w [accessed 30.06.2022].

Baider, F. (2020). Obscurantism and Conspiracy Theory: Contempt in Online Debates Focused on Vaccination. *Revue de linguistique et de didactique des langues (LIDIL)* 61. https://journals.openedition.org/lidil/7652 [accessed 30.06.2022].

Baider, F., and Constantinou, M. (2020). Covert Hate Speech: A Contrastive Study of Greek and Greek Cypriot Online Discussions with an Emphasis on Irony. *Journal of Aggression Language and Conflict*, 20(8): 262–287. https://benjamins.com/catalog/jlac.00040.bai [accessed 30.06.2022].

Baker, P. (2006). *Using Corpora in Discourse Analysis*. London: Continuum.

Baker, P., Hardie, A. and McEnery, T. (2006). *A Glossary of Corpus Linguistics*. Edinburgh: Edinburgh University Press.

Bartmiński, J. (2009). *Stereotypy mieszkają w języku* [Stereotypes Live in Language]. Lublin: Wydawnictwo UMCS.

Breeze, R. (2011). Critical Discourse Analysis and Its Critics. *Pragmatics*, 21(4): 493–525.

Cegieła, A. (2012). O retoryce pogardy i wykluczenia w polskim dyskursie publicznym [On Rhetoric of Contempt and Exclusion in Polish Public Discourse]. *Poradnik Językowy*, 9: 14–25.

Cheng, W. (2013). Corpus Based Linguistic Approaches to Critical Discourse Analysis. https://www.researchgate.net/publication/262070226_Corpus-Based_Linguistic_Approaches_to_Critical_Discourse_Analysis [accessed 13.08.2019].

Del Pinal, G. and Reuter, K. (2017). Dual Character Concepts in Social Cognition: Commitments and the Normative Dimension of Conceptual Representation. *Cognitive Science*, 41: 477–501.

Domselaar, van I. (2018). The Perceptive Judge. *Jurisprudence*, 9(1): 71–87.

Feliksiak, M. (2007). Społeczna percepcja przemocy werbalnej i mowy nienawiści. Raport stanu badań [Social Perception of Verbal Violence and Hate Speech]. Warszawa: Centrum Badania Opinii Społecznej. http://www.mowanienawisci.info/wp-content/uploads/2014/04/K_074_07.pdf [accessed 30.01.2019].

Gervais, M. and Fessler, D. (2017). On the Deep Structure of Social Affect: Attitudes, Emotions, Sentiments, and the Case of "Contempt". *Behavioral and Brain Sciences*, 40: 1–18.

Gorczyca, A. (2019). Przemyśl tylko polski. Wszystko, co czerwono-czarne, kojarzone jest tam z UPA [May Przemyśl Be Only Polish. Everything That Is Red and Black is Associated There with UPA]. *Magazyn Wyborczej* (online), 15.06.2019. [accessed 30.01.2019].

Górski, R., and Łaziński, M. (2012). Reprezentatywność i zrównoważenie korpusu [Representativeness and Balance of Corpus]. In Przepiórkowski, A., Bańko M., Górski R., and Lewandowska-Tomaszczyk, B. (eds.). *Narodowy Korpus Języka Polskiego* [The National Corpus of Polish] (pp. 25–36). Warszawa: Wydawnictwo Naukowe PWN.

Ikuenobe, P. (2011). Conceptualizing Racism and Its Subtle Forms. *Journal for the Theory of Social Behaviour*, 41(2): 161–181.

Ikuenobe, P. (2018). The Practical and Experiential Reality of Racism: Carter's and Corlett's Realism about Race and Racism. *Journal of African American Studies*, 22: 373–392.

Jaszczyk-Grzyb, M. (2021). *Mowa nienawiści ze względu na przynależność etniczną i narodową w komunikacji internetowej. Analiza porównawcza języka polskiego i niemieckiego* [Ethnically and Nationally Motivated Hate Speech in Internet Communication. A Comparative Analysis of Polish and German]. Poznań: Wydawnictwo Naukowe UAM.

Khoo, J. (2017). Code Words in Political Discourse. *Philosophical Topics*, 45(2): 33–64.

Kilgarriff, A., Baisa, V., Bušta, J., Jakubíček M., Kovář, V., Michelfeit, J., Rychlý, P., and Suchomel, V. (2014). The Sketch Engine: Ten Years on. *Lexicography*, 1(1): 7–36.

Klemensiewicz, Z. (1985). *Historia języka polskiego* [History of the Polish Language]. Warszawa: Państwowe Wydawnictwo Naukowe.

Knobe J., Prasada, S., and Newman, G. (2013). Dual Character Concepts and the Normative Dimension of Conceptual Representation. *Cognition*, 127: 242–257.

Korolko, M. (1998). *Sztuka retoryki* [The Art of Rhetoric]. Warszawa: Wiedza Powszechna.

Kraus, M. W., and Keltner, D. (2013). Social Class Rank, Essentialism, and Punitive Judgment. *Journal of Personality and Social Psychology*, 105: 247–261.

Kulesza, W. (1984). Zniesławienie i zniewaga [Insult and Defamation]. In Kulesza, W. (ed.). *Ochrona czci i godności osobistej w polskim prawie karnym – zagadnienia podstawowe* [Protection of Honour and Personal Dignity in Polish Criminal Law – Basic Issues] (pp. 167–168). Warszawa: Wydawnictwo Prawne.

Lakoff, G. (1987). *Women, Fire, and Dangerous Things*. Chicago: University of Chicago Press.

Leslie, S.J. (2015). "Hillary Clinton Is the Only Man in the Obama Administration": Dual Character Concepts, Generics, and Gender. *Analytic Philosophy*, 56(2): 111–141.

Linde-Usiekniewicz, J. (n.a.). Wybrane problemy rozpoznawania językowych cech „nawoływania do nienawiści" [Selected Issues in Detecting Linguistic Features of "Calling for Action"]. http://www.otwarta.org/wp-content/uploads/2015/07/EKSPERTYZA-J%C4%98ZYKOZNAWCZA_J.-Linde-Usiekniewicz.pdf [accessed 30.01.2019].

Mahmoud, S., and Bahareh, M. (2017). U.S. News Media Portrayal of Islam and Muslims: A Corpus-Assisted Critical Discourse Analysis. *Educational Philosophy and Theory*, 49(14): 1351–1366. https://doi.org/10.1080/00131857.2017.1281789 [accessed 30.01.2019].

Meibauer, J. (2013). Hassrede – von der Sprache zur Politik [Hate Speech – From speech to Politics]. In Meibauer, J. (ed.). *Hassrede/Hate Speech. Interdisziplinäre Beiträge zu einer aktuellen Diskussion* [Hate Speech. Interdisciplinary Contributions to Current Discussion] (pp. 1–16). Gießen: Gießener Elektronische Bibliothek.

Meibauer, J. (2021). *Exploring the Linguistics of Hate Speech*. A Lecture Given at the Conference "Linguistic and Social Aspects of Hate Speech", 22.03.2021, the University of South Denmark, Denmark.

Miceli, M., and Castelfranchi, C. (2018). Contempt and Disgust: The Emotions of Disrespect. *Journal for the Theory of Social Behaviour*, 48: 205–229. https://doi.org/10.1111/jtsb.12159 [accessed 30.01.2019].

Niekrewicz, A. (2017). Słownictwo określające tożsamość narodową i rasową w społecznościowych słownikach języka polskiego [Vocabulary Describing National and Racial Identity in Community Dictionaries of the Polish Language]. *Język. Religia. Tożsamość*, 1(15): 47–57.

Ohia, M. (2013). Mechanizmy dyskryminacji rasowej w systemie języka polskiego [Mechanisms of Racial Discrimination in Polish]. *Przegląd Humanistyczny*, 5: 93–105. https://www.ceeol.com/search/article-detail?id=9430tail [accessed 30.01.2019].

Orpin, D. (2005). Corpus Linguistics and Critical Discourse Analysis: Examining the Ideology of Sleaze. *International Journal of Corpus Linguistics*, 10(1): 37–61.

Partington, A. (2008). The Armchair and the Machine: Corpus-Assisted Discourse Research. In Torsello, C. T., Ackerley, K., and Castello, E. (eds.). *Corpora for University Language Teachers* (pp. 95–118). Bern: Peter Lang.

Peisert, M. (1992). Nazwy narodowości i ras we współczesnej polszczyźnie potocznej [Names of Nationalities and Races in Contemporary Everyday Polish]. In Anusiewicz, J., and Nieckula, F. (eds.). *Język a Kultura* [Language vs. culture], vol. 5. (pp. 209–216). Wrocław: Wydawnictwo Uniwersytetu Wrocławskiego.

Przepiórkowski, A., Bańko, M. Górski, R. L. and Lewandowska-Tomaszczyk, B. (eds.) (2012). *Narodowy korpus języka polskiego* [The National Corpus of Polish]. Warszawa: PWN.

Reuter, K. (2019). Dual Character of Concepts. *Philosophy Compass*, 14: e12557.

Shelby, T. (2002). Is Racism in the "Heart"? *Journal of Social Philosophy*, 33(3): 403–418.

Siuciak, M. (2004). Etymologia wyrazu Murzyn [Etymology of the Word Murzyn]. http://www.fil.us.edu.pl/ijp/poradnia/baza_archiwum.php?POZYCJA=180&AKCJA=&TEMAT=Etymologia-&NZP=&WYRAZ= [accessed 30.01.2016].

Sketch Engine (2021). https://www.sketchengine.eu [accessed 30.06.2022].

Słownik języka polskiego (SJP) na podstawie *Słownika 100 tysięcy potrzebnych słów* [Dictionary of Polish on the Basis of Dictionary of 100 Thousand Useful Words] (2005). Bralczyk, J. (ed.). Warszawa: PWN.

Smoleński P. (2018). Ukraińcy się boją: W Przemyślu kibole dostali zielone światło. Wykrzykują: „Znajdzie się kij na banderowski ryj!" [Ukrainians Are Scared. In Przemyśl Football Hooligans Were Given Green Light]. *Gazeta Wyborcza*, 24.02.2018.

Strani, K., and Szczepaniak-Kozak, A. (2022). Online Hate Speech in the UK and Poland: A Case Study of Online Reactions to the Killing of Arkadiusz Jóźwik. In Monnier, A., Boursier, A., and Seoane, A. (eds.), *Cyberhate in the Context of Migrations* (pp. 21–62). New York: Springer International Publishing/ Palgrave.

Stubbs, Michael (1997). Whorf's Children: Critical Comments on Critical Discourse Analysis (CDA). https://www.uni-trier.de/fileadmin/fb2/ANG/Linguistik/Stubbs/stubbs-1997-whorfs-children.pdf [accessed: 13.08.2019].

Szczepaniak-Kozak, A., Jaszczyk, M., Szejbal, A., and Putyra, Ł. (2015). *RADAR Interview Analysis Report Poland*. RADAR Elearning Platform. http://lnx.radar.communicationproject.eu/web/htdocs/radar.communicationproject.eu/home/dokeos/main/document/document.php?cidReq=RAD01&curdirpath=%2FINTERVIEWS [accessed 30.01.2019].

Śmigulec-Odorczuk, A. (2012). Interview with Brian Scott. Jeśli nie Murzyn, to kto? [If Not a Negro, Then Who?]. http://wyborcza.pl/duzyformat/1,128008,12342014,Jesli_nie_Murzyn__to_kto_.html [accessed 29. 01. 2021]).

Taylor, C. (2008). What is Corpus Linguistics? What the Data Says. *ICAME Journal*, 32: 179–200. http://sro.sussex.ac.uk/id/eprint/53389/1/what_is_corpus_linguistics.pdf [accessed 30.01.2019].

Trump, D. (2011). Time to Get Tough: Making America #1 Again. Washington: Regnery Publishing.

United Nations Strategy and Plan of Action on Hate Speech (2019). https://www.un.org/en/genocideprevention/hate-speech-strategy.shtml [accessed 30.06.2022].

Van Dijk, T. (1995). Elite Discourse and the Reproduction of Racism. In Slayden, D., and Whillock, R. K. (eds.), *Hate Speech*. Thousand Oaks, CA: Sage.

Van Dijk, T. (2015). Critical Discourse Analysis. In Tannen, D., Hamilton, H., and Schiffrin, D. (eds.). *The Handbook of Discourse Analysis* (2nd ed.) (pp. 466–485). Hoboken: Willey-Blackwell.

Wang, G. (2018). A Corpus-assisted Critical Discourse Analysis of News Reporting on China's Air Pollution in the Official Chinese English-language press. *Discourse & Communication*, 12(6): 645–662. doi:10.1177/1750481318771431.

Wąsikiewicz-Firlej, E. (2019). Metaphor and Metonymy in Business Discourse. Open University Lecture delivered at Adam Mickiewicz University (11.12.2019).

Winiewski, M., Hansen, K., Bilewicz, M., Soral, W., Świderska A., and Bulska, D. (2017). *Mowa nienawiści, mowa pogardy. Raport z badania przemocy werbalnej wobec grup mniejszościowych* [Hate Speech, Contempt Speech. Research Report on Verbal Violence Against Minority Groups]. Warszawa: Fundacja im. Stefana Batorego.

Wodak, R. (2015). Saying the Unsayable: Denying the Holocaust in Media Debates in Austria and the UK. *Journal of Language Aggression and Conflict*, 3(1): 13–40.

Woiński, M. (2011). *Przestępstwo art. 257 k.k.* [Offence Under Article 257 of the Criminal Code]. Warszawa: Instytut Wymiaru Sprawiedliwości.

Reference corpora

The National Corpus of Polish (PSEN). http://www.nkjp.uni.lodz.pl/.
The Polish Parliamentary Corpus (PPC). https://kdp.nlp.ipipan.waw.pl/query_corpus/.
Polish Web 2012, plTenTen12, RFTagger (Polish Web 2012). https://app.sketchengine.eu.

Tailor-made corpora

Jaszczyk-Grzyb M. (2020). A corpus compiled for the purpose of her Ph.D. dissertation. Available at request: mj55083@amu.edu.pl.

Ukrainiec and banderowiec. A corpus available at Sketch Engine: https://app.sketchengine.eu/#sketchdiff?corpname=user%2FAnnaKozak%2Fukrainiec_i_banderowiec&tab=basic&lemma=banderowiec%20&lemma2=Ukrainiec&lpos=-n&showresults=1&showSketchDiffVis=1.

ABOUT THE AUTHOR

Anna Szczepaniak-Kozak occupies the position of an Associate Professor at the Institute of Applied Linguistics, Adam Mickiewicz University in Poznań, Poland. Her research interests are within the field of applied linguistics, particularly interlanguage pragmatics, foreign/second language instruction and studies of hate speech and radicalisation. She is the author of four books, the co-editor of seven monographs, and the author of more than 50 papers. Currently (2020–2023), she is the main coordinator of the MaMLiSE project – Majority and Minority Languages in School Environment (mamlise.amu.edu.pl). The project aims to support school teachers in delivering effective instruction in linguistically heterogeneous classes as a response to challenges which migration society posits.

7

Focus group interview in the ecological perspective on language study: An insight into critical language awareness of L2 users with regard to translingual practices of plurilinguals

Hadrian Aleksander Lankiewicz

ABSTRACT

The aim of this chapter to integrate focus group interview methodology into language research, in particular into the search for the manifestation of critical language awareness (CLA) among plurilinguals. The author confines its study to translingual practices, which are perceived not only as an "instinct" resulting from the knowledge of many language systems by one mind (multi-competence) but are perceived as CLA, empowering them as plurilinguals. The analytical framework for the research invokes the so-called "narrative turn" and the tenets of ecolinguistics, as breaking the rules of the positivist way of conducting linguistic research, which is incompatible with the dogma of the post-modern era. Referring to the concept of interdisciplinarity, the author applies the focus group methodology, derived primarily from social sciences, to the study of applied linguistics and ultimately reflects on its suitability and benefits for the research area.

Keywords: focus groups, critical language awareness, translingualism, ecolinguistics, plurilingualism, multilingualism

7.1. INTRODUCTION

Language research of the so-called discursive turn has incorporated the analysis of human narratives as legitimate narrative knowledge (Jameson, 1984: xix), validating the manner of data collection, the data itself and the method of data analysis. Hence, the methodology of the social sciences and humanities postulates the notion of the "narrative turn" (De Fina, 2009). Yet, much narrative-based research is still executed according to positivist epistemology and structural tenets (see the criticism of earlier versions of Grounded Theory, Charmaz and Bryant 2010, Charmaz, 2017).

The assumption of human agency and activity, typical of the "post perspective" necessitates a knowledge building paradigm, de-vesting the researcher from their centrality and scientism, which requires the application of recognized scientific methods informed by normativity and the rigour of parsimony. Additionally, the face validity of any research entails the need to take account of the dynamic nature of phenomena to integrate the observer and the observed. To allow for the indeterminacy principle in research, it is also important to approach any problem via participatory action research.

One type of research methodology promoting active experimentation is a focus group based on discussions and interaction among selected individuals moderated by the researcher. The role of the researcher as a "facilitator" or "moderator" makes this method markedly different from traditional interviews and allows obtaining data different form traditional one-to-one interviews. This method or technique, as it is inconsistently referred to, has been known since the 1940s in sociology or psychology, but has become very popular across other disciplines such as education, communication and media studies, feminist research, health research and marketing research (cf. Nyumba et al., 2017: 21).

The rationale for this methodology is very much compatible with ecolinguistic research to account for the phenomenological orientation of any research endeavour since, as Kramsch (2002a) metaphorically puts it, it is impossible "to tell the dancer from the dance". Such an approach helps maintain ecological validity and additionally postulates an inherently critical/ethical stance towards doing academic research (van Lier, 2004: 168). I apply it to the study of the critical language awareness (CLA henceforth) of L2 learners/users with regard to the notion of legitimization of translingual processes of bi- and multilingual language users and resulting empowerment of the L2 user (Lankiewicz et al., 2016). The application of qualitative data analysis techniques pertaining to framework analysis (see Rabiee, 2004, Srivastava & Thomson, 2009) as more suitable for focus discussion groups than interpretative phenomenological analysis (cf. Fade, 2004), offers invaluable insights into the critical language awareness of L2 users.

The findings highlight the highly (inter)subjective and dynamic nature of the method and its data analysis techniques. The chapter ultimately presents an array of methodological advantages derived from the application of this methodology to this kind of research. It, among others, underscores a non-reductionist way of data collection and its analysis and, on the other hand, helps to delve into the critical language awareness of L2 users, envisioned here as an attitudinal and perceptual continuum in which, on the one end, we have a linguistically uncritical mind which believes that language is a structurally fixed monolith, geographically defined, communicatively neutral and unambiguous as well as normatively unequivocal and, on the other end, a critical mind presupposing that language is open-ended, subject to synchronic change from one user to another, the result of social practice, and as such laden with ideologies. Therefore, CLA is seen to be transformative in nature, regarding linguistic practices engaged in the meaning-making process. Since our attention is focused on plurilinguals (people operating various linguistic systems in various sociocultural contexts), we perceive language more as an active process and ultimately supersede the notion of language with that of languaging (García & Leiva, 2014: 204), or more precisely translanguaging (Mazak & Carroll, 2017: 3ff).

7.2. THEORETICAL BACKGROUND FOR KEY NOTIONS

7.2.1. Ecological metaphor to language study

In this subsection, my intention is not to present the outline of the historic development in ecolinguistics, but rather to communicate succinctly the ideology beyond ecolinguistic thinking, which made language study swerve away from more traditional thinking about language as a self-contained abstract domain. I aim at stressing the tenets of ecolinguistics to accentuate its novelty and particularity.

The so-called ecolinguistic paradigm to language study emerged toward the end of the 20th century and was inspired by two separate strains of thinking. The line inspired by Einar Haugen uses ecology as a conceptual metaphor for language study to account for "dynamic processes, which can be observed in language contact situations both at the societal and individual level" (Fill, 2001: 43). In turn, the line inspired by M. A. K. Halliday is understood in a more biological sense (Fill, 2001: 43), putting emphasis on the role of language in solving environmental issues. Critical discourse analysis is a reification of this thinking.

The two above-mentioned schools functioned independently, side by side. However, at the turn of the 21st century, there appeared calls for a more comprehensive and integrated conceptualization of ecolinguistic thinking. They were articulated in the writings of the proponents of ecological thinking in linguistics, trying to look for a more synthetic vision of ecolinguistics. The elaborated vision of this integration is presented in the state-of-the-art article by Steffensen and Fill (2014). They offer a platform for various approaches in the form of the Extended Ecological Hypothesis (Steffensen, 2011) and a naturalized view of language. In this perspective, "[l]anguage, socioculture and behaviour are deeply and irreversibly intertwined with nature, or rather: linguistic and sociocultural resources and behaviours express species-specific ways of being natures" (Steffensen & Fill, 2014: 19). In other words, language is seen as a semiotic process (meaning making), not independent from the sociocultural or environmental realm of human existence and it is viewed as the constructor of reality. An integrationist perception of ecolinguistics is also envisioned by Alexander and Stibbe (2014), who view it as "ecological analysis of discourse (...) a discipline that studies inclusively the relations of humans with other humans, other organisms and the natural environment". In this perspective, language emerges as one of the factors that shape these relationships (Wąsikiewicz-Firlej, 2017: 39).

The ecological metaphor has inspired many (sub)disciplines such as ecocriticism ecopoetics, ecofeminism, ecopsychology, esosociology, political ecology or environmental communication (cf. Wąsikiewicz-Firlej, 2017: 19) and has already firmly established its position in language studies. In linguistics, it is dubbed the ecology of language (Haugen, 1972/2001), "ecological linguistics" (Fill, 2001), or "ecological analysis of discourse" (Alexander & Stibbe, 2014). It is also applied in the field of language acquisition and language teaching (Leather & van Dam, 2003, Kramsch, 2002b, Lankiewicz, 2015), or educational linguistics (a term promoted by van Lier, 2004).

Being fully aware of the fact that any concise presentation of the novelty of ecolinguistic thinking is inherently fallible and incomplete, I will only accentuate issues having significance for this chapter.

Most importantly, ecolinguistics perceives language as a living tissue, pointing to its non-fixity (linguistic signs present only affordances in the semiotic processes which are effectuated by language users in particular contexts). Both the signifier and the signified are subject to changes. Consequently, this line of thinking underscores the agency of language users as creators of meaning on the one hand, and the shapers of the language system on the other. Translanguaging practices of plurilinguals, or an ecological coexistence of languages in multilingual societies, conform to the dynamic processes (Fill, 2001: 43) mentioned in the definition of ecolinguistics. In this perspective, translanguaging is seen as a result of a natural coexistence of languages in one's mind (multi-competence; Cook, 1991, or an instinct; Li, 2011) resulting in the application of linguistic repertoires to perform two basic language functions – communicative and representational. While the former emanates linguistic hybridity, the latter entails perceptual and cognitive changes.

Another aspect of doing research inspired by the ecology metaphor, vital for my considerations, is its critical perspective. Van Lier (2004: 168) interprets it as an imperative for research to be contextualized or "situative", conforming to the rules of ecological validity, and it should be intervention- and change-oriented. In my case, this translates into the application of qualitative analysis of data, its detailed contextual analysis and the selection of an adequate methodology as well as the fact that the research findings offer the vision of empowered plurilinguals rather than incompetent L2 users.

7.2.2. Background to focus group interview

Focus group methodology has been present in the field of social sciences and marketing since the 1940s and was developed by two American scholars, Paul F. Lazarsfeld and Robert K. Merton. The prelude to the focussed interview (Merton, 1987: 554), as it was called back then with an insistence on double "s" in the spelling, was Office Radio Research. With the USA forced to take active part during World War II, both scholars were engaged in a project launched by the US Army as consultants led by a prominent sociologist, Samuel Andrew Stouffer, working on survey studies on soldiers, measuring their attitudes (hence the ever-evolving project was tentatively called the Morale Division). As Merton recollects, "I found myself interviewing groups of soldiers in Army camps about their responses to specific training films and so-called morale films [...]" (1987: 554). Ultimately, the procedures applied in the research were published by Merton and Kendall (1946).

Focused interview (I will apply the more frequent spelling in our descriptions) was applied both to individual and groups to investigate collective behaviour and social contexts of mass persuasion or identification of public distrust. Methodologically, Merton points out that the focus group interview, despite its basically qualitative character, required also quantitative data for the verification of new hypotheses resulting from that qualitative data, and purports that "much of focus-group research today as a growing type of market research does not involve this composite of both qualitative and quantitative inquiry" (1987: 557). Concluding, Merton (1987) points out two important things about this methodology.

In the first place, the scholar accentuates the terminological conflation between focused interview and focus group interview, the originators of the methodology never used the latter. Thereby, he points to methodological discrepancies between the original procedures and the ones used in marketing – not necessary in the academic field of marketing (cf. Morgan, 1996, McQuarrie, 1990) – which Merton (1987: 564) dubs "obliteration by incorporation", standing for the fact that neither the name of the method nor its original procedures come into play. For example, the initiators of focused interviews did not automatically apply this methodology in groups, and considered the limitations and benefits of implementing it for interviewing both groups and individuals.

In the second place, focused interview methodology has never been confined to market research. It was of a generic type to be used for the analysis of qualitative research "by those who are attempting to understand the problems involved in subjective or motivation research in whatever field it may lie" and, in his opinion, it "may help us gain an enlarged sociological and psychological understanding in whatsoever sphere of human experience (Merton, 1987: 565)."

This methodology has evolved, and many researchers have experimented with focus groups in their own way (Morgan, 2001: 144). There are two different approaches to focus groups, inclusive and exclusive ones. While the former sees most group interviews as variants of focus groups, the latter reserves the technique of focus groups to one kind of group interview (Morgan, 1996: 131). Some researchers propose a typology of group interviewing (Frey & Montana, 1991, Khan & Manderson, 1992) to the point of discontinuity with the original intention, as claimed by Merton (1987), yet both typologies exclude from this methodology "naturally occurring conversations in ongoing interaction" (Morgan, 2001: 141). Less obvious, among researchers, is the postulate for focus groups to be based on directive interviewing and a structured question format (cf. Krueger, 1993, Morgan, 1988, Stewart & Shamdasani, 1990). Therefore, it is accentuated that "the more common practice is to treat the focus groups as a wide-ranging method in which the researcher has a variety of options for conducting the actual interviews" (Morgan, 2001: 141), and consequently some researchers adopt an inclusive approach (Morgan, 1996: 132).

Reflections on the application of focus groups or focus group discussions (as the method is most frequently referred to) have been presented in research manuals accentuating the qualitative character of this methodology, to say nothing about numerous other articles on the topic. Merton's fears regarding focus groups have been somewhat dispelled by more contemporary publications pertaining to focus group discussions, which recognize the fact that this qualitative methodology is many a time followed or preceded by quantitative surveys to allow for statistical generalizability. Very rarely it is used as a stand-alone technique and some researchers even recommend triangulation for justifying conclusions from this type of research (Nyumba et al. 2017: 29).

The apparent discontinuity put forth by Merton (1987) is, however, visible in variant applications of this methodology, referred to as the focus group interview, focus group or focus group discussion (I will use the terms interchangeably). While the element "focus group" seems to be stable in the name of the method, defining it in terms of an interview or a discussion makes the big difference, and ultimately boils down to different approaches to the role of moderators, of how much they intervene during the meeting with the group and, possibly, how controlled or structured the discussions are. In other words, as Smithson (2000: 104) claims, the definition of focus groups shows "a tension between participant-researcher interaction and interaction between participants".

Nonetheless, more contemporary publications warn against conflating group interviews with focus group discussions. Nyumba et al. (2017: 21), invoking Smithson (2000), posit "a fundamental difference between these two techniques". Similarly, Parker and Tritter (2006: 25–26) accentuate, it is essential not to confuse focus group discussions (synonymous with focus groups) with group interviews, a situation in which a single researcher interviews many respondents at the same time. The cited authors state the two terms are not commensurate with each other. The biggest difference is in the research dynamics. While in the group interview the position of the researcher is central, the questions are asked individually to different respondents, in focus groups the position of the researcher is peripheral and envisioned as that of facilitator or moderator, to foster discussion of an inter-relational character among participants, rather than having them relaying answers in an individual way to the researcher.

Focus group discussions have become generally more accepted in applied sciences than in qualitative academic research (Morgan, 2001: 145). However, with time focus group discussions became a popular method in social studies. Accordingly, there appeared textbook publications by Morgan (1988) and Krueger (1988/1994) for social studies, including marketing. This methodology crossed to other fields, for example, focus groups received attention also in a special issue of Qualitative Health Research (Carey, 1995, mentioned in Morgan, 2001: 145).

Morgan (1996: 130) presents the general characteristics of focus group interviews, and by extension focus group discussions, in the following way: (1) it is a method of data collection, (2) it "locates the interaction in a group discussion as the source of the data" (ibid.), (3) it anticipates an active role of the researcher in groups sampling and determining the topic of the discussion (Morgan, 1996: 130).

This methodology maybe used as a main method, or triangulated with other methods or research techniques. Sometimes, however, it is used as an exploratory, qualitative stage for the development of survey instruments (Fowler, 1995, after Morgan, 2001: 144). Morgan (1996: 133–135) offers examples of research in which focus groups were paired with other methods, most frequently with in-depth, individual interviews and surveys. This, in a sense, allows for Merton's (1987) objections regarding the use of this methodology, save the order of application. In some instances, individual interviews preceded focus group discussions, and the latter served as a check-up for conclusions drawn from former analyses.

Focus groups met also with criticism as qualitative research, in comparison to ethnographic interviewing (cf. Agar & MacDonald, 1995) and, as Morgan (2001: 145) stresses, established qualitative researchers in social sciences were not eager to apply this methodology.

Apart from applied marketing, focus groups methodology has been frequently used in academic research in social studies (cf. Morgan, 1996: 132), many a time allowing for crossing the traditional boundaries in doing research. Marketing's legacy of focus groups is visible in development and evaluation of various programs delving into among others, substance abuse, educational reform, family planning, spread of HIV/AIDS (cf. Morgan, 1996: 132–33). In this chapter, I try to apply this methodology in the field of linguistics. Judging from the Scopus data base, I dare to say that focus groups are infrequently used in academic language research.

7.2.3. "Telling the dancer from the dance": ecological metaphor in language study and its methodology

Claire Kramsch (2002a), commenting on the application of the ecological metaphor to language learning and acquisition, alludes to William Butler Yeats's poem "Among School Children" and in particular its closing line "How can we know the dancer from the dance?". In the context of the ecological perspective on researching language learning, the phrase is interpreted as seeking a way out of the old dilemma between acquisition and socialization. Briefly, for language study, the ecological perspective is interpreted as the inability to dissect language from the user, and therefore Kramsch criticizes the traditional perception of what language is, the way it is studied, and the way its learning is conceived. Hence, she postulates the need for an incorporation of a new metaphor, that of ecology. In the introduction to the edited volume, Kramsch construes it methodologically as follows: "The metaphor, which captures the dynamic interaction between language users and the environment as between parts of a living organism, seems to offer a new way of bringing together frames from various disciplines to illuminate the complex relationship under investigation (2002a: 3)." And as she continues, since language learning and language use in the era of globalization (social-cultural diversity of industrialized societies) has crossed traditional conceptualizations of language as such, it needs new research categories and new methodologies. Variation became a central category for language acquisition, and it can be applied, by extension, to language study in general. Language research inspired by the ecological metaphor focuses on local interactions of various kinds between linguistic repertoires and contexts in the process of meaning making, which underscores the agency of the language user.

Epistemologically, this holistic and "relational way of seeing", in which you "[p]ull one string, metaphorically speaking, and all the others will move in response" (van Lier, 2010: 4), but at the same time a "reflexive way of seeing" (beyond well-engrained frameworks and categories, such as language user vs. language learner, cf. Firth & Wagner, 1997; Kramsch, 2012) requires, according to Kramsch (2002a: 8), a phenomenological stance. She translates this basically philosophical tradition into an empirical dimension. She draws on selected concepts to demonstrate their ramification for understanding the language learning process as researched and presented by contributors to the volume edited by her. It would not be misleading to claim that this epistemology is eagerly accepted by broadly understood ecolinguistic research (van Lier, 2004; Frayne, 2015; Cowley, 2019).

In most general terms, phenomenology is a school of thought that questions the Cartesian dualism of separating mind and body. In contrast to rationalism, phenomenology in its various strands renders any form of consciousness embodied, meaning it is inseparable from the body and the world. The dictum of *cogito, ego sum* ("I think, therefore I am") in empirical studies was supported by the Newtonian mechanistic paradigm, which dominated scientific research in the Western World. Phenomenology is perceived very often as a breach of this tradition. Edmund Husserl, the father of this philosophical school, took human experience as the starting point for the study of reality, which is available to the human consciousness as phenomena. Hence, the only access to reality is via perceptions, judgements and emotions. More important, however, for my considerations, are the implications of phenomenological tenets for linguistic research driven by the ecological metaphor. It is important to stress here that ecolinguistic research is no way uniform. Different authors accentuate its different properties, and recommend different methodologies. Van Lier (2002: 193–219), proposes some models to effectuate ecolinguistic research and points out the suitability of methodologies based on "action research (or other intervention studies), case studies, ethnographies, and forms of collaborative research" (p. 208). Focus discussion groups may be classified as a kind of collaborative research based on emic data, generated by "insiders" of a particular "culture" (Magill, 1993: 105).

Again, depending on the research theme, authors articulate its various ecological aspects. Additionally, some may not explicitly refer to phenomenological foundations, yet this school of thought is implicit in their considerations. Therefore, the generalizations presented here are not in any way complete and exhaustive, they are rather selected and aligned in such a way as to underpin the ecological tenets of focus group discussion methodology. My further deliberations will be contained to two basic umbrella terms, which include other characteristics of the ecology metaphor. They are the dynamic nature of doing research and the concept of ecological validity.

7.2.3.1. Dynamic nature of focus group discussion

The metaphor of ecology evokes, in the first place, the idea of mutually dependent systems which are nested in other multi-scale systems, as hinted at by the application of chaos/complexity theory to language research (Larsen-Freeman, 2002), which may be presented under the term of contextualized or "situative" relationships (van Lier, 2002: 193), and which may be governed by nonlinear cause and effect (Kramsch, 2002a: 16) in a particular time and space. This line of thinking puts all linear context and data reduced studies, governed by the principle of Occam's razor into question, and favours research which accounts for the dynamic nature of phenomena and is compatible with the poststructural era of quantum physics' perception of reality. Ironically, all the philosophical foundations propounding the relativity and subjectivity of perception have been supported by modern physics, shifting it to the same realm of subjectivity, a feature traditionally ascribed to the humanities or social sciences.

Kramsch (2002a: 8), invoking Merleau-Ponty's concept of corporeal schemata, points to the fact that perception, a central ideal in phenomenological epistemology, can only be mediated through one's body, which is a point of reference for all human activities. We may, by extension, apply this to doing research. This boils down to the maxim of situatedness and contextualization (cf. van Lier, 2004: 20), or activity and agency (van Lier, 2010: 4–5). The phenomenological notion of intentionality translates into the fact that linguistic research driven by the ecological metaphor cannot account for all-encompassing objective laws, since we only have access to "intentional worlds" (perceived through our emotions and judgements). In consequence, any truth is intersubjective (in relation to the Other).

Ecolinguistic research also accentuates the mediation of any human activity via language. Kravchenko (2020: 18) puts it as follows: the central issue for ecolinguistic research is "the realization that language is not a tool out there nor a mental organ in the brain but an essential ecological factor that defines us as a biological species, Homo sapiens, in phylogeny and ontogeny". That being said, he requires an additional caveat, namely the abandonment of the positivist vision of language as an instrument for coding and decoding information, and the abandonment of two myths pertaining to language: code fixity and telementation (Harris, 1981). The former stands for Saussure's dualistic semiotics and objectivity of linguistic means (we can express our intentions via objective linguistic means). The latter posits that a human being is able to communicate their thoughts via linguistic resources. Any linguistic research driven by the ecology metaphor requires a more dynamic and relational approach to language, and sees it as a result of social interaction (Harris, 1987). In brief, human beings negotiate the code and its meaning on an everyday basis. As Larsen-Freeman (1997: 147) presents it, in the context of chaos complexity theory, "[e]very time language is used, it changes".

Keeping all the above in mind, and the fact that in researching language-related issues via language (languaging-about-language, Swain, 2006: 96), it is important to see the mediatory nature of language in human activity and cognition. In the context of language learning, Kramsch, invoking (Vygotsky, 1978 & van Lier, 2000) asserts: "(...) meaning lies in relationships between artefacts, persons, and events, not in the objects themselves, language, as one of many semiotic systems, emerges from semiotic activity through affordances brought forth by active engagement with material, social, and discourse processes" (2002a: 20–21). To adjust research to language-related means of the discursive turn, we must be mindful at least of two things: (1) the fact that the deeper meaning of one's utterance may be nested in a broader context and subject to interactivity, and (2) the fact that a meta-narrative (data analysis) is not free of preconceptions, as manifested by constructivist grounded theory.

Focus groups, as a research technique or methods of data collection, relies on the interaction during a group discussion and "acknowledges the researcher's active role in creating the group discussion" (Morgan, 1996: 130). The role of the moderator is essential and based on a pre-established set of questions, which are subject to adaptation during the group interview, depending on circumstances. Thereby, the reliance on a moderated interaction makes this method different from other types of research involving multiple participants. This way, the elicited data is negotiated or influenced by other responders. Elsewhere, Morgan maintains that the moderator's role is not only confined to the discussion, they are individuals who are responsible for "the recruitment process that brings participants to the groups" (2001: 146). They also prepare questions to guide the discussion and many a time they prepare the reports, as it is in the case of the present study. Nonetheless, Janet Smithson (2000) asserts that the unique aspect which distinguishes focus groups from other methods is its interactions, and suggests that it is essential to reflect this feature in data analysis.

Allowing for the fact that language, in the ecolinguistic sense is a living tissue, with form and meaning dynamically co-constructed by the interlocutors who make use of sign affordances, we dare to say that the methodology of focus group discussions accommodates this basic feature of any linguistic practice.

7.2.3.2. *Ecological validity of focus group discussion*

The concept of ecological validity is at the forefront of discussions among ecolinguists. Allowing for the fact that qualitative research is underrepresented statistically by nature, there appears a question of what makes ecolinguistic research representative and applicable to real-life situations. In most simple terms, it may be called a type of external validity, standing for the question of how the study can be generalized to other naturalistic contexts. The notion of ecological validity was triggered by a dispute between two psychologists, Egon Brunswick and Kurt Levin, with the latter criticizing the former for the inadequacy of taking the lab to the outside context to conform to ecological validity. Lewin postulated the situatedness of any research within individual's life space (cf. van Lier, 2004: 168ff). Since than the notion of ecological validity obtained different interpretations. For the needs of the present chapter, it is important to mention Bronfenbrenner's interpretation of the concept. One of the important facets of ecological validity is its phenomenological aspect, "the correspondence between the subject's and the investigator's view of the research" (1978: 33, after van Lier, 2004: 169).

Morgan, in the context of the popularity of focus groups, points out that "it may be an overstatement, but there is undoubtedly a grain of truth to the contrast between using surveys to summarize the views of an entire nation in the 1950s and using focus groups to get closer to the thoughts and experiences of smaller and more specific segments of society in the 1990s" (2001: 142). Ironically, he claims that an in-depth micro study may be more representative than the statistically representative macro research.

In the case of this paper, the focus group is used as a primary method which is not triangulated with any of the possible combinations envisioned by Morgan (1996: 134–5). Ecological research, in principle, is to be limited in its rage, which does not mean that its outcomes may not be interpreted, by analogy, to a broader context. It offers insights into a micro perspective which constitutes a fractal of a bigger whole. In ecological research, an inference may be more effective and accurate by the application of dialogical analogy than a generalization based on indicative thinking, typical of macro-scale phenomena. This potential of ecolinguistic research is accented by many scholars, e.g. Minsky (1990), Johnson (2001) or Kramsch and Steffensen (2008: 27). Its validity does not derive from the representativeness of the research sample but from its situatedness.

7.3. RESEARCH PRESENTATION

7.3.1. Research-related issues

7.3.1.1. *Critical language awareness in the ecolinguistic dimension*

The concept of critical language awareness (CLA) is an outgrowth of the school of critical linguistics initiated by researchers from East Anglia University in Norwich (Fowler et al., 1979) who articulated the need for a closer study of language in its social context "since language is so distinctly a social phenomenon" (ibid.: 1) therefore the job of linguistics was to raise consciousness about how language works in society in reference to the notion of power. They were inspired by Halliday (1978) who argued for language analysis combining texts and social aspects, which found elaboration in social semiotics. Markedly, the consideration of power in language is the extension of the critical school in social sciences, the continuation of the Marxist school of thought, assuming an oppressor and the oppressed.

Critical thinking in linguistics has ultimately evolved into a new branch of studies, referred to as CDA. One of the scholars who focused on the process of the social production of meaning was Norman Fairclough (1995). He replaced "the word language with the term 'discourse analysis' which (...) explicitly encompasses both the social practices associated with distribution and consumption of texts, and the ideologies and power relations which are inscribed in linguistic conventions" (Clark & Ivanič, 1997; 219). In the conclusion to his book *Language and Power*, Fairclough (1989) postulates the development of "'critical language awareness' as a facilitator for 'emancipatory discourse' which challenges, breaks through, and may ultimately transform the dominant orders of discourse ..." (p. 329). Fairclough is credited with the authorship of the notion of CLA, which was perceived as a practical implication from the study of critical discourse analysis for language education (Clark & Ivanič, 220). It became a catchy notion for many language educators and was followed by a series of articles. A milestone in the development of the idea of CLA is the book edited by Fairclough (1992) with a long introduction presenting the conceptualization of the notion. Criticizing "naturalization of language use" and the application of the notion of appropriacy in language teaching, he calls for a more critical approach, beyond skill training, a component necessary for educating responsible and engaged citizens.

In this perspective, any language use is seen as a political act (reflecting power relations in given society), hence an important component of language education is consciousness raising about possible manipulations via language. CLA is certainly a component of language awareness (LA), which pertains to "the awareness of the close relationship between language and ideology. It involves 'seeing through language' in other words" (Andrews, 2007: 12).

The critical aspect of language education (relating to the issues of power relations) is important for any language education inspired by the ecological metaphor, and, according to van Lier (2004) should, among others, focus on relations, quality, value, diversity and activity, to allow for the fact that language learners are not passive receives and consumers of ready-made language chunks but creative agents in meaning-making processes. This applies to L2 language learners, who, according to Wallace (1992: 62) are a classical example of a marginalized group exposed to neutralized tests and ideological indoctrination inscribed in teaching practices and materials.

One of the key elements of the ecolinguistic approach to language learning and teaching is the deconstruction of the notion of what language is. It is no longer perceived as a cultural monument passed from generation to generation but rather as a non-fixed code changed on a daily basis by its users (Larsen-Freeman, 1997: 149), which I refer to as languaging (cf. Lankiewicz, 2014). I would go so far as to say that global languages like English are additionally changed by L2 users. The ecological perception of language has its repercussions for the process of language learning, which for bilingual and plurilingual people translates into the inability to build the same meanings as monolingual native speakers due to their underlying multi-competence (Cook, 1991). Placing the critical aspect of ecological language teaching at the forefront of my considerations, I have proposed the concept of critical ecological language awareness (Lankiewicz, 2015). In this chapter, however, I decided to use the more familiar notion of CLA, which in the context of plurilingualism and the application of translingual practices will be explored via three central concepts in the ecology of learning designated by van Lier (2010), namely relationships, quality and agency. These critical aspects will be discussed in the analytical part of the research below.

7.3.1.2. Plurilinguals and their translingual practices

Research on plurilingualism and multilingualism generates inconsistent terminology. In older publications both terms are used interchangeably but more recently they appear to be used to refer to different realities. While multilingualism pertains to the sociolinguistic reality of the coexistence of many languages in a particular society, used separately by its members, with some being able to speak more than one language, the term "plurilingualism" is basically of a psycholinguistic nature and refers to the fact that there may exist one mind operating more than one language. Despite the fact that contemporarily the two notions designate different phenomena, nonetheless in research dedicated to plurilingualism the individual knowledge of multiple languages is also inconsistently referred to by the term "multilingual". Accordingly, a person knowing more than two languages is both defined as both multilingual and plurilingual, with the former being even more frequent. In this chapter, however, I will consistently use the latter since it entails some repercussions for any linguistic research, as delineated below.

In the first place, plurilingualism breaks with the monolingual perception of the linguistic competence of people who know more than one language. Bi- and plurilinguals are not expected to process any language the same way as monolingual native speakers, which derives at least from the fact that monolingual language processing is undisturbed by any other linguistic data. Therefore, assuming that there are no special areas designated to a particular language, but rather all linguistic repertoires are handled by the same "hardware", interferences between linguistic competences should be frequent and, consequently, the underlying linguistic competence obtains the form of multi-competence (parallel processing of linguistic repertoires). Hence the plurilingual mind cannot work the same way as the monolingual mind and accordingly all L2 users need to be treated individually (Cook, 1991).

Ultimately, the concept of plurilingualism necessitates the redefinition of what language is, since a plurilingual mind does not allow for sterile pathways for different languages, or special storerooms. Research into types of bilingualism, for example, has been basically inconclusive, and any categorization seems lukewarm or highly arbitrary. Even the very definition of what it means to be bilingual is problematic and vague, and in the end only some inclusive definitions are offered which point out the fact that a bilingual person uses two (or more) languages for communicative purposes. Research also indicates that language competence among bilinguals is always uneven, with a better knowledge of one language than the other. All in all, bilingualism is a complex and multidimensional construct that makes clearcut categorical typologies ineffective, such as between compound, coordinate or subordinate bilinguals. Unsurprisingly, more contemporary research posits the end of bilingualism (Widła, 2016) in favour of multilingualism or, more recently, plurilingualism to account for the uneven competences, language processing mechanisms or learning contexts entailed. Eventually, the concept of plurilingualism and multi-competence is more compatible with the conceptualization of language as a continuum of linguistic repertoires rather than as distinct fixed linguistic entities, as envisaged by positivist language theories. In other words, neither multilingual societies nor plurilingual minds are invulnerable to mutual interferences. Hence, clear-cut linguistic entities scarcely represent the socio- or psycholinguistic reality.

An important dimension of mutual interferences between language systems is the translingual practices of plurilinguals.

7.3.2. Context of the study and group composition

The research was carried out on three different focus groups, as suggested by some proponents of the method (cf. Burrows & Kendal, 1997). Two groups were created on the basis of convenience sampling. Since I work as an academic teacher at the University of Gdańsk, I invited six third-year BA students of applied linguistics to be interviewed in a focus group. The selection was based on prior observation of the students during translation classes and their declared knowledge of languages. Similarly, the second group consisted of 6 second-year BA students of applied linguistics who I teach Italian to as an additional language. It is important to mention that students of applied linguistics at the University of Gdańsk major in two languages (English and German), yet they have one additional language (Italian or Spanish) in their curriculum to be mastered at the level of B2 by the end of the BA program. Nonetheless, some of the students, apart from Polish, the native language for the majority of the students, know other languages, too. Some of the students included in the research had lived abroad for a remarkable period of time, or are members of transnational families. Therefore, the repertoire of the translingual practices elicited during the study may extend beyond the languages covered by their curriculum. This method of sampling is not excluded by this methodology, since "focus groups are often conducted with existing groups" (Morgan, 1996: 131, see also Morgan, 1989).

Participants of the third group were recruited from among former language students I have met in my career and who kindly agreed to convene again for the study. They were purposefully selected for the research due to their multilingual skills. The proponents of the method stress that the focus groups moderator should engage in a "recruitment process that carefully matches participants to the recruitment topic" (Morgan, 2001: 149). The proper focus group composition, of respondents closely related to the research topic, may make the work of the moderator easier and lessen the reliance on the heavily structured interview, thereby making an "ideal focus group" (Morgan, 2001: 148). They were five professionals. One person, for personal reasons, could not join the group, in spite of her earlier declaration.

All of the focus group meetings were carried out in the pandemic period via the MS Teams platform and were of an average duration of an hour and an a half, within the time span recommended by focus group researchers (cf. Rabiee, 2004: 656). The proceedings were recorded and transcribed for detailed framework analysis (cf. Rabiee, 2004: Srivastava & Thomson, 2009).

7.3.3. Objectives

For the study, I assume objectives pertaining to two levels. On the first level, I aim at (1) disclosing respondents' language ideologies or language attitudes regarding plurilingualism[1] in order to adjust them to the concept of CLA, to identify the respondents' linguistic mindset, (2) collecting examples of translingualism among plurilinguals and (3) interpreting them as a manifestation of CLA. Doing so, CLA, in its turn, is not measured by means of questionnaires (cf. Lankiewicz, 2015), it is rather derived from respondents' discussions and utterances on the basis of relational content analysis. In other words, data obtained during focus group interviews will be scrutinized for the relationship between examples of translingual practices and respondents' construing them as signs of language ideology, questioning the monolingual approach to plurilingualism. On the second level, allowing for the title of the volume, (4) all research findings will be considered in the context of the applied methodology with reference to research validity and reliability in comparison to more common techniques for conducting qualitative research in applied linguistics, such as individual interviews, questionnaires or observations. This dimension pertains to meta-research, to account for the multidisciplinary investigation of linguistic issues going beyond engrained methodologies. Therefore, methodological reflection will conclude this chapter.

---

1   I understand plurilingualism as synonymous with multilingualism in the psycholinguistic sense, as the knowledge of many languages by one mind.

7.3.4. Methodology

A focus group interview generates qualitative data, in contrasted with quantitative research. This method is often defined as "interpretative and naturalistic, in that it seeks to understand and explain beliefs and behaviours within the context that they occur" (Draper, 2004: 642) and which epistemologically assumes contextual knowledge based on detailed analysis of a limited number of respondents, yet it offers a more holistic view of a problem. Qualitative data interpretation, which constitutes the basis of any ecolinguistic research, relies on inference by analogy, rather than the generalization (Kramsch & Steffensen, 2008: 27) typical of quantitative methodology. Due to the choice of the method, framework analysis is given priority over interpretative phenomenological analysis (IPA) here. The latter is more suitable for ideographic case-study description, in which each case study results in an in-depth description, and then other cases are analysed in turn for common themes and patterns (Fade, 2004: 648). Instead, the focus group interview allows for interaction and discussion (evident in the alternative name of the method), a different approach to data analysis is necessary to account for the dynamic aspect of data. Thereby, this research applies framework analysis (cf. Rabiee, 2004) and relational rather than conceptual analysis of the content.

Accordingly, in this study, looking for CLA pertains to the emic perspective, presenting the respondents' point of view, rather than the etic one (academic understanding of the concept). It is believed here that language ideologies are also an inherent part of any folk theory.

7.3.5. Data analysis and findings

As mentioned by the proponents of framework analysis and qualitative methodology, such as, for example, focus group interviews, I assume the fact that researcher bias is an integral part of this research. This is largely activated by the key questions predefined for the research which were asked by the moderator during the sessions (see appendix). They, accompanied by additional questions during the interviews, have an impact on the process of data collection and interpretation (Rabiee, 2004: 657). Thus, the analytical framework is partly inscribed in this research and is triggered by the collection process (Srivastava & Thomson, 2009: 75). For any qualitative research, in particular the phenomenological one, "[t]he researcher's beliefs are not seen as biases to be eliminated but rather as being necessary for making sense of the experiences of other individuals" (Fade, 2004: 648). However, the researcher's framework is not the only one, key issues and major themes also emerge during data processing, and any of them may change the distributions of interpretative accents. Kruger's analytical continuum allows for this (1988/1994, after Rabiee, 2004: 657).

The data analysis which follows is based on the highly interconnected stages described by Ritchie and Spencer (1994, after Rabiee, 2004: 657), which are "familiarization; identifying a thematic framework; indexing; charting; mapping and interpretation" as well as eight criteria for working out a research heading as the framework, i.e. "words, context, internal consistency, frequency, intensity of comments, specificity of responses, extensiveness and big picture" (Rabiee, 2004: 660). The ultimate framework emerging form the study will be basically thematic (content-oriented), yet the focus group interview will allow me to balance between two types: conceptual and relational analyses of respondents' responses. The analysis includes typescripts and observational notes written immediately after the interviews. Since the researcher also performed the role of the moderator and due to the communication channel used (MS Teams), data pertaining to body language is very limited. It is worth mentioning that all interviews were carried out in Polish, so all the key questions and all cited utterances have been translated into English by me. Initials have been used in such a way as to protect the respondents' identities. They look as follows: group one (MN, NK, VK, AL, MP, CK), group two (MZ, BC, RA, ND, LK, BA) and group three (AN, EN, PL, JR, MK).

The initial questions (1–3) of the interview asked by the moderator in all three groups were aimed to delineate the linguistic repertoires of the respondents. For the two groups comprising students of applied linguistics, it was taken for granted that apart from Polish, their native language, they knew English and German, and either Spanish or Italian. The students' narratives revealed, however, that their linguistic repertoire incorporated additional languages or and dialects such as modern Greek (1), French (3), Czech (1) or Korean (1). They also admit to speaking or understanding some dialects of Polish (4) or the Kashubian ethnic language (3). The respondents also revealed interesting personal histories. Two students were simultaneous bilinguals, because of being members of transnational families (combining Polish with Greek, or Czech), four students were sequential bilinguals, yet with native-like language proficiency (equilingual) due to their long stay in a foreign country, and with a part of their education completed in that country, in this case Germany. The respondents of the third group work for various international companies, travel abroad and use foreign languages on a daily basis, mostly English and German. Some, however, use other languages in their personal and professional life, such as Spanish, Italian, French or Russian. On average, each participant knows at least three languages, with some knowing 4–5 of them (7 students) at different levels of competence, yet used on a daily basis at school, at work or for other communicative reasons, such as chatrooms. All of the respondents are Polish citizens, and Polish is basically their native language.

The rest of the core questions of the interview aimed at covering objectives 1, 2 and 3. Needless to say, the core questions of the interview were inspired by the concept of the heteroglossic perception of multilingualism (Creese & Blackledge, 2011; Li, 2011, 2017). It would be difficult to untangle them and ascribe them to a particular objective, since the respondents' points of view, stances, opinions and linguistic examples appeared in different moments of the interview during discussions. Besides, objective 3 is very much of an interpretative nature, and its pursuit in based on the relational type content analysis. Nonetheless, these reservations do not dismiss the researcher from considering all objectives one by one.

As to the mindset disclosed by respondents, manifested by language ideologies or language attitudes towards plurilingualism considered in the framework of CLA (**objective 1**), there emerged thematic frameworks pertaining to (1) L2 legitimacy and empowerment, (2) the competence of the plurilingual mind, (3) the intellectual and emotional boost of being plurilingual and (4) the perception of success in language learning. I will consider them in turn, articulating additional categories for each theme and supporting them with quotes and contextual clues.

The concept of language ideologies, understood as assumptions about language in general, rather than how a particular language is perceived (Krajewska & Lankiewicz, 2020), is essential for my considerations of CLA (Lankiewicz, 2015), which entails language theories (folk or scientific) regarding what language is and the way it functions, and how these attitudes may influence the process of its learning and use.

The respondents' CLA was probed via their beliefs regarding plurilingualism. It was hypothesized that knowing many languages and practically using them in different contexts shapes a mindset which goes beyond the monoglossic beliefs of a pluralized monolingualism (Heller, 2007). This, in turn, would be interpreted as a sign of a raised level of CLA (cf. Lankiewicz, 2015), nourished by the linguistic background on the one side (all the participants of the study are university gradated of language major), and the personal experience of being plurilingual on the other.

7.3.5.1. L2 Legitimacy and empowerment

The concept of legitimacy and empowerment in language use may be traced back to Fairclough's (1992) criticism of language appropriacy, which in his opinion results in the assumption of the legitimization of particular language varieties in particular contexts. In the field of L2 teaching, the so-called tenet of naturalization, which underpinned the communicative approach to language teaching, guided by native speaker norms, is nowadays frequently criticized by researchers breaking from the normatively oriented tradition in language education. This new strain allows for the agency of a language user beyond the monolingual approach to bi-and plurilingualism (van Lier, 2004; Kramsch, 2012; Lankiewicz, Wąsikiewicz-Firlej & Szczepaniak-Kozak, 2016; Lankiewicz & Wąsikiewcz-Firlej, 2016; Mazak & Carroll, 2017) inspired by the concept of multi-competence (Cook, 1991).

This theme was deliberately triggered by the construction of the research questions and there is extensive evidence in the frequency and extensiveness of respondents' comments in all three groups. One of the key categories appearing within this theme is the issues of the native speaker, which in the context of plurilingualism boils down to the issues of (1) whether the competence of a bi- or plurilingual person can be compared in any way to that of the monolingual language user or (2) whether any L2 language leaner is able to obtain native-like proficiency, and (3) whether native-like proficiency should be the goal of L2 language education.

For the respondents, the category of the native speaker, despite its sociolinguistic adequacy, seems vague in terms of the linguistic normativity still celebrated so widely in the educational context. Many of them underscore the existence of linguistic heteroglossia within any language, even one so seemingly homogenic as Polish. To illustrate, "…it would be difficult to find a single person who speaks perfect Polish, or any other language" (MN), "I do not know which [declension] case is sometimes correct in my native language" (IR), or "My granny makes so many mistakes and uses some regional words that our relatives from the north of Poland sometimes do not understand her". Nonetheless, they do not reject the idea of the existence of language correctness and the validity of the native speaker model in language learning when they say, "I always try my best to imitate native pronunciation as much as possible" (LK), or "My pronunciation depends on who I am taking to, with natives of a language I try to be as correct as possible, as they were my teachers, when they say something good about, say, my English I am happy, but at work communicative efficiency is more important" (AL). At the same time, for the great majority of them native-like proficiency has never been an ultimate goal for language mastery. They agree that the imitation of native pronunciation is a very personal attitude related to someone's character, motivation, learning attitude or personal goals. Yet, they point at examples where exaggerated hypercorrectness has the reverse effect, for example, "My friend from the Philippines tries to speak so carefully in Polish that the effect becomes comical, unnatural, larger than life" (MP).

The nodal issue of whether one can learn L2 on the level of a native speaker receives a different approach in the two student groups and the one consisting of former graduates. While the responders of the former still express some hopes of nearing native-like competence, the member of the latter make very personal references, judging their actual proficiency and presenting personal experiences to argue for the negative answer to the question. At the same time, they claim to be satisfied with their linguistic qualifications and skills, and "speaking with an accent" is not a problem. In contrast, members of the student groups make claims of the kind, "It is only a matter of motivation and dedication" (MN), "Actors sometimes have to learn a particular accent and they are very successful, sometimes they perfectly imitate a foreign language" (CK), or "I came across a guide in Egypt, who learned

Polish within two years, and if it were not for his looks I would have mistaken him for a Polish person" (VK). However, the latter comment met with the rejoinder of another respondent who experienced a similar situation while visiting Tunisia, but, as she claimed, when she started asking the guide questions he could hardly understand them. This triggered a discussion in one of the student groups of what it means "to be taken for" for a native speaker. Is it only accent (understood as pronunciation) or anything else, for example, fluency or communicative efficiency? Students in this group started to moderate their opinions regarding the feasibility of learning an L2 on a native-like level. Ultimately, it was agreed that basically accent is the most distinctive value in recognizing native speakers, but since it is not so important for language competence, providing an utterance is intelligible, ultimately it became questioned as a desirable goal for L2 learners. The respondents of the graduate group unanimously agreed on the illusion of obtaining a native-like accent, and accentuated strong points of being non-native speakers while being plurilingual "I do not give a damn whether anybody takes me for a native or not, what counts is my fluency and the fact that I can easily express myself in a particular language" (AL), or "I know four languages including my Polish, a British native speaker usually knows only English, why should I feel worse" (MK).

The comments mentioned above are related to the category of being a legitimate L2 user, not a constant learner, as criticized by Firth and Wagner (1997). Respondents undoubtedly perceive themselves as language users in the first place, still being students, regardless of their proficiency level. Even students who claimed to know the basic levels of a language claimed not to be afraid of using it in communicative situations. It is rather the educational milieu which intimidates them, due to the exaggerated attention to correctness, celebrated in particular by some teachers of German. The majority of respondents is aware of their own agency in the process of language learning: "learning a language is my own choice so if decide to learn, it is for a reason" (AL), "I use language with the first words I learn" (VK), or "In the classroom there is little communication, but outside, any single word in a foreign language is not used for a decorative value but to communicate something, language proficiency does not matter to be called a language user" (EN).

The issue of being either a competent language user or an incompetent learner is delved into indirectly via the respondents' language beliefs, with the assumption that accepting certain language behaviours of others reflects their linguistic mindset. Accordingly, my respondents in all three groups basically accept the fact that neither the flight attendant's announcements, nor the automatic messages of telephone operators (as presented by the moderator) have to be communicated in a native-like fashion. Although they point out that heavily non-native language may impede comprehension, or in some cases poor language competence may be a sign of a lack of professionalism, they argue that "we all speak with different intonation and some of us have nice voices, others not" (AB), "if the communicated message is intelligible, why would there be any fuss about pronunciation or grammar correctness, this is not a school" (LK). This linguistic tolerance is particularly strong among professionals of the third group, informed by their personal experiences. Why the two student groups articulate some reservations regarding the respect and comfort of the listener, the professionals clearly underscore the coexistence of different dialects in any language and some manifest the fact that language is not a national property, "both English and Spanish, for example, are used internationally, even natives speak versions of them hardly understood by others" (PL), "My English is mine, my Italian is mine and I do not aim to be either British, or American, or Italian" (EN). There are also voices in all three groups, which accentuate the fact that a plurilingual person cannot be perceived the same way as a monolingual person. A more tolerant attitude towards different non-native "accents" and clear articulation of independent attitudes to language use, a derivative of autonomous attitudes in language learning (cf. Benson, 2011) have been inspired by everyday personal experiences of plurilinguals using their linguistic resources in an unbridled way and functioning outside an educational context. As they say "in my professional life I have no time for thinking about correct pronunciation, I need to be efficient in talking to people. Besides, who cares" (PL), "Whenever I use any language, my thinking is not restricted to it (...), I seem to live in a multidimensional perspective" (JR), and "I want to be myself in any language I speak (...) I rarely speak one language at a time, they mix (...) and this is the real me, I can't help it" (MK).

7.3.5.2. Competence of the plurilingual mind

The theme of the competence of the plurilingual mind has undeniably been triggered by the core questions of the interview. The categories that emerged during the discussion reflect the very personal experiences of a plurilingual person on the one hand, and on the other, as I can assume, have contributed to the respondents' beliefs regarding what it means to know a language in the first place and what it means to know many languages at the same time for the person and for the communication process. The data obtained in this respect allowed me to pinpoint four categories.

Linguistic fluidity is one of them. It can be understood in two different ways. Firstly, as the perception of language beyond a self-contained semiotic system, as a flowing network of signs, changeable from person to person. Linguists define it as the non-fixity of language codes (Harris, 1981). Secondly, it entails some sort of continuity between languages (inscribed in the evolution and spread of speech marked by similarities). Both categories may by envisioned by the notion of languaging or translanguaging (cf. Lankiewicz, 2014). This, in turn, boils down to the agency of a language user, who in the communication process makes use of all available semiotic resources in the signification process. Using the ecolinguistic line of thinking, it is important to admit that signs are perceived only as affordances beyond the well-defined entities engrained in the dyad of the signifier and the signified as presupposed by structural linguists. Ecolinguistics accentuates the role of the interpretant, a notion introduced by Charles Saunders Peirce in his triadic theory of the sign, pertaining to the relation between the signifier (sign) and the signified (object). In brief, the meaning making process is never complete since "a sign signifies only in being interpreted" (Atkin, 2013).

My respondents, accordingly, claim that "knowing many languages changed my thinking, I seem not to be confined to my native mentality" (JR), "the fact that I switch between languages opened my eyes to language issues, I am more creative (...) I am not afraid of experimenting and guessing" (EN), "the meanings of foreign words for me is what I think they mean but other people may have different things in mind" (AL).

Closely related with linguistic fluidity are the categories of contextual adjustment and linguistic confidence, which emerge from the data. My respondents underscore the fact that being multilingual is more than knowing many languages separately. They notice that code switching is an everyday practice for them, but it is not confined only to changing the language. It entails the use of many language codes simultaneously, and this, in turn, has an effect on their native language. A they say "I have problems with switching between languages and I often mix words and grammar" (AB), "When my clients asks me to explain the product to them, often I am not able to explain it in Polish but in other languages I find it easier, strange" (JR), "I know that my Polish is now full of language calques but I can't help it, even if I try to be very correct" (MK), "sometimes I have problems with the grammar of my native language (...) there are moments that my friends laugh at my accent when I speak Polish" (VK). Thereby, students confirm their translanguaging practices and an underlying multi-competence, rather than the competence of discrete languages. Interestingly, some of them maintain to be "lost in the language web"(EN) or "linguistically unstable", with the latter meaning "confused, precarious and labile" regarding the use of linguistic resources. Nonetheless, regardless of their claims, my respondents seem to be context sensitive regarding the use of their linguistic repertoires. To illustrate, one of them says, "the way we communicate depends on who we talk to. I share a flat with a foreign roommate, she is Ukrainian and knows languages, so when we speak, we rarely use one language. It is easier, funnier and more efficient (...) Sometimes, I think that I understand her better than my Polish friends, I mean, I know what she means" (MP).

Significantly, my respondents, particularly in the student discussion groups, initially, seemed to refrain from using the term of being multilingual, instead they used the notion of "speaking/knowing many languages". When confronted with the problem by the moderator, they claimed to be timid and cautious not to be criticized for hubris or showing ungrounded "overconfidence, where there is still so much to learn" (RA). As the discussion develops, they are more eager to admit their plurilingual competence, regardless of their proficiency level for each language. Ultimately, they are willing to define their multilingual proficiency in terms of practicality and usefulness, rather than correctness and native-like authenticity. They unanimously state that it is difficult to keep languages separate, in the era of globalization, even if one wanted to. In this regard, they largely agree that is better to know more languages in a communicative way than have a native-like proficiency of one foreign language because, as they maintain "I can make comparisons and I understand better my Polish grammar" (MN), or "I am more open as a person, I can see that language and culture are entangled and possibly I am a more sympathetic and sensitive communicator" (MK). Accordingly, despite some initial reservations regarding code-meshing (Young, 2004; Canagarajah, 2011a), elsewhere called translanguaging (Canagarajah, 2011b, 2013; García & Li, 2014), my respondents ultimately accept non-native announcements on a telephone answer machine or by a flight attendant (as elicited by one of the questions) as long as they are intelligible. Tellingly, one of them underscores "onboard an airplane is not a language classroom" (MZ), while another one states, "knowing more than one language you cannot think the same way as a monolingual person" (IR). Thus, they admit their dynamic translingual potential (García & Li, 2014).

7.3.5.3. Intellectual and emotional boost

One of the thorny issues in considering bi- and multilingualism is its impact upon the development of cognitive skills. In the literature of the early +20th century dedicated to L2 acquisition, especially that related to an early start in language learning, some scholars communicated the possibility of the negative impact of exposure to a new language, in terms of cognitive confusion and lower scholastic achievements. More contemporary research has dispelled earlier concerns and points to an intricate relationship between language learning and non-verbal cognitive skills (cf. Woumans et al., 2019). It also articulates that bilingualism enhances both the cognitive and linguistic development of children (cf. Bialystok, 2017) and delays the onset of dementia in older age, slowing cognitive ageing (cf. Bialystok et al., 2012). Despite the muted effect of bilingualism on cognitive skills, as signalled by broader research, my respondents clearly accentuated the benefits derived from plurilingualism on their intellect. Interestingly, this theme was not directly triggered by any of the questions. It emerged as a side effect of considering whether it is better to know one foreign language well or many languages in a moderate way. It recurred frequently and extensively enough to be included in this analysis.

My respondents in all the groups verbalized the significant advantages of being plurilingual with respect to the process of thinking, which I framed within the macro category of cognition. They claim that plurilingualism offers an insight into a linguistic dimension "it is easier to learn new languages with all this experience" (EN), "it is difficult to understand for me how people may be linguistically untalented since for me it is only a matter of choice which language to learn" (MK), "I can see through languages, they are all much the same" (LK) in the form of metacognitive skills. They also stress the fact that language learning entails a particular mindset and shapes the process of thinking, as stipulated by the theory of relativism. Some of the respondents were exposed to many languages at a very early age, others learned them through the process of socialization, which additionally influenced their thinking processes. As argued by Perlovsky (2013) the process of thinking requires both language and cognition (a detailed discussion on the relationship between language and cognition is beyond the scope of this paper), which he perceives as "separate but closely integrated abilities" (p.1). In a nutshell, he claims that language can be learned without much experience, which, in turn, is fundamental for cognition. If, however, language is to perform a cognitive function, the connections between language and cognition must be developed and maintained via motivations, which he calls emotions. Further, he posits, "these emotions must be in addition to utilitarian meanings of words (...) must "flow" from language to cognition, so that language is able to perform its cognitive function of guiding acquisition of cognitive representations, organizing experience according to cultural contents of language". His dual computational model of the relationship between language and cognition subscribes to the ecolinguistic vision of developing a personal voice in L2 (van Lier, 2004: 208).

In the vein of language learning as a lived experience, my respondents affirm, "thanks to the knowledge of many languages I do not seem to think like a typical Polish person, since every language offers a different perspective, it sees reality in a different way. For example, now I can see that Polish, my native language, is less optimistic than English, we had a lot of examples during our translation classes" (MP), "learning a language is learning its culture and we can see that things may look different to other people" (RA), "I can see that some foreign words have additional connotations and slightly different meanings, so it is difficult for me to find a suitable Polish word. That is why, borrowing words from another language is not bad when I speak Polish. I cannot imagine using a different word than 'briefing' in my company. The Polish equivalents 'odprawa' or 'spotkanie organizacyjne' are not the same. In a corporation we think differently" (AB), "When I speak Italian or French, I seem younger [laugher]. Well, I use French expressions in Polish because they are sexier [laughter]" (ND).

7.3.5.4. *Perception of success in language learning*

Traditionally, success in language learning is measured by tests measuring the internalization of various language aspects according to operative standards established by external authorities both in an oral and written form. Internationally recognized certificates are based on this way of testing. More recently, however, with the concept of student autonomy, and the application of the ecological metaphor to language learning, the perception of success has been drastically redefined and approached from the learner perspective (Lankiewicz, 2018a). In this approach, success depends on the learner type (the level of control over learning process), personal objectives, personality factors, as well as the level of critical language awareness among language learners, which conditions the whole process of language acquisition (Lankiewicz, 2015).

An essential consideration in the perception of success in language learning is the social-cultural conditions shaped by late modernity, such as globalization, technocratic polices, availability of ICT-based communication channels and a new mindset affecting the role of language in its place in societies. Europe would be most spectacular in this regard, where unification processes and human mobility across borders has contributed to, for example, the emergence of multilingual societies and necessitated plurilingualism (the knowledge of more than one language). The last notion is crucial here, since it calls for the redefinition of the vision of what language is and how it is learned. It entails (trans)languaging processes and implications derived from the concept of multi-competence (Cook, 1991). This line of thinking renders the measurement of success in language learning evasive, and delegates it to the individual realm, conditioned by attitudinal factors far beyond traditional "objective" and external assessments of language skills.

As to the respondents' opinions, their reasoning regarding success in the language learning of plurilinguals can be considered within three additional categories: communicative authenticity, adequacy of pedagogical development and evaluation of plurilingual repertoires, and language mixing practices.

The group discussions indicate that plurilingual respondents, despite the separation of the knowledge of particular language competences in the educational milieu, notice the fact that being a plurilingual and having experiences in the use of many languages has changed their perception of what it means to know a language. To illustrate, "years ago, when I started learning English I thought that I dreamed of learning to speak it like a British person, so I imitated the accent and everything, now what matters is to be fluent enough to express myself" (IR), or "...when I moved to Germany and started learning German, I understood that I will never speak like a German person, if only because of the fact that I also speak Polish, but this does not mean I am not able to communicate what I want in German" (PL).

The responses of some of the respondents can be construed this way that they legitimize their communicational authenticity in foreign languages via the fact that languages are used for the satisfaction of personal goals via the linguistic repertoires at their disposal. The notion of "authentic communication" or "authentic language use" is interpreted by them as an articulation of personal meanings, rather than native-like, pragmatic suitability. As they say "I prefer to know more languages, instead of one on a very high level, and be able to speak to different people in their native languages. If I use only English, the whole communication is very artificial (...) it is like visiting a country through the bus window" (AB). Respondents definitely notice that learning languages through socialization results in a different competence, but this does not discredit language users who learned languages through the process of instructed acquisition, "I lived for 15 years in Greece and I know the knowledge of this language is different from my knowledge of German and English, which I learned at school, but now I use them more than Greek and I am not afraid of using them" (AL). They also indicate that in the globalization era "you can learn a language with a good accent via the Internet. My teacher of German asked me many times if I had lived in Germany because of my accent, but in reality I had watched a lot of German tv channels" (MN). The same respondent makes an interesting observation regarding the communicative authenticity of plurilinguals by pointing out the fact cross-linguistic authenticity is impossible, because "watching an Italian film in the original language and in Polish we experience a different climate and we know that the interpretation of the same film can be slightly different" (EN). It triggered a discussion which could be concluded with the statement that monolingual authenticity is unattainable for plurilinguals who naturally switch perspectives, as it is evident in this comment, "I am authentic any time I use English, for example, but for a German or an English person my language [she means her English as an L2] may seem strange, but English is used in so many different ways by many people so why should I be intimidated. They should appreciate the fact that I know a foreign language, they may not know my native language (...) I cannot think and speak the same way as they do, with language there comes a culture. Can I be multicultural? I am basically Polish even if I know other cultures a bit" (VK). As plurilinguals, not keeping up national standards, they perceive themselves as linguistically successful people, regardless of academic requirements and evaluations.

In the group discussions, my respondents point to the inadequacy of pedagogical development and evaluation of plurilingual repertoires. At large, outside university, they naturally switch between languages and use their linguistic repertoires freely, whereas an academic milieu requires a total separation of linguistic resources. During a language class any influence of other languages is automatically pointed out by the teacher and either laughed at, "if I pronounce something in a German way" (ND), or subject to criticism and correction, "teachers will not let it go if somebody uses a word or structure not belonging to a particular language, it is treated as a mistake" (VK). In the discussion that follows, the respondents seem to understand pedagogical practicality for teaching languages separately, "you cannot accept all linguistic oddities, after all we attend a particular language class" (MP). They are aware of the fact that pedagogical practices are governed by linguistic normativity, but they also remark that there are moments during classes that the correction is not necessary, since both the students and the teachers share the same languages and everybody knows the message being communicated. They also argue that sometimes the occasional use of a word from a different language is intentional, to accentuate additional meanings. To illustrate, "when I borrow words form other languages describing cuisine I do it with a purpose. In Polish we also use the word 'weekend', not 'koniec tygodnia' because we do not have an exact equivalent in our language to communicate the same idea. It is not only the end of the week, it means also freedom, fun, respite and relaxation. Some words have simply more precise meanings or connotations" (CK). As they maintain, these intentional uses, however, are rarely appreciated in the educational setting, even if the teachers themselves are often plurilingual. Both in the student groups and the one composed of professionals, it was admitted that the acceptance of all borrowings across languages should not be accepted in general because it leads to "contamination of languages, linguistic sloppiness and educational wishy-washiness" (ND), yet there are certain contexts in which linguistic shortcuts are welcome, especially if one is plurilingual, "at school, if you use an English word speaking Polish, they say it is incorrect, but in a corporation context it is a reality, a part of corporate language, to say, 'o ósmej mam briefing' (I have a briefing at 8 o'clock). If you want to substitute it with 'spotkanie' or 'odprawa' it is not the same. There some reasons behind the use of these borrowings" (MN). The respondents also mention that their success in learning a new language is conditioned by their knowledge and experience of other languages. Thereby, their plurilingualism contributes to their higher language awareness of linguistic forms. As they say "every language is in a sense specific and one learns it in a slightly different way but there are also some similarities of grammar forms, for example, I would never have expected that the knowledge of German grammar could be helpful in learning Italian. It helped me a lot." (CK). The respondents present a lot of comparative details but their detailed presentation is beyond the scope of this paper. In brief, they all see linguistic awareness or knowledge about language (KAL) as a strategy for learning new languages, deciphering meaning or as a means of avoiding communication breakdowns. To specify, "sometimes I use words or grammar from other languages when I am not sure how to say something in the target language, using some Italian grammar or words in Spanish, or vice versa helps me to maintain a conversation with native speakers, it is better than to say nothing or say something in Polish. Of course, occasional use of English is also very helpful" (NK).

Language mixing practices is another category articulated by my respondents both in the context of their success in language learning (as highlighted above) and as a feature of being a plurilingual. Code switching or language mixing contributes, in their mind, to their communicative efficiency. Consequently, in general terms, they agree that mixing languages cannot be seen as a negative phenomenon. Instead, they see their language repertoires as capital to draw upon to be a successful language user. It can be exemplified by this extended opinion, "I guess for me sticking to one language is problematic, I cannot help it. To express what I mean I frequently switch between languages, it is very difficult to communicate culture-related issues in one language, you will always come across the lack of words or expressions or simply they may not be adequate. I share a flat with a Ukrainian person, she knows communicative English but is trying to improve her Polish. On the other hand, I know some Russian [she obviously knows English and German as a student of applied linguistics]. You would have to hear our conversation. It is a language mess but we understand each other well and we both learn something new linguistically every day. Maybe it is better this way" (ND). All in all, the respondents perceive their success in learning and its use beyond its measurement in terms of monolingual competence. They appraise their linguistic repertoires and see them as a factor contributing to enhanced language awareness.

Research objective 2 pertained to collecting examples of translingualism among plurilinguals. As mentioned in the theoretical underpinning, in this category I put all practices resulting from the use of all linguistic repertoires by multilinguals in a single utterance from typical code switching to transfer and interferences between languages, as conceptualized in the notion of multi-competence (Cook, 1991). This, in turn, in accordance with the heteroglossic understanding of plurilingualism/multilingualism, indicates that the linguistic repertoires of speakers who know more than one language influence each other, and they are shaped in time and space (Creese & Blackledge, 2011; Li, 2017). Since this is a transversal notion, in this chapter I have already mentioned some examples of this practice, discussing other themes. Without doubt, this research corroborates the theoretical considerations of the ubiquity of this phenomenon among plurilinguals. The discussion regarding translingual practices is explicitly triggered by questions included in the group interviews. The majority of examples of translingualism are simply declared by students reflecting on their use of linguistic repertoires, but some of them appeared during the discussion and caught the attention of the moderator. They became the subject of additional consideration by the respondents.

In all three groups, it was explicitly declared that translingual practices are part and parcel of plurilingual minds. The respondents claim that none of the languages belonging to their linguistic repertoires is free of influences. This also includes their native language, which for all of them is Polish. Moreover, they also distinguish details of using translingual practices from simple code switching (e.g. "My English swearing is 'midway', when I am really angry I swear in Polish", PL), via intercomprehension (e.g. "sometimes people talk to me, say in English, and I answer in Polish, because they know what I mean", EN) to transfer and interferences altering the linguistic systems at their disposal. It would be beyond the scope of this paper to mention all of them. I will confine the description to illustrative examples of linguistic transfer and interferences. In this regard, my respondents express the following claims: "I very often confuse grammatical structures between languages, adding, for example, English Present Simple third person endings to German verbs, or the exact translation of some idiomatic expressions from one language to another, sometimes it works, sometimes it doesn't" (LK), "sometimes, speaking Korean with my online friends [the student states she belongs to an online group of people learning this language], it is difficult for me to find the exact expression and I use an English word to be sure to be understood" (NK), "While I was still in high school, I thought that the ending 'en', for example, makes Polish words German. My father does the same thing now when he speaks to our German family, or he simply uses a Polish word with German pronunciation, it is really funny but it happens to me very often they I pronounce English words with a German accent [she moved to Germany in an early age and attended part of her schooling there]" (VK), or "my Polish parents pronounce some Greek words in a strange way, it causes a lot of funny situations and we [children] tease them for this" (AL). The respondents point out that a part of translingual practices are used to compensate for communicative incompetence in any of the linguistic repertoires, or the early stage of language development. Sometimes, these hybrid forms are echoed by members of the family or a group to contribute the familylect (language of a specific family) or ecolect (a language shared by people living close together).

Tellingly, during the discussion interviews, which were carried out in Polish, the respondents frequently resorted to translingual practices. The moderator identified them and pointed them out to the discussant for consideration. As it turned out, the respondents' native language is full of hybrid forms, deviating from the accepted linguistic norm. The focus of consideration here is only the forms (grammar) and vocabulary which might have been influenced by other languages. I disregard all regionalisms. It needs to be highlighted here that the Polish language varies regionally and socially. Accordingly, it was agreed that some seemingly Polish words were used in a particular context with the wrong meaning or outside their pragmalinguistic and sociopragmatic appropriacy, e.g. *ekstra* (additional vs. extraordinary), *dokładnie* (precisely vs. exactly), *wykonać telefon* (a calque from English meaning to make a phone call). Most examples were probably influenced by English. Interestingly, when pointed out, they were not considered hybrid by some of the respondents, only on second thought, was their oddity confirmed.

Some respondents used strange inflections, e.g. *ona była z narodowości niemieckiej* (the use of the preposition "z" is unwelcome here, or *nie wyczuwają od niej innego akcentu* (again, the preposition "od" should be substituted with "u" in correct Polish). Both expressions may be influenced by English prepositions – "of " or "from"). There were lot of other instances in which the accent was influenced, mostly by English or German, or students simply used hybrid expressions, or forms of foreign extraction, e.g. *należy zrobić z tym ordnung* (the last word of the Polish expression was substituted with its German equivalent, Ordnung), or *arbajtować* (a German verb "arbeiten" adapted to Polish grammar). The discussion in one of the groups was concluded with the comment "how can we learn foreign languages perfectly if we make so many mistakes in Polish" (MP), followed by an awareness-raising observation that "if someone knows two or more languages they will surely influence each other, even their native language, there is no way to stop it" (AL). The respondents also admit that the use of some words is dictated by a stronger, more explicit meaning, precision or emotional load connoted by them. Tellingly, one of the respondents says. "I have never heard my mother say the Polish word 'zapalniczka' (cigarette lighter), she uses the Russian equivalent 'зажигалка'. When I asked her why, she recalled her childhood memories. Russian was an obligatory language at school and a lot of Polish people used some Russian expressions because they sounded funny to them" (NK).

In concluding, it needs to be stated that the translingual practices of multilinguals are not only influenced by cross-linguistic inter-references or by linguistic shortcuts but some of them are motivated by an additional, or more precise meaning, or simply motivated by the emotions connoted by them. Hence, I would put forward the claim that, from the ecolinguistic point of view, the meanings of plurilinguals cannot be equated with those of monolinguals.

Research objective 3, pertained to framing respondents' translingual practices into a manifestation of CLA. To achieve this, I apply relational analysis, by analysing the context of the respondents' utterances or relating them to each other. It is believed that an inherent meaning may reside not in concepts, but in the relationship between them. The trigger question in the discussion contains the transversal issue of what it means to be multilingual with regard to language learning and language use. The discussion was tuned in such a way to make respondents focus on the problem of language mixing, a phenomenon identified as typical of multilinguals (García & Li, 2014, Canagarajah, 2011a; 2011b; Li, 2011). Based on my earlier research on critical language awareness (Lankiewicz, 2013, 2015; Lankiewicz & Wąsikiewicz-Firej, 2016), suggesting that the knowledge of many languages may result in higher critical language awareness, I try to explore in this research whether the respondents' justification of the use of translingual practices may be interpreted as a manifestation of CLA. To do this, I will try to rely on proximity analysis, which is to see whether and how often issues related to translingual practices co-oc-cur with issues pertaining to CLA.

I am fully aware of the problem of the subjectivity of the search for the manifes-tation of CLA. First of all, it is laden with ambiguities and its interpretation may be as bottomless as the perception of irony, in the sense that depending on what our mindset is we can see different levels of it and never be sure of touching the core. Therefore, to allow for academic rigour, I assumed that the vicinity of certain words in the comments justifying the use of translingual practices by multilinguals may indicate a level of CLA. As mentioned in the presentation of key research no-tions, CLA will be searched via the concepts' relationships borrowed form van Lier (2010). Any word or expression used in the discussion which may be considered synonymous with one of these or contained in the conceptual category designated by these words will be classified as a manifestation of CLA.

My respondents basically disclosed their CLA mindset pertaining to plurilin-gualism (see description of objective 1), which they see as more than a collection of parallel competences for individual languages (monoglossic perception of multilin-gualism). Their beliefs and examples of personal experiences presented to support them are indicative of a heteroglossic understanding of their plurilingual compe-tence (Crease and Blackledge, 2011; García & Li, 2014). Now, I will try to trace how closely this mindset is related to plurilingual practices as a manifestation of CLA designated by relationships, quality and agency (van Lier, 2010). All of them con-tain an aspect of CLA in the ecological sense.

The notion of relationships pertains to physical, social and symbolic worlds (van Lier, 2010: 4) and it stands for an eagerness to make use of the linguistic potential (affordances) to engage in different activities to see how uses of language are shaped by social relationships. In the case of translingual practices, I will pursue how the re-spondents relate themselves to these worlds in terms of power, and how eager they are to change the conventions of discourse as L2 users, and how far the mastery of the standard may empower or disempower them. Being critical in this regard does not need to mean the total repudiation of cultural norms, but rather indicates how the knowledge of a good form, or the transgression of the form may contribute to social equality.

The idea of quality in language education entails the problem of how education-al standards contribute to the personal well-being of multilingual people and how educational practices reflect the natural process of language learning and use. It also pertains to the measurement of success in the educational context and personal satis-faction with teaching methodology. In general, all aspects relating to the process of language learning and teaching would be contained in this notion, including room for freedom of expression.

The last macro category of agency is related to such issues as autonomy, motivation and investment (van Lier, 2010: 4). It translates into personal "setting objectives, pursuing goals and moving towards lifelong learning, learners need to make choices and employ agency in more self-directed ways" (ibid.: 5). In brief, it stands for the awareness of the need to take responsibility for one's learning process and the evaluations of its results, which Benson (2011) sees in terms of control.

This group of interrelated co-occurring concepts (conceptual matrix) was pursued with a particular question asked by the moderator (MO) in the group interview to show how co-occurring opinions may be construed as a manifestation of CLA. This way, I pursue a collective mindset, rather than an individual level of CLA, which ultimately would be problematic to measure in a collective interview, since responses are related to each other. To illustrate this, I will present the technique applied to the analysis of the answer to one of the key questions. The reader needs to keep in mind the fact that earlier utterances have been recontextualized in the transcript and they appear in a different order in all three groups. A contextual relationship analysis allows us to "open a widow" into the category in question, namely CLA.

A main query of the group interview was question 8, supported with additional points (see appendix) asking respondents to mention situations from their own experience, or the observation of other people, that the languages they know influenced each other to produce any hybrid forms. If respondents' statements appear in the context of other utterances, they are simply followed up with the explanations or comments of the other discussants. For example:

PL: My English swearing is "midway", when I am really angry I swear in Polish. Well, it is normal for me. I think the native language always dominates unless we are native bilinguals. Foreign words gain meaning when used in natural situations in our lives, only then do they mean something to us, they are not artificial (coded as agency).

MA: True, I do the same. My German "Scheisse" is not that bad, it is like a punctuation, or a pause, it does not mean much to me. But sometimes I use it speaking Polish, because I do not want to be so vulgar in my language.

AB: Would you swear like this in the presence of a German person?

MA: If they do so, why shouldn't I. I do not have to be nice as a user of a foreign language, do I? (relationships, transgression of the norm)
        ...

MO: Do you always keep to the language of the conversation, respond in English if it is carried out in English?

EN: Sometimes people talk to me, say, in English, and I answer in Polish, because they know what I mean. For example, as a student I did it very often with my English teacher after class. We had a very crazy one. At school she always used English with us. She was furious with me, but it was not natural to speak English in the hall (relationships, transgression of the rule).

...

LK   I very often confuse grammatical structures between languages, adding, for example, English Present Simple third person endings to German verbs, or sometimes I directly translate some idiomatic expressions of one language into another, sometimes it works, sometimes it doesn't (agency, autonomous play with the language)

BA: Interesting, because it happened to me when I started learning German after English. Now, I do not know why but I use some English expressions speaking German. Well, everybody knows English now anyway, but German teachers always correct me.

BC: They are teachers! They understand what you mean but a German class must be in German! They always demand all explanations in German, but for me it is natural to translate things between languages, it helps me to learn words and phrases (freedom in learning).

BA: Me too, I always translate between languages, it is so natural for me, why can't I learn words and phrases my own way? (quality, freedom in learning).

These are only illustrative fragments which point to a level of CLA of the multilinguals in two different groups (one student group and that of the professionals). In this part of the research, the coding has a very interpretative character and pertains to the concepts used in the analytical categories. Carrying it out only for question 9, I was able to identify examples with the following ratio for each group (27/13, 28/12, 33/16). The ratio stands for a translanguaging example vs. the manifestation of CLA. This analysis, juxtaposed with the results obtained for other research objectives, may modestly suggest that plurilinguals, due to more extensive insight into linguistic systems through their own experiences, may naturally demonstrate a higher degree of CLA than monolingual learners.

7.3.6. Discussion

As the author, I need to make an important caveat that the understanding of CLA is approached from the perspective of the ecological metaphor in language learning. My considerations are limited to three small groups of respondents (n=17). I believe, however, that the application of the focus group interview helped to account for the ecological validity of my research. Therefore, I assume that the research results may be interpreted by analogy to other research contexts with plurilinguals in focus.

As to the research results, they are compatible with my own earlier findings regarding CLA and its influence on language learning (Lankiewicz, 2015), which in the present study finds its manifestation in the language ideology of plurilinguals, who seem to perceive language in a less normative way (cf. Lankiewicz, 2016). This, in turn, is reflected in the processes of translingualism in the psycholinguistic sense, as an instinct typical of plurilinguals (Li, 2001), as evidence of multi-competence (Cook, 1991) and/or in the sociolinguistic sense (cf. Creese & Blackledge, 2011; García & Li, 2014) as an everyday practice reflecting social-cultural tensions, including the issues of power inscribed in the notion of CLA and the empowerment of the L2 user (cf. Lankiewicz et al., 2016; Lankiewicz & Wąsikiewicz-Firlej, 2016).

The present study, due to the application of group discussion methodology, additionally allows us to get an insight into the multilingual mind in a collective way and discloses both plurilinguals' language ideology and their translingual practices, which I ultimately interpret in the framework of CLA, conceptualized in the ecolinguistic sense. Inductively, it can be stated that the sampled plurilinguals demonstrated a level of CLA which empowers them as L2 users. With some caution, by ecological analogy (Kramsch & Steffensen, 2008: 27), it may be claimed that plurilinguals are naturally predisposed to evince a higher degree of language awareness (LA) due to the knowledge of many language systems and CLA, by virtue of the tensions imposed by the simultaneous operation of linguistic repertoires in various contexts.

7.3.7. Conclusion: Research horizon extended

As I have indicated in the historical background to the chosen methodology and its ecological validity, the focus group interview provides a good fit for researching ecolinguistic issues. The pursuit of the manifestation of CLA in translingual practices needs to allow for the ecological validity of the chosen method. For Bronfenbrenner (1979: 33, after van Lier 2004: 169) "ecology" necessitates phenomenological validity, standing for the "correspondence between the subject's and the investigator's view of the research situation" and research situatedness or deep contextualization. These points of view are of particular importance for delving into the issue of CLA, which is of an inherently interpretative and subjective nature, as mentioned earlier. In this respect, focus group discussion constitutes a "research method that is respectful and not condescending to your target audience" (Morgan, 2001: 142) and helps to articulate "thoughts and experiences" (ibid.) as well as offer potential for "in-depth knowledge of a specific situations" (Krueger, 1988/1994, after Morgan, 2001: 145).

Measuring someone's CLA in the general sense is a very tricky issue, since one needs to be aware of the intentions behind any language use. For example, only selected non-conformist, non-standard or creative use of linguistic repertoires may be classified as the manifestation of CLA of plurilinguals. Others may be simply the result of code-meshing or deficient proficiency. What means they can be considered as a sign of critical linguistic thinking is the context and motivation behind their use. Focus group discussion allows for this feature by the fact that one's utterances are motivated by those of others, and the researcher may relate them to each other to reconstruct the conceptual matrix of interrelated co-occurring concepts, which was the case in this study.

The above observations correspond with another key characteristic of doing ecolinguistic research, which consists in its critical perspective, by which van Lier (2004: 169) means "an approach [...] to a state of affairs that applies an explicit and overt rational, moral and ethical stance to the treatment and documentation of that state of affairs...". He also adds that any ecological research "must be intervention and change oriented" (ibid.). In this study, considering the research objectives, I tried to accentuate that the application of linguistic repertoires maybe motivated by conscious choices, additionally driven by personal attitudes, which may be indicative of CLA. Hence, translingual practices may be considered as a manifestation of CLA only if they are juxtaposed with a language ideology contained in personal attitudes. The development of the latter, in turn, may be indicative of the quality of education in an era of ubiquitous neoliberal tenets in language pedagogy (Lankiewicz, 2018b).

Additionally, the critical aspect of doing ecolinguistic research, argued by Lier (2004), consists in the fact that the reflection sessions in which the respondents participate are not only informative for the researcher (offering insights) but also awareness-raising for the participants. They may reshape their original opinions during the discussion, or may ignite additional comments which a traditional one-to-one interview or an observation would not offer. In other words, focus group discussion methodology allows for the agency of the reviewed, swerving from the positivist epistemology and structural tenets in doing linguistic research, as signalled in the introduction to this chapter. In a one-to-one interview the responses may be influenced by the researcher and ultimately be biased, while the application of the methodology of group discussion offers a more participant oriented point of view, so vital for gaining an insight into somebody's CLA. Needless to say, my respondents frequently modified their initial opinions being guided other participants of the discussion or the researcher's additional question. In the transcript, I identified many expressions synonymous with this claim "when Natalie was talking, it came to my mind that ..." (VK). Accordingly, Morgan exemplifies the use of focus groups as "empowering 'clients'", giving them "a fair degree of control over their own interactions" (1996: 133).

Last but not least, the rationale behind focus groups as "smaller-scale projects" (Morgan, 2001: 145), pertaining to specific situations (Morgan, 2001: 145) with the stress on the movement into qualitative methodology is markedly ecolinguistic. Respectively, the micro context in doing research is accentuated by the proponents of linguistic research inspired by the ecosystem metaphor with the claim that the study of a "unit" has some reference to "the larger complex system" (Kramsch, 2002a: 23) and may be informative for the macro-scale.

Thereby, I would say that the application of ecolinguistic tenets based on deep contextualization and relations and focus group methodology, in which participants have a degree of control over their own interaction to the study of the manifestation of CLA among plurilinguals, offers a potential to gain some insights into the cognition processes underlying translingual practices. The findings allow me to claim that the meshing of linguistic repertoires is not only subliminal and instinctive, as it surely is, but also that the "knowledge about languages" (KAL) results in greater critical awareness, empowering plurilinguals.

REFERENCES

Agar, M., and MacDonald, J. (1995). Focus Groups and Ethnography. *Human Organization*, 54: 78–86.

Alexander, R. J., and Stibbe, A. (2014). From the Analysis of Ecological Discourse to the Ecological Analysis of Discourse. *Language Sciences*, 41: 104–110.

Andrews, S. J. (2007). *Teacher Language Awareness*. Cambridge: Cambridge University Press.

Atkin, A. (2013). Peirce's Theory of Signs, *The Stanford Encyclopedia of Philosophy* (Summer 2013 Edition), Edward N. Zalta (ed.). URL = https://plato.stanford.edu/archives/sum2013/entries/peirce-semiotics/ [accessed 14.01.2022].

Benson, P. (2011). *Teaching and Researching Autonomy in Language Learning*. Second edition. London and New York: Routledge.

Bialystok, E. (2017). Second-Language Acquisition and Bilingualism at an Early Age and the Impact on Early Cognitive Development. In Tremblay, R. E., Boivin, M., Peters, RDeV, (eds.). *Encyclopedia on Early Childhood Development* [online]. https://www.child-encyclopedia.com/second-language/according-experts/second-language-acquisition-and-bilingualism-early-age-and-impact. Updated: September 2017 [accessed 17.11.2021].

Bialystok, E., Craik, F. I. M., and Luk, G. (2012). Bilingualism: Consequences for Mind and Brain. *Trends in Cognitive Sciences*, 16(4): 240–250.

Bronfenbrenner, U. (1979). *The Ecology of Human Development*. Cambridge, MA: Harvard University Press.

Burrows, D., and Kendall, S. (1997). Focus Groups: What are They and How Can They be Used in Nursing and Health Care Research? *Social Sciences in Health*, 3: 244–253.

Canagarajah, S. (2011a). Codemeshing in Academic Writing: Identifying Teachable Strategies of Translanguaging. *The Modern Language Journal*, 95(3): 401–417. https://doi.org/10.1111/j.1540-4781.2011.01207.x [accessed 14.01.2022].

Canagarajah, S. (2011b). Translanguaging in the Classroom: Emerging Issues for Research and Pedagogy. *Applied Linguistics Review*, 2: 1–28. https://doi.org/10.1515/9783110239331.1 [accessed 14.01.2022].

Canagarajah, S. (2013). *Translingual Practice. Global Englishes and Cosmopolitan Relations*. New York: Routledge.

Carey, M. A. (1995). Issues and Applications of Focus Groups. *Qualitative Health Research*, 5(special issue): 413–530.

Charmaz, K. (2017). Special Invited Paper: Continuities, Contradictions, and Critical Inquiry in Grounded Theory. *International Journal of Qualitative Methods*, 16: 1–8.

Charmaz, K., and Bryant, A. (2010). Grounded theory. In Peterson, P. Baker, E., and McGaw, B. (eds.). *International Encyclopedia of Education* (3rd ed.) (pp. 406–412). New York: Elsevier Science.

Clark, R., and Ivanič, R. (1997). Critical Discourse Analysis and Educational Change. In *Encyclopedia of language and education*. Volume 6. Knowledge about language (edited by van Lier, L., and Corson, D.) (pp. 217–227). Dordrecht, Boston and London: Kluwer Academic Publishers.

Cook, V. (1991). The Poverty-of-the-Stimulus Argument and Multi-competence. *Second Language Research*, 7: 103–117.

Cowley, S. J. (2019). The Return of Languaging. Toward a New Ecolinguistics. *Chinese Semiotic Studies*, 15(4): 483–512.

Creese, A., and Blackledge, A. (2011). Separate and Flexible Bilingualism in Complementary Schools: Multiple Language Practices in Interrelationship. *Journal of Pragmatics*, 43(5): 1196–1208.

De Fina, A. (2009). Narratives in Interview – The Case of Accounts. For an Interactional Approach to Narrative Genres. *Narrative Inquiry*, 19(2): 233–258.

Draper, A. (2004). The Principles and Application of Qualitative Research. *Proceedings of The Nutrition Society*, 63(4): 641–646.

Fade, S. (2004). Using Interpretative Phenomenological Analysis for Public Health Nutrition and Dietetic Research: A Practical Guide. *Proceedings of the Nutrition Society*, 63: 647–653.

Fairclough, N. (1989). *Language and Power*. London and New York: Longman.

Fairclough, N. (1992). The Appropriacy of "Appropriateness". In Fairclough, N. (ed.). *Critical Language Awareness* (pp. 33–56). London and New York: Longman.

Fairclough, N. 1995. Critical Discourse Analysis. London: Longman.

Fill, A. (2001). Ecolinguistics: State of the Art 1998. In Fill, A., and Mühlhäusler, P. (eds.). *The Ecolinguistics Reader: Language, Ecology, and Environment* (pp. 43–53). London and New York: Continuum.

Firth, A., and Wagner, J. (1997). On Discourse, Communication, and (some) Fundamental Concepts in SLA. *Modern Language Journal*, 81(3): 285–300.

Fowler, F. J. Jr. (1995). *Improving Survey Questions: Design and Evaluation*. Thousand Oaks, Calif.: Sage Publications.

Fowler, R., Hodge, B., Kress, G., and Trew, T. (1979). *Language and Control*. London: Routledge and Kegan Paul.

Frayne, C. (2015). Hermeneutic Phenomenology as a Basis for Ecological Critical Discourse Analysis. *Language and Ecology* (pp. 1–19). www.ecoling.net/articles [accessed 05.08.2021].

Frey, J. H., and Fontana, A. (1991). The Group Interview in Social Research. *Social Science Journal*, 28: 175–87.

García, O. and Leiva, C. 2014. Theorizing and Enacting Translanguaging for Social Justice. In Creese, A and Blackledge, A. (eds). *Heteroglossia as Practice and Pedagogy* (pp. 199–216). New York: Springer.

García, O., & Li, W. (2014). *Translanguaging: Language, Bilingualism, and Education*. Basingstoke, UK: Palgrave Macmillan.

Halliday, M. A. K. (1978). *Language as Social Semiotic: The Social Interpretation of language and Meaning*. London: Edward Arnold.

Harris, R. (1981). *The Language Myth*. London, Duckworth.

Harris, R. (1987). Language as Social Interaction: Integrationalism versus Segregationalism. *Language Sciences*, 9(2): 131–143.

Haugen, E. (1972/2001). The Ecology of Language. Reprinted in Fill, A. and Mühlhäusler, P. (eds.). *The Ecolinguistics Reader: Language, ecology and environment* (pp. 57–66). London: Continuum.

Heller, M. (2007). Bilingualism as Ideology and Practice. In Heller, M. (ed.). *Bilingualism: A social approach* (pp. 1–21). Basingstoke: Palgrave Macmillan.

Jameson, F. (1984). Foreword. Lyotard, J-F [1979]. *The Postmodern Condition: A Report on Knowledge*. Translation from the French by G. Bennington and B. Massumi, vii–xxi. Manchester: Manchester University Press.

Johnson, S. (2001). *Emergence: The Connected Lives of Ants, Brains, Cities and Software*. New York: Fordham University Press.

Khan, M. E., and Manderson, L. (1992). Focus Groups in Tropical Diseases Research. *Health Policy and Planning*, 7: 56–66.

Krajewska, M. and Lankiewicz, H. (2020). Language Beliefs and their Influence on the Process of Language Learning. In Lankiewicz, H., Blell, B., and Altendorf, U. (eds.). *Cultural Issues in the Matrix of Applied Linguistics*. Gdańsk. Gdańsk University Press.

Kramsch, C. (2002a). Introduction. "How Can We Tell the Dancer From the Dance?" In Kramsch, C. (ed.). *Language Learning and Language Socialization*. Ecological Perspectives (pp. 1–30). London and New York: Continuum

Kramsch, C. (2012). Authenticity and Legitimacy in SLA, Multilingual, 2.0? An International Symposium across the Disciplines, University of Arizona. 13–15 April 2012. Keynote Address. Web. 3 March http://www.youtube.com/watch?v=VHxxpdc2PoE [accessed 05.08.2021].

Kramsch, C. (ed.). 2002b. *Language Acquisition and Language Socialization: Educational Perspectives*. London: Continuum.

Kramsch, C., and Steffensen S. V. (2008). Ecological Perspectives on Second Language Acquisition and Socialization. In Hornberger, H., and Duff, P. (eds.). *Encyclopedia of Language education* (Vol. 8): Language and Socialization (pp. 17–28). Heidelberg: Springer.

Kravchenko, A. V. (2020). Why Ecolinguistics? *Ecolinguística: Revista Brasileira de Ecologia e Linguagem*, 6(2): 18–31.

Krueger R. A. (1993). Quality Control in Focus Groups. In Morgan, D. (ed.). *Successful Focus Groups: Advancing the State of the Art* (pp. 65–85). London: Sage Publications.

Krueger, R. A. (1988/1994). *Focus Groups: A Practical Guide for Applied Research*. 2nd ed. Thousand Oaks, CA: Sage.

Lankiewicz, H., and Wąsikiewicz-Firlej E. (2016). The Ecology of Empowerment as Manifested by Student Critical Language Awareness. *Konińskie Studia Językowe*, 4: 373–389.

Lankiewicz, H. (2014). From the Concept of Languaging to L2 Pedagogy. In Lankiewicz, H., and Wąsikiewicz-Firlej, E. (eds.). *Languaging Experiences: Learning and Teaching Revisited* (pp. 1–32). Newcastle upon Tyne: Cambridge Scholars Publishing.

Lankiewicz, H. (2018a), Sukces w nauce języka obcego w świetle podejścia ekologicznego, *Applied Linguistics Papers Volume,* 25(1): 99–115.

Lankiewicz, H. (2018b). Is There a Place for "Sowing" in Second Language (L2) Education at the University Level? Neoliberal Tenets under Scrutiny. In Pawlak, M., and Mystkowska-Wiertelak, A. *Challenges of Second and Foreign Language Education in a Globalized World* (pp. 197–213). Cham: Springer.

Lankiewicz, H., Wąsikiewicz-Firlej, E., and Szczepaniak-Kozak, A. (2016). Insights into Teacher Language Awareness with Reference to the Concept of Self-Marginalization and Empowerment in the Use of a Foreign Language. *Porta Linguarum*, 25: 147–161.

Lankiewicz, H. (2013). Teacher Language Awareness at the Start of the Career: Insights into Teacher Education. In Grabowska, M., Grzegorczyk, G., and Lankiewicz, H. (eds). Language and Concepts in Action: *Multidisciplinary Perspective on Linguistic Research* (pp. 135–158). Frankfurt am Main: Peter Lang.

Lankiewicz, H. (2015). *Teacher Language Awareness in the Ecological Perspective. A Collaborative Inquiry Based on Languaging*. Gdańsk: Wydawnictwo Uniwersytetu Gdańskiego.

Larsen-Freeman, D. (1997). Chaos/Complexity Science and Second Language Acquisition. *Applied Linguistics*, 18(2): 141–165.

Larsen-Freeman, D. (2002). Language Acquisition and Language Use From a Chaos/Complexity Theory Perspective. In Kramsch, C. (ed.) *Language Acquisition and Language Socialization: Educational Perspectives* (pp. 33–46). London: Continuum.

Leather, J., and van Dam, H. R. (eds.). (2003). *The Ecology of Language Acquisition*. Dordrecht: Kluwer.

Li, W. (2011). Moment Analysis and Translanguaging Space: Discursive Construction of Identities by Multilingual Chinese Youth in Britain'. *Journal of Pragmatics*, 43(5): 1222–1235.

Li, W. (2017). Translanguaging as a Practical Theory of Language. *Applied Linguistics*, 39(1): 9–30.

Magill, R. S. (1993). Focus Groups, Program Evaluation, and the Poor. *The Journal of Sociology &. Social Welfare,* 20: 103–14.

Mazak, C. M., and Carroll, K. S. (eds.) (2017). *Translanguaging in Higher Education: Beyond Monolingual Ideologies*. Bristol and Blue Ridge Summit: Multilingual Matters.

McQuarrie, E. F. (1990). Review of D. L Morgan, *Focus Groups as Qualitative Research*, and G. McCracken, *The Long Interview*. *Journal of Marketing Research*, 13: 114–17.

Merton, F. K. (1987). The Focussed Interview and Focus Groups Continuities and Discontinuities. *Public Opinion Quarterly,* 51: 550–566.

Merton, R. K., and Kendall, P. L. (1946). The Focused Interview. *American Journal of Sociology, 51*: 541–557.

Minsky, M. (1990). Logical vs. Analogical, or Symbolic vs. Connectionist, or Neat vs. Scruffy. In Winston, P. H. (ed.). Artificial Intelligence at MIT: *Expanding Frontiers,* Vol. 1. Cambridge: MIT Press.

Morgan, D. L. (1989). Adjusting to Widowhood: Do Social Networks Really Make it Easier? *Gerontologist,* 29: 101–107.

Morgan, D. L. (2001). Focus Groups Interviewing. In Gubrium, J. F., and Holstein, J. A. (eds.). *Handbook of Interview Research: Context and Method.* Thousand Oaks, London, New Delhi: Sage Publications (pp. 141–159).

Morgan, D. L. (1988). *Focus Group as Qualitative Research.* Newbury Park, CA: Sage Publications.

Morgan, D. L. (1996). Focus Groups. *Annul Review of Sociology,* 22: 129–52.

Nyumba, T. O., Wilson, K., Derrick, C. J., and Mukherjee, N. (2017). The Use of Focus Group Discussion Methodology: Insights from Two Decades of Application in Conservation. *Methods in Ecology and Evolution,* 9: 20–32.

Parker, A., and Tritter, J. (2006). Focus Group Method and Methodology: Current Practice and Recent Debate. *International Journal of Research & Method in Education,* 29: 23–37.

Perlovsky, L. (2013). Language and Cognition – Joint Acquisition, Dual Hierarchy, and Emotional Prosody. *Frontiers in Behavioral Neuroscience,* 2: 1–3.

Rabiee, F. (2004). Focus Group Interview and Data Analysis. *Proceedings of the Nutrition Society,* 63: 655–660.

Ritchie, J., and Spencer, L (1994). Qualitative Data Analysis for Applied Policy Research. In Bryman, A., and Burgess, R. G. (eds.). *Analysing Qualitative Data* (pp. 173–194) London: Routledge.

Smithson, J. (2000). Using and Analysing Focus Groups: Limitations and Possibilities. *International Journal of Social Research Methodology,* 3: 103–119.

Srivastava, A., and Thomson, S. B. (2009). Framework Analysis: A Qualitative Methodology for Applied Policy Research. *Journal of Administration and Governance,* 4(2): 72–79.

Steffensen, S. V. (2011). Beyond Mind: An Extended Ecology of Languaging. In Cowley, S. J. (ed.). *Distributed Language* (pp. 185–210). Amsterdam: John Benjamins.

Steffensen, S. V., and Fill, A. (2014). Ecolinguistics: The State of the Art and Future Horizons. *Language Sciences,* 41(Part A): 6–25.

Stewart, D. W., and Shamdasani, P., N. (1990). *Focus Groups: Theory and Practice.* Newbury Park, London and New Delhi: Sage.

Swain, M. (2006). Languaging, Agency and Collaboration in Advanced Second Language proficiency. In Byrnes, H. (ed.). *Advanced Language Learning: The Contribution of Halliday and Vygotsky* (pp. 95–108). New York: Continuum.

van Lier, L. (2004). *The Ecology and Semiotics of Language Learning: A Sociocultural Perspective.* Boston: Kluwer Academic Publishers.

van Lier, L. (2010). Telling ELT Tales out of School. The Ecology of Language Learning: Practice to Theory, Theory to Practice. *Procedia Social and Behavioral Sciences*, 3: 2–6.

Vygotsky, L. S. (1978). Mind in Society: The Development of Higher Psychological Processes (edited by M. Cole, V John-Steiner, S. Scribner, and E. Souberman). Cambridge, MA: Harvard University Press.

Wallace, C. (1992). Critical Literacy Awareness in the EFL Classroom. In Fairclough, N. (ed.). *Critical Language Awareness* (pp. 59–92). Harlow: Longman.

Wąsikiewicz-Firlej, E. (2017). *On (De)constructing Corporate Identity: An Ecolinguistic Approach*. Poznań: UAM.

Widła, H. (2016). Zmierzch bilingwizmu i jego skutki [The Twilight of Bilingualism and its consequences]. *Neofilolog*, 47(1): 9–19.

Woumans, E., Ameloot, S., Keuleers, E., and van Assche, E. (2019). The Relationship between Second Language Acquisition and Nonverbal Cognitive Abilities. *Journal of Experimental Psychology: General*, 148(7): 1169–1177. https://doi.org/10.1037/xge0000536 [accessed 14.10.2022].

Young, V. A. (2004). Your Average Nigga. *College Composition and Communication*, 55(4): 693–715. https://doi.org/10.2307/4140667 [accessed 14.01.2022].

ABOUT THE AUTHOR

Hadrian Aleksander Lankiewicz is the holder of D. Litt. in applied linguistics and PhD in literary studies, and three MA diplomas (in history, English studies and Italian language and culture). He is currently an Associate Professor and the head of the Department of Applied Linguistics at the University of Gdańsk, Poland. His academic interests oscillate between history, American literature and applied linguistics, with the primary focus on language acquisition and foreign language teaching methodology. In recent years, his research has been inspired by the application of an ecological metaphor to the study of language and its learning. Drawing on the concept of multi-competence and political autonomy in the process of language learning, he concentrated on issues of marginalization, empowerment and legitimization in the use of English as a foreign language.

APPENDIX: GROUP INTERVIEW FRAMEWORK

1. Can you present yourself? Define which languages you know and how long you have been learning and/or using them.
2. In which situations do you use a language different from your native one?
3. Do you know/use your native and/or foreign language dialects?
4. Would you classify yourself as a language learner, or language user of a foreign language?

5. Can a language user of a foreign language speak ultimately like a native speaker? Why?

   Can you totally keep to one language during a conversation?

   Are there any moments when other languages that you know get in the way? When? In which situations?

   What is your reaction when you hear a stewardess speaking a foreign language with a strong native language?

   Should official announcements e.g. on a plane, or those delivered by a telephone operator, be recorded by native speakers? Why?

6. Does the knowledge of many languages change the way you communicate?

7. Would you agree with the statement that people who know many languages use them in a mixed way? Why? How?

   Are you able to mention moments when someone was speaking to you in one language and you answered in a different one?

8. Can you mention situations from your own experience, or the observation of other people, that the languages or dialects you/they knew influenced each other or you/they simply mixed them?

   Do/did language teachers allow you to mix languages? Why?

   Is language mixing helpful or disturbing at school or in a conversation?

   What you would recommend to people learning several languages in the same period of time?

9. Is it good or bad when someone mixes languages? Should we try to prevent it?

10. Is it better to know one foreign language perfectly, or several languages to a lesser degree?

Index

awareness information 6, 30

banderowiec 173, 184, 185, 188, 189,
    190, 192, 193, 194, 195, 196, 197,
    198, 199, 200, 207
bilingual sub-competence 30
Bloom's taxonomy 11, 12

case formulation xiv, 105, 106, 107, 108,
    109, 110, 111, 112, 114, 115, 116,
    117, 118, 119, 120, 122, 123, 124,
    125, 127, 128,
case report xiv, 105, 106, 107, 108, 109,
    110, 113, 114, 115, 116, 117, 120,
    121, 122, 123, 124, 125, 126, 127,
    128, 129
case study 80, 169, 205, 224
cognitive artifacts 9
cognitive definition 84, 85
cognitive load theory 6, 32
collaborative learning 1, 2, 3, 4, 5, 6, 7, 8,
    9, 26, 27, 28, 29, 30, 31, 32, 33, 34
collective knowledge 8, 30
communicative activity type 47, 50, 77
communicative project 35, 46, 47, 48, 50,
    51, 53, 61, 69, 70, 73, 75
concept of situation 9
contempt 172, 173, 174, 176, 177, 181,
    182, 183, 185, 189, 192, 195, 196,
    197, 198, 203, 204, 205, 206

content space 6, 30
cooperative learning 2, 3, 4, 5, 8, 32
co-text 12, 15, 16, 17, 18, 19, 20, 23, 25,
    29, 187, 190, 193, 197, 199
critical language awareness xv, 208, 209,
    210, 219, 220, 223, 238, 245, 247,
    249
curriculum 81, 82, 83, 87, 89, 92, 104,
    169, 222

descriptive concept 174
dialogue xiii, 3, 5, 33, 38, 40, 67, 76, 77,
    78, 82, 83, 88, 89, 101, 103, 142
discourse ix, xii, xiv, xv, 1, 2, 4, 7, 8, 9, 10,
    11, 12, 15, 17.19, 20, 23, 28, 28, 42,
    44, 47, 48, 51, 75, 76, 77, 78, 80,
    81, 82, 88, 91, 104, 105, 106, 110,
    114, 115, 116, 123, 124, 125, 128,
    129, 170, 180, 185, 186, 187, 188,
    189, 194, 195, 198, 203, 204, 205,
    206, 210, 211, 218, 220, 239, 244,
    245, 246
discrediting 182, 183, 184, 191
dual character concept xiv, 172, 173, 176,
    177, 178, 184, 200, 203, 204
duoethnography xiv, 80, 81, 82, 83, 88,
    101, 103, 104,

ecolinguistics 75, 76, 170, 208, 210, 211,
    230, 245, 247, 247, 248

ecological validity xiii, xv, 115, 209, 212, 218, 219, 241, 242
education viii, xi, xiv, xv, 1, 3, 7, 28, 29, 30, 31, 32, 33, 34, 44, 77, 78, 79, 80, 81, 87, 88, 89, 90, 91, 92, 93, , 94, 95, 96, 97, 98, 99, 100, 101, 102, 103, 110, 124, 125, 128, 131, 132, 133, 135, 138, 141, 146, 147, 152, 165, 166, 167, 168, 169, 170, 176, 182, 204, 209, 211, 215, 220, 225, 226, 227, 228, 229, 233, 235, 239, 243, 245, 246, 247, 248
embodied xiv, 36, 37, 43, 45, 78, 79, 132, 143, 157, 158, 162, 168, 216
emotions 85, 132, 136, 139, 141, 142, 147, 148, 150, 154, 156, 157, 158, 159, 160, 162, 163, 164, 182, 204, 205, 216, 217, 232, 239
ethnolinguistics xiv, 80, 83, 84, 102
expert knowledge xiii, 1, 2, 8, 9, 25, 28, 29
external validity 218
extralingual sub-competence 10, 28

face validity xiii, 209
focus groups 140, 208, 213, 214, 215, 218, 219, 222, 223, 244, 245, 246, 247, 248
four perspectives model 105, 106

genre xiv, 11, 75, 81, 105, 106, 108,109, 110, 111, 114, 115, 116, 122, 123, 124, 125,126, 128, 129, 187, 245
group awareness 5, 6, 32
group discussions 140, 213, 214, 218, 233, 234
group interview xv, 208, 212, 213, 214, 218, 223, 224, 225, 236, 240, 241, 242, 246, 248, 249

hate speech xiv, 172, 173, 174, 175, 176, 178, 179, 183, 184, 186, 198, 201, 203, 204, 205, 206, 207

ideologies xii, 131, 132, 142, 165, 199, 202, 210, 220, 223, 224, 226
implicit 41, 82, 158, 176, 179, 181, 216
    explicit 9, 23, 25, 29, 98, 179, 180, 181, 216, 220, 236, 238, 243
instrumental sub-competence 10, 22, 28
    sub-competence xiii, 1, 2, 7, 8, 9, 10, 11, 13, 16, 17, 18, 19, 22, 24, 25, 27, 28, 29, 30
insult 172, 173, 174, 176, 178, 179, 180, 181, 182, 183, 184, 185, 192, 195, 197, 198, 202, 204
interaction xi, xiv, 1, 3, 4, 5, 6, 7, 8, 9, 12, 13, 15, 25, 27, 29, 30, 31, 32, 33, 34, 35, 36, 37, 39, 39, 40, 41, 42, 43, 44, 45, 46, 47, 49, 50, 51, 52, 53, 56, 58, 67, 69, 70, 71, 72, 73, 74, 75, 76, 77, 78, 79, 88, 96, 100, 111, 115, 117, 126, 131, 133, 134, 157, 163, 164, 202, 209, 213, 214, 215, 217, 218, 224, 244, 245, 246
interactivity 5, 8, 15, 35, 36, 37, 39, 40, 41, 43, 45, 46, 49, 50, 69, 70, 71, 72, 73, 74, 78, 79, 218
interdisciplinary xi, xii, xiii, xvi, 47, 115, 126, 208
interdisciplinary xi, xii, xiii, xiv, xv, xvi, 34, 72, 74, 80, 84, 104, 127, 205

language as a skill 36, 74
language awareness xv, 131, 135, 141, 165, 168, 169, 208, 209, 210, 219, 220, 221, 233, 235, 236, 238, 242, 244, 245, 247, 249
    critical language awareness xv, 208, 209, 210, 219, 220, 233, 238, 245, 247, 249
language learning vii, viii, xvi, 43, 79, 131, 132, 133, 135, 156, 157, 161, 162, 163, 165, 215, 216, 217, 220, 226, 227, 228, 229, 231, 232, 233, 236, 238, 239, 241, 242, 244, 246, 248, 249

language portrait xiv, 131, 132, 141,
    142, 143, 144, 145, 146, 147, 150,
    152, 155, 162, 163, 165, 166, 168,
    169
languaging x, xv, 35, 36, 37, 38, 39, 40, 41,
    42, 43, 46, 49, 50, 51, 52, 53, 54, 55,
    56, 57, 58, 59, 60, 61, 62, 63, 64, 65,
    66, 67, 68, 69, 70, 71, 72, 73, 74, 75,
    76, 77, 78, 79, 161, 162, 163, 167,
    170, 210, 211, 217, 220, 229, 230,
    231, 233, 241, 245, 246, 247, 248
legitimacy 226, 246
    empowerment xii, xvi, 142, 209, 226,
    242, 247, 249
linguistic behaviour 36, 38, 41, 43, 49, 88,
    167
linguistic repertoire x, xiv, 130, 131, 132,
    134, 135, 141, 142, 143, 146, 152,
    154, 157, 159, 160, 161, 162, 164,
    166, 168, 211, 215, 221, 222, 225,
    230, 234, 236, 237, 242, 243, 244

metaphor x, xiv, xvi, 15, 17, 18, 75, 79, 98,
    110, 112, 114, 126, 132, 138, 141,
    142, 143, 144, 148, 154, 156, 157,
    158, 159, 160, 162, 164, 165, 166,
    167, 168, 175, 183, 206, 209, 210,
    211, 215, 216, 217, 220, 233, 241,
    244, 249
metonymy 183, 184, 195, 206
militarionym 183, 195, 197, 198, 199,
    200
multilingualism x, xii, 133, 141, 165, 166,
    168, 169, 208, 221, 222, 223, 226,
    231, 236, 239
multimodal x, xi, xiv, xvi, 35, 37, 38, 39,
    43, 44, 50, 51, 75, 76, 77, 78, 79,
    110, 132, 142, 143, 144, 157, 161,
    162, 164, 165, 166, 168, 169, 170
multimodal approach xiv, 44, 132, 161,
    162, 164, 165
Multimodal Interaction Analysis 44

Murzyn 174, 175, 205, 206

normative 162, 172, 173, 176, 177, 178,
    184, 185, 190, 194, 196, 198, 199,
    200, 202, 203, 204, 210, 226, 242

phenomenological xii, 41, 72, 128, 209,
    215, 216, 217, 219, 224, 242, 245
phenomenological validity 242
phenomenology 216, 246
plurilingual xii, xv, 130, 131, 132, 133,
    134, 135, 142, 143, 145, 155, 157,
    158, 159, 161, 162, 163, 164, 165,
    166, 167, 168, 169, 208, 210, 211,
    220, 221, 222, 223, 226, 227, 228,
    229, 231, 232, 233, 234, 235, 236,
    238, 239, 241, 242, 243, 244
plurilingualism xii, 131, 132, 133, 135,
    157, 165, 167, 169, 208, 221, 222,
    223, 226, 227, 231, 232, 233, 235,
    236, 239
polyglot repertoire 134
projective techniques xiv, 130, 131, 132,
    136, 137, 138, 139, 140, 161, 162,
    163, 165, 166, 167, 168, 169, 170
psychology ix, x, xi, xiii, xiv, 1, 2, 3, 7, 28,
    32, 37, 44, 46, 76, 77, 78, 79, 84,
    105, 106, 107, 108, 109, 110, 114,
    115, 116, 118, 122, 123, 124, 125,
    126, 127, 128, 129, 130, 132, 136,
    137, 138, 166, 167, 169, 204, 209,
    211, 249

reflection 31, 81, 82, 88, 90, 91, 99, 100,
    104, 128, 131, 132, 141, 143, 158,
    162, 163, 213, 223, 243
relational space 6, 30
Rich Point 10, 11, 15, 18, 19, 22

sampling 214, 222
semantic profile 80, 92, 93
source domain 160, 162

strategic sub-competence 10, 19, 22
symmetry of action 4, 13, 14
symmetry of knowledge 4, 13, 14
symmetry of status 4, 13
synecdoche 184, 195

talk-in-interaction 37, 38, 39, 72
telecollaboration 1, 7, 28, 32
trajectory 42, 45, 47, 49, 51, 71, 72, 134
translation sub-competence xiii, 1, 2, 7, 8,
    9, 10, 11, 12, 13, 16, 17, 18, 19, 24,
    25, 27, 28, 29, 30
translingual xii, 135, 166, 208, 209, 221,
    222, 223, 231, 236, 237, 238, 239,
    242, 243, 244, 245

Ukrainiec 185, 188, 189, 190, 191, 192,
    193, 194, 195, 198, 199, 200, 201,
    202, 207

variation 32, 43, 215
verbal expression 163
visual representation 144, 145, 157,
    164
verbal representation 143
visual portrait 142, 143

xenophobic xiv, 172, 173, 176, 179, 184,
    185, 188, 194, 198, 200, 201
xenophobic hate speech xiv, 172,
    176